Praise for ReQovery

Over the past two years, Katrina Vaillancourt shared her story of entry into and exit from the QAnon conspiracy community with me for a book on which I was working. Her account is brimming with curiosity, insight, and vulnerability. So many of us harbor stereotypes of people who follow QAnon and other conspiracy theories that we forget the very human reasons people turn in this direction. Understanding, however, offers equally human strategies to bring them back. Through her radical openness, Katrina opens a door for those curious enough to listen instead of judging. Her message can help many.

> ~ **Jamil Zaki, PhD**, Stanford professor of psychology, author of *The War for Kindness* and *Hope for Cynics*

Katrina Vaillancourt's *ReQovery* is a compelling, emotionally charged, and ultimately inspiring *tour de force*. This courageous and deeply personal account details Katrina's journey into the dark labyrinth of QAnon as she becomes a true believer who nevertheless finds her pathway out. *ReQovery* is a must-read for anyone personally touched by or studying the challenges of misinformation and ideological extremism dividing our nation and harming the mental health of our people. As a scholar deeply committed to engaging our differences together in deliberation rooted in the fundamental American values we share, I find Katrina's path out of the labyrinth and into recovery to be a powerful call to embrace our shared humanity. Employing Nonviolent Communication principles, which she knows so well, Katrina reveals a potential future where transformation is possible through self-awareness, empathy, and committed engagement with the complexities of searching for the true, the good, and the beautiful together *is* possible.

> ~ **Barbara A. McGraw, JD, PhD**, professor of social ethics, law, public life and politics; director of the Center for Engaged Religious Pluralism at Saint Mary's College of California; and

author of *Rediscovering America's Sacred Ground: Public Religion and Pursuit of the Good in a Pluralistic America.*

In March 2021, as I prepared a webinar entitled "Conspiracy Theories and Political Extremism" for my *Neuroscience and Resonance* series, Katrina Vaillancourt reached out to me. After she shared her writings about her QAnon journey, which deeply moved me, I chose to make her story central to my presentation. As an expert in neuroscience, trauma, and Compassionate Communication, I believe Katrina's story is essential to creating compassion and connection across political divides, especially divisions caused by QAnon.

> ~ **Sarah Peyton,** Nonviolent Communication trainer, neuroscience educator, international speaker, author of *Your Resonant Self* and *Affirmations for Turbulent Times,* and coauthor of *The Anti-Racist Heart*

I met Katrina through my work as a journalist researching QAnon and other conspiracy theories. Her remarkable level of compassion, candor, and commitment to helping others heal was evident from our first conversation. I have found her deeply thoughtful, personally informed insights into the allure of certain disinformation—and its often-devastating human toll—to be profound. Her desire to now turn one of the most difficult chapters of her life into a resource for others is a reflection of the brave and selfless woman I have come to greatly admire.

> ~ **Jess Cook,** reporter, author, journalism lecturer

I connected with Katrina Vaillancourt in October 2020 when she co-facilitated my online group "Across the Aisle," aimed at bridging political divides. I was surprised and inspired by her ease in offering empathetic listening to participants of all political views. Katrina's skill in Nonviolent Communication and her personal journey in and out of QAnon make her story invaluable for those seeking to address political polarization in a way that fosters respect and harmony.

> ~ **John Kinyon,** Nonviolent Communication trainer and mediator, co-founder of Mediate Your Life, author of *Choosing Peace, From Conflict to Connection, When Your Mind Sabotages Your Dreams,* and *Mindfulness in Conversation*

As a certified Nonviolent Communication trainer for over two decades, and a mediator before that, I struggled when two dear friends fell into QAnon in 2020. I had tried everything and still these relationships were suffering. When Katrina reached out to me for support during her recovery, our conversations provided mutual benefit. I offered her empathy, and she gave me insights into QAnon that I couldn't have gained otherwise. This education helped me rebuild and maintain close friendships with those holding different worldviews than my own. May the wisdom of Katrina's personal experience of recovery, as shared in this book, be a beacon of light for all who are seeking to restore relational bonds in the wake of QAnon.

> ~ **Jim Manske,** Nonviolent Communication assessor, trainer and mediator, coauthor of *Pathways to Liberation*

Having spent decades working with over 100 significant new-thought authors and teachers, including Ram Dass, Reverend Michael Beckwith, Marianne Williamson, Timothy Leary, Deepak Chopra, and Neale Donald Walsch, I am honored to introduce a powerful next-generation voice: Katrina Vaillancourt. I have known Katrina both professionally and personally for almost 20 years, and I have watched her consistently bring a depth of wisdom, integrity, and self-reflection to the interactions and relationships in her life. Those qualities served her well in her most unexpected and self-devouring six-month foray into the QAnon phenomenon during the second half of 2020.

She recounts the joy and horrors of that world in intricate detail in *ReQovery*, her first book. On this retrospective journey, the book will undoubtedly serve as a beacon of inspiration for those who have "fallen down rabbit holes," for those seeking to understand how such a thing could happen, and for those who wish to recover from the stress and conflict these experiences often generate.

> ~ **Scott Catamas,** cofounder of the Global Peace Tribe and Love Coach Academy, founder and producer of Awakening World.

ReQovery

ReQovery

How I Tumbled Down the QAnon Rabbit Hole
and Climbed Out

Katrina Vaillancourt

Katrina Vaillancourt & GreenSong Press
Berkeley, California

** Copyright © 2024 by Katrina Vaillancourt. All rights reserved **

Editor: Laurie Masters, GreenSong Press
Cover and Illustrations: Katrina Vaillancourt
(Images originally generated with DALL-E and edited for final use)
Book Design: Katrina Vaillancourt and Laurie Masters
GreenSong Press, Berkeley, California

No part of this publication may be reproduced, distributed, or transmitted in any form or by any means, including photocopying, recording, or other electronic or mechanical methods, without the prior written permission of the author, except in the case of brief quotations of up to three paragraphs for educational, non-commercial, or promotional purposes with proper attribution to Katrina Vaillancourt and the book title *ReQovery: How I Tumbled Down the QAnon Rabbit Hole and Climbed Out,* along with a link to the book's website at:

www.ReQoveryBook.com.

For permission requests to use more than three paragraphs, or for any commercial uses, contact the author via the book's website, providing details about who you are, what content you wish to use, and what your intended purpose is.

Creating derivative works such as summaries, adaptations, recordings, or artistic renditions of this work is not permitted without explicit permission from the author.

In the event of a copyright violation, the author seeks to resolve disputes through restorative justice methods before considering legal action. This copyright statement may be revised periodically to reflect new legal and publishing requirements.

First edition printed in the United States of America
ISBN: 978-0-9913470-5-6
Library of Congress Control Number: 2024911462

This book is dedicated to all the peacemakers of the past, present, and future.

"Peace is not merely a distant goal that we seek, but a means by which we arrive at that goal."
~ Dr. Martin Luther King Jr.

"Peace does not mean an absence of conflicts; differences will always be there. Peace means solving these differences through peaceful means; through dialogue, education, knowledge; and through humane ways."
~ H.H. Dalai Lama

"Peace cannot be kept by force; it can only be achieved by understanding."
~ Albert Einstein

"If you want to make peace with your enemy, you have to work with your enemy. Then he becomes your partner."
~ Nelson Mandela

"Peace begins with a smile."
~ Mother Teresa

"I can't go back to yesterday because I was a different person then."
~ Lewis Carroll, *Alice in Wonderland*

Contents

Acknowledgments i
With This, I Bow Out (Preface) iii
Author's Notes: What You Should Know vii
Introduction: My Motivation to Write This Book 1

PART 1: Before QAnon
Chapter 1: Unusual Stress 13
Chapter 2: Then Came Covid 19
Chapter 3: Discord with Stephen 25
Chapter 4: A Request from a Friend 29

PART 2: My Journey into the QAnon Abyss
Chapter 5: Fall of the Cabal 35
Chapter 6: Bioweapons 49
Chapter 7: Alleged Satanic Manipulators 59
Chapter 8: The Enigma of Q 69
Chapter 9: John F. Kennedy Jr. 73
Chapter 10: So Many Questions 81
Chapter 11: Doing My Research 87
Chapter 12: The Great Awakening 93
Chapter 13: Bill Gates 97
Chapter 14: Mark of The Beast 101

PART 3: Life As a QAnon
Chapter 15: Just Act Normal 109
Chapter 16: It's Not Normal 119
Chapter 17: The Covid Conspiracy 127
Chapter 18: Explosive (Subjective) Truth 143
Chapter 19: Reorienting with Friends and Family 149

Chapter 20: Mending with Stephen 157
Chapter 21: QAnon Week 2 169
Chapter 22: Reestablishing Safety 179
Chapter 23: Unexamined Judgments 187
Chapter 24: Reclaiming Patriotism 193
Chapter 25: Deep in Online Addiction 201
Chapter 26: Fear and Disconnection 209

PART 4: Cracks and Crumbling of my Faith in Q
Chapter 27: Breakdown and Breakthrough 219
Chapter 28: QAnon Themes 225
Chapter 29: It Gets Personal 233
Chapter 30: Bridging the Political Divide 243
Chapter 31: QAnon Cracking and Crumbling 255
Chapter 32: The Fear Roller Coaster Persists 265
Chapter 33: Self-Induced Emotional Torture 275
Chapter 34: Free Yourself from Anxiety 281
Chapter 35: False Evidence Appearing Real 287

PART 5: ReQovery
Chapter 36: Back to Life 299
Chapter 37: QAnon Casualties 309
Chapter 38: Lemons and Lemonade 317
Chapter 39: Healing and Reconciliation 325
Appendix A: Questions and Answers 341
Appendix B: Glossary of Terms from the QAnon Lore 357
Appendix C: Final Reflections and Learnings 363
About the Author 385
Endnotes and References 387

Acknowledgments

I want to thank those whose love and support made this book possible. Thank you, Barbara McGraw, Patrick McCollum, Forrest Landry, Sara Nelson, and Daniel Sheehan for driving home the message that this story needed to be told. Thank you, Jim Manske, Sarah Peyton, and John Kinyon, for holding me through my healing and integration with deep care and empathy as I pulled myself out of the QAnon rabbit hole, initially spinning in shock and shame, uncertain how I'd ever recover. Your open-hearted listening and compassionate coaching made all the difference!

Thank you to the many spiritual teachers I've been blessed to learn from, whose wisdom shared openly helped me to remember that beliefs and one's sense of identity are ever changing with the one exception of the witnessing presence that is here always. Thank you for reminding us all that the true gift of life is the love in our hearts, shared with each other in each present moment.

Thank you to my father, Robert Sals, and mother, Diane Vaillancourt, both of whom read through my manuscript and provided invaluable feedback. Thank you for your unconditional love through it all. Thank you to my brother David Sals and sister Amy Swan, who found ways to stay lovingly connected during my stint in QAnon, even while needing to assert strong boundaries. Thank you to my son, Jadon Seitz, for your consistent love and encouragement, and for being the greatest gift in my life. And thank you to my many extended family members who have consistently shown up in my life with love and support, regardless of our ever-changing ideological differences. I love you all so much!

Thank you, Scott Catamas, for being a close friend through it all. Thank you to the many friends and colleagues who welcomed me back with open arms, providing me with a soft landing as I slowly began to reengage with the community I thought I had lost.

Thank you, Daniel Schmachtenberger, for assisting me with my sense-making and for dedicating your life to understanding and educating the public about the complex and interconnected catastrophic risks on the rise in our modern world, the possibility of life-serving solutions, and the importance of finding and implementing the "third attractor."

Thank you, Laurie Masters, for your curiosity and fascination with my story, consistent empathy, and dedicated work as my Precision Revision editor. Working with you on this project has been a dream come true. Your ability to enhance my original draft with an eye for clarity, flow, and care is beyond anything I imagined possible. Completing this book was not easy. Having you by my side as an ally made all the difference.

And a special thanks to my beloved husband Stephen for sticking this out with me. Thank you for staying close while I was entranced by QAnon, working diligently to help me get my feet back on the ground when so many people were advising you to end our relationship and bid me farewell. I don't know what additional social damage I would have done without you there strongly encouraging me to fully consider the possible consequences of posting QAnon-related content on my social media channels. I thank my guardian angels you stayed with me long enough for me to snap out of the trance and reclaim my life. Thank you! I love you!

With This, I Bow Out (Preface)

This book is a window into a relatively short yet potent chapter in the long arc of my life—a period I would just as soon have buried in the sands of time, to be honest. In it, I share the evolution of my personal thoughts and beliefs through one of the most painfully difficult stages of my life—a six-month "transformation by fire," if you will.

It's been three and a half years since I exited the QAnon rabbit hole, a swirl of "Q drops," QAnon influencers, social media algorithms, and conspiracy theory websites. The experience of shining the light of consciousness on this scramble-brained interlude in my life has been cathartic yet gut-wrenching, and I wish to state clearly at the outset:

It's Over.

In some ways I simply let go of this deeply wounding ordeal, unplugging cold turkey and filing this episode in the past as I've moved forward in my healing process. In others ways I did (and continue to do) the work I have needed to do to ensure my tendency towards online media addiction and QAnon's grip on my mind dissolved.

For the record, my release of this book in no way hints at lingering vestiges of obsession with the fantastical narratives that overtook my psyche for half a year. And yet I am grateful for how the experience has increased my capacity for peacemaking, as bringing empathic presence and supporting the co-creation of mutually satisfying solutions to seemingly intractable relational crises is the work to which I have devoted my life for well over a decade.

My desire in going public with this soul-baring account is to offer a life raft from my broad and compassionate perspective to the throngs of Americans who still find themselves mired in this hellish abyss—and, importantly, to the families devastated by their flabbergasting sea change.

I envision this book serving as a resource for discovering insights and tools in support of greater peace, harmony, and empowerment as we navigate the enormous complexities of intensifying catastrophic risks in an increasingly politically divided and global society of people who are all too often at war with one another. May it illuminate a path toward mutual care even in the face of intense conflict, clearing the way to reconciliation.

I am a firm believer in the adage "United we stand, divided we fall," a sentiment echoed throughout history by numerous leaders, writers, and speakers to emphasize the importance of unity and solidarity in facing challenges or adversaries. I steadfastly believe this is the antidote to "divide and conquer," a common and well-known military and political strategy.

Having fallen into, experienced, and then exited QAnon, I have chosen to tame my once lively political passions. It seems nearly impossible to talk about anything that has been politicized these days without falling into polarity and division unless we confine our conversations only to those who share our basic worldview. This coping strategy pigeonholes the entire diverse population into two silos: "Are you on our side? Or do you break bread with the enemy?"

Part of my strong reluctance to write this book is knowing that my participation in politics has overall been a suboptimal use of my time, amplified my stress, and proved to be an exercise in futility, eventually leading to the full-on life breakdown that I share in this personal narrative. And yet I cannot tell this story without restimulating political discussion. From my perspective, it is a story that must be told.

This book is a chapter of my past, not my present. Moving forward, it is my intention and commitment to walk the talk of my own recovery by

❦ Preface ❦

choosing actions that prioritize integrity, respect, and empathic understanding.

We are at a point in history when sharing ideas that are contrary to other people's political beliefs can quickly escalate into derision and hostility. The simple act of stating a political position risks mocking pushback by those with opposing beliefs and values. They may tag us with slights such as libtard, demoncrat, communist, pedophile, racist, fascist, Nazi, ignorant, batshit, delusional, and the like—terms intended to belittle and dehumanize us.

We may find ourselves lashing out at other human beings, lobbing similarly harsh verbal attacks in emotional reaction to their stated beliefs. We might later feel stressed and exhausted by these blowouts and torn between regretting our actions and digging in with greater self-righteousness—as if the future of the world depends on others agreeing with what we believe to be "right" or true. Despite having been raised to regard name-calling as wrong, so many of us resort to these hurtful and divisive behaviors when caught up in political debates. More disturbing, these escalations around polarized political topics have increasingly led to acts of physical violence.

For these reasons and more, I have almost entirely disengaged from political conversations. I hardly ever watch any news. I don't know many of the horrible things happening in our world, and where I am informed, it is only in a peripheral way. I am not an expert, nor am I here to give you my current political views as they continue to evolve over time. If that's what you are looking for, plenty of others are chomping at the bit to tell you what is "true," what to think, and who to vote for. That is not me. I've done that in the past and have come to recognize the futility of attempting to convince anyone that they should believe as I do. Each of us must find our own way. I trust that each one of us is seeking to discern truth from the barrage of disinformation that sows confusion, frustration, and cynicism, so that we might effectively participate as informed citizens of the world's greatest experiment in government of the people, by the people, and for the people.

Moving Forward

Since 2006, I have been an ardent student of Nonviolent Communication (NVC), a system for peacemaking and reconciliation developed by Dr. Marshall Rosenberg in the 1970s. I began teaching in 2007, and it has since become the primary focus of my professional life. Now, as a certified trainer and mediator with the Center for Nonviolent Communication[1] (CNVC), I am focusing my attention on sharing this deep work, combined with other synergistic practices, in support of healing relationship bonds, particularly within families. Having undergone the journey from far-left politics, down the QAnon rabbit hole, and back to my center, I offer a rare vantage point from which to embody NVC's practices and communicate its core transformational principles to families facing this complex psychosocial challenge. I am all too familiar with the painful political dynamics that can tear apart families, friendships, communities, and ultimately our country, with worrisome implications for the world at large. And yet, I remain optimistic as to the resiliency and innate goodness of the human spirit.

As we navigate these turbulent times, I hope that my story serves not just as a testament to personal resilience but also as a beacon of hope for those feeling adrift in the stormy seas of our current political climate. In sharing my journey, I invite you to join me in embracing the power of empathy to heal and unite us, for our greatest strength resides in the connections found through our shared humanity.

Author's Notes:
What You Should Know

1. Advisory Notice

The following chapters, all the way through "Part 4: ReQovery," delve into a range of topics that are emotionally triggering for many people, especially those who support Democratic politicians and vaccine mandates, as these are the people who felt most painfully impacted by the rise of QAnon. If you are one of those readers, I'm guessing you might prefer to skip over the details in my story that plunged me into the QAnon quagmire. I honor everyone's personal right to choose. I trust you to navigate this book according to your own capacity to engage with this content. And I am sure that it is nearly impossible to grasp the depths of a QAnon trance and begin to have a compassionate understanding for the difficulty of breaking free without a broad panoramic picture of the landscape that consumed the minds of those who fell down this rabbit hole in the first place.

Throughout these chapters, I've included sidebars entitled "Reflections" along with the year, that share something I later learned, or a subsequent personal reflection. Some of them debunk the misinformation that led me down the QAnon rabbit hole, while others add a more complete context. On the other hand, some of them confirm what I would call "uncomfortable facts." I learned a number of disturbing pieces of information along the way that turned out to be true. One example is that Pope Francis did say, "Satan is real. He is evil, he's not like mist. He's not a diffuse thing. He is a person."[2]

Part of my exit from QAnon included separating fact from fiction, which I have not at all been able to do in a comprehensive way as the volume of information that flew past my radar as a QAnon was completely overwhelming to me. Instead, I have learned to accept that there is so much I do not know, and that's okay. To be clear, however, even the darkest confirmed facts in no way prove the larger QAnon narrative.

My aim is to provide an insider's view into how I became entangled in QAnon without dragging you into the same labyrinth. This is not an easy task. You'll need context to fully comprehend and appreciate the many compounding moments and strategies that supported me finding sufficient desire and willpower to exit QAnon in late December of 2020, which I share in parts 4 and 5. But if you experience aversion to reading content in "Part 2: My Journey into the QAnon Abyss" (which covers in fair detail my overnight fall into QAnon between 11pm and 5am on the night of June 12, 2020) or anything else for that matter, please feel free to just skim the chapter headings and subheadings, or jump ahead completely and glean insights from later chapters.

If you experience aversion to any content, please feel free to jump ahead and glean insights from later chapters.

2. On Fictionalization

To safeguard the identities and respect the privacy of individuals involved in my journey, I have altered some names and certain details. These modifications in no way detract from the essence of the experiences we shared. The full names given in this book are included with the consent of those named. My aim is to present a transparent and reflective account without compromising the confidentiality of those who have been part of my story.

Introduction: My Motivation to Write This Book

"You have to write a book about your experience!" one of my mentors, Barbara McGraw, exclaimed to me in mid-February 2023. Her words carried weight with me not only because of our friendship, but also due to her esteemed roles as a professor of social ethics, law, and public life at Saint Mary's College of California. Barbara's extensive work as an author, speaker, and commentator on American identity, the role of religion in public life, and the moral foundations of the American political system made her advice impossible for me to ignore. Still, her suggestion stimulated incredulous laughter in me. "You're kidding me, right?" I retorted, almost reflexively. "Not at all," she asserted. "It's crucial for people to grasp how someone like you, someone totally dedicated to peace, could be drawn into QAnon."

"She's right," her husband, peace activist Reverend Patrick McCollum, chimed in. "This is a book that could be of great service."

They were not the first people to encourage me in this way. My husband (who in 2020 was my fiancé) had broached the topic of writing about my journey repeatedly, as had many others. However, my aversion to taking on this project was tremendous. In the case of this endeavor, I needed to hear it from liberal activists. Their encouragement was immediate and likely would have come earlier if I had risked talking with them prior to early 2023. But I felt too vulnerable to risk broaching this topic with any of them in the first two years after my exit.

I had been resisting the call to share my story openly. After all, who wants to be known for having fallen into one of the most notorious, bizarre, and potentially dangerous social, religious, and cultish political phenomena in United States history?

Yet, after thoughtful discussions with my husband, family, and a handful of friends, all of whom agreed with Barbara and Patrick's perspective, I decided to move past my resistance and tackle this project. Through sharing my personal story, I seek to give you a glimpse into a foreign world in support of whatever desire you might have to better understand how QAnon can hook a person, and perhaps how it hooked someone you love. You'll witness the depth of its psychological grip and potential strategies for aiding loved ones in their reconnection with a grounded sense of reality. Healing fractured relationships and reclaiming the simple pleasures of life become feasible when we step away from futile political squabbles and the exhausting turmoil of conspiracy theories.

Politically Marooned

My QAnon story followed a path familiar to many, in that I was a fervent supporter of Bernie Sanders, but was disillusioned by the Democratic establishment's actions in the 2016 and 2020 presidential election cycles. What I witnessed made me cynical about the party I had loyally supported my entire adult life. I found myself adrift, politically marooned, and infuriated. I believed the values of the Democratic party had been actively undermined by corporate and elite interests, as evidenced by its growing reliance on SuperPACs and the role of superdelegates favoring establishment candidates over grassroots contenders.

Pastel QAnon

My story is also common in that I came in through what is referred to as the "Pastel Q" track, a term coined by a Concordia University researcher. This

❀ Introduction ❀

branch of QAnon, propagated by certain social media influencers, emphasizes child protection and appeals to maternal instincts, alongside promoting alternative health and New Age spirituality. It attracts individuals from the wellness, yoga, and conscious community sectors, resonating with their values and concerns.

> *The "Pastel Q" track emphasizes child protection, appeals to maternal instincts, and promotes natural health and spirituality.*

These topics closely align with several lifelong core interests of mine. I am intrigued by metaphysical beliefs and nonphysical themes commonly explored in New Age spirituality, such as psychic phenomena, angelic beings, and life after death. I've been tuned into natural health since participating in my stepmother's Gerson diet protocol in middle school, and I had my first spiritual awakening at age 18, in which my egoic sense of self dissolved into pure light and I experienced myself as one with all of creation—or as the great Persian poet Rumi wrote, "You are not just a drop in the ocean, but the ocean in one drop." I am also a mother, so protecting children's well-being is a core value and a natural instinct that drives my desire to love and serve all—especially our innocent and vulnerable young people.

Factors Contributing to the Rise of QAnon in 2020

My plunge deep down into the QAnon rabbit hole began on June 12, 2020, shortly after the number of new Pastel Q allegiances spiked and became rampant on every major social media channel. Factors such as the following converged that spring, leading to a dramatic rise in new followers:

- The outbreak of Covid-19 and the ensuing lockdowns, which led to widespread isolation, fear, and uncertainty.
- The significantly increased consumption of news and social media by people confined at home.

- The election-year resurgence of QAnon, which had begun in October 2017 and was gaining momentum in 2020, despite remaining largely unrecognized by the general populace.
- The observations that Donald Trump appeared to be leveraging QAnon rhetoric for his own purposes.
- The release of *Plandemic,* a film by Mikki Willis, which quickly reached millions with its controversial claims about Covid-19.
- The increasingly prevalent content questioning the official Covid-19 narrative.
- The intensity of the US presidential election year, which further polarized public discourse.
- The amplification of social media algorithms, as discussed in the August 2020 documentary *The Social Dilemma,*[3] which exacerbated these issues. These artificial intelligence (AI)-run computational rules are designed to captivate users and maximize their attention, thereby increasing advertising revenue. This is the prevalent strategy for generating profit on these otherwise zero-cost social media entertainment channels. However, it also (inadvertently?) facilitates the spread of extremist content, resulting in real-world consequences.

The interplay of these elements created a perfect storm, leading many, myself included, to align with the QAnon belief system in a cult-like support of Donald Trump. How in the world could this have happened? No political analyst could have predicted this strange turn of events.

A Personal Story

My story is possibly unique in that I flipped allegiances overnight—literally. Additionally, my professional background in Nonviolent Communication (NVC) supports my ability not only to self-reflect, but also to listen to others with care and respect, regardless of how different their views might be from my own. These skills can be transformative when applied to conflict reso-

❀ Introduction ❀

lution. Yet that willingness to hear other perspectives can also make a person more likely to have a flexible belief system, which made me vulnerable to the QAnon phenomenon.

And my story is a rare one, given that I deeply immersed myself in QAnon, subsequently disentangled myself, and am now willing to talk about it. While many people, like my friend Laura, simply got bored of the videos and moved on, it seems that a huge number of those who fell into this rabbit hole remain lost in a trance of online addiction and emotionally charged debates, to the detriment of their friendships and family relations, as well as their mental and emotional well-being.

Readers unacquainted with the firsthand experience of QAnon's seduction, or those who never questioned what they were told about Covid, will come across a plethora of my shifting views that go against their personal beliefs about what is true and scientifically validated. This is particularly the case for individuals with liberal inclinations who rely on mainstream media (MSM) outlets, including CNN, MSNBC, NPR, the *New York Times,* and other resonant platforms to stay informed. The recounting of my transition from a fervent Bernie supporter to a QAnon enthusiast may at times feel significantly uncomfortable as it delves into the media and perspectives that drew me into the QAnon fold.

Encountering ideas that challenge our core beliefs can be disconcerting, a sentiment I know all too well from my departure from both the Democratic Party and, later, QAnon. Yet in any disagreement, understanding and reconciliation rely on the willingness and courage to empathize with opposing viewpoints. This by no means implies that you need to agree with information you deem untrue; however, resolving conflict cannot happen without building bridges of mutual and respectful understanding of each other's perspectives and core values. My empathetic nature provided space for my mind to be open to ideas that led me into QAnon, and it also paved my path out.

Present-Tense Narrative

I have chosen to write this book in present tense for the period between the night I tumbled down the QAnon rabbit hole through to my exit. This means that throughout that part of the narrative, I assert what I believed to be true at the time *as if it were true*. However, the views expressed in this book are not "the truth." They trace the conflation of my thoughts, emotions, values, and beliefs into one all-encompassing and often distorted perspective on the world as I tumbled down this rabbit hole. For six months, I lived as a firm believer before my conviction began to come undone. Then, I embarked on the hard and humbling work of recovery.

This book weaves together excerpts from original texts, emails, and voicemails, breathing life into my story through real-life dialogues with others during my descent into, and emergence from, QAnon.

Annotations and Endnotes

I've peppered this text with annotations in the form of grey-shaded sidebars that serve several purposes but most often provide context and additional information on topics I *did not* vet during my time on the QAnon roller-coaster. These notes were part of the fact-checking I did in my recovery, as I sought to distinguish information backed by reputable sources from information that is not.

I have also woven in many online references as endnotes. While some endnotes go against what I assert in this narrative, they are designed not to prove or disprove my points or belief system, but rather to share with you the information I have seen which led me to the perspectives I share in this story. I have sought to source most of the articles and videos from mainstream sources, as I imagine most of those drawn to read this book lean liberal. However, I have also included articles and videos from other sources when I was unable to find the same content on anything that is considered mainstream. Please feel free to check out the links I've included to get a sense of the information that influenced my thoughts and assessments, and also do your own investigations as you are moved to learn more on any of the topics introduced herein. I have bolded text that I believe could contribute most to mutual understanding of the matters that divide us and added "***" to the weblinks I believe are most essential to visit.

What Matters Most

If this book contributes just one message to the world, I want it to be this, the most important takeaway I can share: We are in conflict with each other based on the cognitive distortions we've been led to believe about each other. But another far more harmonious way of relating *is* possible.

We are in conflict with each other based on the cognitive distortions we've been led to believe about each other. But another far more harmonious way of relating is possible.

I once believed that conservatives were generally full of self-interest, didn't care about the environment, were more into handshakes than hugs and business suits than eco-fashion, and likely did not engage in holistic health practices like yoga and meditation. I thought they didn't care about the elderly, poor, single mothers, or children. I thought they were generally racist and sexist, wanting to return our country to an era of patriarchy and white supremacy.

I have no doubt many conservatives still hold preconceived ideas about people like me, especially as I once identified with what Republicans have come to call the "far left."

Before my entrance into QAnon, I was in the process of unfriending any remaining conservatives in my social network as my beliefs had become so entrenched that they seemed to simply be "the truth." I have come to discover that objective truth is elusive, especially when seeking to find it in the sea of disinformation, distortion, fantasy and lies that permeates both traditional and alternative media these days.

As you follow me on this journey of self-discovery, you'll be given the opportunity to consider the wisdom of so many lessons I learned as I worked to shed light on my unexamined beliefs and prejudices.

Predictable Backlash… (I Feel It Coming)

Despite receiving encouragement from close to two dozen liberal friends and family members to write this book, my resistance was initially impermeable. When asked why I didn't want to do it, the answer was always the same: I felt exhausted and emotionally traumatized at the potential accusations of being a racist, fascist, crazy, delusional nutjob and all the rest of the insults commonly hurled at people who have fallen down this particular rabbit hole. I was unwilling to put myself through that again, especially in the wake of my own recovery from this trying experience. And with the release of this book, I expect all of that will happen again. The more successful this book becomes, the greater the attacks will likely be.

The nature of political polarization and the resulting social conflict in our modern world has sadly increased, especially as we are once again in a presidential election cycle. In addition, the rise in trolling, cyberstalking, and hate speech has turned social media platforms into breeding grounds for unethical behavior. These platforms, which we originally used to connect and communicate with people, have increasingly become cesspools for vitriol and harassment. The triad of online anonymity, group belonging and conformity, and the perceived lack of consequences combine to curb inhibitions and embolden individuals to express hostility more freely than they might in face-to-face interactions. Social media's algorithms, often prioritizing engagement, inadvertently amplify controversial and inflammatory content, exacerbating the problem. This toxic environment not only harms individuals but also erodes the quality of online discourse, creating a pervasive atmosphere of fear and negativity.

Predictably, some people who read this book—and some who will never even bother to—will label me with all of the right-wing stereotypes and build cases to prove that they are right and I am wrong, professing that I deserve all their verbal venom. This is the social conditioning that keeps us all drowning in an ocean of hatred, division, fear, and control, adding to a sense of collective misery, trauma and disempowerment.

Introduction

*Predictably, some people who read this book—
and some who will never even bother to—will label me
with all of the right-wing stereotypes... This is the social
conditioning that keeps us all drowning in an ocean
of hatred, division, fear, and control.*

Does it hurt? Yes. Am I alone in being a recipient of ugly, hurtful speech? Far from it. Did I write this book anyway, knowing that this backlash would be a predictable outcome? Yes, I did.

Why?

- Because many people I love, admire, and trust said that this story needed to be told, that it could help a lot of people.
- Because I care a whole heck of a lot, and if this book can make a difference, it is worthwhile.
- Because I am not willing to allow fear of this backlash to drive me into silence.
- Because I value honesty and transparency.
- And because I believe that in the end, goodness will prevail.

Others, however, will choose kindness. They will choose to focus on my humanity. Those who seek to cultivate empathy in their hearts will "walk a mile in my shoes" as they read these pages, imagining my emotions along the way, and recognizing the universal needs (also known as values) that drove all my choices. They will take note of the circumstances, thoughts, feelings, needs, and intentions I share here, such that they might offer sensitive, perceptive, and appropriate communication that supports me and others who have had similar experiences.

My Intentions for This Book

This story advocates for mutual understanding and compassion, using discernment when choosing what to believe and what to reject, and being open to questioning even deeply held convictions. And it offers practical insights for promoting empathetic connections and establishing healthy boundaries around deeply divisive political issues.

These are my hopes for this book,

- If you have fallen into the QAnon rabbit hole (or any similarly divisive reality tunnel) and are struggling with the repercussions as I did, my intention is that this book might assist you in finding a pathway to recover relationships that you lost as your perceptions diverged.
- I hope this story can help free you from the grips of fear, anxiety, and depression, or from the lure of social media addiction, guiding you back to the essence of life, love, and the beauty that surrounds us.
- I hope it supports compassionate dialogue and renewed social cohesion, helping to dissolve the "enemy images" that drive conflict and lead to violence.
- I hope it helps open up a greater trust that regardless of party politics or ideological differences, human beings are naturally (for the most part) good-hearted, loving, and caring.
- I hope it encourages you to reflect on how your choices of news sources and social media channels may affect your mental health. Uplifting content predictably cultivates optimism, hope, and a more joyful life.
- I hope it highlights the value of unplugging from the screen and plugging back into your life.
- I hope it empowers you to add self-care practices into your daily routine. Doing so frees our energy for enjoying life and being of service to others.
- And finally, my deepest hope is that this book will inspire and empower you to become an agent of reconciliation and peace, effectively counteracting the rise of political polarization.

PART 1:
Before QAnon

Chapter 1:
Unusual Stress

I'm one of those people who normally falls asleep in a matter of minutes, a trait my fiancé, Stephen, often wishes he had. But tonight, the night of June 12, 2020, is far from typical.

In the arid warmth of the San Francisco Bay Area night, my body is buzzing with stress. I cannot believe that despite all Trump's affairs, tax evasions, shady business dealings, coziness with Russia, and an impeachment, he is still president. Despite my ethos of understanding, compassion, and unconditional positive regard for others, I feel nauseous when I hear Trump's voice or see pictures of him. The thought of him securing a second term is terrifying to me. In my decidedly liberal social circles, the consensus is clear: our world cannot afford another four years under the leadership of someone we perceive as racist, sexist, environmentally negligent, and narcissistic, who appears to be grabbing power with fascist intent.

If you had told me that in a single night my politics would flip and I would become a passionate Trump supporter, I would have said that you clearly do not know me. There was no chance in hell that would ever happen… But it did.

Between this night and the next morning, I would come to embrace the core beliefs of QAnon: that the world is ruled by a satanic cabal that harvests a chemical called adrenochrome from innocent children, and Trump is a modern-day hero, working with the "good guys," also known as "White Hats," to overcome evil and bring about a world of peace. These convictions held me in their grip for half a year before I would reclaim what truly matters in life: my holistic well-being, my connection to nature, and a life devoted to fostering love within my family, my relationships, and community.

Conflict with an Ex-Bernie Supporter

On June 5, 2020, just a week before my fateful about-face, I found myself in a heated exchange with my friend Tania, over Facebook Messenger. Once a staunch Bernie supporter, Tania's newfound allegiance to Trump had become intolerable to me, pushing me to the brink of blocking her, along with a couple dozen other Facebook friends. But canceling all these people was counter to my commitment to compassionate understanding. I wanted to try to stay connected, to keep a dialogue going, and perhaps to wake her up from her apparent insanity.

I challenged her, expressing my judgmental (NVC would call it "jackal") viewpoint regarding her understanding of the issues at hand. "Your approach to listening seems superficial, Tania. It's as if anything I send you is dismissed as fake news. The blatant disregard for justice and the surge of white supremacist ideologies under Trump's administration is glaringly obvious, yet it seems to escape your notice. It's disheartening. Your lack of responsiveness makes me question your willingness to engage in a meaningful conversation. It appears you're more interested in converting me than in understanding my perspective. Trump's record is fraught with deception, misconduct, and bigotry, yet you seem to see him as the best president since Kennedy. If you're truly listening, prove me wrong by addressing the substance of what I've shared."

Tania's response the following day only clarified for me her unflinching support for Trump. Exhausted by our circular debates and her refusal to consider alternative viewpoints, I declared my withdrawal from any further political discussions with her: "I can't engage with your political posts anymore, Tania. Despite your good intentions, they're too much for me."

❀ Chapter 1: Unusual Stress ❀

My efforts to keep an open mind and participate in empathetic dialogue, principles I've honed through my work in NVC, seemed futile with Tania. For 18 months, I had tried to bridge our divide, believing in the power of mutual respect and shared truths as the foundation for conflict resolution. While we shared positive regard for each other, we found ourselves at an impasse when it came to agreeing on what was true and what was not, each convinced of our own informed perspectives while dismissing the other as misled.

Tania's shift from Bernie to Trump was a bewildering mystery to me, increasing my fears of a potential Trump reelection and its dire implications for checks and balances, environmental and social protections, and the future in general. My patience and willingness to remain open had reached its limit; I saw no path forward in our dialogue. Despite a shared foundation in our values, our views on Trump's character and leadership were irreconcilably different.

In a final attempt to convey my concerns, I shared an article by Bill Moyers,[4] drawing parallels between Trump's presidency and historical dictatorships under Mussolini and Hitler, hoping it might provoke some reflection on her part.

I could have *never* imagined that only seven days later, I would pivot on a dime and suddenly view the world through her eyes. This overnight radical shift astounded me as much as it horrified my friends, family, and fiancé. To them it seemed inconceivable. To me, it seemed ironically congruent with my core values.

In some ways, my flip was not overnight; it was the culmination of my life experiences, coupled with specific events in the spring of 2020, that primed me for such a drastic shift in perspective.

Feel the Bern!

I was a diehard Bernie supporter in 2015 through the 2016 presidential primaries. To me, Bernie seemed to be the only candidate talking about issues that mattered most to those who were struggling in our country: the increasing wealth gap, the inability to stay afloat with one full-time job, the need for a $15 minimum wage, and the need for universal health care and universal education.

Bernie was championing voices that went unheard or unacknowledged by any other politician. His consistency, integrity, and vision inspired a movement, demanding change. He stood up against the oligarchy and corporatocracy, demanding our government return to its original promise—to serve *all* its citizens rather than a privileged few.

The dream of a more compassionate and inclusive society was one I ached to achieve. The thought of a nation where no mother, child, elder, or vulnerable individual had to endure the hardships of basic survival was what I yearned for.

Betrayal by the Democratic Establishment

However, the treatment of Bernie by the MSM and the Democratic National Committee (DNC) during the primaries left me feeling disillusioned and betrayed. The stark contrast between Bernie's packed stadiums, sometimes reaching crowds of 50,000 people, and Hillary Clinton's modest gatherings that often didn't even fill a high school gymnasium, was undeniable, yet it seemed to make no difference in the outcome. The widespread belief among Bernie's supporters was that he would have overwhelmingly won the Democratic nomination in a fair contest. The suspicion that the DNC and Clinton's campaign had manipulated the process was further fueled by the WikiLeaks release of emails suggesting collusion to secure Hillary's nomination.

The subsequent apology from the DNC[5] felt hollow and did little to assuage my sense of injustice. My perception of Hillary Clinton, Debbie Wasserman Schultz, the MSM, and the Democratic party as a whole was irrevocably tainted by these events. While I shared the anger of many Bernie supporters, their vitriolic chants of "Lock her up!" perplexed me. Was this simply an expression of frustration, or was there more at play?

☸ Chapter 1: Unusual Stress ☸

2023 Reflection – What I Learned

I discovered the origin of the chant "Lock her up" in 2019 when I watched a documentary called *The Great Hack*.[6] This, and the slogan "Crooked Hillary," were crafted by Cambridge Analytica, a data analytics firm known for its expertise in psychological operations and backed by right-wing billionaire Robert Mercer.[7] Trump's campaign enlisted the company[8] to spearhead its social media strategy, capitalizing on a vast data harvest from Facebook[9] and harnessing the ability to influence and manipulate voter behavior. The exposure of the firm's role, not just in Trump's unexpected victory but also in the Brexit vote, led to its legally mandated shutdown. Cambridge Analytica's data was left with the Mercer family.[10]

Following his defeat in 2016, Bernie founded Our Revolution, committed to reshaping politics from the grassroots level. In 2020, I was delighted to see progressive candidates, several of whom had strongly aligned themselves with Bernie, on the Democratic primary debate stage. Marianne Williamson, Elizabeth Warren, Tulsi Gabbard, and Andrew Yang brought fresh progressive perspectives to the debates. Their participation rekindled my hope; it seemed like this would be the year when Bernie's tireless and committed efforts would finally bear fruit within the Democratic Party.

Yet, history seemed to repeat itself, delivering a crushing blow reminiscent of 2016. The DNC and its supporting branch of the mainstream media (MSM) appeared to favor Joe Biden, sidelining every one of the progressive voices. I watched the campaign unfold with a dismayed sense of déjà vu. Andrew Yang was the first to withdraw, followed by Elizabeth Warren and Tulsi Gabbard in March. Bernie was the last progressive standing until April, when he endorsed Biden, the establishment's apparent choice.

This turn of events reinforced my belief that Bernie had been coerced into compliance, marking another election cycle that felt like a mockery of democracy, another victory for the elites. Despite my continued support for

Bernie's ideals, my disillusionment with the Democratic party grew. Bernie's endorsement of Biden felt like a betrayal. The DNC seemed irredeemably corrupt, and the MSM acted as a mouthpiece for elite interests, perpetuating what Noam Chomsky coined "manufactured consent."[11]

Corporate Oligarchy

I had watched a documentary called *The Corporation*,[12] which laid bare the dark underbelly of corporate influence and the concept of "corporate personhood." The Supreme Court's Citizens United[13] ruling in 2010, allowing unchecked corporate political spending, seemed to be the final nail in the coffin for democratic transparency. The influx of dark money[14] into politics, I feared, was eroding the very foundations of our democracy, with oligarchs and private interests wielding undue influence over public policy and opinion.

My trust in the political system eroded over time, but especially over those two presidential election cycles. It became visceral. The perception of systemic corruption, especially in global financial systems, and political allegiance to the elite rather than the common good was not mine alone; it was a sentiment echoed worldwide. In November 2019, the world saw record-high global protests,[15] with tens of millions of people from 114 countries taking to the streets.

Experts have traced the origins of this global unrest to the 2008 financial crisis and the subsequent bailout, which fueled the Occupy movement and its emblematic slogan, "We are the 99%." This movement highlighted a growing distrust in the financial and governmental institutions perceived as catering to the wealthy at the expense of the vast majority. While it seemed unjust to blame merely one percent of the global population, the notion that a minuscule fraction of the ultra-wealthy might be orchestrating widespread economic hardship wasn't far-fetched. This concept of a controlling "cabal" was something I was about to explore further, as I would soon learn many others had already begun to do.

Chapter 2:
Then Came Covid

As 2020 got underway and the world grappled with the onset of Covid-19, originating from Wuhan, China, the global landscape underwent a drastic transformation. The pandemic response enacted widespread lockdowns, effectively stomping out the colossal protests around the globe. This coincidental timing sparked suspicion in me, leading me to wonder about the role of global elites in the emergence and handling of this crisis.

The Coronation

During the early days of the lockdown in California, I stumbled upon "The Coronation,"[16] an essay by Charles Eisenstein, a progressive public speaker, philosopher, and author I had respected for years. Eisenstein proposed that the pandemic-induced measures to enforce isolation were unprecedented. He pointed out that under any other circumstance the public would not consent to the dramatic impacts the lockdown had on our lives and suggested the disturbing possibility that some of these changes might become permanent. This notion resonated with me, and I found myself questioning the legitimacy of these new norms.

Mikki Willis

In April 2020, filmmaker Mikki Willis hinted at an upcoming project that would shed light on corruption within the healthcare system, particularly regarding the handling of the pandemic by pharmaceutical companies and governmental bodies.

I had known of and deeply respected Mikki's work for more than five years. I associated him with the Agape Spiritual Center in Los Angeles, *Conscious Parenting* magazine, an environmental documentary called *Kiss the Ground,* his work with The Shift Network, and most notably, his racial and environmental justice efforts at Standing Rock, North Dakota.

While at Standing Rock, Mikki built alliances with the water protectors,[17] in full support of their basic precept, "Water is life." Knowing of the brutal attacks these indigenous people were enduring, Mikki raised funds to purchase drones with night-viewing video technology. With them he was able to expose the callous use of military force by Tiger Swan, a privately owned international security company.[18] Energy Transfer Partners, the corporation behind the Dakota Access Pipeline project (DAPL), had hired Tiger Swan for "security consulting."

A legal team representing the leaders among the Lakota Sioux indigenous tribe discovered that Tiger Swan's leadership had directed its team to view the water protectors as "jihad fighters,"[19] and was water-bombing them and shooting them with tear gas and rubber bullets in below-freezing temperatures under the cover of night, in attempts to make them go away.[20] I was grateful for Mikki's endeavors to uncover the truth and for his collaboration with federal civil rights attorney Daniel Sheehan. My attention had been captured many years earlier by Sheehan's brilliant work on legal projects, including the Iran-Contra affair and the Lakota Sioux Child Rescue Project; his legal representation of various indigenous water protectors following their unlawful arrests at Standing Rock; and his more than fifty years of unidentified flying object and unidentified anomalous phenomenon (UFO/UAP) disclosure work, including his more recent legal representation of military whistleblower Luis Elizondo.

☸ Chapter 2: Then Came Covid ☸

This collaboration at Standing Rock between two of my favorite modern-day heroes was heartening. Given Mikki's volunteer work at Standing Rock his support of the presidential runs of both Bernie Sanders (2015–2016) and Tulsi Gabbard (2019–2020), I viewed him as a superhero for truth. A man with a beautiful, courageous, and generous heart, I saw him taking bold, decisive action and using his unique gifts to improve the world—all qualities I aspire to grow in myself.

Plandemic

In May of 2020, Mikki released his first "Plandemic" video.[21] It started with an interview with Dr. Judy Mikovits, a PhD biomedical researcher. This interview increased my growing distrust in the MSM Covid-19 narrative. This perspective was further cemented when I watched content from personal transformational guru Tony Robbins, as he posted several videos featuring a panel of seven highly qualified researchers, including an experienced epidemiologist, a Nobel laureate, and several MDs testing and treating patients on the front lines.[22] Every one of these medical experts strongly and openly disagreed with the mainstream narrative, despite knowing that their public challenge of the orthodoxy could cost them their careers, which it quickly did.

Lockdowns and "The New Normal"

The pandemic and the subsequent lockdowns caused job losses for countless people as entire industries came to a screeching halt. My work as a relationship coach was impacted as well. The shutting down of workshop and community networking spaces, coupled with the isolation imposed by lockdowns, heightened my sense of stress and unrest. This period of inactivity and constant online exposure took a toll on my mental and emotional well-being. Yet I felt glued to the news. And what I continued to see on CNN, MSNBC, and liberal-leaning news media outlets deepened my disillusionment with the Democratic party and the MSM's portrayal of the pandemic, particularly its emphasis on vaccination as the sole solution, often championed by figures like Bill Gates, whose cozy involvement with Monsanto[23] had long been a potent point of contention for me.

I perceived Monsanto as a Goliath corporation, among the worst offenders of environmental degradation, and a destroyer of public health. From my perspective, you *cannot* support Monsanto and have any authority as a public health expert; it is an oxymoron. I could not help but to wonder, By what means had Gates become among the most sought after "experts" and a regular guest on the news, advising leaders on how to address this pandemic?

My doubts about the Covid-19 narrative extended to the reported statistics, which I suspected were grossly inflated to exaggerate the threat and heighten the fear in a coordinated effort to coerce the population toward an insufficiently tested new vaccine technology.

My distrust in the media's coverage of Covid deepened when I found this direct quote from the *New England Journal of Medicine*,[24] dated March 26, 2020, in an editorial cowritten by Anthony Fauci, M.D.:

> *If one assumes that the number of asymptomatic or minimally symptomatic cases is several times as high as the number of reported cases, the case fatality rate may be considerably less than 1%. This suggests that the overall clinical consequences of Covid-19 may ultimately be more akin to those of a severe seasonal influenza (which has a case fatality rate of approximately 0.1%) or a pandemic influenza (similar to those in 1957 and 1968) rather than a disease similar to SARS or MERS, which have had case fatality rates of 9 to 10% and 36%, respectively.*

Then, in late May of 2020, the CDC posted a report on its website in which it disclosed a much lower mortality rate than initially feared, a fact that would be later echoed by NPR[25] and the NIH.[26] The new data reported numbers that were less than a tenth of the previous projections that had permeated the news. I believed this should have been huge front-page news, shifting the focus toward protecting the most vulnerable and ending the lockdowns and the push for universal vaccinations, especially for people under age 45, who were shown to be at negligible risk of enduring severe Covid or death.

Chapter 2: Then Came Covid

George Floyd

Only days after this stunning CDC report, the tragic murder of George Floyd on May 25th captured global attention. This incident, emblematic of systemic racism, sparked widespread outrage across the nation, and most especially within the Black community, which had endured blatant and unreported acts of police brutality for far too long. The slogan "I can't breathe," associated with the Black Lives Matter movement in memory of both Eric Garner, who died after police put him in a chokehold, and later Floyd, for an unthinkable 9 minutes and 29 seconds, eerily mirrored the simultaneous plight of severe Covid sufferers, as doctors frantically sought out more ventilators. While I understood these words had become a powerful rallying cry against police brutality and racial injustice, I could not help but notice the irony; it did not seem wise to me to chant an affirmation about the inability to breathe as Covid cases and heightened anxiety were on the rise, both of which could generate breathing challenges.

While I was deeply moved by the global response to George Floyd's death and the subsequent push for anti-racist education and activism, I couldn't help but feel suspicious of the timing. I noted quickly that the MSM had previously failed to pay appropriate attention to the ongoing brutal and clearly racist violence. Now, in a most questionable timing, the topic of blatant police brutality was plastered all over headline news. What I imagined would have been relieving news of the recent studies demonstrating a much lower Covid mortality rate than what was initially broadcast was instead quickly and completely overshadowed by the urgent focus on racial justice. This vital information about the pandemic, which could have alleviated widespread fear and led to a more measured approach to caring for community health, seemed lost amidst the tumult.

Disillusionment

Between the MSM's choices of silence and selective coverage on progressive presidential candidates, and later Covid-19, my confidence in my most frequently visited media channels tanked. To make matters worse, the political party I had identified with all my life had gone astray. I no longer trusted that my concerns were represented by what had become of the Democratic party, which had not only actively worked to undermine non-establishment candidates, but also completely supported the lockdowns, propagating hyperbolized Covid fears while smearing and silencing any dissenting voices. I sensed the MSM had devolved into a load of propaganda, reporting news of a highly biased or misleading nature, telling Democrats what they should think about politicians and policy ideas. It was clear to me these news stories were bought and paid for by the corporations and individuals who would profit most from this pandemic and the political wins their money could buy.

Chapter 3:
Discord with Stephen

During this period, my fiancé Stephen and I found ourselves at odds. Unlike me, Stephen wasn't as deeply invested in Bernie Sanders or as disillusioned by the political process. His career in life sciences, particularly in a role supporting emergency transportation during the pandemic's peak in New York, gave him a front-row seat to the region in our country that was experiencing the worst of Covid-19. His trust in mainstream news and his personal risk assessment led him to eagerly anticipate the vaccine, a stance that put us in direct conflict, especially when he expressed fears for his own safety and upset with my defiant response. I was a clear "hell no!" to the idea of complying with what I viewed as a corrupted vaccine agenda. I have always steered toward natural health solutions and clearly prefer to trust my body's natural immune response over what I perceive to be unnecessary and potentially toxic medical interventions.

Our differing views on Covid-19 were just one facet of our growing tension. The national reckoning with racism following George Floyd's death was another. While I had long been aware of the deep-seated racism plaguing our country, Stephen was less so. He had been raised in a diverse San Francisco Bay Area community, and despite having been best friends with African American classmates throughout his youth and adult life, he found the barrage of news stories painfully revealing. His disillusionment with America's racial injustices grew, affecting his emotional well-being and, in turn, our interactions.

As Stephen grappled with these harsh realities, our conversations became more charged, reflecting the broader societal tensions. We both lamented the state of the nation, attributing the rise in overtly racist incidents to Trump, fearing that a reelection of this man would only exacerbate these painful issues. This period was marked by shared sorrow over the nation's ills, further strained by our individual responses to the unfolding crises.

The relentless stream of distressing news and the prolonged lockdown were taking a significant toll on both my fiancé and me, as was the case for many across the nation. The prospect of the lockdown extending for months, possibly even a year, felt unbearable, amplifying the already frequent and intense conflicts between us. It was not uncommon for me to vent about what I perceived to be a gross government overreach of power and for Stephen to respond in defense of the lockdowns, or for me to go off on the selection of Biden and him to tell me to "knock it off." Our stress levels were manifesting in increasingly reactive behavior, leading to arguments, door slamming, and regrettable words.

No Escape

Previously, during such tumultuous times, I would find solace in stepping away, seeking solitude or support to regain my balance. However, the constraints of the lockdown left me feeling trapped. Where can you go during a lockdown when going hiking, swimming in the ocean, or any other form of escape from one's confines could risk a large fine and arrest?

Amidst this chaos, my sense of disillusionment deepened. I feared the erosion of democracy and the rise of authoritarianism, symbolized by Trump. This imagining haunted my mind as a warning to prepare for the worst—a dystopian future akin to Nazi Germany. The Democratic party, which had been a beacon of hope in my younger years, now appeared to me as an inflexible and corrupt establishment serving only elite and power-hungry interests, leaving only scraps for the people by appeasing their values

Chapter 3: Discord with Stephen

for belonging, inclusivity, and diversity. Politically, I was in a no-win situation. The narrative around Covid-19 was murky at best, and the stringent lockdown measures seemed to intensify societal issues, including domestic violence, addiction, suicide, mental health crises, and many more.

The escalating violence at Black Lives Matter protests, coupled with rumors of civil unrest and reports that Trump might use these protests and the pandemic as an excuse to enact martial law, added to the widespread sense of foreboding. The enforcement of lockdown measures by the police, the financial strain on many, the disproportionate impact on small businesses versus the continued record-breaking growth of large corporations, and the widening wealth gap all contributed to a deep-seated fear and anxiety as all I could imagine was a dark and calamitous future.

And while I didn't trust the official news about Covid-19, I was well aware that it wasn't just a flu. Some people were hit hard by this virus and a few members of my family fit the "dangerously high risk" category. Who was going to die next? Would I be able to see them? Care for them? Say goodbye? Would they die alone in a hospital that barred visitors from entering? These questions plagued me and most everyone I knew. The situation, coupled with my visions of unavoidable tragedies, and the tension with my fiancé, was becoming untenable. It was all terribly wrong.

I had always been told that it was important to stay informed and to talk openly about politics so as to persuade others to vote consciously. I was taught that my vote counts, and voting is how we make a difference. It's how we change what isn't working. Yet, it appeared that despite my best efforts—through activism, donations, and volunteer work—I had made no significant impact on the dire political course we seemed to be on. The overwhelming challenges of the time left me questioning the efficacy of individual action against such vast and systemic issues. I felt completely powerless against a seemingly insurmountable system controlled by a corrupt elite, intent on quashing dissent and consolidating power. This bleak perception of reality dropped me into a state of not only pervasive anxiety, but also despair.

Fate?

Was it fate that on that night of June 12, 2020, amidst a whirlwind of soul-sucking mental and emotional turmoil, I found myself watching a video series that would dramatically alter my political perspectives and outlook? Within the span of just a few hours, my perception of reality underwent a complete transformation, shifting from a state of overwhelming fear to one of deep gratitude and newfound hope. This profound change also redirected my political loyalties, moving me from being a fervent supporter of Bernie Sanders to an advocate for Donald Trump and Q. I became not only receptive to but highly interested in alternative viewpoints, seeking information from sources well outside the mainstream spectrum. My newfound openness led me down a rabbit hole of alternative media, where the lines between genuine news, propaganda, misinformation, conspiracy theories, and fringe beliefs blurred. This eclectic mix of content held my unwavering attention for the next six months, during which I navigated through a haze of media-induced intoxication.

You may wonder how such a drastic shift could occur, how someone with strong progressive leanings and disdain for Trump could suddenly find herself ensnared by outlandish conspiracy theories and aligned with Trump's ideologies. In the pages of this memoir, I will attempt to unravel this complex turnabout and shed light on the factors that contributed to such an unexpected, shocking, and radical reorientation in my political and ideological stance. I will then share with you my personal experience of being in this crazy rabbit hole, and my journey out and home again.

Chapter 4:
A Request from a Friend

At the behest of my friend Laura, I watched the documentary-style video series that would radically alter my perspective. Beginning at a community potluck 15 years ago, Laura and I had forged a strong bond through our mutual interests in NVC, natural health practices, and organic gardening, the serenity of Harbin Hot Springs, and later, our shared enthusiasm for Bernie Sanders and dedication to social justice and anti-racism efforts.

During the lockdown, our friendship persisted through digital means, particularly as we, along with others in our holistic circle, began to critically examine the prevailing narrative around the pandemic, noticing a stark contrast with the viewpoints we encountered through alternative health channels. Our discussions expanded, especially following the tragic event of George Floyd's death, as we delved deeper into issues of racial justice through various articles and videos.

Our text conversation of June 10, 2020 began with casual exchanges, including a discussion of a YouTube interview from the channel TNT in which two Black men interviewed Richard Spencer, coiner of the term "alt-right."[27] I was shocked to see how unapologetically Spencer asserted his identity politics and extremist belief in white supremacy. What I was not so shocked to see was that someone like this strongly supported Trump. Everything I had seen to date led me to believe Trump was a white supremacist as well. This video reaffirmed my belief in the deep-seated issues of white supremacy and its apparent endorsement by figures like Trump.

Laura asked me if I'd seen *13th*[28] on Netflix, about the Thirteenth Amendment and the history of slavery and Jim Crow in the United States. I had watched it the previous fall and expressed my appreciation for the movie. Then, I asked her if she had seen *White Right: Meeting the Enemy*[29] by filmmaker Deeyah Khan and let her know I highly recommended it. She hadn't seen it and expressed immediate interest and gratitude for my suggestion.

Our conversation took a different direction when she brought up *Fall of the Cabal*. She had sent me the link to this video a couple of weeks earlier, and I had ignored it. Once again, she urged me to watch it, saying, "I want to believe that good things could be happening, but it takes me into a complete fisheye lens brain-warp territory."

I must have been too tired or too preoccupied with my own thoughts for that concluding sentence to grab my attention. Whatever the reason, I found myself resistant to prioritizing this series on my watch list. The video thumbnail of the YouTube link, featuring images of politicians, the pope, and the Eye of Providence, struck me as odd, and I lacked the motivation to override my instinctive hesitation.

Reflecting on this chat history now, I see that Laura's remark about the potential for the video series to lead her into a "complete fisheye lens brain-warp territory" stands out. It's a fitting description of what I would experience just 55 hours later.

That Fateful Day…

Two days later, on June 12, 2020, Laura reached out again.

"I finally finished watching *White Right*. Thank you so much for sharing that with me. It's just so obvious that the only way you can hate people is not to know them—not to see them as human. Empathy is everything. Sweet Jesus, it's all such a quagmire. So complicated and yet so simple."

Chapter 4: A Request from a Friend

Ahhh, yes! So true! The only way you can hate people is not to know them, and not see them as human. These words landed as music to my heart. God, I love this woman! Yes! Empathy is everything.

"I'm guessing you chose not to look at the series I sent you," Laura continued. "I wish there were someone to talk about it with. Everybody seems either to swallow it whole or to disregard it wholesale without consideration. I would imagine that there are insights to gain. At the very least, for me, it gives me context for listening to people with seemingly bizarre viewpoints."

Feeling a bit guilty knowing she really wanted me to watch this video, given how she had asked three times and spent an hour of her precious time to watch the video I had suggested only two days earlier, I responded, saying, "Not yet. I'll check it out soon! So long as I remember. If you don't hear from me, feel free to send me a reminder." As a matter of principle, I seek to honor my word, so I put it on my watch list.

That night, as I lay in bed wide awake in a state of full body buzzing with stress, anxiety and despair, sleep seemed far away. It did not help that the sounds of fireworks in our dry and fire-prone neighborhood kept breaking the silence of night. We'd had enough record-breaking fires in the previous five years to fray my nerves for years to come. Even if I could sleep, I felt as if I needed to stay awake until the risk of a fire emergency was gone. So, I figured I'd use the time to watch the series. If only I'd registered her "complete fisheye brain warp" description, I might have watched it at a different time when I was in a less frazzled state of mind. That night, my mind was anything but in a balanced and grounded head space.

This video series was a slippery slope for me in my vulnerable mental state. I was tired of the lockdown I had not consented to, but I did not want to risk arrest or fines either. I had lost all hope that any truly good politician had a chance at rising to the presidency. Democracy seemed to have been demolished, replaced by some combination of oligarchy and corporatocracy. Stephen and I kept bumping heads as our mutual stress levels rose. While I'd been aching for an escape for weeks, there was none to be found.

I needed a distraction. I needed something, anything, to get me out of this state of outrage, despair, and anxiety. The documentary, with its engaging start and sophisticated use of almost hypnotic suggestion techniques, provided the distraction from life I craved.

PART 2:

My Journey into the QAnon Abyss

Chapter 5:
Fall of the Cabal

In my weary state of restlessness, I press play on the first video in the ten-part *Fall of the Cabal* series.

> **2023 Reflection – What I Learned**
>
> The Cambridge dictionary defines *cabal* as "a small group of people who plan secretly to take action, especially political action," which aligns with its common usage in modern English. However, according to Merriam-Webster's dictionary, the word *cabal* traces back to *cabbala*, the Medieval Latin name for the Kabbalah, a traditional system of esoteric Jewish mysticism. While this etymology may not be widely acknowledged or well known, it contributes to the association of the label "the Cabal" with anti-Semitism.

Slide one reads:

> *This documentary was made by researcher and author Janet Ossebaard from the Netherlands, with the aid of countless 'Anons' across the world; It contains thousands of hours of research. I urge you to accept nothing as the truth. Please do your own research and*

double-check everything I present to you. That is the only way to truly wake up and become an independent thinker.

That all seems fine to me. I don't know who Janet is. I assume the "Anons" she's referring to are members of Anonymous,[30] a group of digital hacktivists (hacker/activists) who gained prominence on YouTube during George Bush Jr.'s final term as president. From what I can gather, Anonymous sought to use their hacking skills in support of social justice. I appreciate that she suggests I not accept anything as the truth and instead do my own research if I encounter anything that seems untrue to me. Being an independent thinker is something I value, so this suggestion resonates.

2023 Reflection – What I Learned

There's not much information about Janet Ossebaard online. All I could clearly find is that she was fascinated by crop circles, is best known for her creation of the *Fall of the Cabal* series, and died in the fall of 2023. Her fans question the circumstances around her apparent suicide. The Anons she referred to in her introduction overlap somewhat with the loosely organized hacktivist group Anonymous.[31] While I still do not know who these Anons are, they seem to be anyone who claims to have "intel" which they share as add-ons to Q's posts.

Slide two reads:

I have striven to respect all copyrights of the images used in this documentary. If you believe I infringed on your copyright, please contact me a.s.a.p. so that I can settle things in an appropriate way.

I like Janet more already as this statement shows integrity, which I value.

Slide three reads:

🪷 Chapter 5: Fall of the Cabal 🪷

Warning: I urge you to watch this documentary all the way till the end. You may find the first episodes shocking or even unbelievable, yet at the end everything will fall into place. The final two episodes (9 & 10) contain an unexpected twist, causing you to face the changes ahead of us with Hope and Faith in your heart.

Slide four reads:
The End of the World As We Know It
Things That Make You Go Hmmmm...
Part 1

As the documentary commences with captivating visuals of Earth from space, accompanied by a stirring orchestral score, Janet shares her opening remarks:

We are about to witness one of the greatest events in human history. The world as we know it is crumbling before our very eyes, and the majority of the world population is not aware of it.

Her assertion that longstanding power structures are being dismantled resonate with my observations and the discourse among many members in my community.

Janet continues:

Power structures that have been in place for thousands of years are being taken down as we speak. Soon we will be shown evidence of an elite plan, so evil, so all-encompassing that people will be shocked to the core. This documentary was made to help you deal with what's coming.

My already nervous state of being cranks up a notch. Could Janet be referring to the same elite that Bernie Sanders so often speaks of? Their greed and manipulation of laws, policies, and government does at times seem evil, or at least heartless. I know there are people motivated by greed and selfishness at the top of many institutional structures, but could it be worse than what I sense is going on?

Janet continues:

Is it a good thing? Oh yes! It's the best thing that could possibly happen to us.

I exhale a measured sigh of relief. It seems there's a happy ending to this one. As dark as the world may be, I have usually been able to keep the faith that something wonderful could be on the horizon. Maybe this movie will clarify what I'm missing and help me anchor back into faith that our future isn't a complete impending disaster. I hold out a glimmer of hope, unaware that I am already becoming entranced by Janet's narrative.

Her storyline continues:

But in order to understand and process the quantum leap that we and humanity are about to take, you must understand the reality, so to speak, the timeline that we as a species were placed in, and believe me, you don't have a clue just yet. The evil I mentioned has been working behind the scenes so intelligently, so brilliantly that hardly anyone ever noticed a thing. What I'm going to do is give you a short overview of the things that made me go 'hmmmm'... things that made me start digging for the truth. We'll go from there, shall we? Join me on a journey down the rabbit hole.

Curiouser and curiouser, I think to myself, playfully quoting *Alice in Wonderland,* which happens to be the one movie I watched the most as a child. It is also a theme I would later learn is not only used extensively by Q, but also woven into movies and TV shows such as *The Matrix* and *Star Trek: Discovery.*

California Fires

The orchestra music reaches a crescendo and a new song enters. It's a piano, and the sound is melancholy.

❀ Chapter 5: Fall of the Cabal ❀

"Let's start with the recent forest fires, for instance in California," Janet begins.

Oy! That is close to home, I think as I recall the inferno of 2015.

The massive fire that burned a total of 76,000 acres in Lake County, California, also flattened Harbin Hot Springs just days before my 40th birthday celebration was going to be held there. About a dozen of my dear friends had been traumatized by that experience. One friend was shaking for months after the incident as she and another friend of mine took the risk of driving down a fire road to escape the massive flames. In her trembling and tears she recalled the fire as looking like "the gates of hell."

Needless to say, my birthday that year was quite the opposite of the epic gathering I had planned. As an empath, I too was in tears as I felt the stress, fear, and trauma of members of my community. And my birthday, which was going to be a grand and epic celebration, literally went up in flames.

•••

"Did you know that these fires forgot to burn trees?" Janet asks as an image pops up of a neighborhood flattened by fire with untouched trees lining the remains of those houses.

"That they were capable of cutting through houses?" A new image is shown of a house that strangely has a clean cut. Most of the house is destroyed, but there is a straight line delineating the flattened part of the house, while on the other side of that line, the house appears untouched.

"That they burn trees from the inside out?" A picture of a redwood with flames peeking through from the inside shows on the screen.

"That they were able to lift cars, tilt them, and smash them down?" The next photo shows cars gutted by fire and flipped upside down.

"Are you sure these are ordinary forest fires?" Janet asks.

Then a yellow screen with white words in bold pops up reading, *THINGS THAT MAKE YOU GO HMMMM...*

Compelled by a mix of intrigue and skepticism, I pause the video to verify these extraordinary claims. A quick online search confirms the existence of such images.

2023 Reflection – What I Learned

I did not consider at the time that these images could have been digitally altered. I still don't know how they were initially captured. But I did learn that trees can burn from the inside out when they are struck by lightning, or when the fire around their base finds a weak spot in the trunk.[32] And the explosion of its gas tank can cause a car to flip upside down.

Mercury in Vaccines

The next scene talks about how "we all know" that mercury is toxic, with a graph comparing the parts per million in a vaccine to the parts per million in toxic waste. The vaccines have far higher concentrations of mercury on that graph. Janet poses what to me is an obvious question I've wrestled with plenty of times: Why is mercury, not so widely used anymore but still an ingredient in some vaccinations, okay to inject into children?

2023 Reflection – What I Learned

My subsequent research revealed crucial additional information, which at first relieved some of my concern. The type of mercury used in some vaccines, ethylmercury, is utilized in thimerosal, a preservative added to multi-dose vials of vaccines to prevent microbial contamination. Unlike methylmercury, the form found in seafood like tuna (which is known for its toxicity and potential health risks, particularly affecting the nervous system), ethylmercury is said to be processed and expelled by the human body more efficiently (presumably through the urine or other avenues of excretion, such as feces, sweat, hair, or fingernails), posing significantly less risk of accumulation to toxic levels, as validated in a study by Pichichero in 2002.[33]

    A 2005 study by Burbacher, however, while confirming that the ethylmercury in thimerosal does indeed exit the blood very quickly, found that it easily crosses the blood-brain barrier, delivering mercury directly to brain tissue.[34] An additional published study by Kern in 2019 confirms these second findings, presenting twenty-two studies indicating that ethylmercury converts to highly toxic compounds that

Chapter 5: Fall of the Cabal

> "significantly and persistently bind to tissues in the brain."[35]
>
> I was unable to find any information to clarify why these later studies have not changed the use of ethylmercury in vaccines. I did note that the CDC website asserts that "scientists have been studying the use of thimerosal in vaccines for many years. They haven't found any evidence that thimerosal causes harm."

Geoengineering Aerosols

Janet transitions to discussing chemtrails, a topic enveloped in controversy and speculation for years and which the government has historically dismissed. More recently, however, discussions have emerged around "geoengineering aerosols," a term that seems to sanitize the concept of chemtrails, making it sound more scientifically grounded and less conspiratorial.

My familiarity with the chemtrail theory spans almost two decades. As I've witnessed planes leaving long white lines in the sky, I've pondered the potential veracity of the widespread rumors and conjectures.

2023 Reflection – What I Learned

Geoengineering aerosols are, indeed, a legitimate scientific concept, distinct from the chemtrail conspiracy. These aerosols are part of a broader research field exploring climate change mitigation strategies. The primary components of these aerosols are sulfates, inspired by the natural cooling effect that volcanic eruptions can have by releasing sulfates into the atmosphere. This form of climate intervention remains a topic of intense debate due to its potential implications and ethical considerations.

Conversely, the term "chemtrails" has been co-opted by conspiracy theorists who assert that the visible contrails left by aircraft are, in fact, deliberate discharges of chemical or biological agents for undisclosed harmful purposes. The most compelling piece of evidence I came across was from Kristen Meghan, a former Air Force pilot and industrial hygienist turned whistleblower, who shares her personal experience,[36] highlighting what geoengineering expert David Keith has openly promoted. He believes the strategy of shooting a known hazardous substance, sulfuric acid,[37] into the air is our best and needed solution to mitigate global warming as we work to reduce emissions. Keith openly states that sulfur dioxide, a form of sulfuric acid, is the preferred substance for this purpose.

However, Meghan alleges that the geoengineering aerosols are not "simply" sulfuric acid, and that these trails also emit forms of aluminum, barium, and strontium. The even more concerning testimony of Jim Lee at ClimateViewer News, who has dedicated his life's work to studying the topic of weather modification, corroborates and expands upon her claims.[38] Meghan's claims diverge significantly from the scientific understanding readily available online, which asserts that contrails are predominantly made up of harmless water vapor, a byproduct of aircraft engine combustion.

Lucifer and the Vatican

The documentary proceeds to examine potential satanic symbols within Vatican architecture, beginning with the Audience Hall, drawing attention to its alleged "reptilian" design elements. Janet highlights various architectural features and pieces of artwork within the hall, which she suggests bear resemblance to reptilian creatures.

2023 Reflection – What I Learned

Concerns have been raised about the potential manipulation of photos through wide-angle shots to exaggerate a reptilian appearance in the Vatican's architecture. While there are indeed serpent-inspired elements present,[39] the interpretation of these designs can vary widely. Not being a Catholic, I initially struggled to grasp the significance of these design choices. However, one explanation[40] ties back to biblical symbolism, where the serpent can represent both sin and salvation, as illustrated in John 3:14-15, where the serpent lifted up in the wilderness by Moses prefigures Christ's crucifixion and the atonement it offers.

Janet also comments on a large bronze statue in the Vatican, suggesting that Jesus's hair was purposefully styled to resemble a reptile's head.[41]

🪷 Chapter 5: Fall of the Cabal 🪷

2023 Reflection – What I Learned

The statue in question, located behind the pope in a photo of the Vatican Audience Hall does have a grotesque look to it, and in a certain lighting, the hair does appear to resemble a dinosaur head. This massive piece was commissioned in 1970[42] as a modern statement against the use of nuclear weapons, particularly in the wake of the Cuban Missile Crisis.

The narrative then shifts to the Vatican's involvement with a telescope, which Janet claims is named "Lucifer."

2023 Reflection – What I Learned

The identity of Lucifer in religious texts and traditions has been a subject of debate and interpretation over centuries, and its relationship varies depending on the context and belief system. Scriptures in the holy books of the Abrahamic religions refer to Lucifer as the "Light Bringer" and "Morning Star." He was a cherub or angel, once close to God. Lucifer is often portrayed as having been one of the most beautiful and wisest of all angels, which made his fall to evil particularly tragic and profound.

A *Popular Science* article[43] confirms the Vatican's connection to a telescope with this name, while a 2023 PolitiFact fact-check[44] labels the Vatican's ownership of a "Lucifer" telescope as "false." Whatever the case, the telescope was named by German astronomers and is located at the University of Arizona, not directly affiliated with the Vatican.

My distrust of the Roman Catholic Church has deep roots, informed by historical events and personal family history. I am aware that the Council of Nicaea in 325 AD, under Roman Emperor Constantine, significantly shaped the official Bible, eliminating content that might empower women or promote anything that might suggest that anyone can experience direct connection with the Divine. This act effectively positioned the clergy as essential intermediaries between God and the faithful, a move I've always found unsettling and judged to be a power grab.

Moreover, Constantine's placement of Christian holidays over the top of Pagan holy days[45] in the third century AD seemed like a strategic move to consolidate his power by reducing diverse belief systems into one religious authority under his rule. The subsequent persecution by the Catholic Church against those who sought to continue their ancestral, earth-centric spiritual practices is among the governing abuses of Roman colonialism. Their heartless political and religious leaders branded Pagan practitioners as "heretics" who must be "saved," even through methods of torture. Those who refused to be "saved" by the church were thought to be without souls and were put to death. These aspects of the religious history of the Catholic Church impact me personally due to my ancestral ties to the Cathars,[46] followers of a dualistic Christian gnostic movement who were decimated as a result of Pope Innocent III's crusades.

These historical grievances, compounded by the modern scandal of child sexual abuse within the church, have made me leery of this religious institution. While I respect the core spiritual teachings of all religions, the actions of those in power within organized faiths often seem to betray the very principles they preach.

Personal Note on Jesus vs. the Church

While I hold a general distrust of the Roman Catholic Church as a power structure, this is separate from my view of Catholics, the broader category of Christians, or those who are spiritually inspired by Jesus's exemplary life.

The documentary's exploration of potential satanic symbols within Vatican architecture further fuels my suspicion. Why would such imagery and names be chosen if not to hint at darker undercurrents beneath the church's holy facade?

Chapter 5: Fall of the Cabal

All these sound bites from *Fall of the Cabal*, and my thoughts about them, are flying by me so fast I don't want to take the time to track, much less fact-check anything. I commit to watching this series through to the end without pause. I'll do my research later, honoring my promise to Laura. It makes sense to me to follow Janet's introductory advice to view the series in its entirety before jumping online to check on her claims. This approach aligns with my desire for efficiency, given the rapid-fire presentation of provocative claims. I take mental notes of what I intend to check out later, with particular interest in looking for information on topics I find overly strange or unthinkable.

Janet then asks, "And since when does the pope make the sign of the devil?" while showing the last two popes holding out their pinkies, pointer fingers, and thumbs, making the hand sign that I know means "I love you" in American sign language.

Janet's suggestion that recent popes have used this hand signal to demonstrate their allegiance to the devil strikes me as particularly far-fetched. Her subsequent presentation of well-known public figures using a similar gesture with pinky and pointer finger only does mean horns in sign language. However, this does not necessarily signify support for the devil; more likely, it is a sign of fandom for the Texas Longhorns sports teams out of Austin, Texas. I quickly dismiss this claim.

Throughout my viewing of this first episode in the series, my reactions vary widely—from agreement to curiosity, skepticism, and outright disbelief. Yet, my inability to sleep, the compelling nature of this video's presentation style, and my commitment to Laura keep me engaged. I am repulsed by the content, yet intrigued to discover where this journey through Janet's findings will lead.

9/11

Janet then delves into the 9/11 World Trade Center attacks, a subject I explored years ago through the documentary *Loose Change*,[47] which echoes what has been shared by Architects and Engineers for 9/11 Truth.[48] This exposure led me to question the official investigation of the events.

Disney

Next, the narrative shifts to examining Disney's use of subliminal erotic imagery[49] in its animations, hinting at a deliberate attempt to influence young minds. Having encountered these claims about two decades ago, I recognize the subtle yet unmistakable sexual symbols embedded in films like *The Little Mermaid,* where a castle spire resembles a phallus[50] and a fleeting moment suggests an aroused priest during a wedding scene. While aware of these elements, I hadn't deeply considered their implications or the intent behind them.

2023 Reflection – What I Learned

In response to the controversy, former Disney animator Tom Sito addressed these images in a 2015 *Huffington Post* article, later updated in 2020. His explanations did little to quell the speculation. A more candid insight I encountered on Reddit suggested that animators, seeking amusement in their tedious work, might insert obscure details unlikely to be noticed by most viewers.

Abortion

The discussion takes a darker turn as Janet claims that full-term abortions are legally permissible in the United States, and more specifically New York, using a *New York Post* headline as evidence. She then states that there are doctors who perform these abortions and claim the baby cannot feel any pain. These assertions are deeply troubling to me. I have always been pro-choice, but with limits. I can't imagine any situation in which I would support the abortion of a fully viable fetus.

2023 Reflection – What I Learned

The claim that New York legalized full-term abortions is a distortion of the truth. Following Governor Cuomo's 2019 enactment of the Reproductive Health Act, which codified Roe v. Wade into state law,

Chapter 5: Fall of the Cabal

> misconceptions arose. The Act permits abortions beyond 24 weeks only under specific conditions: either the fetus is nonviable or the procedure is essential to safeguard the mother's life or health.

Migrant Caravan

The documentary then shifts its focus to the 2018 migrant caravan, highlighting the journey of families traveling from Honduras to the US border. Janet presents a map, claiming the caravan traveled over 2,000 miles in 1.5 months, supposedly timing their arrival to coincide with the American midterm elections. She calculates that this meant walking an average of 45 miles a day, pointing out that most travelers were wearing inadequate footwear like flip flops or even going barefoot. She supports this claim with a series of photographs depicting the migrants' challenging journey. Furthermore, Janet alleges that George Soros funded chartered buses for the asylum seekers, making this otherwise unfeasible journey possible for thousands of migrants. She alleges that Soros has an evil intent: to undermine the US economy while gaining fiscal leverage in which he can win enormous windfalls. Janet asserts Soros had actively previously succeeded in a similar finance strategy when he made over a billion while almost breaking Britain.[51]

Reflecting on my own exposure to the caravan through CNN, I realize their stories had always centered on the migrants' dire circumstances and their search for asylum, evoking deep empathy for their plight. The logistical impossibility of such a journey, especially under the conditions described, had never occurred to me until presented in this light by *Fall of the Cabal*, prompting yet another moment of suspicion. Was this organized? Supported? Intentional? What's really going on here?

> **2024 Reflection – What I Learned**
>
> My more recent efforts to uncover detailed information on the logistics of the migrants' journey have been inconclusive. However, while seeking to understand the reality at the border I learned that the crisis is real.

> Between 2018 and 2023, migration patterns and border apprehensions at the US-Mexico border have seen significant fluctuations. In 2018, nearly 467,000 apprehensions were recorded. By 2021, encounters at the border surged to over 1.6 million. The fiscal year 2022 saw over 2.2 million encounters.[52] In 2023, the dynamics at the border evolved further with the end of the Title 42 policy and the implementation of new immigration strategies, leading to a record 2.5 million encounters.[53] As of May 2024, some sources report that more than 7 million illegal border crossings have occurred since Biden's inauguration.[54]

Foreskins in Facial Creams

Fall of the Cabal next scrutinizes Hollywood celebrities for their endorsement of facial creams derived from the foreskins of baby boys,[55] retailing at $650 per treatment. This revelation, though shocking, aligns with my understanding of the medical and cosmetic industry's interest in regenerative properties found in various human tissues. There are stem cells found in a baby's umbilical cord and the placenta. It makes sense that some kind of similarly rejuvenating cells would exist in the foreskin too. However, the ethical implications of cutting off such a sensitive part of the male genitalia, with no consent possible because of the age of the infant or child, then classifying it as "bio-waste" and using it as a source for cosmetic products, deeply troubles me.

Janet's voice continues. She seems to be using a tone of sarcasm when she poses the question, *"What's next? Drinking babies' blood?"*

This hyperbolic leap strikes me as outlandish, emphasizing the video's inclination towards sensationalism. It's way too big a jump from foreskin-derived face cream to drinking babies' blood. It is well beyond my mind to imagine anyone would ever do such an insane thing.

Chapter 6:
Bioweapons

Janet's narrative progresses to suggest that viruses like AIDS, SARS, Zika, and Ebola are patented, implying they are manmade, due to the nature of patent laws. My eyebrows raise reflexively. I don't know what to make of this claim, but it feeds my already strong distrust of our government and what the powers that be might be hiding from us as it relates to Covid-19.

> **2023 Reflection – What I Learned**
>
> The claim that the patenting of viruses like AIDS, SARS, Zika, and Ebola suggests they are manmade is misleading. The patents associated with these viruses generally relate to medical research, such as vaccine development or diagnostic tools, and do not imply that the viruses themselves are artificially created. This misunderstanding often arises from a lack of clarity about the nature and purpose of such patents. For a detailed explanation, you can refer to the Reuters article from October 27, 2020.[56]

The documentary's insinuation about the possibility of bioweapons being developed alongside experimental vaccines adds to my growing wariness, particularly considering the legal immunity granted to vaccine manufacturers under the National Childhood Vaccine Injury Act of 1986.[57] I expect this vaccine will likely be pushed through without sufficient time for safety studies, which under normal circumstances would take at least three years to complete. However, given the context of this pandemic and understandable support for an emergency response, the safety studies will be fast-tracked to complete them as soon as possible.

Event 201

My distrust in our public health authorities is further fueled by the timing of Event 201,[58] a pandemic preparedness drill.[59] This simulation was hosted by the Johns Hopkins Center for Health Security, in partnership with the World Economic Forum (WEF) and the Gates Foundation, starting on October 18, 2019,[60] right around the time some experts[61] determined the novel coronavirus to have first emerged in Wuhan, China. I have seen so many news reporters asking Bill Gates[62] how we should work to get through the pandemic, but all I can think of is how expertly he has coordinated the whole response. This thought fills me with a sense of cynicism.

I think everyone noted Gates's strategy, as I heard people to the left of the aisle repeating this statement with hopeful conviction, and others, like me, repeating it with dread. Gates said Covid would end when "almost every person on the planet has been vaccinated against coronavirus."[63] I couldn't help but wonder, was his global vaccination strategy motivated by public health concerns? Profit motives? A value for control? Or some combination of these factors? Based upon my previous knowledge of his involvement with Monsanto, health does not seem to be anything close to a primary factor.

Mass Surveillance

Janet then presents the notion that our personal devices, regardless of whether they are turned on or off, are embedded with spyware, recording our every conversation. This idea is not new to me, thanks to Edward Snowden's revelations as illustrated in the documentary *Citizenfour*.[64] Still, it invokes

Chapter 6: Bioweapons

squeamish discomfort due to my knowledge of the extensive global surveillance he exposed, run by the National Security Agency (NSA) with the forced cooperation of telecommunication companies. I lament as I recall that these incursions on civilians' private spaces were further welded into law by what seemed to be reactive bipartisan support of the Patriot Act[65] after the collapse of the Twin Towers in 2001.

Monsanto

Janet's narrative shifts to Bayer's acquisition of Monsanto, highlighting Monsanto's controversial history with Agent Orange[66] and its transition to agricultural chemicals post-Vietnam War. The video shows images of heartbreaking birth defects as Janet briefs the viewers on the multifold damages caused by Agent Orange.

This is another concept I have loads of prior familiarity with, given my connection to another friend, Lisa, a passionate environmental activist and health educator.

For years, Lisa has kept me abreast of the horrors of Monsanto, sharing dozens of videos and articles with me. She has alerted me to various lawsuits against the corporate behemoth. She has educated me on how to avoid the growing list of unlabeled GMO foods, ingredients, and products sprayed with the known carcinogen this company produces called glyphosate,[67] the active ingredient in the herbicide Roundup. I became aware early on of a movement called Millions Against Monsanto[68] (now called Billions Against Bayer) and have often referred to this company as many others do, referring to it as "MonSatan." From what I have learned about it, I am more aware of how its products generate death[69] rather than support life. I remember Robert F. Kennedy Jr.'s (RFK Jr.) legal breakthrough against Monsanto in 2018 when he won $289 million[70] for his client who had terminal cancer caused largely by what was proven to be Monsanto's intentional concealment of the cancer-causing toxicity of Roundup. Monsanto's stated mission is to "feed the world," but when your company destroys organic farms, kills beneficial soil microbes, and feeds humans and livestock animals foods grown with highly carcinogenic toxins that accumulate in the body, can that really be viewed as beneficent?

> ### 2023 Reflection – What I Learned
>
> As of January 2024, Bayer spent about $10 billion of the $16 billion it set aside to resolve more than 150,000 cases over Roundup.[71] With these numbers, one might think it unimaginable that Roundup continues to be sold in the United States. However, the revolving doors between Monsanto executives and the Environmental Protection Agency (EPA)[72] have been well documented[73] over the last 25 years. Glyphosate is now an ingredient in a broad list of agricultural products.[74] It is sprayed on most grains, nuts, legumes, and a variety of other produce[75] (even those labeled non-GMO)[76] prior to harvest. Despite its proven toxicity, glyphosate remains legally available for purchase.

Bill Gates

Given my knowledge of Monsanto, Gates's $23 million investment in this corporate monster in 2010,[77] and his active push for farmers in India[78] (and later Africa) to replace their own renewable heirloom seed supplies with these infertile seeds and toxic chemical agricultural products, which led to mass suicides[79] and a 41% rise in cancer,[80] my mind is in a furious tailspin. It's hard for me to imagine how anyone could believe Gates has anyone's health interests at heart.

War Crimes

Janet's last key point in the first 12 minutes of *Fall of the Cabal* is to highlight the fact that President Obama received a Nobel Peace Prize only months after gaining the presidential office. In the following eight years, he invaded seven countries and reportedly dropped a bomb every 20 minutes.[81] "Who on earth was on that Nobel committee?" she asks in a tone of puzzled exasperation.

Chapter 6: Bioweapons

I remember Obama receiving the Nobel Peace Prize. At the time, I was so delighted he was president that I did not pay attention to why he received this prestigious award. I brushed those details off, figuring that being the first Black president was reason enough; it was a triumph that inspired hope of a new America no longer brought down by the legacy of racism and Jim Crow.

I was however dismayed, as were many people I know, as he engaged in war after war,[82] using drone strikes as his primary method of assault.[83] I heard stories that innocent civilians were dying, and I could not understand why Obama would have made these terrible choices. I wanted to believe in everything I thought he stood for: peace, cooperation, diversity, empathy, and a world in which all people are valued and all human lives matter, regardless of nationality or whether or not their countries are members of NATO.

The Military-Industrial Complex

I thought perhaps Obama's previous dedication to conscious and compassionate leadership had been hijacked in some way. Could he have been blackmailed or otherwise meaningfully threatened to act in ways that opposed his stated values and previous integrity? Was no one able to stand up to the powers of the espionage wing of the CIA and the private interests of defense contractors? Dwight Eisenhower's final speech before he left office was one in which he sought to warn Americans of the dangerous rise of this military-industrial complex.[84] Janet's words make me wonder, has it grown beyond all checks and balances? Could it be that even the standing president could not stop the dictates of this brutal war machine?

I can think of no other reason that Obama, the leader I have so deeply admired, and in whom I placed my hope for the future, would do such a thing. Even the reporters in the MSM expressed criticism of his war policies during his presidency.

2023 Reflection – What I Learned

An *Atlantic* article[85] critically examined President Obama's drone strike policies, highlighting the ethical and legal challenges posed by such covert operations. It suggests that Obama's decisions could not have come from naïveté. It alleges Obama enabled a continuation of highly controversial practices by the CIA, undermining the principles he espoused.

The Deep State

I had previously watched Daniel Sheehan's full lecture series "Rulers of the Realm,"[86] an exposé on the dark corruption of mostly unelected officials lurking within our government. In this series, Sheehan, a prominent federal civil rights attorney, highlighted the wholly immoral actions of members of the Bush family and the CIA, lesser-known factual details surrounding the assassination of President John F. Kennedy, and a dozen other related subjects. I wonder, was this lecture series pointing to what conspiracy theorists refer to as "the Deep State"? If it's different, I cannot see the difference at this time.

2023 Reflection – What I Learned

The term "Deep State" typically refers to a supposed secret network of powerful individuals, often within the government or other institutions, who operate behind the scenes to influence political decisions and policy-making processes. The concept suggests that these individuals, who may include government officials, people working within intelligence agencies, military leaders, and prominent business figures, work to promote their own agendas and maintain power, regardless of changes in elected leadership or public opinion.[87] Critics often view the notion of a Deep State as a conspiracy theory lacking substantial evidence.

Chapter 6: Bioweapons

Mainstream Media Silence

"The world is not what you think. And guess what all these things have in common?" Janet asks. "They were completely ignored by the MSM. Not one news channel covered or questioned any of it." The next screen is black with one word in white: *silence.*

The Uniparty

She continues, "And just when I thought I'd seen it all, *this* became president of the United States." A very unflattering picture of Donald Trump is shown on the screen followed by a second photo in which he is making fun of a disabled reporter.

"I always thought there were two political sides in life," Janet reflects. The screen shows a red sign with the word *Left* and a blue sign with the word *Right* as she states: "Left was for the common people; right was for the rich. But I soon found out that my ideas did not reflect reality at all."

She continues, "Obama seemed to have enchanted everybody, including myself, with his good looks and charms, but like I said, he invaded seven countries. He was a Democrat for God's sake! Maybe the left and the right were two wings of the same bird?" she asks as I notice my resonance with her ruminations.

Citizens United

This thought is not new to me. As dark money flooded our political landscape following the horrid aforementioned Citizens United Supreme Court ruling in 2010,[88] it seemed that people with heaping gobs of money had purchased every major politician on both sides of the aisle.[89] While we maintained the façade of a two-party system, I suspected it was more appearance than reality. I would never forgive Justices Clarence Thomas, Antonin Scalia, Anthony Kennedy, John Roberts, and Samuel Alito, or the Koch brothers, for this horrible judicial decision,[90] which destroyed regulations designed to prevent just this scenario. I believe, as many do, that this one decision rapidly decimated our democracy by giving way too much power to corporations and oligarchs. Already they were too interwoven with US regulatory agencies through lobbying, legalized bribery, and revolving-door deals.

Here Janet pivots: "In spite of my leftist upbringing and background and my fierce opposition against Trump, I decided to give him the benefit of the doubt." A couple far more flattering pictures of Trump appear on the screen.

I feel resonance with Janet's past but am immediately disturbed by this shift.

Enemy Images

While I seek to dissolve what in Nonviolent Communication (NVC) are called *enemy images*[91]—evaluative thoughts that cast others as bad, wrong, and deserving of punishment—it has been very hard for me to experience anything but outrage and revulsion whenever I see Trump's face or hear his voice. I find myself however, due to my striving to walk the talk of NVC with integrity, actively working to soften my abject loathing of this man.

Can I learn to "witness" Trump without anger and disgust? I notice I am challenging myself with what seems an extremely tall order. Perhaps with Janet's perspective, I may find something more redeeming about him.

Q: A Ray of Hope

The graphic transition from Trump to the final image uses a circular watery motion that looks very much like an Anonymous hacktivist combined with *The Matrix*. In the center is a hooded figure with the letter Q floating where the face should be, encircled by a sunburst of computer-screen-green ones and zeros set against a black background. Janet's voice enters again, "And then, out of nowhere, rose the enigma of Q."

This character called Q sounds vaguely familiar to me, but I don't know where I have heard of it before. Could this secretive person or persons going by the name Q represent the needed collaborative efforts aiming to dismantle systemic elite-sponsored rot? This notion, while speculative, opens new avenues for revealing the underlying truth behind the complex web of political narratives and power dynamics. A partnership between Anonymous and insiders from various clandestine US intelligence agencies

Chapter 6: Bioweapons

would be an epic combination of talented, well-positioned, and conscious revolutionaries, capable of exposing corruption and restoring power to the people. My body surges with a refreshed sense of hope and excitement.

Only fifteen minutes have passed since I pressed play on part 1 of this 10-part *Fall of the Cabal* series. I am overwhelmed and intrigued by the dense content. The myriad topics, despite their sheer volume and often disturbing material, somehow resonates with me. That, along with the promise of a positive wrap-up, offers a much-needed diversion from the ongoing daily stress of this Covid-19 lockdown that has now entered its fourth month with no clear end in sight. A part of me is eager for any insight that might bring clarity to these chaotic times, or even give me good reasons to diminish my disdain for Trump.

Chapter 7:
Alleged Satanic Manipulators

The Cabal

In the nearly three hours that follow, Janet expands on the points in her introduction, adding more as she weaves together an elaborate and all-encompassing theory of what's "really going on" in the world *and* how humanity will find our way through to a much more beautiful, equitable, sustainable, and peaceful future. Janet sets forth "evidence" suggesting that a dark elite group she refers to as "the Cabal" is actively working to normalize pedophilia,[92] devil worship,[93] and cannibalism.[94] She reveals what she says is John Podesta's art collection, featuring paintings of kids tied up in an empty swimming pool, pointing out that Podesta is Hillary Clinton's right-hand man.

The Clintons

She builds an argument asserting the Clintons have been using their nonprofit to engage in child sex trafficking out of Haiti and for money laundering with dark sources. She highlights Marina Abramovic's satanic art and this woman's potent influence in Hollywood. And she believes Bill Clinton is secretly a cross-dressing worshipper of Satan, as confirmed by a painting owned by Jeffrey Epstein in which the former president is wearing a blue dress and red high-heeled shoes. As for the questionable deletion of tens of thousands of emails from Hillary Clinton's private server, Janet believes Clinton was desperate to hide what WikiLeaks would later reveal: that Clinton secretly worships a satanic god named Moloch and used that email account to engage in child sex trafficking using strange comments about pizza to hide that she was in conversation with Podesta about pedophilia.

These claims are *way* over the top and sound like complete bullshit to me. But I don't skip over anything in this series. I am committed to watching it all the way through to get to the good news.

> **Personal Reflection 2023**
>
> As I did not even consider these allegations could be true at this point in my journey, my later learnings are reflected in chapter 11: "Doing My Research."

Janet believes that for this heartless Cabal, money and power are never enough. These people are authoritarian in nature and want *total power and control*. They don't just manipulate politicians with bribes; they lure them to places like Epstein's Island, where targeted politicians are encouraged to socialize, drink, and get high, which seems normal at this kind of high-profile gathering, until the next stage of debauchery arrives. Once these political leaders are relaxed and inebriated, they are seduced into having illicit relations with underage teens without knowing they've been photographed and filmed along the way.

Fame, Fortune, Bribery, and Blackmail

According to Janet, the Cabal maintains its power not only through bribery, including promises of money, fame, and power, but also through this form of blackmail, which only gets darker as people rise to positions of global power. The Cabal's methods of manipulation mirror what Hollywood portrays as "making deals with the devil." In addition to politicians, the Cabal targets royalty, members of the World Economic Forum, and Hollywood stars. In keeping with this narrative, those who rise higher become

Chapter 7: Alleged Satanic Manipulators

stuck in the Cabal's trap: obey and demonstrate your willingness to bend your actions to their will and you will gain more power, riches, and fame; fall out of line, or try to expose us, and we will ruin you.

While this level of organized manipulation would have seemed beyond extreme to me in the past, I have been struggling to make sense of the greed and corruption I have been seeing for so long. Why don't these people listen to their internal moral compasses like those in my family and extended community do? Aren't most people around the world naturally inclined toward kindness and care? Isn't that the basic nature of humanity? Am I overly naïve?

Jeffrey Epstein

In 2019, I was stunned by the news of Jeffrey Epstein and Ghislaine Maxwell. While he was said to be a financier, there was no clear record of who his clients were except for one, the owner of Victoria's Secret. No one knew for sure how Epstein made his billions.[95] In 2019, some news sources I viewed revealed that underage teens were coerced and sometimes forced into erotic connection with him in his various residences, including his private island. Several women openly accused Epstein of requiring them to have sex with high politicians and royalty. It was well known that he was rubbing shoulders and doing business deals with many of the wealthiest and most powerful people in the world.

My mind is racing with thoughts connected to this video. There's so much corruption at the top. Can this be a major part of explaining how the rich and powerful can make decisions that are so harmful to humanity in favor of personal gain? According to the creator of this *Fall of the Cabal* docuseries, yes, it is.

Satanic Worship and Innocent Victims

As if this alleged scope of elite-level crime and corruption is not bad enough, Janet kicks it up a notch. According to her, members of the Cabal practice the darkest satanic rituals of child torture and sacrifice, extracting and then self-administering an anti-aging potion called adrenochrome, made from the blood of terrorized victims. This name was purportedly chosen because of the fear-induced adrenaline that floods the victim's blood just prior to "harvest." Adrenochrome is said to be untraceable, as it is natural and readily metabolized by the body, leaving no biological evidence that can be discovered through any form of testing.

> ## 2023 Reflection – What I Learned
>
> There actually is a chemical compound created by the oxidation of adrenaline called "adrenochrome,"[96] but it is not what QAnons believe it is.[97] The name and idea of adrenochrome likely caught appeal in QAnon because of its mention in pop culture, having been mentioned in Aldous Huxley's book *Doors of Perception*, the novel *A Clockwork Orange*, and the movie *Fear and Loathing in Las Vegas*. A similar mythical brew is included in the movie *Death Becomes Her*. *Monsters Inc.* has also been cited in connection to adrenochrome.

A full episode of *Fall of the Cabal* is dedicated to this topic of the satanic ritualized abuse of children, including photos and news media showing children who are badly beat up. Some of the pictures show children with "panda eyes," in which the skin around their eyes is a deep shade of purple, almost black, in heartbreaking portraits of their young faces.

These allegations are completely shocking to me. I feel utterly devastated as I see the images and hear the stories flash on the screen. The pain in my chest runs deep as tears are streaming down my face. As I watch this section of *Fall of the Cabal*, I feel entranced in the way people do when they drive past a gruesome car wreck. One can only hope the drivers and passengers survived and are getting the care they need to recover. How on earth could anyone be getting away with harming children as shown in these photos? It's so completely wrong! With all my heart, I need to know something is being done to protect these children. I cannot live with knowing that this is happening to innocent young victims.

Chapter 7: Alleged Satanic Manipulators

Lady Gaga

Next, Janet points out that Lady Gaga painted her eyes in a panda bear likeness in one of her costumes.[98] Many times in this series, she connects Lady Gaga and other Hollywood stars to these alleged satanic practices and consumption of adrenochrome, as she weaves a connection between the Cabal and Hollywood.

2023 Reflection – What I Learned:

While it is easy for many Christians, and perhaps believers of other Abrahamic religions, to view Hollywood's renditions of Satan and satanic practices as evidence that Hollywood is supporting Satan, it is easy for many artists to understand that the play between forces of good and evil, light and darkness, are essential elements of art. And shock, or twisting of traditional meanings of well-known symbols, catches attention and often generates profit.

Janet also shows a video snippet of a news channel from a foreign country reporting on the crime of people abusing children to harvest adrenochrome, and a video of a brother and sister who openly talk with an investigator about how their father cuts off babies' heads and drinks their blood at church. The details of those interview clips are more gruesome than I can repeat. The pictures are hard enough to see, but these videos add a whole new level of shock to my already stunned and disoriented state.

2021 Reflection – What I Learned

The interviews of these two children appear to be real, and their father may have been a seriously twisted human being. I don't know, as I was never able to find clear verifiable context to explain more about this situation. But even if what the children reported was true, it in no way means a global organization is supporting this unconscionable, depraved, and illegal behavior. As for the media report, it came from a foreign news channel I had never heard of. I have every reason to believe it was at best poorly researched and at worst a purposeful propaganda piece.

Make It Stop

Had these horrifying claims been revealed within these first few episodes, I would have turned off the series just as I turn off trailers for horror films, but they were not "revealed" until parts 6, 7, and 8. By then, I was hooked and felt compelled to watch the series through to completion. In the beginning of the series, Janet warned her viewers that the truth was darker than we could imagine but encouraged viewers to watch it all the way through because there would be very good news in episodes 9 and 10. She promised to end on a positive, optimistic, and empowering note. If there is any truth to these horrific and heartbreaking allegations, and it seems there is, I am now desperate to hear her promised good news. Having followed Janet's trail of logic, and the evidence given to her by what I assume are trustworthy Anons, I am feeling more deeply shaken, shocked, grief stricken, and vulnerable than ever. I need some kind of hope to hold onto so as to avoid falling into a complete pit of powerlessness.

The political betrayals of 2016 and 2020 were bad enough. The clear grip of the power elites and their seeming lack of care for humanity and the planet were already looking dire, but the picture Janet is painting is so much worse than I ever could have imagined.

I cannot fall into a deeper sense of powerlessness than the one that has been building in me over the years, most especially in these last three months of the Covid lockdown.

Episode 8 begins with the following quote from an unidentified Anon, a group I still assume to be members of the hacktivist group Anonymous. I'm guessing they've successfully broken into the Cabal's private data. What this Anon has to say confirms Janet's thesis:

Worldwide, children are stolen and sold to the elite pedophile rings. They are tortured, raped, and murdered as part of satanic

Chapter 7: Alleged Satanic Manipulators

ritual ceremonies. The murderers then drink the children's blood and eat their flesh. The blood of children who were severely traumatized before they died contains a natural drug produced by the pineal gland in the brain. Adrenochrome is the highest valued drug in the world. The god they serve is Satan. It is not a God of Love and Mercy.

2021 Personal Reflection

I had not considered until the end of my time in QAnon that this "Anon" could be a random person, or a propaganda generator, who enjoys logging onto the disturbingly bizarre and highly encrypted anonymous message boards called 4chan and 8kun (formerly 8chan), where this QAnon phenomenon began.

2021 Reflection – What I Learned

The accusation of harvesting and drinking human blood has clear anti-Semitic propaganda roots, which I describe more thoroughly towards the end of chapter 29, "It Gets Personal," where I discuss the *Protocols of the Elders of Zion*.

My mind is now spinning on this apparent revelation. I had been aware that the pineal gland naturally produces N,N-Dimethyltryptamine (DMT)[99] at two points in every human's life: upon birth and upon death. DMT is also referred to as the spirit molecule.[100] Many teachers connected to the plant medicine and psychedelic areas of study say this molecule is responsible for our feeling of connection to God, and this DMT can be harvested from plants. It is also naturally produced in humans via the pineal gland under circumstances that do not occur naturally in life. Spending three days in total darkness can elicit this natural experience of DMT secretion in the body, as can specific breathing techniques.

If what this Anon is saying could be true, it's pure evil to harvest the pineal glands of innocent children or any living creature. These allegations of ritualized satanic abuse of children are unthinkable, and the pictures are nightmarish. I am struggling to figure out how to put this new information into perspective. Only complete psychopaths would ever consider doing such a horrific thing to children.

I do believe there are sociopaths who rise to the top of power structures, but could they really be this depraved? Not only to abuse and ritually sacrifice children, but on top of that to use this extreme level of crime to bribe and manipulate politicians, royalty, and other powerful leaders in a direction that perpetuates pain and suffering for lives everywhere? This is well beyond anything I had previously imagined, but I don't have better answers to explain the extreme greed and cruelty I see in our world. All I know is I feel powerless to make it stop. I feel heartbroken as these horrors are planted in my imagination. Someone must put an end to this!

As if my state of stress wasn't high enough before I pressed play on *Fall of the Cabal* only a couple hours earlier, the "evidence" Janet presented has me quaking in shock and dismay. Tears stream down my face as Stephen, oblivious to my distress, sleeps peacefully beside me. It's the middle of the night. As much as I need the comfort I know he would under normal circumstances seek to provide me, I don't dare wake him. We've been in conflict in these last few days. The last thing I want to do is disrupt his sleep. Besides, how on earth would I explain the last two hours of video viewing that have brought me to this fragile state? It's hard to imagine he'd have patience for this. I'm alone with my emotions and all the information I've just received. All I can think now is I cannot tolerate this abuse happening to innocent children. Something must be done to end this violence. Just make it stop!

Satan is Real

"Whether you believe in Satan or not, these people do," Janet asserts.

I now remember a prior clip in *Fall of the Cabal* where Janet quoted Pope Francis as having affirmed "Satan is real. He is evil, he's not like mist. He's not a diffuse thing. He is a person."[101]

Chapter 7: Alleged Satanic Manipulators

> **2023 Reflection – What I Learned**
>
> It is true that Pope Francis has been quoted saying "Satan is real," and "He is evil, he's not like mist. He's not a diffuse thing. He is a person."[102] While this assertion might be surprising to a nonreligious person, many Christians have been raised with the belief that Satan is as real as anyone. That was not my upbringing, and before watching this video, I had never actually thought about the possibility that Satan could have a physical body. I had only thought of him as an archetype.

Could that possibly be true? I know there are spiritual saints and enlightened masters in this world, so is it possible the antithesis energies are also here in human or humanoid form?[103] Is the satanic influence on earth more concrete than I had previously thought?

Sure, Janet's claims are outrageous, and they stretch my imagination into dark recesses where it has never before gone, but I don't have a better answer for why the world is in such a horrible state. I don't have another way to explain the greed and corruption I know must exist among the ruling, ultra-elite class. Maybe the root of all that heartless cruelty actually does come from "God's fallen angel," Satan, and his calculated manipulation of the human race from the dawn of civilization through to present time.

> **2023 Reflection – What I Learned**
>
> I was unaware that "satanic panic," as propagated by QAnon, was nothing new.[104] It is a trend that began in the late '60s. The Salem witch trials and the Crusades could also be considered forms of satanic panic. In both of these cases, unfounded religiously based beliefs about Satan's influence were accepted by the masses as undeniable truth, despite flimsy evidence to back serious accusations against innocent people.

Janet seems to recognize that her claims are over the top. She doubles down, saying many victims have tried to speak up and their cries fall on deaf ears. Why? First of all, the MSM will never publish this information, and second of all, most of those in charge of the higher courts are too involved with the Cabal, too reliant on its generosity, to be able to take down the abusers. She points out the very real and undeniable fact that Catholic priests had been raping children for decades before their abuses were discovered.[105]

My heart is in shambles as the evidence I see presented in Janet's series is not only troubling; it appears something completely sinister could be hiding behind the Catholic Church's façade of virtue and moral righteousness.

The Calm Before the Storm

But then, Janet has a relieving report to share, in contrast to the obliterating scandalous rumors of the previous episode. Her update is not new to me. Around the time she created this series (in July of 2019), Jeffrey Epstein was arrested.[106] While his August 10, 2019 death would silence his testimony, it would be only a matter of time before his guest list would be revealed.[107] Janet reassures us, "Everyone who visited his island will be indicted soon. Think of big names such as Prince Andrew, Bill and Hillary Clinton, John Podesta, James Alefantis, Marina Abramovic, Tony Blair, Mark Zuckerberg (Facebook), Jeff Bezos (Amazon), Erik Schmidt (Google), Bill Gates (Microsoft), Evelyn and Lynn de Rothschild, and many, many Hollywood stars. Is this the beginning of the long-awaited mass arrests [the unsealing of indictments, and the "storm"] Q keeps referring to?"

Many of these names have been mentioned, along with incriminating evidence, over the course of the series, and the idea that the vile people who collude with the Cabal will be apprehended provides me with a ray of hope in an otherwise dark abyss. I am aware of the news of Epstein's arrest in the real world, but hearing that his guest list will soon be released is a huge relief. Maybe the tide is turning. Maybe a great shift in power is beginning to happen. Wouldn't it be amazing if all the perpetrators of organized crime and child abuse were stopped once and for all! That would change the world for the better in one fell swoop.

Chapter 8:
The Enigma of Q

In episode 9, the music adds to the sense of something very good about to happen as Janet returns to the topic of the appearance of Q. She explains, "through the 'Q drops,' hints, clues, and questions are planted like seeds, waiting for humanity, to be picked up, researched, and unraveled." She talks about how this movement, connected to Q, grew on social media channels that were initially set up by the Cabal to track us all. But now these media streams are being used against the Cabal to awaken humanity. Janet points out the evidence she's been shown in support of her assertion that humanity is waking up. Photo after photo shows people en masse, protesting in revolt to the elite powers.

Humanity Rising

As I see the pictures of mass protests flash on the screen, I feel thrilled to see humanity rising. I have seen similar photos before as I kept tabs on the rising protests in the fall of 2019,[108] but I had no idea they had anything to do with Q. Can it be true that these massive protests were the result of an awakening of humanity supported by United States government insiders with Q-level clearance[109] in order to drive the change we need in our world? My heart skips a beat at the thought of it. My internal chemistry has shifted from excess adrenaline and cortisol dumps into a surge of much more pleasurable neurotransmitters such as dopamine, oxytocin, and serotonin. As I am still on the all-consuming emotional roller coaster ride of this three-hour series, I am only semi-aware of the dramatic shift in my personal biochemistry.

> **2023 Reflection – What I Learned**
>
> As it turns out, the photos Janet showed were a combination of the mass protests in 2019, along with the Yellow Vest economic justice protests that began in France in 2018 and spread around the world, and some protests in which people held signs denoting their QAnon allegiance. Most of the protests had nothing to do with Q.

Janet asserts, "A revolution of the people can only work when there is help at the top. That help was never there in the past, but now there is. That's what makes this revolution different. We have an ally at the top. An ally we refer to as Q."

My internal sense feels she's right. Bernie lost because those who held power over him squashed him. "Our Revolution" could not succeed without help from those at the top. Instead, the powers that be aligned themselves in near complete opposition to his campaign. But this revolution, led by Q, has organized support from insiders known as "White Hats." These are the good and morally motivated men and women in high positions of power. Seeing Janet's evidence of how huge this movement has grown in such a short amount of time is thrilling! This revolution to overturn the oligarchy is happening! I feel a sense of hope rising in me.

Donald Trump… Really?

This episode is dedicated to showing evidence that Q is a government insider, also that Q and the White Hats actively chose Donald Trump, supporting him in his win for the presidency so that they could establish the authoritative power necessary to end the Cabal's reign. Janet talks about how Q is posting clues to help humanity join in on this great shift in power.

Chapter 8: The Enigma of Q

She gives examples of how these Q drops, along with actions President Trump has taken, have led to real-world takedowns of corrupt influencers like Jeffrey Epstein and his ilk. It appears Trump and the White Hats are coming closer to pulling out the root of evil that plagues our planet.

While I am perplexed at Q's choice of Trump, according to Janet, Trump has been grossly misunderstood as a result of the Cabal's hold on the MSM. Janet asserts that Trump understands the dark workings of the Cabal and the Deep State they have planted within United States governmental agencies. She explains that he is 100% committed to ending the horrors of pedophilia and child sex trafficking, demolishing the Deep State, and ending the grip the Cabal has on humanity. *And* he has the entire team of Q and the White Hats on his side.

I am at once shocked and heartened by these revelations. I had lost trust in the MSM, but hadn't ever considered that they could be a tool used by a truly devious Cabal in order to manipulate everyone in my left-of-center community with disinformation for purposes of maintaining total power and control.

> **2023 Personal Reflection**
>
> Recall that I was in a highly compromised emotional state when I started watching this series. Looking back at this point in my journey, I realize how ripe and ready I was to hear anything that would restore my sense of hope for the future and faith in humanity.

Janet insists her assessment of Trump's genius is spot-on by pointing out how his strange way of drinking water on two occasions gave us clues similar to those we would find in the Q drops. It led the deep insider Q team to the takedown of the dangerous NXIVM cult[110] and of the Zara clothing company, which had used slave labor to create its clothes. Janet illustrates with a handful of examples how Trump's unusual behaviors and misspellings are his way of partnering with Q to give us clues as to what is going down in the Deep State.

2021 Reflection – What I Learned

Two human tendencies can combine to make meaning (as Janet did) out of every word, action and tweet Trump has ever made so as to align his actions with one's preexisting beliefs. One is *apophenia*,[111] "the tendency to perceive meaningful connections between unrelated things." The other is *confirmation bias*,[112] "the tendency to search for, interpret, favor, and recall information in a way that confirms or supports one's prior beliefs or values."

My mind is spinning from everything I've seen and my heart aches for a renewed sense of hope. Before, I had always thought Trump was an imbecile. But could it be that he's pretending to be one while secretly sending major clues to those who know how to read them? Could it be that he is in fact doing so much more than meets the eye? Could it be that he is taking down sociopathic evil? Is he stopping those who profiteer off of slavery, sexual aggression, the torture and murder of innocent children, and the blackmailing of politicians? Is he stopping the evils of those who would seek to control the entire human population? If Trump is doing that, as Janet explains, I could begin to feel love and gratitude for this man whom I've been judging so harshly these last few years.

I felt enlivened to imagine what I am coming to believe through watching *Fall of the Cabal*. Could it be that Q has gathered all the evidence needed to bring corporate and government criminals to justice? Could it be that Q is working closely with Trump to fulfill a plan to save America? According to Q, the indictments have been written. It's only a matter of time before they will be unsealed. This will be "the Storm," the grand legal takedown of the Cabal. It will "drain the swamp" and rid our world of the immediate impacts of its very worst humans on the rest of humanity.

Chapter 9:
John F. Kennedy Jr.

Return of the King

Part 10 of *Fall of the Cabal* is entitled "Return of The King." The first image is of the words "The Truth Movement" overlaying a blazing letter Q.

Then Janet speaks:

> *When everything we've seen in the previous episodes is presented to the public with undeniable evidence, people will be in shock. The normal way to deal with shocking information is first to deny it and ridicule the messenger, then get scared, angry, or depressed, and finally accept it as the new paradigm. This will take some time.*

What Janet says here feels right. If what she has revealed is the hidden reality behind the massive corruption and greed I have seen in our world, these revelations are beyond shocking; it is deeply disturbing, and something I don't want to believe. I may have to deal with these phases of awakening in myself and be patient and supportive of others as the world wakes up. I may have to work through the intensely uncomfortable process of my worldview shifting dramatically to acknowledge this truth.

Janet's voice continues:

I believe there will need to be a spokesperson to convey to the world what happened. Someone who will be believed by everyone, Democrats and Republicans alike. It cannot be Donald Trump. Democrats will hate him, no matter how much peace he brings upon them. If I were to choose, for the US at least, it would have to be John F. Kennedy Jr.

What? I know that JFK Jr. died in a plane crash in July of 1999… this may be a bridge too far. But then Janet reveals a plethora of evidence, including dozens of photos she has come across, leading her to firmly believe that JFK Jr. faked his death.

She reports that JFK Jr. graduated as a lawyer and swore he would avenge his father's assassination, even if he had to take down the government to do it. In her telling of the story, he ran for the New York Senate seat in 1999, as did Hillary Clinton. But his private plane, which he piloted, crashed into the Atlantic Ocean before the election took place (the clear implication being foul play).

2023 Reflection – What I Learned

JFK Jr. was encouraged to run for the New York Senate in 1999, but he declined the request before Hillary made her interest clear.[113] His career focus[114] remained on his creation of *George* magazine.[115] The bodies of JFK Jr., his wife Carolyn Bessette, and her sister Lauren Bessette were found by the Coast Guard on July 22, 1999, six days after his plane went missing.[116]

Faked Death

Janet explains that JFK Jr. knew in advance that the Cabal was trying to assassinate him, just as they had his father, President John F. Kennedy, in 1963, and his uncle, Robert F. Kennedy, during his run for the presidency in 1968. Janet asserts that after considering his options, JFK Jr. concluded that the only way to escape his own assassination was to fake his death and

Chapter 9: John F. Kennedy Jr.

go deep underground. She said that while he enjoyed flying his private plane, he knew that there were agents among the espionage arm of the CIA who would tamper with the mechanics of private planes. This was their most common means of exterminating politicians who got in their way. Because of this, he always checked the mechanics before flying.

As much as this likely would stretch most people's imagination, less than five years earlier, I had listened to an interview with John Perkins,[117] author of *Confessions of an Economic Hitman*,[118] in which he spoke about his experience working for the NSA. According to Perkins, assassination through meddling with a target's private plane is a tactic the NSA had actively used to take down enemies for decades.

In addition, I had known a man who worked in the military who often spoke about the covert operations he was convinced our military forces were engaging in, including this assassination technique. This news is not new to me. I can only imagine JFK Jr. would have been aware of these covert operations as well. And seeing as his father and uncle had been assassinated, could it be that an entity within our intelligence agencies is actively seeking to destroy the possibility of that family's lineage continuing to hold high seats of political power?

According to *Fall of the Cabal*, on July 16, 1999, JFK Jr. saw his plane had been tampered with. This presented an opportunity to pull off his disappearance plan. As he was closely connected to the government's search and rescue team, he knew he could count on them to claim they found his body while helping him disappear with an undisclosed and top-secret alias. Janet reports that JFK Jr.'s dead body was never verified by family members, who received only a box of ashes said to be his cremated remains. JFK Jr. and his wife, Carolyn Bessette-Kennedy have been living in disguise, working closely with the White Hats ever since.

George Magazine: Survival Guide to the Future

Janet proposes that JFK Jr. planted clues announcing his return in the February 1997 edition of *George* magazine, subtitled "Survival Guide to the Future." The video shows page 8 of this magazine as Janet reads the text, "Buckle your chin strap and hold on as *George* enters the time warp and reemerges in the year 2020."[119]

"Is this John communicating that he will reappear in 2020?" Janet asks.

Pages of *George* magazine appear on my computer screen highlighting the cover, which offers the following headlines:[120]

- "Bill Gates Talks to John Kennedy About Murdoch, Money, and World Domination"
- "Can Politically Incorrect's Bill Maher Make it in the Big Time?"
- "Indictment Day: Will Hillary Get Busted?"
- "Carl Sagan's Farewell Address"
- "Exclusive: The Inside Story of Jimmy Carter's Final Days in Office"
- "The End of Social Security: What's Broken and How to Fix It"
- "Survival Guide to the Future"

Stopping to confirm online that this magazine does exist as described, I feel a rising exhilaration as I imagine a leader like JFK Jr. rising up in power. Wouldn't it be amazing if he is still alive and working to remove the forces that killed his father and his uncle? I have been praying for years for new enlightened leadership. I eagerly anticipate courage and gusto from people running for high office who are capable of healing the political divides, ending corruption, and restoring the most ethical interpretation of our US Constitution so as to reestablish this literary legal masterpiece as the sacred ground that unites all people in our country. I am incredulous but enlivened by the notion of what a man like Kennedy could bring to politics. I know this claim is way out there, but if it is true, I can envision JFK Jr. helping our nation secure a thriving and enlightened democracy. I'd love to find information to confirm that he is in fact alive.

Conqueror of the Darkness

Janet then points out the strange appearance of a man named Vincent Fusca, who began passionately volunteering at Trump's campaign offices. She explains how his name in Latin means "conqueror of the dark." According to her, many people believe this man is JFK Jr. in disguise.

Chapter 9: John F. Kennedy Jr.

> **2023 Reflection – What I Learned**
>
> In fact, Vincent Fusca is not JFK Jr. or Q. He is simply Vincent Fusca.[121] However, Vincent, from the Latin "vincere," does mean "to conquer," and the Latin word "fusca" means dark, swarthy, or dusky.

Where We Go One, We Go All

Next, Janet connects JFK Jr. to Q by pointing out that his father's memorial site from an aerial view is in the shape of a Q. She then shares with excitement that the QAnon slogan, "Where we go one, we go all," was engraved on the bell aboard JFK Jr.'s boat. Clues seem to point to the possibility that JFK Jr. is Q.

> **2023 Reflection – What I Learned**
>
> The bell is from a 1996 movie called *White Squall*,[122] and neither that boat nor the bell ever belonged to JFK Jr.

Alliance for a Vendetta

Janet goes on to say that Trump and JFK Jr. were close friends. She claims that when JFK Jr. appeared to have died, Trump swore he would complete the mission to avenge the murders of both JFK Jr. and his father, President John F. Kennedy.

> **2023 Reflection – What I Learned**
>
> I have found no evidence that Trump and JFK Jr. were ever close friends. They happened to be two wealthy Democrats living in New York. In all likelihood, the photos Janet showed of the two of them together were real, but that proves nothing about the nature of their connection.

Promise of a Beautiful Future

After this massive reveal, Janet goes on to share her vision of the world that is possible—a world with free energy and more equitable sharing of wealth. Earlier in the series, she said we have all the technological solutions we need to solve every problem we face. We have developed free energy technologies, cutting-edge nonpharmaceutical health solutions, and strategies to replenish our air, water, and soil. However, the Cabal has worked to control and hide all the inventions needed to create the world we dream of. Once the patents are freed from the Cabal's control, they will be released, and humanity will be freed from tyranny.

This is all very exciting. The world Janet describes would be the answer to my most ardent prayers. I want to believe it is the world we are moving toward. I want to believe that despite all appearances, that world is not only possible, it is inevitable.

Janet makes her closing statement:

The world as we know it is about to end. What is awaiting us is a world of peace, harmony, liberty, and equality, the dawn of the Golden Age as described in each and every source text.

I have grown to fully trust Donald Trump. He may seem rude, silly, and clumsy from time to time, but he has earned my trust in the past two and a half years as I have followed his every move. He is a genius—a 5D chess player, a man with a huge heart.

My mind quickly generates a rational explanation to help me bridge the chasm between my old assessments of Trump and the ones being revealed to me now. I must have missed this fantastic news about Trump because the MSM had lied not only to me, but to everyone in my family and community, for decades.

Janet's final words are:

There will be a relatively short bridge period in which people can adjust to the new paradigm and its energies. I don't think there will be much chaos. Everything is ready to be implemented. A new

Chapter 9: John F. Kennedy Jr.

banking system, new ways to educate our children, a new medical system without poisonous and addictive chemicals, and so on and so forth."

All we need to do is be patient. Watch everything unfold. Trust in the Plan. Do whatever we can to help others wake up. And remain focused and ready. Ready to assist. Ready to help create a beautiful new world. Some people will wake up faster than others. Remain calm, and in service to all. Or as Q put it, 'As long as you sleep, we will fight for you. Where we go one, we go all!

2023 Reflection – What I Learned

Looking back at the astonishing speed with which I swallowed this narrative whole, I went online to inquire about the phenomenon. Here are some things I learned.

Anxiety, especially heightened anxiety, can impair critical thinking and increase susceptibility to manipulation or misinformation. When a person is experiencing anxiety, they may have difficulty evaluating the credibility of sources or assessing the validity of information as their brains have gone into a limbic "fight, flight, freeze, submit or fawn" state, with no access to a whole-brain response. This makes them more vulnerable to accepting falsehoods or conspiracy theories that promise relief from their distress.

A secondary phenomenon known as *confirmation bias* then kicks in. This is where people selectively interpret information in a way that confirms their existing beliefs or reduces their feelings of uncertainty or fear. Latching onto beliefs that provide a sense of safety, reassurance, certainty, and/or control alleviates discomfort and provides a sense of security, even if it is based on false premises.

Then *cognitive dissonance* piles on. Cognitive dissonance is a psychological response where individuals experience discomfort as a result of holding conflicting beliefs or information and can feel threatened by those who challenge or question their beliefs.

This tendency can manifest in groups through a phenomenon known as *groupthink* or *herd mentality*. In their collective desire for harmony and cohesion, members may suppress dissenting viewpoints, leading to a consensus that may not be based on critical evaluation. This can result in a group collectively embracing beliefs or decisions that might not be grounded in reality.

These natural human tendencies make it increasingly essential for individuals experiencing anxiety to practice mindfulness and actively engage in practices that support critical thinking. When feeling anxious, take extra time to verify information by checking reliable sources. Seek support from trusted individuals or professionals who can provide accurate information and help co-regulate the person in distress.

Despite their expertise, professionals can also fall prey to these proclivities, particularly in fields or environments where there's strong pressure to conform to prevailing theories, practices, or norms. When you need professional help, seek out individuals who demonstrate critical thinking, openness to diverse perspectives, and a commitment to an empathic approach and evidence-based practices.

As is true with everyone, therapists can be biased. Remember, it is not a therapist's job to tell you what is true and not true; it is their job to support your mental and emotional well-being and to assist you to find your own answers. Check their credentials, seek testimonials or reviews from clients or peers, and assess their willingness to discuss various approaches.

A good professional should encourage questions and be open about the limits of their expertise. If they are not sufficiently trained to address issues of high anxiety, mind control, or cult dynamics, they should be honest and refer you to a more qualified professional.

Chapter 10:
So Many Questions

Wow! Wow! Just Wow! What an emotional roller coaster that was, packed with so much information—no way can I come close to tracking all that I've just witnessed. I am compelled to believe much of it, even though I realize that several parts are definitely off base and likely untrue.

Who Owns the Media?

It is easy for me to believe that the corruption in our world is far worse than I could have ever imagined. It is easy to believe that the MSM is deliberately choosing unbalanced narratives in support of corporate agendas and elite power plays, especially given that almost all of our major media companies are owned by only six conglomerates.[123] And it isn't a stretch for me to now view the MSM as a deceptive tool for power-abusing forces.

2023 Reflection – What I Learned

In 1983 there were fifty media companies. By 2012, 90% of all media outlets had been consolidated into only six conglomerates: Comcast NBC Universal, Disney, CBS, Viacom, News Corp, and AT&T.[124,125] The largest stakeholders in all of these media companies are the

Blackrock Fund Advisors and the Vanguard Group.[126] This does not mean they "own" the media, however it does point to a possibility of coordinated influence.

Have Life-Serving Patents Been Confiscated?

It is easy for me to believe that the CIA and the FBI have confiscated[127] all kinds of life-serving patents, including the free energy technologies of Nikola Tesla. It is easy to believe that the oil and gas companies have worked out deals with government regulators and intelligence agencies in order to maximize profits. The power of their money and lobbyists is no secret. And I like the idea that if the government workers, politicians, and nonstate actors who are participating in corruption can be sent to the Guantanamo Bay detention camp and all the confiscated free energy patents and other technologies can be released to the public, we can have all the solutions we need to restore our planet and live abundantly together on earth.

Did JFK Jr. and Carolyn Bessette-Kennedy Fake Their Deaths?

If what Janet's saying is anything close to true, I do want to believe that JFK Jr. and his beautiful wife Carolyn Bessette-Kennedy faked their deaths in order to survive the assassinations all too common in that family's lineage. It seems within the realm of possibility that JFK Jr. would know this and discover his assassination attempt before it happened. He could have gone underground to continue the work of his father.

2023 Reflection – What I Learned

I was completely unaware that there are many who believe various famous people, including Elvis,[128] Michael Jackson,[129] Prince,[130] and JFK Jr.[131] are still alive.

❀ Chapter 10: So Many Questions ❀

Are JFK Jr. and Donald Trump Friends?

And it seems clear to me that JFK Jr. and Trump were friends, given the pictures Janet shared in *Fall of the Cabal*. Maybe Trump had been chosen by the White Hats. Maybe they are working to eliminate the corruption that has festered and spread through the inner workings of our government. Maybe he is actively working to "drain the swamp," as Janet suggests.

> **2023 Personal Reflection**
>
> Looking back at these thoughts of mine, I notice that I had started to turn a blind eye to the investigations into Trump's business practices, including allegations of tax evasion, fraudulent activity, and conflicts of interest. Additionally, there have been inquiries into his potential obstruction of justice, abuse of power, and violations of campaign finance laws during his presidency. Knowledge of these allegations faded into the distance as I tumbled down this rabbit hole.

Only a few months earlier, I had lost all hope with the second-round crushing of Bernie and Our Revolution. Dark money seemed to have won. If Janet's research really did expose something closer to the truth, it would lift a load of despair off my shoulders. I would know that a large group of sincerely good people—true patriots—are highly attuned to the nature of the problem and have been working for at least two generations to devise a plan that will have the best possible chance at taking down the Cabal once and for all.

Could This Alleged Satanic Cult and Adrenochrome Be Real?

I don't want to believe the darkest of Janet's talking points. I don't want to believe the abuse and slaughter of innocent children and drinking of babies' blood is true.

I don't want to believe the disturbing revelations about Marina Abramovic's "satanic art,"[132] especially as she mentored Lady Gaga,[133] and is revered by other Hollywood stars. I don't want to believe John

Podesta's art collection is what Janet says it is. Could Podesta really own a bronze statue of one of Jeffrey Dahmer's beheaded victims and display it openly in his home?[134] And what about the numerous paintings by Serbian artist Biljana Đurđević, of young children tied up in an empty swimming pool?[135] Do those belong to Podesta too? I would feel disturbed to discover that anyone owned such an art collection, but especially someone like John Podesta, as he was Hillary Clinton's right-hand man. Was Podesta ordering children for sex using pizza references as a coded language common among pedophiles? Did Clinton really say she was going to sacrifice a chicken to Moloch? I don't want to believe these revelations have any validity. At the same time, I am drawn into the promise of a better future, and because of that, I am willing to shrug off some of Janet's more outlandish assertions, assuming it doesn't really matter if they are true or not.

And what's with the widespread use of the symbols, in Disney,[136,137] on diapers,[138] on children's toys,[139] on ice cream,[140] in jewelry,[141] logos,[142] and even woven into the pope's clothes[143] that Janet says the FBI has confirmed are used to advertise the underground industry of child sex slavery and pedophilia?[144] I have no idea.

And what's with all these politicians coming together wearing red shoes?[145] Did the last pope also really wear red shoes?[146] Do red shoes really signify allegiance to this so-called satanic cult that is the primary curse wreaking havoc in our world, as Janet says?

All these thoughts and more are extremely disorienting and disturbing. And yet they also appear to be key points to Janet's larger narrative. I don't want to believe them; they're way too dark and bizarre, but I also can't drop the thought: What if even a portion of this is true?

As soon as the video ends, I am compelled to start looking into all these claims online. I want to separate truth from falsehood. That should be easy enough to do, right?

Chapter 10: So Many Questions

2023 Reflection – What I Learned

It wasn't until six months later, as I was on the precipice of exiting the QAnon trance, that I came to the clear realization that it is *not* easy to separate truth from falsehood by way of online research.[147] In addition to (all forms of) the MSM, which is the most obvious and ubiquitous source of propaganda in our country, China, Russia, foreign adversaries, our own FBI and CIA, large corporations, and internet influencers of various stripes all participate in generating propaganda. This includes misinformation, disinformation, AI-generated deepfakes,[148] psychological operations (psyops), phony social media accounts, AI bots, and trolls. These forms of truth-negating information have flooded our channels so thoroughly it is incredibly hard to distinguish what is factually true from what is misleading or false.

Chapter 11:
Doing My Research

Even though it's the middle of the night, I have completely lost interest in sleep. I begin to look up the most bizarre among Janet's talking points, intending to rule out the most outlandish claims from the outset. I am stunned as each of my searches generates multiple pages of content, confirming what I had just seen in her video series. How had this entire world been hidden from me before? My gasps are audible, and my fiancé opens his eyes, notices that I'm still awake, then adjusts his position before falling back asleep.

2023 Reflections – What I Learned

Today, very little of what I saw in 2020 appears in my Google searches, and most of it seems to have been scrubbed from the internet altogether. But some of it still exists on alternative search engines such as DuckDuckGo, Startpage, or Brave, and on newer social media platforms such as Bitchute, Rumble, Parler, and Telegram.

"Spirit Cooking"

I look up "Marina Abramovic satanic art," and images[149] and articles[150] immediately appear, including her use of blood as paint,[151] upside down pentagrams, and her very bizarre "Spirit Cooking" dinner gathering, at which dozens of famous Hollywood stars partook of what appears to be a cannibalistic feast.[152] One of the most striking photos is of Lady Gaga sipping a dark red liquid from a spoon while before her is what appears to be a dead female body in a tub of blood.[153]

2021 Reflections – What I Learned

Months later I would discover that the blood-like substance was actually a thick, red, culinary syrup, and the body was an actress playing dead at a themed art gala at the 20th Annual Watermill Center Summer Benefit.[154] This doesn't settle my uneasiness all that much, but to each their own, perhaps.

John Podesta's Art Collection

John Podesta's strange art collection appears to be verified as well by multiple sources. When I click the images tab on my Google search, I see many pages with art pieces of half-dressed children tied up in various ways. There are close to twenty websites with a photograph of Podesta gathered with other politicians, all wearing red shoes. And the painting of Bill Clinton[155] lounging on a fancy chair in a blue dress and wearing red shoes shows up as I scroll through the pages connected to this search. Geez! It appears this painting had belonged to Jeffrey Epstein.

2023 Reflections – What I Learned

According to a fact check, this particular art collection is not owned by John Podesta; however, his brother, Tony Podesta, does own a number of these art pieces.[156] Jeffrey Epstein did own a painting of Bill Clinton in a blue dress with red women's dress shoes. Its Australian

Chapter 11: Doing My Research

> artist describes this painting as "silly school artwork" she created while completing her master's at the New York Academy of Art. When it sold at the 2012 Tribeca Ball, she was unaware that Jeffrey Epstein purchased it.

As I watch all these search results popping up on my screen I am stunned into silence, with one thought only: *Oh my God... This is all real.*

Pizza, Chickens, and Moloch

I search the Wikileaks records of Hillary Clinton and John Podesta's emails. I find the strange references to pizza and hotdogs by Podesta and other political leaders unsettling. Hillary's comment about sacrificing a chicken to Moloch, however, is the most suspicious of them all.[157] Janet had referenced these when talking about how politicians are actively engaging in pedophilia and child sex trafficking. She asserts that these codewords are common knowledge in the industry:

- Pizza = child
- Cheese = girl
- Pasta = boy
- Hotdog = boy

I had taken note of these bizarre and potentially damning allegations, hoping to find nothing to substantiate them. I don't know what to do with these pages of evidence from Wikileaks, but what remains of the trust I previously had in Podesta, Clinton, and the Democratic establishment as a whole is seriously tanking.

> **2021 Reflections – What I Learned**
>
> I had not previously heard of Pizzagate. Nor was I aware of how thoroughly this conspiracy theory, along with dark and disturbing art collections had been amassed online, (along with everything else supporting QAnon theories) connecting them to top politicians. Erotically grotesque assemblages of art from James Alefantis, Arrington de

> Dionyso, Margi Geerlinks, Patricia Piccinini, Louise Bourgeois, and Biljana Djurdjevis were easy to find. These grotesque assemblages seem to hold an unsettling allure for a number of powerful people.
>
> While I have no way of assessing the authenticity of any of the Wikileaks files, there is reason to believe at least some portion of the leaked documents originate from Russian propaganda campaigns designed to sow seeds of distrust among US citizens.[158]

I look up Moloch and confirm that this Canaanite god is in the *Book of Leviticus*,[159] which is the third book of the Torah and included in the Old Testament. It is believed that the practice of child sacrifice was (and perhaps still is) associated with worship or appeasement of this horned god.[160] My mind is spinning and my heart is racing as I try to put together all the pieces I am learning in this strange new world.

I confirm in another WikiLeaks post[161] that the two symbols of pedophilia Janet had revealed have been identified by the FBI. The published document affirms that these symbols are used by the underground child sex slavery industry to advertise whether they have boys or girls available to potential customers.

I find websites confirming that these symbols and ones like them are or have been used in logos by various politicians, corporations, and even the pope.[162] Are they knowingly signaling their involvement and allegiance to pedophilia and this dark Cabal?

I find the full-length video of the 9-year-old girl named Grace talking to the investigator about the church where her father participated in sacrificing babies and drinking their blood.[163] I also find a video of a similar interview with her younger brother.[164]

Inconspicuous Filter Bubbles

Just about every search I do is producing content affirming the darkest and most bizarre things I had just seen in *Fall of the Cabal*. As I continue these searches, the web of darkness multiplies like a mind virus; content expanding on each of these topics begins to flood my iPhone screen.

Chapter 11: Doing My Research

2021 Reflections – What I Learned

What I didn't know at the time was that artificial intelligence (AI)–driven social media algorithms had identified patterns in the categories of content I had been viewing that were holding my interest, resulting in a **"filter bubble."**[165,166] A filter bubble occurs when social media algorithms curate content that aligns with a user's previous online behaviors and preferences, creating a personalized information ecosystem. This tailored experience can significantly limit exposure to contrasting viewpoints and diverse information, fostering an echo chamber effect. Consequently, **users may find their belief systems and biases reinforced over time, as they are less frequently challenged by alternative perspectives or new information.** This mechanism is well described in the documentary *The Social Dilemma.*[167]

My understanding of the overall QAnon perspective expands with each new point of confirmation I discover along this primrose path. Most everything my social media accounts are suggesting I watch and read next are in basic alignment with what Janet Ossebaard has revealed. However, I am completely unaware of the attention-harvesting AI-driven system feeding me more fear porn aligned with this sudden all-consuming fascination of mine.

Oh my God…

… This is all too much.

Red Pill

Having received the messages of *Fall of the Cabal* and having found hundreds of pages confirming the validity of Janet's presentation, I now find myself viewing the world from a radically different standpoint. This perspective is enlivened by a completely different set of memes than the ones I was resonating with just the day before. I feel I now understand the nature of the dark systemic structures of human domination. From the perspective of QAnon, I have taken the red pill.

The Matrix: Red Pill and Blue Pill

There's a scene in the movie *The Matrix* when Morpheus offers Neo the blue pill or the red pill.[168] Take the blue pill and forget everything: go back to the AI-constructed virtual reality that fools the mind into thinking what you see and hear are real, and experience what has always seemed normal. Take the red pill and wake up to the truth: see with your own eyes what is really going on behind the scenes in the world. Neo takes the red pill and learns the dark reality of the true nature of the matrix, which is a colossal AI robot that feeds off of humans and keeps them imprisoned in a virtual reality. His grand adventure of empowerment and spiritual awakening begins when he chooses to take the red pill. This famous scene is referenced often by others in the QAnon community whom I discover along the way. In QAnon, this reference has a double meaning: the red pill not only aligns you with "the truth"; it also signifies the Republican party. The blue pill, on the other hand, keeps you stuck in illusion and is the color of the Democratic party.

Chapter 12:
The Great Awakening

Only three hours have passed. It's now Saturday, June 13, 2020, in the wee hours of the morning, and I am spinning in both horror and exhilaration, wide awake and in a kind of emotional state I've never experienced before.

In the third slide of *Fall of the Cabal,* Janet says:

You may find the first episodes shocking or even unbelievable, yet at the end everything will fall into place. The final two episodes (9 and 10) contain an unexpected twist, causing you to face the changes ahead of us with hope and faith in your heart.

These words accurately reflect my experience.

Unconsciously Confirming My New Bias

I open my web browser and enter the text "Is JFK Jr. still alive?" My heart jumps for joy as once again my search results in dozens of links, including photos showing what he looks like in present time. He is of course older, but quite handsome. I am presented with ample evidence that JFK Jr. has been secretly attending Trump's rallies and spending time with him between events. The February 1997 issue of JFK Jr.'s *George* magazine, entitled "Survival Guide to the Future,"[169] pops up on my screen. The cover's headlines include titles Janet had pointed out: "Bill Gates Talks to John Kennedy about Murdoch, Money and World Domination," and "Indictment Day: Will Hillary Get Busted?" I note that these clickbait titles (though the term didn't exist in 1997) bear an uncanny resemblance to present-day news headlines. How had JFK Jr. come up with these in 1997? Was he blessed with the gift of precognition?

I am enthralled with my new belief that JFK Jr. is either Q or is part of a collective of White Hats who together are Q. And that together with Donald Trump and the White Hats, he has devised the Plan, and they are executing on it even while we sleep. Despite the appearance of total devastation, which is beginning to lead so many people into feelings of nihilism, forces of good are working overtime behind the scenes. Truth and justice shall prevail!

Fulfillment of the Prophecies

Janet had said in her closing statement, "The world as we know it is about to end. What is awaiting us is a world of peace, harmony, liberty, and equality, the dawn of the Golden Age as described in each and every source text." Having researched so many of Janet's claims, these final words now land with greater credibility.

The idea of a promised Golden Age, a time of utopian paradise, is not new to me, nor are the prophecies from various traditions. I recall a song I sang repeatedly in my youth called "Age of Aquarius" by The 5th Dimension: "When the moon is in the seventh house and Jupiter aligns with Mars, then peace will guide the planets and love will steer the stars." This planetary alignment, which holds great significance among astrologers, had happened once since the 1969 publication of the song, at what was called the Harmonic Convergence, in August of 1987. And the phenomenon was slated to repeat itself very soon—in July of 2020.[170]

It seems we are finally exiting the dark ages of the Kali Yuga and entering the Satya Yuga,[171] the Age of Supreme Truth, the birthing of the Golden Age, as revealed in Vedic scriptures. I know this aligns as well with the Mayan calendar, whose 5,126-year cycle ended on December 21, 2012.

Chapter 12: The Great Awakening

I am also aware of the Rainbow Warrior prophecy of many North American indigenous tribes[172] and the Eagle and the Condor Prophecy,[173] which originated in South America and is gaining traction and building cohesion among indigenous tribes around the world. In addition, during my three years as an active member of the Baha'i Faith, I had come to learn about the promised coming of the Most Great Peace.[174,175] These are some of the source texts that point to what Janet affirms is happening now—the fulfillment of ancient prophecies with the essential assistance of Q, Trump, and the White Hats.

Janet characterizes Trump as a "5D[176] chess player." It seems he is working with a stellar team to take down the Cabal and dismantle the systems of control they've placed on humanity. Perhaps he is even working with fifth-dimensional spiritual forces.[177] Even though these ideas stretch my mind yet again into domains I had previously held at arm's distance or vehemently rejected, I find my mind is open and receptive to thoughts that the world is not at all what it seems.

As this promise of the Golden Age settles into my body, I easily drop decades of fear-producing thoughts. I am filled with a renewed sense of hope, trust, and faith in God, the Omnipresent, the Omnipotent, the All-Loving, the All-Knowing, the All-Wise, the Divine Designer of the Universe and of All Life.

Love permeates my body and swaddles me as a childhood song, "He's Got the Whole World in His Hands," arises in my mind. My inner child is squealing with sheer delight. I am in awe of it all, enjoying the vastness of peace as I feel it throughout my body. Wonderment fills my mind. Fear is gone. I can hardly contain myself. I am bursting with joy. My psyche and body relax as a vision of the future now appears bright and beautiful. All that remains is wonder, and gratitude.

I am eager to put these feelings of abounding love into action. What can I do to actively participate in the Great Awakening? How can I assist in waking friends and family members out of their collective trance? I don't know how to start, but I am certain it is not with "Hey, did you know that the news channels you are watching are lying to the public? Did you know Trump is not a racist, sexist, or Hitler wannabe and that he's actually a good guy working with JFK Jr. and the White Hats to defeat evil in our world?" No. That is definitely not the way to start. Not in my community.

Chapter 13:
Bill Gates

2023 Reflection – What I Learned

The Q drops never mentioned Bill Gates, but *Fall of the Cabal* did. That mention, in combination with my distress over the coming mRNA vaccine and my previous distrust of Bill Gates, led me into a deep-dive exploration into the Covid-19 rabbit hole.

The sun will be rising in a couple hours. I take pause from my research on *Fall of the Cabal* and find myself once again staring into the darkness of our unlit room. I feel restless as my mind is buzzing with all this new information, which has already turned my world upside down. I am bouncing with enthusiasm while trying to lie still in our bed. As a matter of habit, I pick up my phone once again. This time I click my Facebook app.

Opening Facebook is like opening the fridge when I'm not hungry. But in that case, I simply close it with little time wasted. My experience of Facebook is different. Opening it is an unconscious habit. But once I start scrolling, twenty minutes or more can fly by before I realize my brain has gone into a limbic hijack once again. In the early hours this morning, it is easy for me to get hooked.

Today, Saturday, June 13, 2020, is #ExposeBillGates day on Facebook. I don't know who started it, but this call to action has motivated at least several of my East Coast Facebook friends to get an early start on their day. One post is particularly captivating to me. It is an infographic that reads "A Man of Great Influence."[178] In the middle is Bill Gates, and around him are all the organizations, corporations, and nonprofits to which this infographic asserts he has contributed exorbitant dollar amounts. The comments on this post contain a link to a four-part Corbett Report series called "Who Is Bill Gates?"[179]

I feel a small burst of fire rise in my body as I imagine what this documentary might reveal beyond some of the nauseating details about his way of building Microsoft and his current supposed philanthropic projects. This man seems to lack a humanistic code of ethics, and I am eager to learn more as I press play on this two-hour documentary.

Microsoft Monopoly

Bill Gates accumulated plenty of critics as he built his mega-tech company, Microsoft. While most Silicon Valley programmers in the '80s shared their source code openly, Bill grabbed the code, changed it, made it his own, then built a monopoly, violating antitrust laws in order to dominate the market.[180] My already-negative assessment of this man only intensifies as I learn of his past business dealings.

Global Health Organizations

James Corbett sheds light on the massive outpouring of money, totaling close to $9 billion, from the Gates Foundation to global health agencies.[181] He highlights Gates's donations to the World Health Organization (WHO), to which Gates is the second largest donor after China,[182] the Centers for Disease Control (CDC),[183,184] and the National Institutes of Health (NIH)[185,186] and his cofounding and funding of the Global Vaccine Alliance Initiative (GAVI).[187]

Chapter 13: Bill Gates

Public Education

Gates has poured money into educational facilities[188] and media outlets. He spent $233 million developing and implementing Common Core educational standards for all United States public schools, which have since been adopted by many private schools as well.[189] Johns Hopkins University,[190] the Imperial College London[191] and the University of Oxford[192] have all benefited from Gates's generous grants and donations, and Gates channeled at least $2 million to the Massachusetts Institute of Technology (MIT), following a directive from Jeffrey Epstein.[193] Corbett claims he has also funded news reporting and fact-checking groups for the BBC, NPR, NBC, Al Jazeera, *The Guardian, The Atlantic,* the Center for Investigative Reporting, and dozens of other media outlets.[194]

Unelected Power

Corbett's next question is the obvious one: given all these contributions, does Gates have too much influence on the way we are handling the Covid pandemic? And if he does, would any of these news organizations risk questioning or criticizing his approach? It's hard for me to imagine they would. Rather, it seems Gates is yet another unelected person of enormous power who could be considered part of the Deep State.

W. Gates and Eugenics

I am already aware of Gates's ties with Monsanto, but Corbett weaves a connection between Gates and the eugenics movement,[195] which has gone quiet for decades. Eugenicists aim to improve the human gene pool through selective breeding and the discouragement or prevention of reproduction among those considered to be genetically undesirable. (But who gets to decide what is and is not desirable?) This movement has led to the marginalization, discrimination, and in extreme cases, forced sterilization and genocide of members of "inferior" races, profoundly violating their human rights and dignity.

Corbett points out that Bill Gates's full name is William Henry Gates III, and that the Eugenics Society lists a member named W. Gates. Could this be Bill's grandfather? Corbett says many among the global elites have spoken about an "alarming overpopulation problem" and actively come together in secret meetings to talk about how to address this alleged dilemma. He says that these elites no longer talk about eugenics; they couch the topic in public health, as a decoy to the real issues they are discussing.

Quantum Dot Vaccines

Corbett then reveals information on Gates's quantum dot vaccines, developed at MIT.[196] This technology creates an invisible-ink tattoo[197] made of undisclosed substances, which is readable by a mobile phone app. Corbett likens this tattoo to a bar code, a comparison I find very uncomfortable, given what I remember from childhood about the biblical mark of the beast.

Chapter 14:
Mark of The Beast

The mark of the beast comes from the Book of Revelation. I had seen a documentary TV show about it in the mid-'80s that made a deep impact on me. From Revelation 13:6, the text reads, "And the second beast required all people small and great, rich and poor, free and slave, to receive a mark on their right hand or on their forehead, so that no one could buy or sell unless he had the mark—the name of the beast or the number of its name. Here is a call for wisdom: Let the one who has insight calculate the number of the beast, for it is the number of a man, and that number is 666."

Another point from Corbett connects this revelation with Covid, causing my head to spin, especially given *Fall of the Cabal's* references to Satan. HR 6666, the TRACE Act (Covid-19 Testing, Reaching and Contacting Everyone), had been introduced to Congress in May of 2020.

2023 Reflection—What I Learned

There is a House Resolution 666 practically every year in Congress. HR 6666 is less common, but still a repeated number over the years. The number 666 does not hold the same superstitious consideration in Congress as the number 13 does in hotels and high-rises, which rarely have a 13th floor. 2019 and 2020 were not anomalies.

I have every reason to believe the quantum dot vaccines are highly unlikely to be deployed in the United States anytime soon. And I imagine that microchipping technology has not yet become small enough to be included in the upcoming Covid vaccines, but I don't know for sure. At the same time, I have seen microchips the size of rice grains being used in human bodies in the past—like a strange growing fad.[198] People lined up years ago to get chipped so they could wave their hands to unlock doors at work or to purchase snacks from a vending machine. And I remember being horrified when in 2017, I read an article from *USA Today* titled *You Will Get Chipped... Eventually.*[199] I am aware that powerful technologies such as the ones in our smart devices, are increasing in their capabilities while shrinking in size as the field of nanotechnology grows. Could these microchips already be small enough to fit inside a hypodermic vaccine needle?

Surveillance Technologies

But then I realize that the surveillance can occur by technologies that aren't injected. It could be a required wearable technology,[200] for example, like the headsets Chinese children are made to wear, which scan their brains to see if they are paying attention during class.[201]

It doesn't take me long to find the patent Corbett had shown in his exposé on Bill Gates. Patent #WO2020060606A1 can be readily found by anyone on Google.[202] I quickly create a mnemonic to memorize this number: "[New] World Order 2020 666 A.I." It was filed by none other than Microsoft in 2019. The abstract to this patent reads:

> Human body activity associated with a task provided to a user may be used in a mining process of a cryptocurrency system. A server may provide a task to a device of a user which is communicatively coupled to the server. A sensor communicatively coupled to or comprised in the device of the user may sense body activity of the user. Body activity data may be generated based on the sensed body activity of the user. The cryptocurrency system communicatively coupled to the device of the user may verify if the body activity data satisfies one or more conditions set by the crypto-

Chapter 14: Mark of the Beast

currency system, and award cryptocurrency to the user whose body activity data is verified.

I wonder, Will this device be external or internal? What is its intended use? It seems within reason to believe this patent could be connected to Bill Gates's project to create digital ID2020[203] as a biometric global identification system[204] designed to track every human on the planet.[205]

Social Credit System

According to Corbett's theory, the Cabal's overarching plan is to roll out vaccine passports, which will be used to validate whether or not a person can participate in public life, keep their job, take public transportation, go to school, take a flight, etc., very much in line with China's social credit system.[206]

Fear arises once again, along with new questions: Is the Cabal so threatened by the rise of Q that it is speeding up the timelines and planning on culling the human population using the panic of the pandemic to introduce and normalize emergency-authorized mandatory vaccinations? Will it then try to enslave what remains of humanity? I have seen videos showing how the social credit system effectively controls the lives of large swaths of Chinese citizens.[207] They reveal a modern-day manifestation of Orwellian dystopia.[208] It's no longer fiction; "Big Brother" is alive and real in China. This mass surveillance technology is coupled with a rating system that offers immediate perks for "good" behaviors—and punishment for unapproved ones. It knows when a person has volunteered their time to a charity, but also when they've jay walked, rolled through a stop sign, purchased alcohol, or spoken critically about the Chinese government. It watches and listens to everything.

Every action is scored, and stepping out of line garners swift consequences, including slow internet service, the inability to book a flight or purchase business-class train tickets, and even being barred from enrolling your kids in high school and higher education. The government might even take away your dog. Furthermore, companies are encouraged to check social credit scores before hiring. If you've been blacklisted, you may not be able to maintain employment, and you will not enjoy the same ease around compliant friends and family who don't want to risk their scores being lowered by association with you. (This "social" aspect of the social credit control grid is its lynchpin: no enforcement is required when your social circles perform this function aptly).

As of 2017 the Chinese Communist Party (CCP) had imposed such punishments more than seven million times, and blacklisted individuals' names, faces, and addresses were emblazoned on billboards throughout the areas in which they lived.[209] Public shaming and denial of financial instruments such as credit cards and loans are more ways in which a person with a low social credit score might be punished in China—without notice and without possibility of redress.[210,211]

Is This Pandemic a Warm-Up?

Is the Cabal using this pandemic as a means for setting us up to install a similar system of total surveillance and authoritarian control here in the United States? Could we be forced to receive injections, or quantum dot tattoos, against our will, under the guise of an emergency "public health" mandate? From what I can see, including the movement toward a central bank digital currency[212] and the consolidation of power granted to the World Health Organization,[213] the answer is yes.[214]

These thoughts increase a sense of urgency in me. Darkness, lies, and manipulation cannot win this battle. Love, truth, and goodness must prevail.

I realize I cannot hold my new revelations secret. I cannot simply stay quiet about my new gratitude for Trump and Q, which I know will not be at all welcomed in my social circles. I need to act fast to get the people I love to see that these vaccines are potentially deadly. I feel a surge of energy and a burst of joy as I realize I can jump on this #ExposeBillGates bandwagon. It is an obvious entry point for helping my friends and family wake up to the sinister vaccine agenda that Gates, Fauci, and heads of the WHO, CDC, NIH, NSA, and others are propagating. I expect my community's understanding of Trump and Q will naturally take hold after they can see the truth

❀ Chapter 14: Mark of the Beast ❀

about this pandemic. I believe I can be effective in my efforts to expose that truth.

With awakening the masses and saving the lives of those I love in mind and heart, I make my first #ExposeBillGates post. I am intentionally discrete about my new faith in Q and support for Trump, but not at all discrete about my concern over the way the pandemic is being handled or my distrust of the coming vaccines.

PART 3:

Life As a QAnon

Chapter 15:
Just Act Normal

It's Saturday morning, June 13, 2020. Stephen stirs awake shortly after 7 a.m.

Just act normal, I coach myself, despite my radical overnight flip.

"Good morning, My Love," I say to Stephen, but I am not my normal sleepy self.

"Good morning," he responds in a groggy tone, "Did you sleep at all last night?" he asks.

"I didn't," I reply, "but I'm feeling ok. I'm sure I'll catch up later."

It's nearly impossible for me to relax into our ritual morning snuggle. On the one hand, I am excited by my new sense of hope and faith, and on the other hand I know that when I choose to share this news with Stephen, it could be explosive.

While part of me trusts the Plan, I know it won't take care of smaller details like the well-being of my friends and family. I've got to talk them out of their eagerness to get vaccinated. In addition, mainstream news portends "the worst" fire season ever. While I do not trust the MSM to be honest, I do believe that when they predict events like massive fires, they are likely right, as their news channels are run by the same dark elites who ensure California will be ablaze. I know in my bones this fire season will be a doozy. I want to prepare for the worst and encourage others to do the same.

To make matters worse, Covid is spreading, and hospitals are becoming increasingly overwhelmed. I imagine a fire season in which people are being displaced from their homes, breathing polluted air, and jamming themselves into temporary shelters where this virus will likely spread rapidly. It's a perfect recipe for tragedy, and I don't want to be anywhere near it.

It's now 7:40 a.m. Stephen is sitting in his favorite leather chair, enjoying his morning coffee, and catching up on news. He looks up from time to time and tracks my movements from room to room, scrolling on my phone and on my computer.

"What's with you today?" he asks. "You're acting really weird and it's unsettling to me."

"Nothing," I quickly respond, avoiding eye contact as I pick up my mug and bring it to the kitchen. The excuse of doing a little bit of house cleaning seems like a good way to disappear for a bit. But when I reenter the room, he asks that same question again. I know it is obvious that it is not "nothing" that is going on. I am clearly hiding something, and this is highly unusual, as we have an agreement to be open and honest with each other. So, when he asks again, I answer with more transparency. "I don't want to talk about it right now," I say. That is not the answer he wants to hear.

"It's not about another guy, is it Katrina?" He asks.

"No." I respond quickly. "There's no other guy, My Love."

He presses on, "Then what is it, Katrina?"

"I just don't want to talk about it right now," I say as I avert my eyes.

"But you will tell me what is going on with you and why you are acting so strange, right?"

I feel a twinge of confrontation on the rise and try to calm it. "What do you mean I am acting strange?" I ask.

His response is quick. "You seem wired. Your eyes are wide, and you don't seem to stop moving, except when you are fixated on Facebook or whatever keeps grabbing your attention. You can't seem to sit still, and you

Chapter 15: Just Act Normal

have been avoiding me all morning. You didn't sleep at all last night, and you seemed to be on your phone all night doing something. What was so important, Katrina? I don't know what's going on with you, but it's very uncomfortable to be around you right now."

"Do you want me to leave for a bit then?" I ask, hoping for an excuse to step away.

"No. I want you to calm down. I want to know what's going on. And I want to feel like you are here and present with me."

I hear a tone of exasperation in his voice. Tension had been building between us for months now, only growing in the recent weeks. It seems this strain could be reaching a crescendo.

I can't find it in myself to calm down. Instinctively, I take a deep breath. What should I say to him? How might he react?

Expose Bill Gates

"I noticed your Facebook post too," Stephen continues. "Did you really need to do that? I know you don't trust Bill Gates or the vaccines, but other people do. When you put yourself out there like this on Facebook, you're going to upset a lot of people. You keep telling me how important community is to you and how difficult it is to be in isolation. Do you really want to be driving your friends away with posts like this?" He sounds incredulous.

As much as I am trying to restrain myself from saying anything, Stephen's comment hit a nerve. My reaction pours out despite my efforts to thwart it. "Stephen, I don't trust the coming Covid vaccines at all. Have you seen the deformed children in Africa and India who received Bill Gates's so-called vaccines? You know he's in bed with MonSatan, and you know how I feel about that company." The feeling of disgust permeates my facial features as I can hardly talk about this agrochemical company using its proper name. "There's nothing trustworthy about Bill," I continue. "Why is a successful computer guy suddenly the spokesperson for global health? I don't trust him, and I don't trust the massive influence he has, or his clear agenda to vaccinate the world. I will *not* get vaccinated, and I hope you won't either."

"Come on, Katrina. You're overreacting," he exclaims. "As you know, I've been working in life sciences for decades. Any pharmaceutical product must go through extensive and rigorous safety testing before it is used on the population. The process of moving a new drug through the FDA and into the market is not an easy one. Once a drug is approved, we know it is very safe. Of course, there are always rare potential side effects, but the protections these vaccines will offer will far outweigh any risks. You need to get over this, Katrina. I don't want to die from this virus because you refuse to get vaccinated."

"Red light!" I state firmly, feeling intensity in my eyes and tightness in my body. Red light is a signal Stephen and I have agreed to use to stop an interaction that is going downhill fast. If it were a lesser discomfort, I might have called "yellow light," in which case we agree to slow down and tune in to see if we are able to make eye contact and get in touch with our love, care, and respect for each other. We have found this is a good litmus test, measuring our capacity in any given moment to stay connected in a productive way while proceeding with a difficult conversation. However, this conversation is stirring big emotions quickly. I need to bow out and re-center myself with a promise to return to this topic later.

2024 Reflection – What I Learned

Vaccines are classified as "biologics," not pharmaceuticals.[215] They are not held to the same rigorous standards as other pharmaceutical products seeking to come to market, and far less so when granted "Emergency Use Authorization."[216] The *British Medical Journal* called the Covid vaccine studies "hardly blind," expressing concern over the noticeable pain in the arms of eight times as many test subjects who received the vaccine, versus the placebo.[217]

Polarization

Meanwhile, the comments are piling up on my #ExposeBillGates Facebook post. It's easy to see who is reacting to my post, who is seeking to engage in

Chapter 15: Just Act Normal

a caring manner, and who can see the dark truth and the brilliant beam of hope I am now seeing. The rush of interactions with my post feels wonderful and enlivening, in contrast to the isolation I've been feeling for months now. Even the more negative ones fill me with hope, as I trust that with care, persistence, and patience, I'll be able to turn these people around.

Some of the first comments include:

"Nooooo! Not you too… Bill Gates is one of the good guys!"

"Thank you for sharing the truth, Katrina!"

"Sorry, Katrina, you're way out in the weeds on this one. Almost every point in your post can be easily tracked back to one or more conspiracy theories. Bill is doing amazing things for our fellow humans."

"First, they (the Right) went after George Soros, now it's Bill Gates. The world is complicated, Katrina, and you can't make an omelet without breaking a few eggs. If you're interested in knowing the truth, do your research on the Gates Foundation with legit—not conspiracy-oriented—sources. They've helped save over a hundred million lives and they have provided countless educational opportunities."

I am not at all surprised there are so many who don't see what I see. I know they've all been brainwashed by the MSM. And I'm grateful to discover which of my friends are already awake to reality. I am eager to respond with engaging questions as this is what I understand Q does; drop hints, clues, and questions. I am hopeful that I might create cracks in what I believe to be my community's mass hypnosis. To those who are already awake, I add a heart to their comments, or drop them a personal note so we can celebrate the good news discreetly.

I respond to most everyone, and my responses make it increasingly obvious to the community around me that I have fallen headfirst into the QAnon rabbit hole. It doesn't take long for most people to realize that nothing they are saying in their attempts to snap me out of it is getting through to me.

A Softer Tone

Stephen seems unhappy with me, and I am not eager to connect with him. I slowly take inventory of my surroundings, a practice I've learned that assists with calming a trauma response. My small golden-framed Mother Mary catches my eye, her heart radiating love. I see photos of our family placed around our home. My eyes are drawn to our statue of an angel with her hands in prayer, a symbol that in India accompanies the greeting "namaste," which roughly translates to "The Divine in me sees and honors the Divine in you." I feel the beauty of this sentiment as I gaze upon her. I glance around at the plants I tend with loving care and feel gratitude for the warmth they add to our home. Our Casa d'Amore (House of Love) is filled with reminders of all that is sacred, and I am soothed by these visual reminders of values I hold dear.

While I still resist reconnecting with Stephen when he approaches me to revisit the conversation, I am willing to reengage with a softer tone.

"Stephen, my love, I know you are feeling deeply concerned, sometimes fearful, that the coronavirus could end your life prematurely. I imagine it scares you when I say I am not willing to take the vaccine because you have a need for safety and well-being, not only for yourself, but for everyone you love. Am I coming close to expressing what's going on for you?" I ask as I connect to him with a soft gaze and gentle touch.

"Thank you, Katrina. Yes. I am very unsettled by how many people are getting very sick and dying from this virus. I would never force you to do something that you don't want to do, but I am afraid that your choices could kill me. I don't know what to do with that. The vaccines won't be available for a while, so we don't have to figure this out today, but I hope in time you will trust that they're safe and worthwhile. Until then, I hope you don't take any serious risks with your health and mine."

"I hear you," I respond. "I love you and I want you to be healthy for decades to come. I am washing my hands, using hand sanitizer, and wearing a mask at the grocery store. I don't think I'm taking any real risks. And I acknowledge that I can have a significant emotional reaction when I think you might try to force me into any kind of medical procedure against my

Chapter 15: Just Act Normal

will. Thank you for reassuring me you would not do that. I'm glad it will be a while before these vaccines are rolled out."

In this moment with Stephen, I am longing for ease between us, as the strain is clearly hard on us both, and we are stuck in this house together for the unknown duration of the continued lockdowns.

What I am not able to do is to slow my mind. It is running a mile a minute, processing all the weird, concerning, and fantastic content from *Fall of the Cabal*, James Corbett's series on Bill Gates, and all the web searching I did over the course of the night.

"Katrina," Stephen continues, "there's something else going on for me too. I'm very concerned about your engagement on Facebook. I'm reading all your comments, and you seem to be really out there. I know you don't like Bill Gates and of course he's made mistakes, but really Katrina… accusing him of wanting to microchip the population?! You are creating meaning where meaning does not exist, and you are clearly upsetting people in our shared community."

I am agitated but silent while listening to him. We've shared so little joy in the last few weeks, and escalating conflicts seem to be increasingly unavoidable. I can only imagine it will continue in this way until he "wakes up" too, drops all his stress about the false threat of Trump's presidency destroying our country, and we are back on the same page together again. I want that so badly.

Blue Pill

As tension with my beloved is on the rise, I find myself building resentment toward the MSM, whose leadership I believe to be the evil cause of his "blue pill"[218] trance. The blue pill is a stubborn and misguided system of belief that is cultivated, fed, and hardened by the MSM, which drives reactivity against anyone who disagrees with its orthodoxy. I quickly find myself aligning with the anger I would hear in Trump's voice as he calls out the "fake news." I believe Stephen's mind has been captured by a horrible liberal-elite propaganda machine. I want those lies to stop and those bad-faith actors forcefully restrained from committing more harm. I want a global population educated about the real news around them with the kind of honesty, integrity, truth, and transparency that Walter Cronkite embodied as "the most trusted" news reporter in America for a solid 19 years.[219] I am resolved to be patient with Stephen, to find our way through this as we come to discover the truth together.

Stephen's tone increases in intensity. "Katrina, I am trying to be patient and reasonable with you. I don't know what's going on, but you're acting strange, and I don't feel safe around you."

Wow. I don't know what to do with that. Sure, we don't agree on everything, but how on earth could he not feel safe around me? I've never shown any signs of physical violence or even name-calling. At my worst I have raised my voice and pounded pillows.

"You know I would never physically hurt you," I reassure him. "So, what do you need from me so that you can feel safe around me?"

"I need you to calm down and act normal." He responds using what I would call his business tone of voice.

"As much as you'd like me to, I can't calm down. I have too much energy inside of me right now. I could get on the treadmill to see if I can work it out, but it's hard for me to sit still right now."

Stephen shakes his head and walks away. I am sad to experience our disconnection, but relieved for a bit of space.

Keeping Secrets

I manage to get through that first day without revealing to Stephen that I am overjoyed with my new and deep-seated belief that Trump is saving us all from a very sinister future of genocide and human enslavement. What I do not manage to do is to find a way we can go to sleep on good terms. That night, once again, I am lying in bed, wide awake. This time I am both stressed about the tension I am experiencing with Stephen and exhilarated by my new lease on life. The future is not doomed. Trump and the White Hats are in control, and they will put an end to corruption, allowing us to create a future I can hardly wait to see.

Chapter 15: Just Act Normal

My giddiness over the good news keeps me scrolling and clicking into the night on everything I can find to confirm my newfound faith in Trump. I chat with my small yet quickly growing group of QAnon friends. Our conversations are enthusiastic, and we share the relieving joy of seeing the true source of evil and trusting that it will be dismantled. We celebrate the great news about Q, the White Hats, and the surprising brilliance of Donald Trump. We share links and videos with each other, some of which are conspiracy related, and others of which are simply conservative news stories, interviews, and speeches given by Trump. We feel thrilled as we consider the possibility that JFK Jr. is alive and in hiding, and we give each other virtual high-fives by texting our QAnon mantra, "Where we go one, we go all!" (Or WWG1WGA for short.)

What a whirlwind it is. I have been a QAnon for less than 24 hours and my life feels so much different than it had just the day before. *Thank God!*

Chapter 16:
It's Not Normal

It's been only twenty-four hours since I pressed play on *Fall of the Cabal*. I should be tired, given zero sleep the previous night. However, restlessness keeps me bright-eyed all night once again. Escalating conflict between Stephen and me makes it uncomfortable to lie in the same bed. I maintain distance, distracting myself on my phone. My eagerness to learn more compels me to watch videos and read articles all night, looking up anything and everything my mind is curious to delve into.

I choose to watch videos I see connected to the #ExposeBillGates hashtag. One is from channel France 24 with Vandana Shiva, world-renowned Indian scholar, environmental activist, and author,[220] in which she is highly critical of Gates.[221] Another video, previously entitled *Speak Truth: A Doctor Exposes Bill Gates Wicked Agenda*[222] validates what I saw in *Meet Bill Gates*[223] from *The Corbett Report,* as does one from journalist Del Bigtree called *The Coronavirus Agenda*.[224] They are excellent videos, and I quickly add them to my Facebook comment thread, furthering my argument that this man is dangerous.

Social Media Conflict

Comments on my post continue to roll in. One acquaintance, Rick, commented, "Katrina, you are promoting far right-wing conspiracy theories that are absolutely and easily verifiably false but will help serve the oligarchy and Trump. Why are you helping and supporting Trump?"

Another friend Lauren jumped in, "Hey Rick, you know I love you. Please please please look deeper."

I try to engage with Rick, staying on the topic of the Covid vaccines while mostly ignoring his assertions that I was unknowingly supporting the far right. Sure, I now support Donald Trump, but I would never support the hatred and bigotry of the far right.

In our back and forth I write,

> For those who trust in the quickly created, briefly tested, rapidly disseminated new mRNA Covid vaccines, and don't mind being guinea pigs, it may make sense to just go with the proposed solution. I would think this would be especially true for those who believe these shots will end the pandemic, including the horrible lockdown we are all made to endure for who knows how long. I myself don't trust the safety or efficacy of these experimental vaccines, and I do trust my immune system. I want to wait at least three years to know what the long-term side effects are. And while you may not agree with me, I hope you can at least understand my rationale for feeling this way. When this vaccine rolls out, if I decide to decline it, will I be able to keep my job? Get a new job? Fly on an airplane? Go to a grocery store or restaurant? Take public transportation of any kind? How far will this thing go? And is it possible that by the time we find out, it will be too late?

In Rick's final comment to me he writes,

> First of all, I feel your concern and love for so many. And I know that core is where all of this is coming from. And because of that, I apply my mind and heart to trying to discern the truth, just like you do. I also have the benefit of medical training that helps me discern truth from conspiracy theory. And I know that most anti-vaxxers' fears are based on conspiracy theories that are not truly based in fact. So, with love and caring for all, and with my lifelong dedication and professional training, preserving health and life in

Chapter 16: It's Not Normal

everybody, I feel compelled to defend life and health when that is threatened. And I believe that any promotion of false right-wing conspiracy theories threatens the life and health of all. So, I try to speak out against these dangerous falsehoods. Though I do get a bit riled up about this stuff and can get too ferocious in my protector mode. I apologize if I've done that.

While I am unable to meaningfully receive or digest any feedback that asserts I am spreading conspiracy theories or unknowingly supporting the far right, I am grateful for those in my community capable of returning to love and compassion when triggered, as Rick did. I believe it has become common knowledge that people tend to be uncharacteristically harsh, judgmental, and cutting in social media commentary, and even more so when they have no deep personal connection with the people they are interacting with.

It is puzzling to me that most of my community seems content with the mainstream narrative, as I see posts highlighting notable experts who are strongly questioning and clearly challenging that orthodoxy. Among them are ex-Pfizer vice president and allergy and respiratory researcher Michael Yeadon; Dr. Robert Malone, holder of the nine original mRNA vaccine patents ; Dr. Michael Levitt, Nobel Prize winner in chemistry; Dr. Eran Bendavid, an infectious disease physician and professor of medicine at Stanford; Dr. Alan Preston, a former professor of epidemiology; Dr. Michael Roisen, chief medical officer at the Cleveland Clinic; Scott Jensen, MD, US senator; Dr. Martin Kulldorff, professor of medicine at Harvard; Dr. Sunetra Gupta, professor and epidemiologist at Oxford; Dr. Jay Bhattacharya, professor of medicine at Stanford Medical School; and Dr. Christiane Northrup, an OB/GYN made famous by one of her patients, Oprah Winfrey.

All these eminent authorities in their fields are in clear dispute with the mainstream-driven so-called scientific consensus surrounding Covid. And they are not the only ones. Dozens of other doctors, researchers and scientists are openly challenging the Covid narrative as well. If I am wrong about this, these top-level academics, scientists, and doctors are too.

Social Relocation Begins

The abrasive remarks from my "blue pill" community make the kind, supportive, and loving comments of my new and growing "red pill" community all the much sweeter. These new friends are becoming my emotional lifeline. They can see me, understand my concerns and my pain, and celebrate my courage in speaking up. It is clear and evident that I am not alone.

Over the course of these 24 hours, I can identify at least a dozen of my 3,000+ Facebook friends who I assume to be politically left and who are seeing the world as I am seeing it. Those numbers quickly grow over the next few weeks as I discover more and more of my preexisting friends who are aligned with most or all of my newfound QAnon beliefs. I actively seek out friendships with more people who share my new worldview, feeling joy at what I see as a grassroots movement that is growing quickly.

> *Over the course of these 24 hours, I can identify at least a dozen of my 3,000+ Facebook friends... who are seeing the world as I am seeing it.*

I lie awake most of the night, catching only a couple hours' sleep. YouTube consistently has at least a half dozen interesting videos on the suggestion list, and the more I watch, the more my new worldview cements in my mind.

Emergency Preparedness

At 5 a.m., I figure I have been in bed long enough. It's time to get up.

"Where are you going?" Stephen asks.

"I can't seem to fall back asleep," I answer. "Unless you want to snuggle, I'm going upstairs so I won't keep you awake too."

On days when Stephen and I have experienced conflict the evening before, he is usually able to reset himself at night and return to a heartfelt connection with me the next morning. He often wakes up before me, and in the rare times that I am awake early, he welcomes me for a long morning snuggle, which I generally love. Cozying into him and feeling the warmth

Chapter 16: It's Not Normal

of his body and his arms wrapped around me is something we both look forward to. His lack of interest in cuddling this morning is telling.

At the top of the stairs, I see a mailer I had set aside from our local fire department. It is designed to educate our community about the high likelihood of a significant fire season ahead with a checklist supporting every household to get prepared. Included are a list of items to pack in the event of evacuation, and information about how to clear vegetation to make our yard as fire safe as it can be. I do additional online research and post a more comprehensive checklist to my Facebook page, encouraging friends to buy N95 masks, as their cloth masks would do nothing to filter toxic smoke-laden air. As it turns out, N95 masks are very hard to come by. Due to the pandemic, most supplies have gone to various medical facilities. However, I locate a little-known seller in Bali, which offers masks made from 100% organic plant fibers. I share the link with friends and family, encouraging them to stock up.

I am glad we took down seven Italian Stone Pines in our back yard a couple of years ago. Those trees are not only brittle and prone to collapsing in ways that could have damaged our neighbors' yards; they are also highly flammable. When those trees go up in flames, they become massive fireballs. But we still have twelve Italian Cypress trees edging two sides of our home. It doesn't take much research to see that these trees could also easily light up like matches, creating a mass of flames several times larger than the trees themselves. I want them gone. While Stephen does not initially agree with me, he opens to the idea a couple days later after men from our local fire department confirm that should any of those trees catch fire, they will seriously damage our home.

While I am working through our fire preparedness checklist, I notice Stephen is finally up from his slumber.

"What are you doing?" Stephen asks as he reaches the top of the stairs.

"Oh, I'm just cleaning the house, and looking to see how we can prepare for the fire season this year," I respond, trying to be nonchalant.

"Are you concerned about the upcoming fire season?" he inquires.

"Of course I am," I say firmly. "For well over a month the news has been predicting that this will be the worst fire season California has ever seen. We've had four massive fire seasons in the last five years. I have so many friends who are still traumatized by the loss of their homes. Others have had very close calls with those fires. Ashley and François narrowly escaped. Remember?" No doubt my tone is less than nonchalant as the fear I am feeling is becoming increasingly apparent in my nervous behavior.

"Katrina, sweetheart, I think it's a good idea to do reasonable preparation ahead of the fire season, but please do not get bent out of shape. We've been fine these last five years and we will be fine this year as well."

His words are not sufficiently reassuring. While it is true that we have been unscathed by the previous fires, we can't assume that our good fortune will continue. Our home is not in as much of a danger zone as many of our friends, yet I am well aware that a mile away from us are acres of public land with dried up, dead trees and hundreds if not thousands of madrones, whose leaves and bark are so oil-laden that when they ignite they burn intensely, leading to more severe fire behavior. If that place went up in flames, who's to say our neighborhood and home would survive? Do I push back to try to drive home a sense of urgency? Or let it go for now so as not to engage in yet another conflict with Stephen? I feel torn between these two strategies seeking to serve different needs. I do not want to sacrifice some of my needs in order to meet those of others; I want it all—ease and harmony with Stephen, and safety during the fire season.

I am unaware that Stephen is reading my body language as I contemplate what to do and what to say. My head is tilted down, and occasionally I look slightly to the left or right as I consider options.

Heightened Concerns

"What's on your mind?" He asks.

Sometimes I wish he were less attuned to me. Do I respond? Or brush it off with an "Oh, nothing"? As my tendency is to be open and honest, I take a risk to share.

"Stephen, I am very concerned about the upcoming fire season. You know how much I've been shaken during the previous fire seasons. And you've seen the condition of the trails down the street. There are dead trees everywhere. What if the fires are so severe that the fire stations cannot

Chapter 16: It's Not Normal

handle it all? And what do we do if we have to evacuate our home? I can prepare us with a grab-and-go box, but do you want to be staying in a shelter along with dozens if not hundreds of others when there's a pandemic that's killing people?" I figure it is good leverage to amplify his own fear about dying from Covid to get him onboard with my increased interest in exiting California for the fall. "Why go through all that fear when we can simply get our home as fire safe as possible and go somewhere where fire is not a concern?" What I do not express to him is my concern that these fires are being intentionally lit by an evil Cabal.

"Katrina," he begins with a tone of frustration and exasperation in his voice, "You are really overreacting to the threat of fire. What's going on with you? You didn't sleep at all two nights ago, you hardly slept last night, and yet you are wired with energy like you're high or something. You are not acting like yourself. And to be honest, it's wearing on me. It seems you might be having a mental health breakdown, and that is concerning to me. I want you well, Katrina. I want us well. As I said, I'm all in favor of fire safety, but please, calm down. Take a breath or meditate or something. Maybe take a nap. I'm sure you need one."

My heart sinks. What can I do? He doesn't seem to be taking my concerns seriously. Just breathe, relax, and meditate?! His suggestions seem to be dismissive of my concerns. While that's great advice for calming stress, it's not how you respond to real-world threats.

But I *am* stressed, and I need to relax. So, I sit down for a break in my day and click my Facebook app because... well... it's habitual and I'm addicted.

New York Nurse

My Facebook post has generated more topics to research. One lady, whom I quickly add to my friends list, posted an hourlong video highlighting an undercover nurse named Erin Olszewski.[225] She expresses that she was thrilled with the successes that her team had generated treating early Covid with hydroxychloroquine, zinc, vitamin D, and ivermectin at a private hospital in Florida. She hoped to bring these protocols to a public hospital in New York. However, the New York hospital was set in its protocol and, according to Olszewski, that protocol was killing people.

She reports that many people in this impoverished New York neighborhood were coming to the emergency room in fear that they might have Covid. But they were not suffering from Covid; instead, they were suffering from anxiety, which presents with the similar symptom of shortness of breath. When a new ER patient's Covid test comes back negative, the patient is held for days at a time, in case they might have been exposed to someone with Covid while waiting with a room full of others in emergency care. According to Olszewski, these patients are tested every three days until the result is positive, in which case they are put on a respirator until they die, with no ability for their friends or family to see or contact them.

While this nurse found the Covid protocols enforced by management at the New York public hospital to be concerningly poor, she also expressed understanding that many of these nurses are clinging to their jobs to pay the bills and are unlikely to go against management's decisions even when, from her perspective, it is clear as day and captured on video that what they are doing is wrong.

"Just Following Orders"

There's a word in the German language for this kind of unethical compliance: *"amtssprache,"*[226,227] a term used by Nazi soldiers to describe what made them obey actions in support of genocide. "I was just following orders," was the common refrain.

For me, this compelling video is yet another confirmation of my long-held belief that the MSM is hiding the truth about this virus and successful early treatments, while the "healthcare" system is incentivizing inflation of the positive Covid test count and death count. My heels are fully dug in on this topic. What I am seeing leads me to believe something horribly wrong is unfolding around this plandemic. This is greed at its worst. This is a manifestation of evil.

I tumble deeper down this rabbit hole.

Chapter 17:
The Covid Conspiracy

Having taken space from Stephen, my mind continues to spin on all the information I am learning. I am working overtime to make sense of it all, and in particular the Covid madness that has overtaken both my world and the world at large.

The Cult and the Hunger Games

As I follow the thread of this rabbit hole, a Rose/Icke interview teaser catches my eye on my YouTube feed. I go to the London Real website and press play on *Rose/Icke 1: The Truth Behind the Coronavirus Pandemic, Covid Lockdown & Economic Crash*.[228] In this video, Brian Rose, London Real founder and CEO, expresses his belief in the scientific method and the efficacy of Covid vaccines, as well as his choice to comply with government mandates, before asking Icke for his thoughts on current events.

Icke begins,

For 30 years, I've been warning people in my books and everywhere I can that this world is operated by a Cult (Icke's term for the Cabal) that has no boundaries. The Cult is at the core of the system in China, America, etc., etc. This Cult wants to create a beyond-Orwellian global state in which a tiny few people dictate to everyone else. It's not classic fascism; it's not classic communism—

it's technocracy. The ability for that to happen is through smart technology and AI. The idea is that everything will be connected to AI. This is what the Internet of Things (IoT) is about. Eventually the human brain will be connected to AI, and thus whoever controls AI will be driving the perceptions of humanity, which can be done from a central point, through this global smart grid. I call this the hunger games.[229] *They also want a completely cashless society, in which everything is digital currency run through this central smart grid.*

He continues,

Now, I've written about the way they do it, which I call Problem—Reaction—Solution. They covertly create a problem and use the mainstream media to tell the public the version of the story they want you to believe. Then they move to stage two, which is fear. It is the stage of control. In stage two, they use the mainstream media once again to generate a demand from the public, or at least an acceptance from the public, that something needs to change to solve the problem. At that point, the cabal who created the problem offers solutions they have prearranged to address the problem they covertly created. This is how the Cult controls the population in the direction of their choosing. This is how they lead the human race step-by-step closer to this technocratic society they are actively building.

Know the outcome, and you'll see the journey. If you don't know where this world is being taken by this cult, then everything seems random: coronavirus, random; climate change, random; economic crash, random. But when you know where we are being taken, when you can see this hunger games structure of society,[230] *then the apparently random events become clear stepping stones to that outcome.*

I have read *The Hunger Games* series and watched the movies.[231] I remember how eloquently they spoke about the dystopian future our civilization seems to be moving toward—a world in which the filthy rich live off

Chapter 17: The Covid Conspiracy

the forced labor of impoverished populations. Icke's words are hitting home, especially in light of the steadily growing wealth gap, which people I deeply admire, including Bernie Sanders and Robert Reich,[232] have highlighted so potently.

Icke continues,

Let's take all of that and apply it to the coronavirus and see what's happening now and let people decide for themselves if they think that the coronavirus hysteria ticks every single box of that goal.

After setting the stage, Icke spends the next half hour expanding on this point. He maintains that the coronavirus is not dangerous for everyone; it poses a clear threat only to certain segments of society, especially the elderly and people with compromised immune systems. Many people have only mild to manageable symptoms and quickly build natural immunity.

Kary Mullis and PCR Tests

Almost everything Icke is presenting resonates with what I now believe with regard to Covid-19 as I double down on my resolve to question the lockdown and the vaccine agenda. This video fascinates me. I am eager to listen to the next interview, *Rose/Icke 2: The Coronavirus Conspiracy: How Covid-19 Will Seize Your Rights & Destroy Our Economy*,[233] which was first released in April 2020, nineteen days after the first.

In this second video, Icke explains that the PCR "test" being used widely to diagnose Covid does not (and cannot) verify the presence of a virus. It verifies only the presence of genetic material that is *similar to* SARS-CoV-2. Icke says that the PCR tests are being used to inflate the Covid infection and death statistics in order to scare the public into believing this to be a deadly virus (problem) so that they will enthusiastically embrace (reaction) the vaccines (solution).

I pause to do a bit of research on these claims. Here's what I come up with: PCR stands for "polymerase chain reaction." This method was invented by biochemist Kary Mullis in 1984 and won him a Nobel Prize in 1993.[234] Mullis (who died of heart and respiratory failure in August 2019) was highly critical of Dr. Anthony Fauci, saying in a recorded video, "Fauci knows nothing about medicine and should not be in the position he is in," and "He's got a personal agenda, and he does not mind going up on television and lying directly in front of the camera."[235]

Mullis also clearly stated that the PCR is not a diagnostic tool; it should not be used to search for a virus, or to diagnose anything whatsoever, as it can amplify genetic material enough to find anything you want to find.[236] The CDC's current recommendations instruct testing facilities to run the samples through 40 cycles of amplification.[237]

2021 Reflection – What I Learned

In August 2020, a number of researchers showed that the level of amplification routinely used in Covid PCR testing generated false positive results as high as 90 percent. A *New York Times* article by journalist Apoorva Mandavilli reports that Juliet Morrison, a virologist at the University of California, Riverside, said, "Any test with a cycle threshold above 35 is too sensitive. I'm shocked that people would think that 40 could represent a positive. A more reasonable cutoff would be 30 to 35, she added." Harvard epidemiologist Dr. Michael Mina concurred, saying he "would set the figure at 30, or even less."[238]

Dr. Anthony Fauci himself stated "If you get a cycle threshold of 35 or more, the chances of it being replication competent [i.e., live/infectious] are miniscule… if somebody does come in with 37, 38, even 36, you've got to say it's just dead nucleotides, period."[239]

None of us were told (and if you asked, they couldn't tell you) how many amplification cycles were used in the PCR tests we all took. While this does not prove the Covid case count numbers were inflated, it does give reason to believe they might have been.

Icke suggests we should watch the media's choice of language and notice how many times new reports say that someone died "after testing positive for Covid." This does not mean they died *from* Covid.

☸ Chapter 17: The Covid Conspiracy ☸

I discover that in April 2020 Deborah Birx, MD, coordinator of the White House Coronavirus Task Force, instructed health institutions in the following way: "If someone dies with Covid-19, we are counting that as a Covid-19 death."[240] They might have died of cancer, a heart attack, or a car crash; however, if their PCR test results at the time of death come back positive for the SARS-CoV-2 virus, they are added to the Covid death count, despite 90% of them being false positives.

I feel my frustrations rise as I gain evidence leading me to conclude that the WHO, CDC, NIH, and White House Coronavirus Task Force are actively exaggerating the Covid case count and death count in order to herd humanity toward mass vaccination, despite the actual estimated Covid infection fatality rate being only 0.4%. I believe the Cabal/Cult is driving fear and mass compliance with the lockdowns and the vaccine. Icke asserts the lockdowns will be over when the Cult has accomplished everything it wants, destroying businesses and creating increased reliance on government handouts.

Censorship and Other Abuses of Authoritarian Power

The third interview, *Rose/Icke 3: 1,000,000 People Fighting for Freedom*,[241] was broadcast in May 2020. In his introduction, Rose shares that 46 days ago they broadcast Rose/Icke 1, and the episode immediately went viral and was watched ten million times. He continues,

> 27 days ago, we broadcast the second interview, which had 65,000 concurrent viewers, with an expectation to reach 40 million views, making it the largest video podcast in human history. Thirty minutes later, that livestream video was deleted and banned on YouTube with no explanation and no communication.

Rose announces he is now livestreaming on his new censorship-free platform, an independent broadcasting system created by the people and for the people.

Rose then turns to Icke and says,

In the last episode, you spoke of the Covid-19 misdiagnosis, the misclassification of deaths, further dangerous technology rollouts, the vaccine agenda, economic totalitarianism, and the weaponizing of fear.

He continues,

The next day a BBC article broke the news, and the representatives of YouTube accused you of being a Covid-19 denier and subsequently deleted ten of your videos and my personal vlogs from our YouTube channel. Instagram, Facebook, and Dropbox followed suit by deleting and banning more of our videos, and then London Real was entirely deplatformed from YouTube and Vimeo without explanation. But we fought back and continued to host both episodes to millions of viewers while suffering very sophisticated malicious attacks on our platform.

At that point I had enough, as I believe in the fundamental right of freedom of speech," Rose shares with a passion, *"so I decided we can no longer count on any third party for broadcasting. Eleven days ago, we began crowdfunding to create the digital freedom platform, which has now raised over a million dollars worldwide to promote freedom of speech and freedom of the press. It's been an incredible vote of confidence in what we are doing.*

I am stunned by Brian Rose's introduction. This mass censorship appears powerful and well-coordinated. Given how much evidence I have seen in support of Icke's assertions about the end goals of the Cult, and the way those ideas mirror what Q says about the Cabal, and the many statements Bernie Sanders has given about the elite, and Trump and others have said about the Deep State, I'm inclined to align with the idea that this Covid crisis is a power game designed to keep the rich at the top and everyone else at the bottom in society, with a rapidly vanishing middle class. I find the trajectory of these financial dynamics concerning.

❦ Chapter 17: The Covid Conspiracy ❦

2024 Reflection – What I Learned

Many people believe that the current dwindling of middle-class America is the direct result of an ongoing Marxist takeover.[242] In theory, Marxism champions the proletariat and the idea that the working class can assemble to overthrow the ruling class, thus freeing themselves, reclaiming power and self-governance.

However, in practice we have seen again and again that revolutionary lower-class uprisings against those with wealth has not led to a sovereign people. The vacuum of power has consistently led to authoritarian communist takeovers—most infamously those of Joseph Stalin in the Soviet Union[243] and Mao Zedong[244] in China,[245] but also Cuba, North Korea, Vietnam, Czechoslovakia, Great Britain, Cambodia, Laos, and East Germany.[246] Stalin deliberately exterminated six million of his own people, and nine million in total if you count those killed through his policies.[247] Mao Zedong killed somewhere between forty and eighty million citizens in China during his reign. While some of the Marxist theories sound good in concept, they have had clear pitfalls.

This Rose/Icke video series continues to confirm what I have come to discover in the last few months, but especially over these last few days. The roots of my gratitude for Q continue to deepen. I know freedom of speech is a cornerstone right in our US Constitution and is essential to a healthy functioning democracy. The attack on London Real is disturbing to me, especially on top of other forms of media control I see happening in mainstream news and on social media channels. Who is in control?

Icke begins his response to Rose with "Welcome to my world," before describing his experience of similar tactics used against him all his life. He asserts that if the Cult is going to get away with controlling our world, the puppet masters have to start by controlling our perceptions. He continues by reviewing content from the first two videos saying,

> *There is a global network that works through secret societies with literally satanic roots that has a structure in place to dictate from a central point down into even local communities.*

I don't remember Icke's conspiracy theories pointing to satanic roots, but to be honest, I didn't pay much attention to him when I first listened to him at the New Living Expo over a decade ago. Today, I note that his research and Q's intelligence seem to point to the same conclusion. I feel excited by that thought, as I would love to find more solid evidence for these claims that feel so true.

Icke argues that the Cult is not doing this for money. They are driven by a desire for complete control. He talks about networks that have been created to dominate all the systems: government, finance, the media, etc., stating that they are all part of what is now known as the Deep State. He asserts that they are now seeking to control the medical systems and Big Pharma, saying this is going on in every country; they are all working the same agenda, the same blueprint.

Mechanisms of Control

I discover that *Rose/Icke 4: We Will Not Be Silenced*[248] has just been published today, on June 14, 2020, so I keep going. Icke reveals that he's been ridiculed for his work for over 30 years, but rather than being a victim to the mockery or censorship of his research, he is now finding new social media platforms that are not censoring speech. He continues to talk about how life is not random. All things are connected.

From the point of view of spiritual oneness, I resonate with this possibility. My favorite children's book is *All I See Is Part of Me*,[249] and I feel a sense of celebration as I consider the inherent interconnection of all of the Universe. After all, it is the uni (meaning one) verse (or phrase in a song), and so many spiritual masters talk about the mysterious and wondrous beauty of our inherent unity with the totality of creation.

Icke points out several contradictions in the way the pandemic is being managed. It's okay to protest with Black Lives Matter, but it's not okay to protest the lockdowns or to gather in any other groups. Churches are being shut down, but bars remain open. Why is that? Icke asserts it all serves the agenda of the Cult, saying:

Chapter 17: The Covid Conspiracy

What is allowed, encouraged, and promoted serves the agenda, and what is suppressed, demonized, and prevented challenges the agenda. It's so simple, and that's why there is madness, but there is method in the madness.

I feel alignment in my deep distrust of government authority. My inclination to rebel is supported and further fueled by Icke's willingness to speak out. Brian Rose's increasing engagement and enthusiasm to join in the fight against the censorship and vaccine agenda enlivens me. I am comforted by the idea that, if I am ridiculed, it's because I am speaking truth to power. I will not let the Cabal win. Where we go one, we go all.

Icke continues by sharing nondenominational spiritual wisdom before weaving back to argue that the Cult is working to divide people and destroy families in order to maintain control, in classic "divide and conquer" fashion. He states with passion and confidence that the same family bloodlines that were behind commercialized slavery are now funding Black Lives Matter in a war against White people, in order to shame, humiliate, and disempower them. He says that the Cult is pressuring poor White people to "get on your knees and confess your white privilege" because this is not a race war; it is a class war against all of us, and in order to win that war, it has to divide and rule the masses, which far outnumber the relative few at the top of the Cult's power structure. If we rise up together, their game will be over.

We've been in class wars for some time. This continues to be one of Bernie Sanders' top talking points. The divide between the mega-rich and everyone else is atrocious and growing worse. Of course, this Cabal is working to conquer us ordinary people so it can maintain its power and wealth, regardless of the costs. Cabal members work in the same way as crony capitalists—their prime aim is to secure the highest possible quarterly profits, despite the cost to humanity or the environment. If they believe they can get away with it, they'll do it.

Icke says that the restrictions will continue with the rise of vaccine passports and legally enforced mandates against those who do not comply. The Cult will fabricate food shortages to increase dependence on government handouts and further pressure compliance. They will fabricate a second wave of virus, as the news is already predicting. I am stunned at hearing how evil the Cabal, or the Cult as he calls it, can truly be.

All in all, Icke asserts that what he really wants is a world in which people are free, regardless of race, class, or any other differentiating feature. I want this too.

To my eye, this Rose/Icke video series affirms what I learned in *Fall of the Cabal*: the Cabal is an ancient cult that uses propaganda and mind control techniques to manipulate people. Icke claims that some methods include repetition. A lie repeated many times by a perceived authority among large groups of people will eventually be perceived as the truth among those collectives. Another technique is to induce trauma in order to take the conscious mind offline so that ideas can be planted in the subconscious.

2023 Personal Reflection

It didn't cross my mind that induced trauma could be precisely what happened to me as I was watching *Fall of the Cabal*. By sharing detailed stories and images of child abuse, the series planted all kinds of ideas in my subconscious mind that I would have never considered before.

Some mind-control techniques Icke cites are similar to other forms of propaganda such as those designed by Edward Bernays, Sigmund Freud's nephew, whom Icke references in his interview. I learned about Bernays's tactics several months ago while watching a documentary called *The Century of Self*.[250] I understand how most decisions we make are driven more by our subconscious conditioning than by our present-time consciousness. Bernays cynically used his knowledge of the subconscious to entice women to smoke in 1929, thereby doubling profits for the tobacco industry. He did this by convincing feminists to light up cigarettes as an act of emancipation during New York's Easter Parade, sensing that this act of

Chapter 17: The Covid Conspiracy

defiance would catch wind among the greater feminist movement, resulting in a new wave of customers for his client, George W. Hill, president of the American Tobacco Company.

This devious tactic of using symbols and imagery that hook our subconscious and get us to think, believe, and act on impulses we would not consciously think, believe, or act on makes sense to me. It also makes sense that through subconscious manipulation techniques, a dark group of elites could have been controlling masses of people throughout the ages. It seems as though only in the present time people can see this for what it is—manipulation and control. As more and more of our population gains awareness of the workings of the subconscious mind and manipulative techniques used in propaganda (both perpetrated by and exposed by social media), we empower ourselves to choose consciously rather than be puppeteered by others. As we become increasingly committed to questioning authority and undoing our unconscious conditioning, we can and will (I hope) step forward in life with gradually more conscious and life-serving choices.

2024 Reflection – What I Learned

Some people have made a study of the art and science of mind control. Jason Christoff is one such person. He has multiple videos that show various mind control experts and experiments at work, demonstrating how easy it is to hack people's minds so they conform to subtle suggestions while believing they are thinking for themselves. He also offers coaching and education for those who want to increase their immunity to these tactics.

The must-see video linked at the end of this sentence is queued to a 6.5-minute clip in which three prominent young social media influencers are challenged to create a unique Instagram selfie in 5 minutes, using any of 50 random props and 20 themed rooms to film in. To their astonishment, all three of them create the *same image* in the *same room* with the *same* hashtag![251]

In retrospect, whether intentionally or unintentionally, I do believe Janet Ossebaard employed some of these techniques in *Fall of the Cabal* as well.

All of the content I am watching and absorbing deepens my conviction that Covid-19 is undeniably a "plandemic." Is an occult group of elites using predictive programming, as originally suggested by Alan Watts?[252,253] Was the 2012 Olympics opening ceremony an example of this form of mass manipulation, foretelling the coming of Covid-19 and its impact on communities and hospitals?[254] Is the Cult intentionally using movies and the media to inform us of what it is going to do before it does it? Is it using propaganda and mind control in its own twisted way: creating what it asserts is sufficient consent to treat humanity in ways that intensify pain and suffering?

Could it be that the Cabal is also using symbolic representations like the logos known to the FBI as pedophilia symbols to target the subconscious minds of humans?[255] Was it intentional or just coincidence that Google named two of its products "Adreno" and "Chrome," and that its logo comprises three sixes forming a circle?[256] Are there times when the sign language for "horns" is actually used to publicly yet covertly pledge allegiance to Satan?[257] Are face masks along with the six-foot distancing being used to train the latest facial recognition software?[258] Is the Cabal also using masks to subconsciously program us to shut our mouths and stop talking and fear each other?[259] And is it a coincidence or by design that six feet is the prescribed amount of distance, creating a fixation on sixes all around us?[260] Who came up with this six-foot recommendation anyway? Janet Ossebaard posed all of these questions and more in her densely packed three-hour *Fall of the Cabal* series. So many images from those videos continue to rise in my memory.

2024 Reflection – What I Learned

In January 2024, Dr. Anthony Fauci testified in front of Congress, saying he did not know where the six foot "social distancing" came from, that it was "likely not based on any data," and that it "sort of just appeared."[261]

❧ Chapter 17: The Covid Conspiracy ❧

I trust I am finally seeing "The Truth." I am putting together all the pieces. I am solving the puzzle, the world's greatest mystery of why there is so much pain and suffering in society. I see the workings of evil, and I know we will awaken humanity to these critical truths. We will rise up together and resolve this problem once and for all. Despite the darkness inherent in what I'm learning, my body is high on dopamine as I connect the dots I am gathering from all my QAnon-related sources.

Conversation-Ending Labels

Everything I am learning is so thrilling to me. I wish I had more people I could talk to about it all. I can't wait to reconnect with Laura. I start by sending her a link to the video of the undercover nurse.

"OMG!... That video" she writes.

"I know, right?" We are both blown away.

"It's such a process every day," Laura continues. "I see dozens and dozens of things like this all the time. But the video will be on a YouTube channel that people call conspiracy, so they won't watch it. In fact, they literally won't even think about it. They just start wagging their fingers... How is it that nobody can sit in the "both/and" gray area and see that there can be a horrific virus and a giant crime syndicate going on all at the same time? They act as if one negates the other."

While I have only ventured into this new worldview for a couple of days, I am already painfully aware of ways in which so many topics I believe need more visibility are quickly squelched with the "conspiracy theory" memeplex, including "misinformation," "right-wing propaganda," and "anti-science," especially when talking about anything to do with Covid. The Wuhan lab leak theory, the use of ivermectin and hydroxychloroquine, people daring to question the effectiveness of masks or the upcoming mass rollout of a new mRNA vaccine technology, and even advice coming from nutritional experts who echo what has been known for decades—taking vitamin C, vitamin D, quercetin, zinc, spending time outdoors and exercise can boost one's immune response against viruses... Yet, all of these Covid-related topics are swiftly slapped with the conversation-ending labels quickly made nearly synonymous with the overall evaluation of "conspiracy theory."

I wonder,

> What the heck is going on? Why isn't there room for open expert debate, which is the literal foundation of good science? Wouldn't it build public trust to have transparent dialogue in the shared desire for separating truth from falsehood? Why won't Dr. Anthony Fauci and Bill Gates engage in a live debate with Drs. Jay Bhattacharya, Sunetra Gupta, or Martin Kulldorff, all renowned experts from top-tier universities, and outspoken critics of the government's response to Covid?[262] Or with RFK Jr., who has made childhood health and environmental issues his life's work?[263] I don't want to be fed one side of the argument and told I have to buy into it, especially when another side is being actively censored, deleted, and mocked. Why are droves of high-level PhDs and scientists being erased, losing their jobs, their social media accounts, and their access to PayPal, Venmo, Stripe and other payment processors? Who is behind the mass censorship of speech? Who is rolling out these financially punitive measures?

This frustration compels me to look deeper into the origins and original meaning of the word "conspiracy."

The Latin Roots of "Conspiracy Theory"

A theory is defined as a supposition or a system of ideas intended to explain something, especially one based on general principles independent of the thing to be explained. But what of conspiracy?

The word *conspiracy* breaks down into two elements of Latin origin: *con* means together or with, as in congregate or connect. *Spire* means to breathe. (*Inspire* means to breathe in or to give life. *Expire* means to breathe out or to end. *Respire* means to breathe again, as in *respirator*.) *Spire* also derives from the Latin word *spiritus*, meaning spirit, as it is in the word *spirituality*. And so, the literal definition of *conspire* is to breathe together or to breathe together in spirit.

I find it completely ironic that this conclusive accusation, which literally means "to breathe together" is on the rise in a time when "I can't breathe"

Chapter 17: The Covid Conspiracy

is a trending vociferous refrain, in remembrance of George Floyd and in support of Black Lives Matter.

I don't know how the definition of conspiracy shifted from breathing together to its current-day definition: a secret plan by a group to do something unlawful or harmful. The only thing I can find is the use of the word in the Roman Empire era, to describe those who gathered with the intention to usurp the power of the emperor.

2024 Reflection What I Learned

A scanned PDF document found on the cia.gov website entitled "Countering Criticism of the Warren Report,"[264] relays that members of the CIA, including director Allen Dulles,[265] conspired to kill President John F. Kennedy and then cover it up.[266] (Dulles later headed President Johnson's Warren Commission, which investigated the very Kennedy assassination.)[267]

This same group appears to have popularized the modern use of the term "conspiracy theory" as a way of silencing those who dared to question the original official Warren Report.[268] This was most widely seen in Richard Hofstadter's popular *Harper's Magazine* article, "The Paranoid Style in American Politics," written in 1964, the year after Kennedy's murder.[269]

Chapter 18:
Explosive (Subjective) Truth

I Support Trump(!?)

On the third night after pressing play on that notorious documentary, *Fall of the Cabal,* I get a few hours of sleep. Stephen is up well before me, and so I take my time before heading upstairs.

As Stephen and I value honesty and openness in our relationship, we intentionally schedule times to share what we call "withholds," which are communications that have, for whatever reason, been left unsaid. Through this practice, we endeavor to maintain trust and clarity in our mutual connection. It is with this intention that I walk upstairs, working to calm my nerves once again as I prepare to reconnect with Stephen.

I am not eager to tell Stephen that I now support Donald Trump, and this is a clear withhold. I feel pressure building in me, as I've been holding onto this potent secret for three days. That is a long time for me. Maintaining this level of secrecy is uncomfortable. I want to honor my commitment to clearing withholds with my fiancé; yet I struggle to figure out an artful way to do it. How might I soften the blow? I don't know. As a result, my approach is more like standing on the edge of a cliff, hoping that the unseen water below will catch me as I jump.

"Stephen, you have expressed to me several times that I am acting differently and that it seems something has changed. There is something that has shifted in me, so I want to be open with you and put it out on the table. My fear is that you might react, and that could drive a wedge between us, and my hope is that by sharing we might start to address the distance I know we've both been feeling. I'd like to think that by sharing this we might start finding our way back together again."

"Thank you, Katrina. So, what is it?" He asks.

"Well," I start, "I watched a documentary a few nights ago, and it's caused me to view many things differently."

"Okay. Go on," he says to me with a look of fatigue, yet engagement in his eyes.

And so, I continue. "This documentary showed me how our media has been lying to us. It's been getting us to believe things that are not true, about politics, Covid, and the Republican Party," I continue.

"Media is biased," he replies, "but it's quite a claim to say broadly that the media is flat-out lying to us, Katrina."

Stephen has a pragmatic mind, and while at times he negates my intuitive side, I generally appreciate his grounded perspectives and do my best to meet him there. It does not seem wise to tell him about *Fall of the Cabal*. I need a quick pivot. The only idea I am able to conjure up is to share with him what I learned yesterday from yet another video called *Hoaxed*,[270] which seeks to prove that the mainstream news is lying to the public. This might be a first stepping-stone to the larger conversation. But I am far from confident this will work.

Tentatively, I continue the process of revealing my truth to Stephen saying, "I hear and understand that it's a bold claim, and I imagine you'd like to believe that you can generally trust that the news is honest, but I've come to understand why so many Republicans are calling it 'fake news.' This documentary showed so many small snippets of what the news tells us is true, then showed a fuller context to demonstrate how reporters are twisting facts. Whoever is giving the reporters content to cover, they are completely intentional in how they contort information. This cannot be

Chapter 18: Explosive (Subjective) Truth

explained away by saying they are merely highly opinionated. I've seen so many examples of flat-out false news stories. I can't trust our mainstream news channels anymore," I explain.

"Really, Katrina?!" He sounds exasperated. "You know, between this and everything you are posting on Facebook, I'm starting to think that you are secretly supporting Trump. Tell me that's not so."

I am caught like a deer in headlights. His request for me to denounce Trump is so clear, but in my heart of hearts, I can't do that. It would be a lie to deny my newfound appreciation for Trump and the changes I believe he is working tirelessly to establish on behalf of all people everywhere.

"Stephen, with all that I've recently learned, I do support Trump. I know that is a huge change." Stephen cuts me off before I can continue.

"What the fuck, Katrina?! You're kidding me, right? Did you really just say that you, of all people, support Trump?!"

He is clearly well beyond dismayed. Is he approaching livid? I don't know, but my nervous system is now in a state of freeze as my limbic brain decides that I am not safe in Stephen's presence. My eyes look down, and my breathing becomes almost nonexistent.

Stephen walks out the front door, slamming it behind him.

I am shaken deeply, scared and alone. Vulnerability overwhelms me as I curl up in a ball on the sofa. How in the heck am I going to get through this one? Usually when I experience complex life challenges, I turn to my dad or one of a few select best friends whose wisdom, care, compassion, and mentorship I value, but all of them think Trump is a dangerous con man, and it's predictable that any of them will think I'm out of my mind. Thanks to their shared blue-pill trance, they'll be more likely to try to correct me with MSM-sourced videos and articles than to understand what I'm going through and the new clarity I have found. Who can I turn to now?

I take a risk and call my dad. He's consistently been the safest person for me to talk to, no matter what the topic has been, and he has a dozen or more Republican friends who are "snowbirds" to the warm climate in which he lives. He might understand. He might even wake up! The thought of it fills me with hope.

My hopes, however, are dashed in the conversation with my dad, but it is okay. I knew he was unlikely to open his mind to these new ideas and see politics in a radically different way on a first call. It's not like he's ever had anything good to say about Trump, as the information streams he consumes has led him to the firm conclusion that Trump could well be Hitler 2.0. He does, however, provide emotional comfort as I relay to him the challenges and rising strain I am experiencing with Stephen. He also agrees to watch *Fall of the Cabal* soon and reconnect with me once he's watched it so we can talk about it. That's as much as I can hope for in this initial call. I appreciate his care and feel excited at the possibility that this video series might help my dad see what's really going on in the world. It would mean so much to me to have him as an ally as we work together to wake up the rest of our family before they walk into this horrible vaccine trap set by the Cabal.

Immediate Consequences

An hour later Stephen is back. Tension escalates quickly.

"Katrina, I don't know who you are anymore. Last week you were still all about Bernie and Our Revolution. Today you're supporting Trump, a man whom you've previously despised. You've hardly gotten any sleep and you are acting weird. I don't know if you've just had a mental health break or what's going on, but this isn't right. I can't stand to be around you like this. Your energy is off. If it doesn't change back quickly, if you don't return to normal, one of us will have to leave for a time." His voice is insistent, and the sharp look in his eyes, and tense muscles in his neck and face, tell me he is serious.

If one of us needs to leave, it will logically be me. I have more work flexibility, and I have friends who might let me stay on their couches. He needs the stability of our home office for his demanding work.

But I know I can't just wave my magic wand and make my beliefs change overnight. I know they had flipped just a few days earlier, but that was different. The words "I was blind but now I see," ring through my mind as I give thanks for what I am experiencing as amazing grace. I took the red pill and now feel, for the first time in my adult life, that I see the truth behind

Chapter 18: Explosive (Subjective) Truth

the veils of deception. There is no going back. But clearly it would be a miracle if Stephen comes around any time soon to see the intentional trickery in the MSM and the truths they are hiding.

Trust in the Plan. God's got you! I repeat in the silence of my mind to generate faith, courage, and confidence. This is the time of the Great Awakening, and I know that I am among the earlier ones to wake up. The truth is coming out, and eventually everyone who survives the coming battle against humanity, driven by the Cabal, will wake up to the truth I have been blessed to find! My inner sense of righteousness is firm, and this way of seeing reality stokes strength and patience while keeping love very much alive in my heart. I will do my best to save Stephen and my friends and family members from the dark and sinister plans of the Cabal. My commitment to this task is wholehearted. I know I can't force anyone to wake up; everyone gets to choose for themselves. All I can do is my best and leave the rest to my Higher Power. I comfort myself with these thoughts.

Stephen, however, seems unable to find any comfort or inner peace with my sudden transformation. The tension in his brow and tone of his voice communicates repressed anger beyond anything I've previously seen in our five years together. For the most part, he keeps his space, occasionally approaching me with more words of outrage and disbelief, demanding that I change back to the Katrina I was before that fateful night. Our every interaction rocks me deeply. I find my body trembling and needing to dig deeper into my newfound faith: Trust in God. Trust in the Plan. God's got you.

It seems that just as I am able to settle myself down, Stephen walks past me and raises his voice again, slamming a door on his exit. It's so hard to recover from these constant assaults on my nervous system, but I am committed to staying as centered as possible. I'll be of no use to our world if I am falling apart too. I remember the words Janet Ossebaard shared in the final episode of her 10-part series: "The normal way to deal with shocking information is first to deny it and ridicule the messenger, then get scared, angry, or depressed, and finally accept it as the new paradigm. This will take some time." Clearly, Stephen is in the phase of ridicule, fear, and anger. Just breathe, I tell myself again. Trust. Stay firm in what you know to be true. This will take some time. Trust in the Plan.

While Stephen has never been violent with me, his escalations outsize what I would generally expect. I wonder if perhaps I've never seen him at his worst. Could he be capable of losing his temper in a violent way? Am I safe? I certainly do not feel safe, and that fear only escalates over the course of the night.

The next day I quietly pack my bags and find a moment in the afternoon when he is distracted with his work. I get in the car and drive away. I have no idea when I will return. All I know is that I cannot live with this level of fear and stress for another day.

Chapter 19:
Reorienting with Friends and Family

I don't have much of a plan. I'm hoping I can couch surf with friends who are willing to host me then head to Sedona in early August to escape before the fire season begins. I can hardly wait to get there. The land feels enchanted. The red rocks are majestic and restorative to my spirit. It is only a full day's drive away, so I figure I will not be trapped somewhere unable to get back home, as it seems unvaccinated people may be barred from flights. Fire dangers in Arizona are low, and a new QAnon friend who lives in a nearby city says she can connect me to others who think like we do and could possibly get me a job if I want to settle down long term.

It's amazing to me to see how much my social circles have changed over the last week since my flip into QAnon. I've been losing connection with friends and family as they react to my Facebook posts and commentary, but so many new friends have been popping out of the woodwork. Their ability to see what I am seeing and to empathize with the social challenges I am experiencing is like a lifeline. I don't know what I'd do without them.

Most of my new friends are Republicans, some are Libertarians and a few dozen were Bernie supporters like me. Previously, I had held a bias that Republicans are generally closed-minded, poorly educated, all about money, selfish, and racist. Is it really any surprise that my bias was informed by the MSM? No wonder I previously had no Republican friends to speak of. It's stunning, humbling, and heartwarming to discover that the people I am meeting are kind, warm, open, compassionate, care about minority groups, and want the remaining racism in our world to be undone too. Most of them are very much like me when it comes to our social and political values; however, I'm unsure how many of them believe in Q. I'm not eager to ask just in case I might be ostracized once again, similarly to the way I am being ousted by my old community.

> ***It's stunning, humbling, and heartwarming to discover that the [Republicans] I am meeting are kind, warm, open, compassionate, care about minority groups, and want the remaining racism in our world to be undone too.***

As I check out their profile pages it becomes readily apparent to me that these Trump supporters enjoy hugs, yoga, hiking, festivals, organic food, and are engaged in finding ways to live a more sustainable life, with care for the earth, animals, and each other. I'm not only amused by this realization, but also stunned at how thoroughly the MSM has brainwashed me to believe otherwise. What captures me the most about these people is the empathy they share with me for the social challenges I am going through with my friends and family after my politics flipped. It's easy for them to understand what I'm dealing with. They have endured harsh judgments from liberals, who regularly accuse them of being racist, sexist, ignorant, homophobic, fascism supporters, etc., and who refer to them as "deplorables."[271] These are all accusations I am beginning to receive as well.

Most of these new friends have given up on the hope that liberals might actually listen with respect or see them clearly. They understand liberals are caught in the trance of believing the lies of the MSM, so they try not to take it personally. But after a while, this kind of disrespectful treatment would wear on anyone. It's understandable that those who have endured insults based on political prejudices lose their patience, resulting in some who are more aggressively reactive to left-of-center politics than others. Given my

Chapter 19: Reorienting with Friends and Family

experiences with Stephen and a handful of others in my community, I can see how easy it is to become hardened and how tempting it is to lash back out of pain and anger. It's been only a week for me. It's been years for so many others.

Now I Understand

I am excited to reconnect with Tania, who several days ago was the only Trump-supporting Facebook friend with whom I was willing to stay connected.

On June 16, 2020, I get a short Messenger note from her.

"Hello Love," she writes.

"Good to see you again Sister!" I exclaim. "What a ride this has been, and it's only been seven days! New knowledge can seriously shake everything up." I take a pause before continuing. "It seems my relationship might end. Stephen thinks I've flipped and in a way he's correct. I took the red pill and am seeing life through an entirely different and *much* clearer lens now. I've been mostly undercover so-to-speak about my personal revelations. I love my friends and family and my community, and if I told them Trump is the greatest president of all time, their fear of him would be projected on me and they'd be less open to hearing what I am sharing. But who knows. Like it or not, I just can't hold this stuff in!"

"Don't be afraid to share the truth," she responds. "You might be surprised how many others are awake and looking for the courage to speak up, or who may be awakened by your revelations. It's happening fast! Sending you lots of love!"

I feel heartened, deeply heard, seen, and celebrated when I read her response. It is such a sweet contrast to the conflict happening at home. Stephen and I are texting a bit, but I am far from ready to talk to him.

Standing Up and Taken Down

As if I am not already deep enough in the QAnon and adjacent Covid-19-questioning rabbit holes, deeper, deeper, and deeper I go. With each new bit of information I read or watch on YouTube or see in my growing number of newly focused Facebook feeds, I become increasingly convinced I am right. I see the truth. I need to wake others up before it is too late. I become increasingly bold on my Facebook posts. On June 20th, I post a piece titled "Robert Kennedy Jr. Exposes Big Pharma, Fauci and the Danger of a Covid-19 Vaccine."[272]

2021 Reflection – What I Learned

The Center for Countering Digital Hate (CCHD), a nonprofit that purports to "stop the spread of hate and lies online," accused RFK Jr. of spreading "Covid-19 anti-vaccine misinformation and conspiracy theories," ranking him at #2 on its "Disinformation Dozen" list.[273] CCHD is funded by a host of dark money groups.[274,275] The White House used the "evidence" generated by this nonprofit, health officials, and the FBI to pressure social media companies, including Facebook, Instagram, YouTube, and Twitter to deplatform everyone on the list, successfully removing Kennedy and several others.[276]

The documentation CCHD gave to "prove" that RFK Jr. is a danger to public health and must be completely censored consisted of screenshots of his social media posts showing links to the following articles from his nonprofit, Children's Health Defense:

- "Home Run King Hank Aaron Dies of 'Undisclosed Cause' 18 Days After Receiving Moderna Vaccine"[277]

- "Tip of the Iceberg? Thousands of COVID Vaccine Injuries and 13 U.S. Deaths Reported in December Alone"[278]

- "Health Officials Push Pregnant Women to Get COVID Shots, Despite Known Risks"[279]

- "653 Deaths + 12,044 Other Injuries Reported Following COVID Vaccine, Latest CDC Data Show"[280]

Each of these articles is cited and rigorously fact-checked by RFK Jr's team of medical professionals, scientists, and attorneys.

Chapter 19: Reorienting with Friends and Family

> I cannot help but wonder: If the truth is self-evident or can at least be proven, why are these arguments being actively hidden by our government? This begs the question: How can we know for certain who is propagating misinformation?

The engagement on this post is far less than what I had received on my previous #ExposeBillGates post, but I don't let that bother me. Half of the people who respond are supporters, cheering me on, while a few others post comments like "Spreading more conspiracy theories again?" I feel irked, but I'm starting to get used to it, and I am taking it less personally. Ridicule, anger, and denial are now predictable reactions to my truth-telling.

My close friend Amanda quickly comments on the RFK Jr. link I posted.

> *30 seconds into this video I could tell it was nonsense. Just the fact that he's rambling that this virus is some sort of hoax, and that people don't need to stay home to slow the spread should have set off your bullshit alarm. People are dying over this. You are the one that needs to educate yourself Katrina. There are thousands upon thousands of scientists that have devoted their lives to studying this stuff. These are the people we need to be listening to, not some crackpot who has a theory. Do you really think that all these people including Bill Gates are somehow in cahoots to what, take over the world? What is Bill Gates' motivation to do something sinister with a vaccine? Money? He is already one of the wealthiest men in the world and there are a lot easier ways to make money. Seriously Katrina—you are choosing the wrong people to trust. I realize that you have an aversion to science, but science = truth. It can be proven.*

Ouch! That was far from the kind of friendly banter we usually have. I know she can't see what I'm seeing. I argue with her in my mind:

Aversion to science?! I don't think so. I'm all for discerning objective truth from untruths. Science can equal truth when every aspect of the scientific process is done transparently, and when scrutiny and debate over the scientific method and respective results are welcomed. There must be a commitment to maintaining a lack of bias. But lack of open discourse between scientists who have come to different findings and therefore disagree with one another, lack of engaging in an open process to determine how their findings could be so radically different? That's scientific dogmatism—not science.

From what I can see, scientists whose findings support a vaccine agenda are being highlighted in MSM headline news, while those who question the safety and effectiveness of the vaccines are being silenced and deplatformed. And the safety studies in progress are not being shared with the public. What do these vaccine companies have to hide? If they want us to trust in their products, why not be totally open and honest with us? Maybe their vaccines are not proven to be as safe and effective as they want us to believe. Maybe the truth would be bad for profits and harm the push for herd immunity via vaccination. But most people in my community don't share my concerns. They believe those who are being silenced are simply a relatively meaningless minority, and wrong.

2023 Reflection – What I Learned

In September of 2021, a group of scientists and medical researchers successfully sued the FDA under the Freedom of Information Act to force the release of hundreds of thousands of documents related to licensing of the Pfizer-BioNTech Covid-19 vaccine. Representing the group, attorney Aaron Siri fought for expedited release of the data the FDA relied upon to license the product. Despite the FDA's repeated promises of "full transparency" with regard to Covid-19 vaccines, including when licensing Pfizer's Covid-19 vaccine, the agency requested that the completion of this disclosure be delayed until at least

Chapter 19: Reorienting with Friends and Family

2096—a total of at least 75 years.[281] Note that people who took the shots would be elderly or deceased and unable to petition for redress with the FDA's preferred timeline should the documents reveal errors in the agency's assessment of the safety and efficacy of the Pfizer Covid vaccines.

In an historic legal victory, the group won the lawsuit, which forced the FDA to produce the documents at a rate of 55,000 pages per month, as opposed to the 500 pages per month it originally sought. As of July 2024, the full release is not yet complete.

Tony, an acquaintance, responds with

Amanda is correct here. You continue to be incorrect. In my opinion, you are so incorrect that you are actively causing harm. You claim to have love and respect. All I see from you in these kinds of posts is a profound disrespect. As such, I need to distance myself and protect myself from you. As Amanda has pointed out, you have not actually educated yourself, instead, you are spewing complete nonsense. Right now, you are the problem with your insane, truly insane, and horrific ideas about the world. I've spent a bit of time today, and quite a bit of time over the last few days reading your posts. They are almost indistinguishable from the worst of alt-right talking points. To put it bluntly, you are wrong. And you are being willfully ignorant.

Double ouch. I know I have posted information on Bill Gates, and the Covid agenda, including the frightening future possibility of an authoritarian governance like "Big Brother" in Orwell's *1984*, but alt-right? And disrespectful? What have I done that fits in either of those categories? If anyone is being "willfully ignorant," it's these two. How can anyone not see?! That fact is stunning to me. The Cabal's use of the MSM to brainwash the public is more potent than I could have previously conceived.

Tony then replies to Amanda, "You have way more patience than I have."

To which she responds, "I don't. I am stepping away now too. Too many other things to be worked up about right now."

I lost these two and at least one other on this thread. I guess I'm being blocked just as I had been blocking others in the weeks leading up to my flip in perspective.

My heart aches as I begin to contemplate that waking people up could be much harder than I hoped it would. Despite my love, care, and commitment to get to them in time, I might fail. As a result, so many people I love might fall victim to the mass genocide leading to the Orwellian 1984 scenario the Cabal has planned for humanity. I continue a commenting spree. I don't want to accept that I have lost these people from my life, and possibly from life itself. I feel desperate to wake people up.

I write back. "I love you both! I hope you know that. I know this is a very uncomfortable topic for both of you and that you'd feel more comfortable with your current beliefs than considering the dark picture I am presenting here. But if this darkness is real, then we are on the verge of falling into a totalitarian surveillance state."

"I am in no way against all vaccinations," I continue. "I have taken plenty—by choice. I am against mandatory vaccinations. There are plenty of reasons we should have the right to choose what does and does *not* go into our bodies. There are natural ways to boost our immune systems. There are pharmaceuticals that can help too—short of vaccinations."

Tears fall from my eyes as my vision of the future is moving from one of profound hope and conviction that we would cocreate a heaven on earth together quickly in a Great Awakening, to the possibility that I might lose everything I value the most and everyone I love. I can't let it play out that way.

Chapter 20:
Mending with Stephen

I know texting is generally not an optimal form of communication of emotional content, but when taking space due to conflict, Stephen and I have found it can be a way to stay connected with less potential for escalation. While we are physically apart, we maintain our rituals, sending each other daily good morning and good night messages. But I'm giving off less of an affectionate vibe and more of a business tone, as I feel guarded. I am not about to change that without good reason. I remain committed to getting out of California for the fire season. Seeing as Stephen thinks it's a crazy idea and says he won't go along with it, I let him know I'm prepared to go without him. He has no interest in leaving our home or relocating to a Republican state during the pandemic, despite the regular warnings that this fire season will be record breaking. He'd much rather stay home and if a fire comes, defend our home. And if we are to go anywhere, he does not want to be in Trump country. However, while I maintain a guarded and confronting tone in our text exchange, his tone is softening.

Usually in our morning text messages, he calls me "Beautiful," and I call him "My Love." But in our current state of conflict that would feel forced and inauthentic.

"Sorry not to see 'My Love,'" he responds to my greeting on the morning of June 20, 2020.

I feel petulant. "I don't want to write 'My Love' when I am not trusting that you truly love me for who I am." I then continue. "As for our disparate political viewpoints, I would like to ask you to read everything I posted this morning sometime today in your efforts to understand where I am coming from."

"I am reading all your posts, Katrina. And I do love you," he states. "And again, I wish you could hear me more clearly. It was not your political view that was upsetting me. It was your energy. For what it's worth, I am watching the 10-part series you recommended to your dad."

I respond with, "Thank you for taking time to watch that video, to seek to understand me, and stop judging me." I continue by expressing what he cannot see. "When I am away from you, my energy is entirely different. You can ask anyone who has talked to me or seen me. No one else is reacting to me like you have."

"You had a couple of days that were over the top and I believe you recognize that," he retorts.

"Fair enough," I reluctantly admit, reflecting upon the fact that I only slept about four hours in total over the last three nights.

He adds, "That in combination with everything else you threw at me was more than I could take."

I am not ready to empathize. Instead, I inform him. "Part of my 'energy' is my fear of your reactions."

He texts back, "Okay, I hear that."

His willingness to acknowledge my experience helps me to soften.

He continues: "And your bounding excitement in one moment and shouting expletives about Bill Gates the next moment was really hard to take."

I am still not ready to reflect on the impact my words and actions are having on my fiancé. "Bill Gates IS evil," I snap back. "Don't try to convince me otherwise."

Chapter 20: Mending with Stephen

I cling to my claims as Stephen tries his best to reason with me and build a bridge back to reconnection.

"Truth is truth," I add with conviction.

"I am not trying to convince you of anything." His words land as an attempt to reassure me. "And funny you say 'truth is truth' because truth is very hard to find. It depends on your source. But I am not here to contest your views. I'm trying to understand them."

"Thank you for considering my perspective," I respond. "I do hope you will truly come to understand. Honestly, without you 'getting' it, I don't see us lasting. I cannot unsee what I've seen. I cannot go back to ignorance."

My imagination draws images of what I believe is the predictable future. I see devastating fires, people being displaced from their homes and sent to crowded temporary housing with smoke-filled air resulting in higher Covid cases and deaths. This would be followed by a massive push for mandatory vaccinations, along with vaccine passports, and loss of livelihood and basic rights for those who do not comply with the vaccine agenda. I see this as the beginning of a society of mass surveillance, leading to a dystopian technocratic future as early as 2030, one etched into my mind by the World Economic Forum's ominous assertion "You'll own nothing and be happy"[282]—unless We the People rise up and fight back. *Do not comply!*

I can't imagine how Stephen and I will be able to navigate the upcoming social, political, and global challenges together if we cannot agree on the facts. We must be on a similar enough page when talking about what is happening in the world. Without this basic shared reality, our life strategies will be at odds with each other.

"Let me say it again," he writes. "My reaction, frustration, and anger in the last day or two before you left was in large part due to the energy that you were putting out, and your lack of sleep. On top of that, imagine hearing the major shift that you have now told me about."

He has a point there. No doubt I would have flipped my lid if our roles were reversed. If he had become the Trump supporter overnight, the old me would have been yelling at him in total reaction and disgust. I would have been desperate to convince him that Donald Trump is a Hitler-wannabe—a fascist threat. That assessment would have taken precedence over my long-standing aversion to Bill Gates. But now that I've awakened, I see how my previous beliefs were largely informed by brainwashing. And Stephen is still brainwashed.

Stephen continues texting. "And imagine what it was for me to hear your plan to live somewhere else for the next four or more months without me. Can you imagine how I might react to that? How anyone might react to that!?"

Ok... another good point, I silently acknowledge to myself. Of course, he's upset with the idea that I would take off for several months without him. But I feel like I must stand my ground on this one. I am *not* willing to stay in California.

"Yes," he continues, "my frustration boiled over and I slammed doors. I'm sorry you became frightened by that outburst. As for your views of the world, I keep coming back to this question: How does it affect us in our day-to-day lives? There are many things we agree on and others we don't. But that does not have to affect how we live and thrive together."

"Thank you for your apology," I text back. "And there are several things I need, or I will naturally want to distance myself from you. 1) Fire safety: prepare our home and plan to be safe from the fires this fall. 2) Politics: we can't have a happy relationship if we are endlessly arguing about politics. 3) Anger management: you've acknowledged that your depression of these last few months has built to a breaking point, and you've been unconsciously lashing out at me with unkind and sarcastic comments. That must stop."

Stephen's response is swift. "I am doing 1 and 2 and I am open to 3, but don't currently have a plan of action for that."

We agree to end our conversation here and pick up where we left off in the morning.

The next morning, he lets me know he has completed watching *Fall of the Cabal* saying, "I understand your enthusiasm. I am happy to speak with you about it—and again, wanting very much for that to be in a place where we are in a loving connection." These words are woven into beautiful

Chapter 20: Mending with Stephen

expressions of continued love; however, I am quick to dismiss his shows of affection.

"I am here. I am committed to us. I am committed to your well-being," he writes. "I am committed to ensure that *if* we cannot work things out, you will be okay. *And* I am nowhere near a point where I think that we are not great together." I imagine Stephen is seeking to send me love, understanding, apologies, and renewed commitments with the hope that I might be willing to be with him again and to remember who we are to each other. Yet I feel resistant to his outreach.

Stephen backs his commitments in action. He researches workshops that specialize in anger management so as to reduce the possibility of his emotions boiling over again. He lets his therapist know that this is the topic he wishes to begin working on in their upcoming sessions. As it turns out, anger management is one of the specialties this therapist offers. Ron is skilled in helping men discover the underlying sources of their angry outbursts and has extensive experience training them in better ways to process those feelings so as not to harm others.

2021 Reflection

In late December of 2020, upon my exit from QAnon, I learned that Stephen had immediately turned to his therapist, asking how he might handle the fact that I had been sucked into QAnon. Ron suggested that Stephen's best approach for rebuilding connection with me was to imagine that my quick and dramatic change was very similar to the dynamic of becoming a born-again Christian. I might be forever changed. And while Stephen could seek to build bridges of understanding with me, arguing about my new belief system would not be fruitful. It would likely result in a tremendous amount of additional pain and suffering for us both, leading us on a quicker path to separation.

No wonder Stephen's turnaround and interest in *Fall of the Cabal* had happened so fast. Stephen's commitment to accept that I was in a new worldview, combined with his commitment to practicing anger management, were two steps in a positive direction for our relationship.

In this first week apart in June 2020, Stephen takes my request for fire safety seriously. He begins looking for professionals to remove the twelve Italian Cypress trees lining our home. This is no small project, and he is far from excited about spending such a chunk of change to get the job done. But he recognizes it's vitally important to me, and so he is willing to act on it, especially if it helps us stay together and gives us a chance at the life we have dreamed of.

Again, he reassures me that he will never force me to receive a medical treatment, including a vaccine. He asks that we wait and see how things play out, reminding me it will be at least six months, if not much longer, before we will even have the option to get the shot. With that, he suggests that it doesn't make sense to decide whether either of us will or will not take it until the formulation for this injection is complete, and comprehensive safety testing information is available. He reassures me that he will honor my choice when it comes to my body.

These three commitments are soothing to receive, and as my heart begins to reopen, I return to adding "My Love" to my messages.

Follow-Up with My Dad

"Please let me know when you've gotten through all ten videos," I write my dad, hopeful I might at least get him to wake up with me.

He responds,

My Dear Katrina, I've seen enough of it to identify it as a QAnon narrative. Whoever 'Q' is, he or she is a highly intelligent conspiracy theorist who has created an Internet-based platform that is as addictive as a video game. It is built in a way that convinces adherents that any evidence submitted against its broad-ranging theories is further proof that an evil Cabal is actively working to hide the truth from the public. In effect, any attempt to disprove these theories can be twisted and used to validate them! And for adherents, they are not theories at all, but an aggregate reality that the benighted masses just don't have a clue about, to their ultimate peril.

🪷 Chapter 20: Mending with Stephen 🪷

I do not have ears to hear this, and I virtually block it out of my mind. My ability to understand the valid points my dad is making will not become accessible to me until after my exit from this QAnon trance six months later.

He continues,

> *I know that presenting you with facts and evidence that contradicts what's in these videos will be pointless. Because if you're buying into this worldwide conspiracy mindset, then anything I, or any family member, or any friend who doesn't subscribe to the 'evidence' presented in these videos as well as a vast network of supporting websites, will be viewed as innocent dupes of the all-powerful, evil elite who have created a mirage of false narratives to enslave the world—and especially little children for erotic exploitation. The sad outcome all too often is that the conspiracy theory adherents become alienated from friends and loved ones alike, and soon find themselves isolated, fighting for the Light in a dark and scary world.*

2023 Reflection

If only I could have heard his warnings. My father predicted my future accurately. In only a couple months after identifying with QAnon, I would feel more frightened and alone than I've ever felt in my life, as old friends I thought I could count on were no longer there for me, and new friends were too new for me to feel the depth of connection I needed. I did not revisit this text exchange until I began writing this book in early 2023. While I was a QAnon, I had been wrapped up in an emotional conviction that blocked ways in which I normally listen to and relate to my dad, whose wise counsel has often guided me.

> *Sweetheart, in the interest of objectivity, please consider studying the history of QAnon by going to sources outside the QAnon network, if for no other reason than to gain a broad perspective from political historians such as Richard Hofstadter.*[283] *American*

politics has a long history of this kind of thing. It's called 'apocalypticism.'[284] *Read about it; it is eye opening.*

While I'm addicted to doing research, I am not the least bit interested in looking into some guy named Richard Hofstadter or apocalypticism. I just want the world to wake up from the nightmares I see are being caused by an evil source. I just want a thriving earth—a world that works for everyone. That's all. I search for nothing my father suggests in his message to me. Had I done so, it would not have taken long to see that the QAnon-related stories I was caught up in were nothing new.[285] Many of the exact same conspiracy theories, with slightly different dressing, had been around throughout time.

Dad continues,

The most important thing to ask ourselves when we're drawn to any belief system, be it social, political, or spiritual, is 'Does this system resonate with my deepest heart's values and bring me joy, inspiration and peace right now?' And 'Is the prevailing narrative one of brotherhood and sisterhood, God in everyone, no separation?' Or is it 'good versus evil, the blind versus those who see, and the need to uncover and fight against evildoers to help usher in a utopia?'

Bingo! I think to myself. I feel a very deep sense of certainty that Q is a force for unification of goodness throughout all humanity. The vision of peace and the creation of a modern Eden on earth is resonant with my deepest heart values. If anyone can bring about this beautiful future in which darkness and corruption is brought to a final end, I am confident it will be this movement rising from a mysterious government insider source called "Q."

"No matter how all this evolves," dad writes, "you are my daughter and of course have my love, dear Katrina. This will not change no matter how far apart we may drift from time to time in terms of thoughts and beliefs."

I feel extremely disappointed that Dad has not watched all the way through, but also touched by his clear love for me.

Chapter 20: Mending with Stephen

"Dad, this *is* a loving revolution. It *does* align with my deepest heart values. It is about truth and love. It is about ending corruption so that the goodness in humanity has a chance to prevail. Please please please watch the whole series as you promised you would," I beg him. He excuses himself from the conversation.

The next day we connect via FaceTime.

"Dad, I need to have a deeper conversation about *Fall of the Cabal* with you. I know it's impossible for you to understand me unless you can see what I'm seeing. I don't know how to continue our conversations without having that shared context. It's like we are speaking in two different languages."

"I understand how much this would mean to you, Katrina, and I simply cannot get myself to watch it." His resistance to this series is evident by the way his face twists up when speaking these words. "That video is so toxic. It makes my stomach turn and isn't good for my well-being. When I tried to watch it before, it had an impact on my entire day. That's not how I want to spend my precious time. I'd much rather focus on my practices of meditation and service to others. That's what brings me joy."

I persist. "Can't you please just watch it through? I know there are gut wrenching horrible scenes in that series, but it paints a picture of what's really going on in the world, and we cannot change anything unless we know what we are dealing with."

"Katrina, how can you take that video seriously? To me it's simply offensive. Do you really think Obama, Pope Francis, and the Dalai Lama are pedophiles and satanists?"

"There were some crazy-sounding accusations in those videos... I know... So, she's got some things wrong. But if you watch the whole thing, I think you will still see what I have seen—the corruption, the Cabal, and the ways in which Q is helping us all see how bad it really is so that we can rise up together and put an end to all that actively seeks to cause harm in our world."

"Okay, I'll watch it," he offers, as it is evident to him how much this means to me.

Yayyy! I celebrate this breakthrough as our call completes.

Although Dad is still resistant, I am hopeful this might be the beginning of his awakening. After all, he was willing to watch parts of that video series. He had also scanned some other media I had sent him, other articles about Trump's environmental efforts, his combatting of child sex trafficking, and old interviews he had given in which he shared his political perspectives. Dad agreed Trump was not entirely bad. And while I think he might be taking steps in my desired direction, it doesn't take long before he feels a need to assert some kind of boundaries on our back and forth.

I write,

Dad, I know you've always thought Trump was a dangerous, power-hungry man, but he's not. He's completely committed his life to the benefit of our country and to a positive future for all beings everywhere. He is ushering in a new era of peace and prosperity for everyone!

He responds,

Katrina, I love you, and I know your life is motivated by love and compassion and a desire to make the world a better place. I will always know that about you and will always love you. But I just can't understand how it is that you think Trump could contribute to that kind of a world, nor do I have the patience to read or respond to everything you are sending me. And even if I did, it would never change my mind. I think you know that as a person of Jewish lineage, I was at one time fascinated by the rise of Hitler. How was it that one man could persuade so many good people to commit genocide against all the Jews?! It was unfathomable to me, so I studied it. And what concerns me is that Trump is doing all the same things Hitler did. His presence as president poses a serious threat to America.

I've heard the argument that Trump is following Hitler's playbook[286] more than I care to remember, but I don't understand what basis the MSM

Chapter 20: Mending with Stephen

is using to validate this serious accusation against him. All I can see are the smear campaigns in which they take snippets out of context and twist his words to build their case. It seems obvious to me that the Cabal is doing everything in its power to take him down, and this is even more reason for me to back him up. Trump must be a serious threat to their power, otherwise they wouldn't be attacking him daily. He must be ruining their plans to create a global technocratic totalitarianism[287] in which humanity is enslaved and the only ones who live freely are the elite who hold control over everyone else.[288]

I remain confident that I am right, and my dad is incorrect, misinformed, or brainwashed in these matters. I want to respond in a defensive manner, but he has clearly stated that he is not open to hearing any more. It's rare that he has needed to establish a boundary in our conversations. In fact, I do not remember him ever before doing so. So, I bite my lip and think to myself, Oh Dad, if you could only see. Trump is not following Hitler's playbook. It's the Cabal who wants us to believe he is. Those elites have been able to purchase every other president, but because Trump has all the money he needs, he cannot be manipulated, purchased, or otherwise told what to do. He's the only one who can stand up to them and put an end to the legalized bribery and corruption that has become normal to our political systems.

I intend to share this response with Dad later, but now is not the right time. So, I take a different approach. I write,

Thank you for letting me know you need to have a boundary with this stuff. I can get very worked up and passionate, and I understand my new appreciation for Trump is incomprehensible for you and for everyone else who knows me. Thank you for seeing my heart. That means a lot to me. I love you so much and I am grateful I can talk to you when I don't feel safe talking to anyone else.

"Of course, Katrina," he responds. "I love you and want to be there for you whenever you need someone to talk to."

Chapter 21:
QAnon Week 2

No one among my community is waking up, regardless of how ardently I have been trying to get them to see what I am seeing via my many forms of outreach. Despite my best efforts to build openness, Stephen and my dad are showing no sign of budging. I do not know what to do with that, as I desperately want them by my side, in this new world with me.

Meanwhile, I have several friends unfriend and block me on Facebook, with a couple dozen others openly expressing their being upset at my continued doubling down on Bill Gates. Their comments include:

"No! Don't buy into this garbage! There are perfectly factual and legitimate reasons to dislike Bill Gates. Choose one that's not part of the QAnon death-cult."

"Always remember and never forget, conspiracy theories are not facts."

I see a long reply from a friend. He's trying to talk sense into me. He completes his comment with, "In the case of this conversation, I've been blown away by how many people in your community love you enough to wade into this discussion and address this with care and respect. You inspire a lot of loyalty."

It's true. I know I've earned their love and respect over the years with heart-centered interactions I've had with each of them. That loyalty is evident in most of our exchanges despite the difficult topics we are now engaging in. Over time, however, some of my friends lose their patience with our conversations. I wonder if perhaps I am inundating them with too many articles and videos from the whole new world I have found, but I don't know how else to answer some of the questions they pose or to substantiate the points I seek to make. Whatever it is, it's painful, as I see mean-spirited judgments of me in the commentary to me and to each other, including "lost cause," "delusional," "a pawn of the alt-right" and "supporting white supremacy and fascism."

Don't they know me? I cannot fathom how members of my community could even think these things about me, much less accuse me publicly on a comment thread of my Facebook page.

My heart sinks. It hurts. I love these people. I am trying to help them see what's really going on. The effectiveness of the Cabal's propaganda is so much stronger than I imagined. I must start facing the possibility that I may not succeed in waking people up before the vaccine rolls out. How many will die before the world wakes up and defeats this sinister group? Heaviness weighs on me as I once again consider the possibility that the Great Awakening is not happening as fast as I'd hoped.

Fortunately, there are a few brave souls who continue to show me love and support on this Facebook post.

Joy writes:

I'm getting tired of seeing people shaming others for their beliefs. At this point, I don't care as much about whether I agree with a person. I care way more about whether they can present their disagreement without playing the 'I'm right, you're wrong, I'm wise and you're stupid' game. It's getting old. Katrina, you have every right to speak what you believe to be true. I see you doing that with a lot of grace, and I appreciate you for it.

Thank you, Joy! It's so soothing to receive supportive comments like this—to be seen and heard. My longing for understanding and community are met as I read comments such as these—of which there are few.

Chapter 21: QAnon Week 2

My friend Stuart is engaged in this comment thread as well. He admits he had been sucked into believing conspiracy theories for over a decade and had only recently exited. He responds to Joy in a confronting way:

> When words turn to violence, I care far more about people staying alive than I care about the hurt feelings of people spreading this stuff. Would you say the same thing if the KKK was at a high school trying to convince people of a dangerous belief? Are you okay with all the Sandy Hook parents who already dealt with the tragedy of losing their little children, having to deal with conspiracy theorists giving them death threats? What you're suggesting is that words have no power. When people are spreading misinformation that leads to deaths, they should be held accountable.

Stuart makes good points that I would have jumped on board with prior to my QAnon flip, but I cannot hear them any more than I can hear the Trump/Hitler analogy. Why would he bring up the KKK and Sandy Hook when I'm talking about vaccines and health? I see no connection between his comments and anything I've posted. It's clear to me that concurrently controversial topics are being weaponized and politicized: if any topic can be associated with President Trump, it is certain to be dismissed out of hand and never considered on its merits.

Joy responds:

> Yes, we are all entitled to, and responsible for, expressing what we feel convicted to share. But when someone 'speaks their truth' by condemning, shaming, or judging others for their beliefs, THAT is violence. I'm suggesting that words DO have power, and now more than ever is a time to get clear within ourselves about our personal values—then come together with others with an attitude of curiosity and flexibility. I personally am choosing to stay flexible and open to differences with a value for exchanges with people who can meet me in a field beyond right and wrong.

I love Joy's response. I don't recognize at the time that Joy and Stuart are speaking on two different levels. Stuart is presenting his concerns over collective damages that are at the very least influenced, and at times clearly caused, by people's belief in various conspiracy theories—especially the ones which support enemy images, hate and violence. Joy is talking about Stuart's personal communication with me and pointing out an impact Stuart doesn't care to acknowledge at the moment, although under different circumstances, I have no doubt he would. His immediate concerns over the physical safety of marginalized groups are overriding his sensitivity to my heart or care for our friendship.

Both friends have some training in Nonviolent Communication (NVC). I can tell Joy is applying these principles to this debate, sharing a quote from Rumi, "Out beyond ideas of wrongdoing and rightdoing, there is a field. I will meet you there." This idea has been used many times to encourage NVC students to set aside their tendency to evaluate statements as right and wrong, which in our culture carries the implication of deservingness—of either reward or punishment. Dr. Marshall Rosenberg taught that both notions are actively used to maintain authoritarian power structures in society.

In the context of NVC, this poem instead encourages students to practice empathy as an avenue to embody what practitioners call "compassionate consciousness." The most basic practice is to reflect on these two questions: What might this person be feeling as it relates to what they have shared? What might this person be wanting? To answer this second question, an NVC practitioner might refer to a list of "universal needs," which are understood to be the drivers or motivators for the actions we take.[289]

However, Stuart is making an argument that empathy has limits. There are more extreme situations in which basic NVC "boundaries with compassion" or "protective use of force" might be insufficient. There are social dynamics in which a less politically correct and honest form of expression might be more appropriate. While Joy's comments are seeking to encourage values of the heart in this debate, Stuart is sounding an alarm. He is

Chapter 21: QAnon Week 2

convinced that a different strategy is needed to address certain topics that are driven by conspiracy theory and hate groups. I can't hear any of what he's got to say in a meaningful way right now. I am grateful for Joy's choice to continue asserting the principles of NVC on this comment thread. I feel delight in my sense of sisterhood with her in these challenging times.

Stuart, who is also a writer and passionate social activist, continues to engage:

> *My biggest issue is people acting like they KNOW. Look, I didn't automatically debunk these conspiracy theories. I believed them myself for more than a decade. But I've done tons of research on the other side, and it was almost laughable how easily some of them are debunked in the actual medical and scientific communities (which most conspiracy theorists don't spend any time studying). I've changed my mind from 'knowing,' to 'I don't know,' but if I had to guess, I'd imagine that millions of doctors and scientists got in it for pure reasons. The fact is that if 99% of them agree on certain things like the scientific method and peer-reviewed studies, I'm more likely to trust them than I am to trust random internet people reposting QAnon conspiracies. It just seems like a logical gamble. For example, if someone you loved needed surgery, you would want to go with someone who's an expert at surgery, who's going to take a surgical approach that has a track record and has been studied and reviewed. I doubt that you would go with an Internet meme instead, right? It's the same thing for me. The problem is that QAnon conspiracy theorists are cult-like with their beliefs. You're talking about being rigid. These people are like the extreme religious nuts that just want to force their 'truths' down everyone's throats.*

Stuart loses patience with Joy after a few more exchanges and continues to post to me on the main thread with very long comments in his efforts to get me to see what he sees. Over the next couple of weeks, he revisits my Facebook posts to give it another go. He engages diligently, and when he finally concludes that nothing he is saying is getting through, he exits with this:

> *Katrina, you're a rookie in the conspiracy world. I see you're in 'new relationship energy.' You are passionate in your conviction that this is 'the one' and you have blinders on to anything that challenges that view. Once again, I was in it for over a decade and there isn't a single point you made that I haven't studied much more deeply than you have. I once believed all these topics myself. Hopefully, someday you'll have the same true awakening that you're being emotionally and mentally manipulated. Hopefully, you won't lose all your friends and family before that happens.*

If I can't hear it from my own father, there's no way I can hear it from anyone else, despite the reality that I am losing friends quickly. A couple of family members are unwilling to talk to me. That has never happened before in my life. How could this happen in a few short weeks?

I also read comments such as "For fuck's sake, knock it off already with Bill Gates. He's the target of disinformation campaigns." And I receive an occasional show of support for my Bill Gates post: "Yes, Katrina! You nailed it!"

Reconnecting with Stephen

While Stephen's tone of love, generosity, commitment, and acceptance continues with consistency in the days that follow, a full week passes before I am willing to see him again. Over the course of our time apart I reported to him many times that my nerves are still on edge. I understand I am prone to quickly entering a stance of self-protection and self-defensiveness when I think about the possibility that I might say something triggering to him and he might have another angry outburst. However, on June 25th I am feeling an increased sense of safety in our text exchanges.

"Stephen, sweetheart, I'm still feeling uneasy about reconnecting with you, but I'd be willing to get together for an hour or two. We can meet up at Sarah's house."

Chapter 21: QAnon Week 2

"Really Katrina? Do you really need a chaperone to feel safe around me?!"

"I do initially," I reassert. "As I have said many times, I have not been feeling safe with you. I am grateful your tone has shifted, but I was shaken by our last contact, and my nerves won't settle unless I have another friend within hearing distance."

"Fine," he acquiesces. "Whatever you need to feel safe. I just hope we can have some time that is just for us. I love you, Katrina. I want us back."

Five hours later he texts me, letting me know he'll be arriving in two minutes. I feel a combination of gratitude and nervousness as Stephen walks over to greet me. Our eyes meet. Then mine instinctually avert his. He pauses his stride, opens his arms, and asks, "May I offer you a hug?" I step forward, still looking to the side as I place my head briefly against his chest for a warm but not melting hug. The tension of my guarded stance is obvious. Stephen accepts the sensitive space I am in. As I feel his commitment to love, gentleness, and openness, my guard softens. We spend several hours together. He asks if I would be willing to listen to a recording we had created less than two years earlier.

It is a recording of happier times. We were sitting together on the beach while on vacation. I asked him if he would be willing to share with me what he views as my strengths, my weaknesses and in what ways people in general know they can count on me. These questions came from a homework assignment during my participation in a Landmark Education course called the Self-Expression and Leadership Program. In this conversation, Stephen expresses admiration for my multitalented nature, especially in the arts, including singing, dancing, painting, sculpting, gardening, etc. He appreciates my intelligence, noting my knowledge in areas of alternative health, fitness, spirituality, and transformative practices, and my passion and skill in NVC.

I notice my heart feels increasing warmth as I listen to this recording. I hear the joy in my voice and my occasional giggle. I remember the smile on my face, and my natural tendency to cozy into him when times are sweet between us.

"The next piece I wish to share with you is both a strength and a weakness," he begins in the next phase of this recorded conversation. "I don't like this word, but I don't know what else to call it. You tend to be naïve. It's hard to call it a weakness because I also see it as a beautiful idealism with which you view life and all that is possible. It's a dreamer quality and I value that in you, so it's hard to call it a weakness, but…" he pauses in a moment of contemplation.

"It depends on how it plays out?" I offered as I considered this challenging aspect of my personality that others had pointed out to me before.

"Yes, you could say that," he responds. "It's a childlike quality that allows you to see the world with eyes of love, and to hold a vision that peace is possible. This way you view life causes you to be very warm and openhearted with people around you, and that is a quality most people who meet you can see very quickly. However, your naïveté has also led you to trust some of what I believe are tall tales, as well as people whom you later realized were not trustworthy. That's where these strengths can become a weakness. There are times you have believed people's tall tales at face value. You hold people in their highest light, even when they don't deserve it. Because of this, I fear that childlike innocence you hold can be used by others in ways that could be, and at times have been, manipulative. I don't want to change this quality in you because it goes hand in hand with this idealism you carry, which I love, but I do wish to protect you from those who would lead you astray or cause you harm."

As we sit in my friend's guest room listening to this recording, I hear the truth in his words.

In this recording, when Stephen recounts the ways in which people know they can count on me, he highlights my commitment to empathy, my desire to be warm and open to everyone, and my love for family. He recalls aspects of my life history, noting times I sacrificed my personal needs in order to be present, loving, attentive, and caring with a member of my family in need. It feels amazing to be so deeply known, seen, loved, and appreciated by this man. It feels reassuring that he could see that this is still, and always

Chapter 21: QAnon Week 2

has been who I am—not someone disgusting or repulsive, as he had described me ten days previously, but someone absolutely lovable.

In the recording, Stephen then asks me to share with him what I view as his strengths, weaknesses, and how people know they can count on him. "There are so many strengths I could list, including your ability to solve complex problems, or to envision a goal, create a plan of action to attain it, and discipline yourself with the kind of consistent follow-through necessary to fulfill your plan and make dreams into realities. And you have an amazing sense of touch. I just love being in your arms. And in this moment, the strength I am feeling most moved by is how deeply you listen, how deeply you care, and how deeply you love me."

He smiles at me as he hears these words, and both his and my smile broaden as we hear his voice in this recording: "I love you, Katrina. You are my beloved!"

Then my voice comes in with: "Thank you My Love. I feel that! And I love you too!"

We hear smooching in the recording before my voice comes in again. "Are you ready to hear what I view as your weaknesses?" I ask.

"Sure." He responds.

"I notice you have a hard time saying 'no' to people when you feel at all responsible to them. One way I've seen this is in your work. You rarely take a day off."

"I think you know how demanding my work is, Katrina. I can't just ..." he begins.

But I cut in. "I know it's hard to take time off, but sometimes you really need it, and it's not like the whole world will fall apart without you. If you don't get that time off, you get increasingly stressed, irritated, and exhausted, and when that happens, you are more likely to have a shorter fuse not only with me, but with people in general."

We engage in a short dialogue about this dynamic and the real challenge it is for him and for us before getting back into the last question. "I believe people know they can count on you for many things," I begin, as I talk about his great hugs, his ability to listen, ask excellent questions, offer guidance and support, and express care. I save the biggest one for last. "People in your close circle know they can count on you to be there in the event of an emergency; to listen and to provide practical support. You often have the foresight to know what they want and need before they do. I remember how you did that for my mom when my stepfather underwent major surgeries followed by a month of rehab. You rented a place for her to stay so she wouldn't have to drive over an hour each way day after day to be by his side. I cannot begin to tell you how much that touched my heart. I've seen you show up in meaningful ways in support of each of my family members and a number of our friends when they've hit a rough spot, and I know all the people in our family and close community can count on you for that. It is a tremendous gift that I don't take the least bit lightly."

My body has relaxed a bit in our time together, and Stephen continues by expressing his commitment to me and to us. He reassures me that he does not want to try to change my mind. He wants only to understand me and to figure out how we can get back into a harmonious flow with each other.

Chapter 22:
Reestablishing Safety

The next day I feel safer communicating with Stephen. I send him several videos and articles that have caught my attention. While I am hopeful that I might get him to see the world as I am seeing it, I am also testing him. I need to know that he is truly open to understanding my new worldview, that he is not only willing to hear it without reacting negatively, but can engage with material I am seeing in an intelligent and constructive way. The videos and articles I send him are my litmus test to know how safe I would be if I choose to return home. I don't want to feel like I am walking on eggshells and cannot talk about matters that are important to me.

What I send him is only a small portion of all the information coming across my screen in my extensive daily online scrolling. One is a video seeking to prove that masks don't protect a person from viruses, in which a man uses a vape pen to demonstrate how permeable all masks are to particles as microscopic as a virus.[290] Another is a satire from comedian JP Sears, called *How to Get Angrier at People You Disagree With*,[291] which has brought much-needed comic relief to the crazy conflicts that seem unavoidable if I say anything about Bill Gates, or question masks or social distancing mandates. It seems many of my old friends cannot help but to spin out in anger quickly, hurling insults at me, but clearly, I am not alone in that experience.

I also send him information I am finding on the origins of the Antifa movement,[292] which originated with Stalinists,[293] who were against the fascist threat they saw in Hitler. And, I send him an article titled *The Pedogate Crackdown*, which claims that due to Trump's war against child trafficking, 51 of 76 missing children in Michigan had been found by the police.[294] My heart celebrates this victory, which I see as proof of Trump's work to end human trafficking, especially child trafficking, striking at the heart of the Cabal's criminal network.

I am eager to show Stephen what I believe to be "behind the curtain." I'm likening my awakening process to Dorothy's discovery in *The Wizard of Oz* of the "Great and Powerful Oz." This ostensibly fearsome "wizard" turns out to be just a shrunken old man, pretending to be far more formidable than he is. Driven by my desire to know "the truth" and my emotional zeal for Q, I actively question everything I previously thought I knew and seek to "connect the dots" as other QAnons who discovered Q long before me have learned to do.

I send Stephen an article about China's loans to third-world nations in Africa, seeking to increase his awareness of China as a growing threat to the US. Stephen is aware of this threat but encourages me to trust that it is not nearly as immediate as I am perceiving it to be.

I send him a copy of a photo said to be Obama's original Kenyan birth certificate stating, "This of course could be faked, but so could a Hawaiian birth certificate."

2021 Personal Reflection

I am embarrassed to admit that I was actively questioning Obama's place of birth.

🪷 Chapter 22: Reestablishing Safety 🪷

"Okay," he writes back. "You have given me loads of material to work through and I will do so, but please be patient. My day is full." A moment later I see, "On the birth certificate thing… I don't know. Honestly, I have some skepticism about the photo you just sent me claiming to be Obama's original Kenyan birth certificate. So now we have competing certificates. Don't know which is real and which isn't. Are you now of the opinion that Obama is part of the Cabal? We should talk about this stuff live though. I don't want text to be misunderstood. I am listening and learning."

I am delighted with this response. Stephen has not reacted negatively. He expressed openness and was engaged. Sure, the idea of Obama being born in Kenya or that he is in cahoots with the Cabal requires a stretch of the imagination, but my imagination has been quite stretched over these last couple weeks.

I respond. "I know it's a lot and your day is quite full. And yes, let's talk about this stuff when we are together. I also would like to ask you to keep much of what we're talking about here confidential. I understand you have told a few close friends and family members that you think I might be having a mental health breakdown or something. I assure you I am not. And it's been painful to hear that you've talked about me this way to others."

As I've connected with people in my life, some are aware of my political flip, and most are not. When they express concern for my well-being, as influenced by Stephen, I am able to quickly reassure them that my mental health is sound. I do this by focusing more on explaining the conflict I am experiencing with Stephen while grossly underplaying my giddy enthusiasm for Q and my newfound allegiance as a QAnon.

I continue texting. "I'm not saying this to make you wrong. I know you're concerned about me and perhaps trying to build support around me, but it has created unnecessary tension for me with people including members of my family. Unfortunately, people who think that all the stuff I am presenting to you is unfounded can quickly become frightened when their beliefs are questioned. It's as if I am questioning their identity. I have seen many friends and family members double down in their certainty, asserting they are informed by factual, accurately reported, and scientifically validated sources, and that what I'm presenting is plainly wrong. If I stick with the conversation and try to engage in respectful debate, many get angry. Those who know me more as an acquaintance than a close friend can go low and simply attack not only my thoughts, but also who I am as a person. It's like they've completely forgotten who I am." I feel heavyheartedness and frustration as I recount the growing list of interactions in which I have been made wrong, ridiculed, and accused of being a conspiracy theorist, a quack, anti-science, an anti-Semite, etc. over the last couple of weeks.

I am starting to feel weary of the number of negative comments and messages I am receiving from people on social media. In my own certainty, I am doing my best to stay active in my efforts to wake people up. But I also modulate my comments, knowing I am pushing the edge of people's comfort zones, trying not to push too far. I know that the reality of the pandemic and other social and political factors are already stressing everyone out. While I believe my work to wake them up is essential to their survival and our collective future, I do want to be as gentle and compassionate as I can.

"I think you know how much I love my family!" I write Stephen. "It's important that I can have a different perspective and give voice to it without fear that I could lose their love overnight. I'm very much in my heart. My mind is clear. I understand why this scares them so much. I'm a bit bold on Facebook, but in our personal connections I want to be a whole lot gentler. Our love is way more important than getting them to understand what I'm saying. At the same time, I am planting seeds with everyone as I find this information critically important to understand."

I firmly believe the majority of my friends and family are worried and reacting negatively because I am questioning everything they believe to be true and asking them to make the extreme and (I feel) necessary perceptual adjustment I recently made. That is not an easy shift, and I have compassion for the situation they are in; blind victims of brainwashing as I had been only a couple weeks earlier. Considering my new beliefs appear to them to be entirely against everything they stand for, it is understandable that their psyches will fight to hold on to what is familiar, even if that means trusting in the litany of the MSM's lies.

❦ Chapter 22: Reestablishing Safety ❦

I do not have room in my mind to consider another obvious possibility: Could I be trying to save them from nonexistent threats? I am unwilling to accept that my communications are unwanted and are stimulating intense agitation in the people I love, who are already highly stressed from all the chaos and uncertainty happening in our world. I can't fathom that their urgency to save me from my QAnon trance could be as intense as my urgency to save them. I am so set on my mission that I am unwilling to see that my continual outpouring of the new content I am seeing is, from their point of view, a boundary violation. It's easier for me to imagine it's their brainwashing than the much more likely possibility that they are extremely disturbed that I am obsessively committed, not only to sharing my views, but also to trying to get them to agree with me and join me in questioning the Covid narrative and exploring QAnon rabbit holes.

"Anyway, I hope I can trust you with confidentiality." I repeat in my note to Stephen. This is not the first time I make this request and it will not be my last. "Please let me know how this lands for you. I love you!"

2023 Personal Reflection

Looking back from 2023 I can see the horribly challenging bind I put Stephen in. My needs for safety and confidentiality were unbending, as were my needs for self-expression, connection, and partnership with him. I was asking him to handle a lot of information and absorb the impact of it all with only his therapist to talk to. I did not feel safe with the idea of him talking to anyone else who might think I had lost my mind. When I received word that he had reached out for support from my family members and our shared friends, I felt like my boundaries were being violated and I would become agitated quickly—sometimes potently so.

I continue sending Stephen articles, many of them from Fox News, critical of New York Governor Cuomo's handling of the pandemic and accusing him of making decisions that inflated the Covid death count.[295] I send him videos of Trump's old interviews: one with Jay Leno in December 1999,[296] and another of him as a newlywed with Melania on Larry King Live.[297] As a new and enthusiastic Trump fan, I find these interviews endearing and interesting. I'm hopeful they might soften Stephen's view of Trump. However, his perception remains unchanged (a fact he does not dare share with me). He is committed to working this through. He knows that anything he says condemning Trump will only drive me away. He's consciously and actively choosing connection over conflict.

Over the course of my two weeks away, Stephen has made great strides demonstrating his commitment to addressing the three areas I told him I need. He has taken out the dozen Italian cypress trees and expresses willingness to leave California with me for the fire season. He has shown that I can talk politics with him without these topics escalating into conflict. I trust he will not force any vaccines on me, and I appreciate his willingness to learn more about immune-system-boosting supplements as well as banned pharmaceutical treatments. His engagement with anger management techniques has also come a long way in a short period of time.

In late June, Stephen is eager to share with me a potent insight he had in one of his therapy sessions, one that shifted his relationship to his anger, increasing his ability to act consciously rather than taking it out on me. He recognizes that as a child, it was not safe for him to ask for what he wanted or needed. Doing so would consistently generate a painful response or reaction from his mother who was overwhelmed with her full-time job and four kids to raise, and his father who believed corporal punishment was a necessary tool for training good behavior in boys. Because of this, Stephen learned to repress his feelings when something hurt. Of course, people can't stuff their feelings without causing them to build up and explode or at least come out sideways through sarcastic remarks from time to time. These mini (and sometimes not so mini) explosions were driving me to distance myself from him.

Stephen's therapist suggested he practice paying attention the moment something doesn't feel good to him and see if he could simply say "ouch" as a way of acknowledging his frustration. With him engaging in this

Chapter 22: Reestablishing Safety

practice, I can be alerted to when something I do or say lands in a hurtful way. We can communicate about it before it builds into something bigger.

Stephen is eager to engage in this practice, and I am grateful every time he follows through. I prefer to know when something I've said might have struck him as insensitive or uncaring. I want to know when he feels hurt by something I've done so I can become more attuned and we can have higher quality interactions, less stress, and be more loving with each other.

With this new awareness and practice in hand, we feel an increased confidence in our ability to stay connected. Stephen's tendency to build up anger and express it in unconscious and hurtful ways diminishes and becomes an occasional "oops." On July 2, 2020, I am very happy to return home.

During these two weeks away, I have been on Facebook and YouTube at least eight hours a day, absorbing massive amounts of information and exchanging notes with new QAnon friends. I continue my efforts to awaken those liberal friends who I perceive may be more open to questioning mainstream narratives. However, I keep losing more and more friends along the way. It's a high price, but I am determined to look out for their best interests. I trust that as the world awakens, they will come to understand why I did what I did and thank me for it.

Chapter 23:
Unexamined Judgments

In early July, 2020, an article, *Anatomy of Delusion: How Otherwise Conscious People Descended into the Darkness,*[298] makes the rounds on Facebook. This article was written by Stanford graduate and founder of The Shift Network,[299] Stephen Dinan. I first learn about this article when my close friend Scott posts it on his Facebook feed. It is obvious he's referring to me as he posts, "One of my dearest friends has gone down the rabbit hole, and it's been so difficult for her family and friends." A QAnon friend brings this post to my attention writing, "How dare your 'friend' accuse you of being delusional and descending into darkness."

Later in his comments, Scott clarifies,

> *I was referencing my friend who has taken this 180-degree turn that has led to her own sister and other friends distancing from her. I'm not condoning or judging it, but it seems very sad to me. I have counseled many people that lost family and friends when they joined a cult or left the cult. Many organized religions have a similar cult-like quality: the belief that they have a unique glimpse into the truth which makes followers feel special. I see similarities within this thread: the idea that some people know the truth and the other ones*

are delusional idiots. That does not resonate with me as a healthy dialogue.

All I can hear is this: Either my friend called me delusional, asserting I have descended into the darkness and joined a cult, or he's accusing me with no evidence whatsoever of calling others "delusional idiots," or both. *Ouch!*

One of the comments Scott receives in response to his post is this:

The real issue is that when you go down the rabbit hole, Trump is seen in a whole new light. Many can't let their programmed beliefs about him go. They are fully locked in TDS (Trump Derangement Syndrome).[300] *Therefore, anyone who has been guided down the rabbit hole is considered a delusional conspiracy theorist by those not able to take a deep dive to discover why they hate him with such committed venomous tenacity. This article is written from a place of 'spiritual superiority' as Stephen Dinan claims to know what's happening with all of us poor, delusional, lost souls. That is total BS, and anyone who claims 'to know' is not coming from a place of wisdom in my opinion. I agree with others who have criticized the article here. It is divisive and is trying to explain why tens of thousands of spiritual people along with others are waking up to a reality that has shocked even the most open-minded ones.*

I agree. Yes! This is spot on! I "like" his comment and put in a friend request.

It is easy to distinguish Trump supporters from Trump haters when reading the comments on this post. Scott expresses surprise and concern about some of the divisive and attacking comments that stream in as reactions to his post, adding the following afterthought:

What I do know about is relationships. That is my field of study and understanding. I don't see relationships improving with these dramatic beliefs, debates, and arguments. I see them being very divisive. It's heartbreaking. I posted out of concern for what is creating a lot of separation. None of us KNOW who killed JFK, or

Chapter 23: Unexamined Judgments.

exactly what the truth is around 9/11, or the historical truth about Jesus. But most of us have strong beliefs. And sadly, different beliefs about Jesus have led to scores of wars and the deaths of millions over the past 2,000 years. Let's not make that tragic mistake in our current relationships with family and longtime friends.

As I am still feeling the emotional impact of my name being implied in this post, I cannot see that Scott, in his follow-up comments, is seeking to be neutral, inclusive, and nonjudgmental; this is his attempt to share wisdom that might support stronger relationships in these deeply polarized times. For years he has been one of the few people I have called, other than my dad, when I have been in distress and needing support. But today his comments do not land as neutral. They appear to me to be a direct attack.

A mutual friend takes time to comment on Scott's post:

You don't know, Scott? Oh, well, let me tell you, Trump is an incompetent buffoon with none of the many qualities the president ought to have and all the defects he or she should not. He is a sick man. That, my friend, is the truth about the President.

I notice my urge to defend Trump when reading this comment. I am well aware that a political war is going on and conversations that touch on Trump or dozens of other topics have become intensely divisive. Many of my Republican and QAnon friends constantly criticize and condemn Obama, Biden, Pelosi, Alexandria Ocasio-Cortez, Diane Feinstein, and many others. This mutual friend has written comments to my posts, in a similar Trump-bashing vein, while also attacking my character. While I seek to have patience, I also need to reduce the impacts of this kind of verbally abusive behavior in my social media feed, which I gladly do with a quick click of the unfriend button.

At this point I'm more than a bit bruised by the arguments I have been enduring online and in conversations with many people who I thought were my friends. It hurts to be told I am crazy or delusional, or that I support racism, homophobia, transphobia, anti-Semitism, and fascism. "That couldn't be further from the truth!" I state out loud, even with no one around. I feel as if I am screaming inside.

I know I am intelligent. When it comes to the attacks accusing me of being a racist, I know I've got more close non-White friends than most White people. And transphobe or homophobe?! I have enjoyed ongoing connections with at least a half-dozen folks who have hormonally and/or surgically transitioned their physical gender to match their sense of inner identity. I have had dozens of sweet connections with people who identify on the "gender spectrum," and I know these people have felt safe, appreciated, and respected in my presence. The idea that I am homophobic is ludicrous, especially as I have had plenty of gay friends, and I've dated women. Ethnically, I am half Jewish, and I take pride in my roots. And fascism?! How ridiculous is it to me that anyone could believe I support fascism? The thought is completely absurd. I am exasperated that my friends, who I thought knew me, cannot see me clearly.

Anything questioning the official Covid narrative has been firmly associated with QAnon, ensuring that no rational discussion can be attempted. Anti-Trumpers have been encouraged by the liberal media to use dehumanizing, character-bashing labels in response to anyone who posts anything questioning Dr. Fauci or Bill Gates, or supportive of Trump or ideas connected in any way to QAnon. The propaganda campaigns are coloring my community's view of me so deeply that they think my core values have changed, despite having no evidence whatsoever to back their evaluations of me. It seems that if I mention any topic they don't want to discuss, they tie it to Trump then reject it out of hand. It is rare for anyone in the anti-Trump world to contemplate for any duration an argument that might have merit.

I am astounded by this and can hardly stand to be in contact with them anymore, despite my commitment to do my very best to rescue them. At the same time, I have to humbly admit—only a few weeks ago I had many off-based biases about Republicans. How erroneous is it that I have believed they were generally uneducated, racist, and uninterested in natural health, yoga and meditation, and all about generating profit regardless of the cost

Chapter 23: Unexamined Judgments.

to our air, water and soil? I have always considered myself open-minded and inclusive, but I have been blind to my unexamined, judgmental assumptions. Now that I see through their eyes and understand their views and values, I share the pain and frustration they feel regularly as those on the left project their unsubstantiated and dehumanizing evaluations onto me and anyone else who dares question the mainstream narratives.

My heart is in pain. I need emotional care, comfort, connection, partnership, and hope. I find the reprieve I need among other QAnons and conservatives who have also experienced the avalanche of insults from "the left" (as they commonly refer to everyone left of center.) Previously, I have thought that my Democratic and progressive friends belonged to the party of compassion, inclusivity, tolerance, and love. Some of them do. A precious few are kind to me, and others have simply gone silent, but my overall experience here is *far* from respectful or empathetic.

This is especially infuriating because I have seen no QAnon content at all that clearly supports racism, sexism, homophobia, or fascism. In fact, I've seen the opposite. However, my attempts to point this out to my old friends are not heard. They seem to think they know what kind of content I am seeing better than I do. I shake my head, disheartened at the complete blockades to any kind of communication that might bring about understanding, compassion, and connection.

Gratefully, I can turn to comedian JP Sears to lighten things up. I have been amused by his "Ultra-Spiritual" skits from years prior, as they made fun of my community in ways that even New-Age hippies like me find entertaining.[301] He even lives close by in Marin County, so those skits are inspired by a unique San Francisco Bay Area subculture. It feels healthy to be able to laugh at ourselves rather than taking ourselves too seriously. I don't think I've ever laughed so hard as when I watch one of his skits in late March, 2020, *What To Do When You Run Out of Toilet Paper*,[302] during what some called the "toilet paper apocalypse" in the early days of the Covid lockdowns.

Stephen appreciated JP Sears' humor back in those days as well, but since that time JP has clearly taken the red pill and is showing up with a new angle shaping his sense of humor. On this day, as I am licking my wounds, I press play on his "Blue Pill People" video.[303] I love it when comedians can make me laugh at realities that are otherwise painful and hard to tolerate. Prior to this awakening of mine, I regularly tuned in to John Oliver, Bill Maher, and Trevor Noah. Now, Bill Maher is the only one of that crew whom I still enjoy watching. JP, however, has me laughing full force at an experience that is truly troubling to me. I am grateful I can watch so many videos from his channel. He's got a vast selection that make fun of the Covid lockdown policies, fact checkers, the MSM, and the rapidly escalating divisive insanity happening in conversations between liberals and conservatives. While I find JP's humor refreshingly hilarious, Stephen and many others in my community have come to detest the new content.

Chapter 24:
Reclaiming Patriotism

While Stephen and I are challenged by the ongoing tension between us, out in the world life is still happening and my online engagement continues to take up most of my time. Conservative news outlets report that Black Lives Matter protests are increasingly out of control.[304] Businesses are often looted, and cars and buildings are set on fire. Bystanders who get caught up in these protests are getting injured, and other protests escalate into riots. Most of my left-of-center friends seem to blow off the concerns I express about the rising violence and destruction of property, saying that as a White person, I should not be critical of these events, but rather I should show more compassion for Black people's outrage as expressed in whatever means these protesters deem is necessary. However, I tend to align with my conservative friends who say that arson and looting are crimes that have no excuse. Rage can be expressed without damage to property or people. There are better ways to protest racism and police brutality than to burn up car lots, smash and loot local businesses, and harm people.

In some of these protests, various statues are toppled or beheaded. While I understand and support actions to remove symbolic reminders of slavery's legacy, I have mixed feelings about the statues of two of our founding fathers, George Washington and Thomas Jefferson, coming down. I deeply admire these brilliant men who founded our country, and yet they did own slaves, which I find atrocious, even though it was considered normal during their time. I have also read articles saying that Mount Rushmore is under threat, as it also "celebrates other slave owners."[305] It seems many leaders associated with Black Lives Matter think it should be destroyed.[306]

2024 Reflection – What I Learned

There is still controversy as to whether Mount Rushmore should stand as a patriotic monument or be removed due to its symbolic association with slavery and the inability of the US government to honor treaties and Native Americans.[307]

I might have jumped on this bandwagon before QAnon, suggesting that Mount Rushmore be redesigned with faces of indigenous chieftains. But *Fall of the Cabal* revealed to me that the Cabal is seeking to stomp out patriotism in order to make our country weak. Janet's research led her to assert that our love for our nation is the only way we will find the strength to continue to fight for our freedoms and for the promises made in our Declaration of Independence and United States Constitution. Without patriotism, we will lose the will to defend ourselves from those who would seek to destroy us—terrorists both foreign and domestic. I understand the passion and logic on both sides of this debate, and yet given what I've learned about the importance of patriotism, I stand on the side of maintaining this monument.

My research leads me to a videotaped interview with a former Russian KGB[308] agent, titled *Yuri Bezmenov Warns America About Socialist Subversion.*[309] As a result, this perspective is further cemented in my mind. In this video, Bezmenov exposes the way the KGB has actively engaged in psychological warfare against the United States since the Cold War, using a strategy they call "ideological subversion" or "active measures." His basic explanation is as follows:

Chapter 24: Reclaiming Patriotism

> *The goal is to change the perception of reality of every American to such an extent that despite the abundance of information, no one is able to come to sensible conclusions in the interests of defending themselves, their families, their communities and their country. It's a great brainwashing process that goes very slow and it goes in four basic stages.*

This statement from Bezmenov shakes me deeply. It seems people have little ability to discern fact from falsehood. Given confusion caused by ideological subversion, how can we responsibly evaluate issues in service to solving the many complex and serious challenges we are facing today? We must resolve well over a dozen catastrophic risks,[310] and we need to understand our problems with objective clarity in order to have any chance at forming effective solutions.

In this interview, which was recorded in 1984, Bezmenov explains that demoralization is the first stage of the KGB's four-stage plan to destroy the United States from the inside. Step one is to eliminate our sense of patriotism, make Americans feel disgusted with the history of our own country, and embrace communist ideals. All the way back in 1984, Bezmenov said that the demoralization campaign had already been completed. He said that if we could see what had already happened and actively work to turn the tide, it would take a minimum of 15 years to correct this problem.

He said the second stage is destabilization, which is happening fast due to the rise of Marxist and Leninist ideas. The third stage will be a crisis, which can happen in as short as six weeks. Following that will be a fourth and final stage, a violent change of power, structure, and economy, as humans adapt into what he calls "normalization." Bezmenov said this is the full system. The end goal of ideological subversion is a world communist system. He said, "The time bomb is ticking. You will have nowhere to defect to. This is it. This is the last country of freedom and possibility."

> **The time bomb is ticking. You will have nowhere to defect to. This is it. This is the last country of freedom and possibility.**

2023 Reflection – What I Learned

In July of 2023, I learned that presidential candidate RFK Jr. shared my concern about the possible rise of a world communist system. On July 16, 2023, *The Atlantic* published a hit piece on Kennedy.[311] Other MSM outlets followed suit. Shortly thereafter, congressional Democrats ironically attempted to censor his testimony from a congressional hearing on the topic of censorship.[312]

When their efforts to ban him failed, the left tried to label him an anti-Semite, taking short but accurate quotes from Kennedy completely out of their original context. For example, Debbie Wasserman Schultz asserted that Kennedy had "made light of the Jewish people's genocide" by quoting him as having said "Even in Hitler's Germany, you could cross the Alps into Switzerland. You could hide in an attic like Anne Frank did." However, in full context, Kennedy said:

"What we are seeing today is what I call 'turnkey totalitarianism.' They are putting in place all of these technological mechanisms for control that we've never seen before. It's been the ambition of every totalitarian state since the beginning of mankind to control every aspect of behavior, of conduct, of thought, and to obliterate dissent. None of them have been able to do it. They did not have the technological capacity. Even in Hitler's Germany, you could cross the Alps into Switzerland. You could hide in an attic like Anne Frank did."[313]

I am not surprised by these liberal MSM political attack tactics used against Presidential candidate RFK Jr., as I had seen the similar methods used against Donald Trump, Tulsi Gabbard, Marianne Williamson, and others.

I am secretly hopeful JFK. Jr. might make his presence publicly known at Trump's Independence Day speech. What an epic reentry to the world that would be! I feel a surge of joy as I entertain this hope.

Independence Day

I have never identified myself as a patriot. In years prior, I would not place my hand on my heart during our national anthem, as I viewed our country

Chapter 24: Reclaiming Patriotism

as an atrocious warmonger and could not find any way to feel supportive of our massive military presence and involvement in the decimation of people around the world. However, after I came to understand that a key strategy of the KGB's (Russia's secret police) long-term plan to destroy the United States from the inside is to undermine the population's sense of patriotism, my love and appreciation for our country and for the brilliance of our founding fathers has increased. I know of no other place in the world that has a constitutional republic with so many protections for the freedoms and voices of its citizens as we have. We were given carefully designed checks and balances of power so as to maintain a governance that is of and for the people. In QAnon, I have learned exactly what Bezmenov asserted: If the United States falls, democracy everywhere in our world could fall. That thought scares me.

On July 4, 2020, I post an art piece of the word *Love* colored in with the American flag, to my social media feed. Along with this image I write:

While I was taught something about the virtues and values of the forefathers of our country, it was overshadowed by what I learned of our endless wars, and the crazy amount of taxpayer money that goes to our military. In my formative years, I gained an understanding about the genocides of our native peoples, and the way the CIA planted crack in Black neighborhoods, destroying lives and rounding up an extraordinary number of our Black brothers and sisters while strengthening the military and prison industrial complexes. I mourn what happened in Vietnam and am angry at Nixon for making marijuana illegal so he could round up the many pot-smoking war protestors and further imprison minorities in our country.

While I was taught something about Washington, Jefferson, Adams, Roosevelt, Lincoln, and Kennedy, and understood them to be heroes in the story of our American history, I had lost sight of their significance over time. In more recent years, that knowledge has been somewhat erased—practically forgotten—as I have been reminded of the truth that had always been there: Washington, and other White men of his time 'owned' many Black people, who were forced to work for them as slaves.

I know that while men of Washington's time did not have the awareness we do now around racism, and the self-evident truth that all humans are created equal, this truth, although declared with conviction, was not believed, or accepted among most White people in 1776.

I mourn that part of the past. And still I celebrate that Washington managed to create an army out of farmers and defeat the greatest military power of that time—led by King George of England, who was known for his brutality against all who were disloyal to him.[314]

There would be no United States of America—no 'Land of the Free'—without George Washington. He could have made himself into a king, but he chose to put into practice the principles of a democratic republic; a vision that he and other educated men established together as visionary leaders of that time. This piece of our shared history as Americans is quite remarkable.

I know there is a popular movement building to destroy Mount Rushmore, fed by righteous rage. But destroying this monument is also wiping away the gifts that these four presidents gave us all. It is choosing to see them ONLY for their shortcomings and to ignore the sacrifices they made for us.

So much beauty has arisen from this nation. OUR nation. We created the first car, the first airplane and successful flight, the first landing on the moon, incredible cinema, jazz, blues, and gospel, brilliant computer technologies, and so much more.

Let us NEVER forget all that is good while we seek to correct and make amends for what has been harmed or broken.

We are waking up, and possibly on the verge of becoming a truly great nation in which Black lives matter. Native American lives matter. Latino lives matter. Puerto Rican lives matter. Muslim

❀ Chapter 24: Reclaiming Patriotism ❀

lives matter... people of every minority and majority color, culture, and creed—matter.

Our country was born as a result of the men and women who longed for freedom and sovereignty from the oppressive rule of King George. And they won that freedom on the Fourth of July, Independence Day. Our national birthday.

Let's not lose sight of what is good and right about the USA. Let's hold our Declaration of Independence and Constitution as sacred documents that are the blueprints for the United States of America which IS possible so long as we hold the vision, strive to fulfill it, and don't give up on it or let other countries destroy us from the inside.

Yes, we've got work to do.
Yes, we must end all forms of racism and sexism.
Yes, we must care for our mother the earth.
Yes, there is a lot of righteous rage alive in our communities at this time.

But no! It's not time to create riots, burn, and destroy things. It's time to protect ourselves from those who would destroy us from the inside. Those who are hell-bent on destruction must be stopped so that those who are committed to beneficence and to life, liberty, and the pursuit of happiness may prevail. United We Stand.

The handful of responses I receive on this post come mostly from people I know are aligned with my new belief system. I've only been a QAnon for three weeks and already my online social life has shifted dramatically, as my old community is practically silent.

JFK Jr. does not show up at Trump's speech. But that's okay. I'm sure there's a good reason for it, and I eagerly await the day he reemerges in our world.

That night, it is hard to sleep. Not only am I disconcerted about the possible downfall of our nation, I am also distressed about the fire risks in dry California. Due to the pandemic and mandatory social distancing, there are no major fireworks displays, so people have purchased their own. And despite the fact that setting them off is illegal in the dry and fire-prone area where we live, the blasts are going off until 4 a.m., keeping me on high alert all night.

The next morning, I thank my guardian angels there have been no major incidents. Despite the high fire danger, neighbors continue lighting fireworks most nights for the remainder of the month. My eagerness to get out as soon as possible stays strong.

Chapter 25:
Deep in Online Addiction

Stephen and I get on the road to Arizona one month later. It's been seven weeks since I became a QAnon adherent. It seems we have found a flow, although it's still rocky from time to time. One week after our arrival among the beautiful red rocks of Sedona, massive fires break out in California. Friends report the air to be so thick with smoke that it appears to be night in the middle of the day. The intensity of these fires further validates my sense that I am tuned in to the truth and preparing appropriately while others are not paying close enough attention.

My social media posting becomes increasingly infrequent as Stephen gently and regularly encourages me to become more conscious of how painful it is to be losing friends with each post. I don't know if those relationships will ever be repaired. I know I can't blame people for blocking me, as I was living in their blue-pill mindset less than two months ago. I, too, blocked people much like the person I have now become. It seems some people might just be too deep in the MSM trance. Will they ever come around?

I thank God for having dropped *Fall of the Cabal* in my lap at the right time so that I can now see this mass left-of-center trance for what it is. I wish I knew how to be more effective at sharing that same blessing with others.

At the same time, the social losses hurt. So, I curb my Facebook posting and begin to work on accepting the possibility that most everyone I love might die at the hands of the Cabal, and I may not be able to do anything about it. While I am not able to fully calm my impulse to post content backing my views around the virus and coming vaccines, I am able to moderate it only in consideration of the predictable social consequences. Maybe, just maybe, there's some bit of hope that something I post will get through.

My posts tend to include unifying spiritual principles as shared through memes and wisdom quotes. I also post several political comments in which I share conservative views while trying to present them as important to understand for the sake of political bridge building. "United we stand, divided we fall" is at the bottom of all these posts. Almost no one from my former community responds in a positive or supportive way to these posts. To my utter dismay, accusations that I am supporting racism and fascism continue to flood in, along with more personal assaults on my character. People I once knew as my loving community fall silent; I wonder if I have been shadowbanned by new Facebook algorithms. The initial elation I felt when I became a QAnon believer is fading.

Healing in Nature and Community

I spend less time on devices and focus more energy on enjoying life, cutting in half my eight to ten daily hours of online consumption. This is easier to do in Sedona where the Covid lockdowns are not nearly as severe as they are in California. Hiking trails are open, and a wonderful large community gathers at least twice a week to dance outdoors, unmasked and joyfully sharing smiles, hugs, and laughter. Small businesses remain open throughout the pandemic here. A return to something close to normal is profoundly relieving to me; I break down in tears as the stress of my time in California begins to unwind from my body. My new community wraps me up in hugs as they can only imagine how difficult living in the San Francisco Bay Area must be.

Stephen and I are thrilled to discover that people here generally don't have much interest in talking about politics. I am happy to discover a handful of new friends whose beliefs resonate with my own. Despite being online less, I am fully engaged in my new worldview and eagerly sharing notes with new friends about the crazy world of the Cabal. Stephen feels ill at ease with Arizona's lax Covid precautions. My enthusiasm for hugs and hanging out with QAnon or otherwise Trump-supporting friends is another cause for stress in his world.

One of the empowering statements I have used at difficult times in my life is: "Breakdowns lead to breakthroughs!" Yet the breakdowns Stephen and I keep experiencing seem relentless and are exhausting.

Discouraged

My energy continues to dissipate from the initial high of "waking up," as I realize others are not also "popping like popcorn" as I imagined they would. While I keep looking to find the perfect news article or scientific report that might create cracks in their certainty, nothing seems to work. My conservative friends are all astounded at a Yale study[315] performed over the summer to determine which intervention techniques would be most effective for coercing people to get the Covid vaccine. This study tests "persuasive" (what I would call manipulative) methods, including use of embarrassment, guilt, and anger; exhortations to "trust in the science," leveraging the desire for economic security and freedom (which have been drastically reduced by the lockdowns), and publicly shaming vaccine-hesitant people for their "lack of bravery." Forms of shaming proved to be most successful techniques. The study also sought to determine how to apply peer pressure to increase willingness to take the jab.[316] I share this study with my community, but my liberal friends show no interest whatsoever.

I am hopeful that the second film in Mikki Willis's *Plandemic* series, *Plandemic 2: Indoctornation*,[317] released in August 2020, will changed the minds of at least a few of my friends and family, but it seems no one in my community is giving that documentary an ounce of credence. It is quickly dismissed as "conspiracy theory" and "disinformation." If these videos fail to help them see what's really going on, what will?

I trust that eventually I will be redeemed when the operation called "the Storm" is in full swing, and the White Hats complete their task of rounding up all the criminals and those engaging in bribery and corruption. This is how they will "drain the swamp." And I know I'll be redeemed when JFK Jr. comes out in support of Trump. I trust that day will come. How could it not? If JFK Jr. faked his death and is seeking to take down the Cabal, and if Trump's upcoming campaign is essential to the fulfillment of the Plan which has been created over the course of decades by the White Hats, then JFK Jr. needs only to reveal himself at a rally and voice his support for Donald Trump. Then an unstoppable wave of support will emerge. All the pieces will fall into place, and we will be saved from the dreaded plot of the Cabal's New World Order.

Meanwhile, perhaps I can help Stephen see that Trump is not a racist. Perhaps I can show him videos comparing Trump to Biden in that regard. Surely Biden's sponsorship of the Crime Bill[318] should be incriminating enough, as is the statement he made in 2007 that Obama is "articulate and clean."[319] Perhaps I can help him see how the news reports accusing Trump of racism are lies propagated by the MSM.

I was moved by Trump's tribute to George Floyd,[320] and I noticed that while it could have been a unifying message, it was completely buried by the MSM. Is there a chance Stephen might be willing to hear it even though it is Trump speaking? By signing the First Step Act into law,[321] Trump ended the worst impacts of the Crime Bill,[322] which disproportionately put Black nonviolent offenders in prison. Trump made permanent a commitment of $255 million in annual funding for historically Black colleges and universities.[323] Trump's daughter Ivanka is married to Jared Kushner, an Orthodox Jew. She converted to his religion to marry him. How could an anti-Semitic father support that? I've seen Trump in pictures where he seems to be loved by Jesse Jackson,[324] Al Sharpton,[325] Spike Lee,[326] Snoop Dogg,[327] Oprah Winfrey,[328] and many others.[329] He nominated the first Black woman for promotion to general in the US Marine Corps.[330] I've now seen dozens of Black people who have taken time to express in various forms of online media that they do not agree with the depiction of Trump as racist.

Chapter 25: Deep in Online Addiction

Tension rises between Stephen and me as we continue making the mistake of talking politics way too often. Both of us have fallen into the habit of reading the news in the morning. Our news choices are quite different. If either of us slips and makes just one brief political comment, it sparks a heated debate between us—one that escalates quickly and never ends well.

After escalating conflict to a point of needing to take space once again from each other, Stephen texts me: "What you support is viewed by your community, your family and me as having racist leaning if not outright white supremacist motivation. Whether you agree or not is not the point. We will believe what we believe. There is such a thing as guilt by association, Katrina. I fear you are blind to that."

I am so tired of Democrats accusing all Republicans of being racist. I see plenty of evidence in defense of the argument that while some conservatives clearly spout racist rhetoric, most, including Trump, do not. Stephen has not listened to Trump's full speeches as I have. I now hear what Trump says in a much different context from the twisted narratives spun by the MSM. I have seen so many videos of Trump relating to people of all different cultural and religious backgrounds. He treats them with respect. I discover videos of transgender people, cross-dressers, gays, and lesbians who do not view him as a homophobe, and countless Black people who do not believe he is racist. This is especially apparent in the dozens of videos I watch from the Walk Away campaign[331] and Blexit[332] on YouTube. Even with my enthusiastic and open sharing, Stephen firmly believes Trump's interactions and official meetings with people of various skin melanin levels, religions, and cultural backgrounds are him "acting in ways that are required by his job, but otherwise completely inauthentic."

It seems I cannot win this debate. And despite Stephen's best efforts, neither can he. We take sides, entering regular painful and intensely polarized debates about who is right and who is invested in disinformation on this and many other topics. We both conclude that it is better to keep our politics to ourselves rather than trying to engage with each other, although we find it nearly impossible to do this while maintaining a sense of connection and emotional intimacy. As a result, I feel like we are drifting apart.

The differences between the way stories are told on the right and the left sides of the political aisle infuriate me. Why is the country falling apart over these debates? Why is this war of words manifesting in my relationships with friends and family? Why can't we do what mediators and conflict resolution experts suggest and seek to understand the perspectives and experiences of both sides in search of the bigger picture, more representative of the whole truth? It's no wonder more and more people believe we could be on the verge of a civil war.

My conversations with Stephen might go better if we can take them out of red versus blue. But given all the news each of us is reading, that seems impossible. Between this and other heated arguments, our mutual exasperation becomes unbearable. We question whether we can endure this relationship. Is our love strong enough to stay together despite radically different views of reality?

My heart feels broken. The lockdowns have created far more isolation than I can handle. It seems no one can hear me except my new and quickly growing QAnon and Trump-friendly community. These new friends are the only people who seem willing to listen, understand my heart, and empathize with my pain. They are there for me. With them is where my desperate needs for connection, love, understanding, and belonging are met. Outside of that I feel so alone—an outcast.

My new QAnon friends, most of whom are also former Bernie supporters, become my social lifeline. I am resigning to the likelihood that the friends I have had for decades might not wake up. I might have to let them go and build a new community with my new friends who can see through the deceit streaming in through the MSM. They are awake to the inner workings of the Cabal. I trust my new friends have a much better chance at surviving the upcoming cataclysmic changes and challenges than my old friends do.

The Answer

I continue engaging in hours of online "research" every day. I'm excited to watch the latest interview between Brian Rose and David Icke. This one is

Chapter 25: Deep in Online Addiction

Rose/Icke 5: The Answer.[333] In this video, I come to understand that the Cult uses face masks to subconsciously command people to cover their mouths and remain silent, rather than speaking up. The Cult can test their in-development human tracking systems by noting who does and does not comply with face-mask protocols. Icke talks proudly of his refusal to wear a mask and encourages everyone to follow suit, saying that our noncompliance is the most immediate way we can step into our collective freedom. *Noncompliance is key.*

My willingness to wear a mask drops away as I proudly enter shops and grocery stores mask-free. In Arizona, masks are recommended but not required. It feels amazing to be stepping into my power, and to see others who are doing the same.

Hooked

I am unable to pull myself away from my screen despite my fiancé's encouragement to spend time in nature, relieve stress by dancing, or offer Compassionate Communication sessions on a donation basis at a local café. He reminds me regularly that life happens off-screen. His constant reminders are the only thing helping me find any semblance of balance at all. I choose once again to reduce the number of Facebook comments I post in places that are visible to my community.

Instead, I join a couple red pill groups, "Trump 2020" and "JFK Jr. Lives!" and I follow various QAnon and "Follow the White Rabbit" pages, where I experience shared reality with other followers. This allows me to process the new information I have been discovering with people who see politics the way I see it. It's also a way to distract myself from the pain of having lost connection to most everyone I love. I find deep solace in regular connection with red pill people, in contrast to the venom I continue to receive from my old Facebook community. I feel a need to connect in social circles where I am wanted, seen, and appreciated. Who doesn't want that?!

Stephen fluctuates in his willingness to talk politics with me. Sometimes he's got no space for it, but then he sees how I distance myself from him and he tries to open the subject again. At the present moment, he is open to understanding my political views. I am eager to grab this precious opportunity and show him everything I'm learning. But with the volume of content I've been reading, watching, and digesting, that desire is impossible to fulfill. I know I am seeing patterns that point to the truth. But how can I get this knowledge across to Stephen when he gives me only brief windows of receptivity?

I send Stephen more articles and videos that are passing through my social media stream. What I keep learning about the Cabal reconfirms what I learned from a documentary called *Zeitgeist: The Movie*,[334] which I watched in 2007, and in the *Thrive Movement* series[335] by Foster Gamble. Those films led me to distrust our global finance system and believe banking is essentially run by eight families including the Rockefellers, Rothschilds, and Morgans. I want to be sure our finances are aligned for the coming changes, so I send Stephen articles predicting the next collapse of the economy.[336] I send him a video showing what American "preppers" are doing to prepare for worst-case scenarios[337] and an article about the underground luxury bunkers that billionaires are buying and building.[338]

I send him articles about hydroxychloroquine trials showing positive results for treating Covid.[339] I send him various Trump interviews, especially ones I believe clearly demonstrate that Trump is not racist or fascist. I send him the trailer for *Hoaxed*,[340] a documentary that seeks to prove to left-of-center voters that the MSM is all fake, driven by six media company owners, and heavily sponsored by Big Pharma and the military-industrial complex. I send him information on what I believe to be the real story and danger of Antifa and its link to George Soros. I send him updates on the Ghislaine Maxwell story. I send him a video of Candace Owens titled *Democrat Laws Negatively Impact Minorities*.[341] I send him George Carlin's *It's a Big Club and You Ain't in It!*[342] appreciating this short comedy skit for directly summarizing everything I am trying desperately to get across to him. I send him an article citing a way in which China could melt the US power grids using an electromagnetic pulse weapon.[343] These are only a fraction of what I send his way. I'm hoping that in all of this, he will begin to see the patterns too.

In return, Stephen sends me a couple of articles on various beautiful travel destinations.

Chapter 26:
Fear and Disconnection

It's been two months since my QAnon awakening, but only a couple weeks since having the green light to share articles and videos with Stephen. He lets me know it will take a while to get through all of it. My onslaught of sharing continues and his tolerance fades to a point in which he has little capacity left to manage his bottled-up frustration with all the triggering content I send his way. We enter into a short, yet productive conflict.

Self-Reflection

"Katrina," he says, "Why on earth do you feel compelled to share all of these links with me? What value does any of this add to our lives? Why does any of this matter?"

I have to pause for a moment as this is not a question I have been considering at all while scrolling endlessly through various Facebook and YouTube feeds, or Google and DuckDuckGo searches. I quiet my mind as I listen for my answer to arise from within... What is driving my urge to share?

I take this moment to pause and feel into my body. I notice I am grasping for some sense of certainty. I want something more I can count on. I need safety, security, and stability. I don't know how to attain that in such an uncertain world, as I am perceiving multiple looming threats—variations on the way Armageddon might roll out. I feel I need to stay informed and plan ahead to the best of my ability in order to generate some sense of safety.

These needs have become my primary emotional drivers. They have partially eclipsed other needs, such as love, friendship, belonging, esteem, and self-actualization. How can I pay attention to these secondary needs when I am overwhelmed with fear for our very safety?

"Katrina, we are safe. There is nothing major to fear," Stephen expresses in an exasperated tone.

"How can you say that?" I quickly retort. "You hardly see any of what I'm seeing. The media you watch keeps you in a trance that blinds you from the actual growing threats that are on the horizon!" I respond with my arms flying about for emphasis.

With little gas left in his tank, yet a deep-hearted commitment to keep on trying, Stephen chooses to respond empathetically to my fears and need for safety. His voice becomes a bit slower, softer, and his eye contact more intentional as he says, "Katrina, I love you. I want to help you to know that you are safe… that we are safe, and that I am always doing my best to look out for you." I feel my body relax a bit as his care reaches more deeply into my being.

"Thank you, Stephen," I say as my body relaxes into his embrace. "I know you want to keep us safe, and I also know that you do not see the world as I am seeing it. You do not see the threats that I see coming. But you saw how I was more alerted to the California fires than you were, and you've agreed it was better that we got out when we did. I see other challenges ahead, and I need to know that we're on the same team. You've expressed a concern that you believe I'm getting swept up in all of this stuff. You think it could become divisive to us. And I'm afraid that if I see danger and you don't, I'll need to prepare and make decisions that you will not understand or approve of. That could divide us."

In all my online surfing, I haven't taken the time to slow down and feel what's happening in my body. Tears fall from my eyes as I realize I am feeling truly vulnerable and have been for some time. My social media

Chapter 26: Fear and Disconnection

addiction, and the dopamine hits I receive from confirming my cognitive bias, have been helping me avoid that feeling of vulnerability.

Negotiating a Better Balance

Another week passes and it is mid-August, only nine weeks into my life as a QAnon. Stephen is despairing of the hope that I will ever be willing to put aside my endless social media consumption, be present to the full reality of my feelings, question my allegiance to the QAnon belief system, and address my emotional state.

In this moment, it feels good to be in Stephen's arms and to feel his care for me. We sit quietly, enjoying each other's companionship. A few minutes later, Stephen offers a suggestion. "Katrina, I understand that a number of the articles you read, and videos you watch, are stirring up concerns about what the future might bring. Of course you want to know that we are as prepared as we can be so that we can navigate those challenges as they arise."

"Yes. Thank you." I affirm, relaxing more deeply into his arms.

Stephen continues: "As you know, my work has got me in front of my computer all day. As much as I care about you and want to understand what is stirring up fear in you, I have very limited capacity to spend more time reading articles and watching videos after a long day's work. I also need our weekends to decompress and enjoy life. It seems you are simply sending me everything that catches your interest."

"I'm not," I respond in a defensive tone. "I'm just sending you the ones I feel most strongly about." I notice feelings of angst and urgency in my body. I am still unable to relax.

"Okay. I hear that, Katrina," his voice is calm. "And it's still more than I can handle. Which of the articles and videos that you've sent me do you believe are important for me to read for the purpose of being able to plan our future together? What do I need to know in order to address your concerns and need for safety?" he asks.

I take a moment to flip through some of the headlines I've recently sent him. He has already addressed my concerns about a possible impending economic collapse, and given his ability to understand finances, I choose to trust his knowledge of our financial systems as a way to reduce my concerns.

We have already talked about the realities of climate change and have considered our options including where we might live and what measures we might take to prepare for a possible natural disaster. He has already addressed my fear of the vaccines and supports my desire to study alternative health strategies. We have argued about the nature of Antifa and George Soros and ultimately agreed that this is not worth arguing about, as neither of us can sufficiently prove our own point or disprove the other, and it has made no immediate impact on our lives. He encourages me to trust that China is not an immediate threat, and if something were to happen, it would likely be in the distant future. He does everything possible to encourage me to release my fears, relax, and enjoy life.

It helps, but my fears continue to stick to me, much like the clinging pain I have felt after accidentally brushing up against stinging nettle. I don't know how to let these fears go. The uncertainty in our world is eating away at me, keeping me in a perpetual state of anxiety.

Stephen wants to enjoy life, as opposed to engaging with me in the practically nonstop content I send him. He lets me know he is willing to make himself available for up to two hours a week, in which he will give his full attention to reviewing and responding to whatever articles or videos I want him to read and understand. We choose the day and time together. He asks that we use the remainder of our time to relish quality time together.

This seems a reasonable way to seek balance. It encourages me to begin looking at the content I'm reading and watching with greater discernment. I know I have only this precious two-hour weekly window we have agreed to. So I ask myself, How might Stephen react to this content? Will he find a way to immediately debunk it using fact-checks he trusts and I do not, as he has done with so many others I have shared? I am motivated to check my sources sufficiently so that I can succeed at sharing with him content that might impact the way in which we plan for our future together.

As I begin to fact-check various articles and videos in the way I imagine he will reflexively do, I realize there isn't much I trust will be worth sharing

Chapter 26: Fear and Disconnection

with him, as I am finding it exceedingly hard to prove or even create a sufficient argument for most of it. I am not consciously aware of it, but this practice of sorting out solid articles and videos begins reengaging my ability to slow down and think critically.

I find it hard to keep my comments to a once-a-week schedule and am regularly saying things under my breath almost every time Stephen says anything that could trigger a QAnon association in me. Politics, Hollywood, entertainment, and news are all conversational landmines for us.

Losing Family Connection

Ten days after our arrival in Arizona, Stephen and I have a massive breakdown. I try calling my dad, but he doesn't pick up, as his wife is napping. Instead, he sends me a text.

"How are you doing, honey?"

I'm not well.

> *Stephen is talking to his therapist right now. He got angry and said I was brainwashed. He accused me of being a racist too—three times, even though he knows how much I care about people regardless of skin color. He sees my support of Trump as incomprehensible and atrocious. Can you believe he's accusing me of supporting racism and fascism?! He threatened our relationship repeatedly. I guess I am a racist because I pointed out that Kamala Harris' parents were not citizens when she was born. They were just visitors here, and so it's not a completely clear-cut path for her to be vice president.[344] There has never been a clear Supreme Court ruling on this issue... If saying that makes me a racist, that's ridiculous.*

2023 Personal Reflection and What I Learned

I was unaware that my statement of fact about Kamala Harris's parents is connected to a larger far-right disinformation campaign commonly known as "birtherism,"[345] which encompasses more than Harris. While

> I did not recognize it at the time, what I was doing fits the definition of a classic "Motte and Bailey" logical fallacy;[346] I was pointing out something factual, modest, and easy to defend, which was however conflated with a much more radical topic.

My texting continues. "This morning Stephen said he might go back to California without me. He's saying we can try again in six months to see if we still want to be together. He is entirely pushing me away. I love him! I want to be with him! I want us!" I write.

My dad responds, "I believe Kamala Harris's qualifications to run as vice president are indeed clear cut, Katrina. Why would you take up this issue?"

I respond.

> *I don't like Harris. She was not in my top seven picks in the primaries. I do not like what I learned of her choices as California's attorney general.*[347,348] *And I don't see it as clear cut. It doesn't make sense to me that someone who was born here to two noncitizens on temporary stay should be qualified for the highest office in our country. But who cares? I don't need to argue about it.*

And while I say I don't need to argue about it, I continue.

> *I just posted a comment on a friend's Facebook post saying, 'Did you know her parents were not US citizens when she was born?' Stephen then took up a fight with me publicly on Facebook. But I can drop it. I don't really care, but he did. The rest of our day was crap—he was angry at me all day. I tried to be loving and respectful. He just kept calling me names and making threats. I had to call a red light and end the conversation. So, we were silent and avoided each other for most of the day—until he was willing to soften again.*

"Sweetheart," my dad implores, "this political stuff is torturing him! For love's sake, I would beg you to resign from politics. Leave that to warriors

Chapter 26: Fear and Disconnection

who don't mind jeopardizing friendships and loving relationships for the sake of some righteous cause, whatever it might be."

This does not make sense to me, as I have always been engaged in political discussion with my family. "How is it that different views are 'torturous'?" I ask.

"Because some views are incendiary!" he exclaims.

I respond with a screenshot of the definition of "incendiary."

In·cen·di·ar·y
adjective: incendiary
(Of a device or attack) designed to cause fires.

"You both perceive my views as designed to create metaphorical fires? And the MSM is benevolent?" I write back. The thought of my dad's perception has my head spinning, as from my perspective, it is completely opposed to the truth.

He implores me once again.

Please drop out of politics and live your life with Stephen. It would be beyond tragic if everything blew to pieces. Pursuing this political path is wreaking havoc on Stephen's psyche, with lots more to come as election day approaches. It may just burn him out, and you could find yourself lonely, sad, confused, and alienated with a lot of repair work to do if you don't just shove politics in the garbage can. From my perspective and the perspective shared by everyone in our family, your political narrative is derived from extremist right-wing memes that have gone mainstream thanks to the cunning, destructive and traitorous thug in the White House who's jeopardizing the entire American experiment. The nation is enduring a bone-crushing existential crisis. And if you continue to passionately engage in it, endorsing a narrative that for the most part is the polar opposite of everything we believe, then your perspective (irrespective of its merits) will more than likely end up severely wounding some of your most cherished relationships. Can't you see, it's just not worth it?

The truth is I cannot see this. The part of my mind that controls my sense of identity and belief system, the part of my psyche that clings to QAnon to create a sense of hope in this otherwise terrifying reality, the part of me that thinks that I understand what's really happening in the world and am actively participating in the solution, does not want me to see what my dad, Stephen, my friends, and my family are all seeing. I continue to view myself as being on the righteous and truthful end of all these debates. They are brainwashed. I am clear. And in the end, truth will win, and I will be redeemed.

Dad continues:

There's no reason why you can't have your opinions about anything and everything. But taking these opinions public serves no good purpose whatsoever. You won't be able to convince anybody that your narrative is right, and theirs is misguided, just as they have not been able to convert you to their way of thinking. So, what's the point?

I snap back,

No one in our family just 'shoves politics in the garbage.' We have always been politically active—giving voice to what we believe in. Mom has made several political posts today. That's how we were raised. That's how we've always been. Would you suggest any of my siblings also avoid posting anything political right now? Or just me because my politics are different?

I am feeling frustrated and disheartened as I perceive myself to be singled out and no longer an equal member of my own family. I question whether I still belong or if I am becoming an outcast to all my previous social circles, including this most important one. My text message to my dad ends with a sad face emoji. Tears fall from my eyes as I write "I guess I'm alone in this." I've never felt so misunderstood in my life.

PART 4:

Cracks and Crumbling of my Faith in Q

Chapter 27:
Breakdown and Breakthrough

I choose to stay connected to my dad through topics he is willing to engage in: California fires, and news on alternative Covid treatments. I am grateful we can stay connected, as I don't feel like I can talk to anyone else in my family without risking negative reactions and fallout.

Wearing Thin

Conflict with Stephen remains high for days, and both of us are wearing thin. In late August, I write my dad, "Stephen continues to affirm that we could have stayed in California, saying that my fears are irrational. He's saying that I am crazy and delusional, and I need to fix my tendency toward fear and overreaction, or our relationship is over. I am tired of being called crazy and delusional by my 'beloved.' He might pack up and drive away. At this point I am so tired of his threats, I told him if he's going to keep threatening to leave, he should just go. He said I am pushing him away and that if he goes, it's forever."

An hour later I add to the message to dad, "Looks like I must get better about keeping everything he might disagree with to myself. I pray that it doesn't squash our intimacy. It's a lot to hold all that I am learning inside and not share. I don't know how to carry all this alone and still feel emotionally and physically open to him as we used to be. But if I don't keep my political thoughts to myself, he'll pack up and leave."

The next morning, I report that Stephen and I are doing better, and a week later I report we are again on the brink of separating, as Stephen has informed me he is on the "razor's edge" of packing up and leaving. This time he is feeling outraged that I am unwilling to socially isolate for fourteen days prior to his scheduled trip to see his newly born grandson. Needless to say, I am not invited on this trip.

We are grateful to have emergency access to a couple's-coaching session with our mutual friend Scott, who is steeped in NVC teachings. Scott and I have worked through the difficulty we had with each other after he posted the article by Stephen Dinan a couple months back. Stephen and I need someone to assist us through these emotional escalations, and Scott has proven to be skilled at helping us through these breakdowns. In the first session, I come to terms with the fact that Stephen vehemently opposes my political ideology. He's done his best to endure it but can't stretch like this anymore. I have to cool it down or our relationship will end.

In the second session we talk about Stephen's upcoming trip and negotiate a balance that is workable for both. I am free to enjoy light social connection outdoors with no hugs and only short conversations at a minimum three-foot distance. Stephen feels okay with this, as there is generally a good breeze outdoors, reducing the chance of Covid exposure. He asks me to stay upwind of any conversation, which I am amenable to. It is a compromise we are willing to make in consideration of each other's needs—mine for connection and his for his family's well-being.

It's awkward for me to maintain social distance from my friends for this two-week period, as hardly anyone else maintains precautions at the outdoor dances we attend. My boundaries seem unusual and unnecessary to them. But I follow through on my agreement with Stephen. When asked, I let friends know my husband is going to see family and they feel vulnerable about the potential of contracting Covid. My friends are respectful of my boundaries and generally understanding. For me, this is a temporary and

Chapter 27: Breakdown and Breakthrough

acceptable price to pay so that we can maintain sufficient stability in our relationship.

I know that in addition to working weekly with a therapist, Stephen has been reaching out to a handful of our mutual friends and family members trying to bolster support to talk sense into me and to maintain his sanity.

2021 Personal Reflection

Months after my QAnon exit, Stephen would reveal to me that in this initial span of time, a half-dozen people he had consulted not only empathized with his pain and struggle, but also told him they would not blame him at all if he chose to leave me. One of our mutual friends, Stuart, who himself had been a conspiracy theorist for over a decade, went so far as to insist that I was a lost cause. He spent more than an hour trying to convince Stephen to end our engagement and let me live out the natural consequences of my new QAnon beliefs.

Stephen chose to double down on his commitment to stick with me despite the stress and strain he was enduring. The thought of letting go, allowing me to drift deeper into the direction I was heading was heartbreaking to him.

I am grateful Stephen chose to push through, and yet I understand he could not endure this stress forever. What I was not aware of was that he had committed to giving our relationship his best effort for six months. He decided that if he saw no meaningful improvement after that time, he would likely lose his willingness to continue putting in this kind of effort and we would have to go our separate ways. Almost three months had passed since my entry into QAnon, and there was no end in sight.

First Mini-Breakthrough

Our relationship continues to fray for another several days. While not a breakup, this is a serious breakdown as we can hardly tolerate being in each other's presence. Both of us are desperate for the other one to come around.

After yet another break from each other, Stephen suggests, "Rather than arguing about whose political view is right and whose is wrong, can we talk about what we know for sure is objectively true, and what we cannot be certain of?"

"That sounds like a good idea to me." I respond.

We acknowledge that reading the news gives us stories of what is going on, but there is generally no way for us to confirm that the "facts" stated in the news are objective at all. Each of us tends to trust certain sources and distrust others. We can see how each news organization is rated on Media-BiasFactCheck.com,[349] but to be honest, the ratings on this website don't mean much to me. I figure anything with "fact check" in the name has been corrupted in some way by the Cabal's influence.

Still, we can agree that new stories can all be questioned and that fact-checking the news is a long and difficult process, sometimes impossible. So why are we arguing about stories we are reading when we could be doing better things with our time? Is it so important to be right? Or can we loosen our hold on trying to win an argument in order to prioritize feeling connected and happy together?

Having established the folly of arguing over things we cannot prove, Stephen extends an olive branch.

"I am willing to consider the possibility that the way I am seeing the world could be wrong." He says.

A burst of joy erupts in my being. *Oh my God! Yes!* I exclaim inwardly and inaudibly. Maybe this is the beginning of his opening to finally seeing the truth!

"Thank you." I respond with a glowing smile.

He takes a long pause before continuing. "Are you willing to meet me there? Would you be willing to consider that while you're feeling completely certain about your political views, there's a possibility that there is information you are seeing that could be wrong?"

"Sure. I'm willing to meet you there," I respond immediately. It is only fair to meet him there. However, I can't currently imagine truly doubting

Chapter 27: Breakdown and Breakthrough

my position. For now, I am hopeful that this is the beginning of Stephen's entrance into my fold. In the meantime, that optimism provides me with a bit more peace of mind.

While this might seem like a small agreement, as we both take it to heart, we are able to argue less and enjoy our time together more. I take my commitments seriously and am increasingly willing to acknowledge when I come to see that some of the things I have believed are inaccurate or just plain wrong.

Chapter 28:
QAnon Themes

Child Sex Trafficking and Pedophilia

Stephen also takes his commitments seriously. He acknowledges that some aspects of the QAnon narrative are painfully true, but as he points out perhaps grossly exaggerated. Neither of us have been aware of how rampant human trafficking verifiably is. His heart strings are pulled into an agony similar to mine when I introduce him to Operation Underground Railroad (OUR).[350] I had learned about this nonprofit through Tony Robbins, who created a special YouTube segment introducing the work of OUR as he encouraged his followers to contribute to this organization that frees children from sex trafficking and helps to rehabilitate them.[351]

As I look into this organization, I learn that since 2013, OUR's operations and aftercare efforts have led to the rescue of over 6,000 survivors and the arrest of over 4,000 predators. How is it that we never even knew about this dark and massive industry that is competitive in size and scope to drug trafficking? Stephen says he would like to donate to this organization. It feels good to be on the same page on this issue.

Of course, my interest in this dark subject goes well beyond Stephen's. On September 2, 2020, Q posts "How is blackmail used?" Following the question, Q posts an extensive list of 45 Democratic and 44 Republican politicians and activists who have been found guilty of sexual acts with underage kids.[352] I begin fact checking the list and find local news articles affirming conviction reports of 27 of the first 28 names listed. I do a random pick of others on the list and find verifying news on them as well.

This list is astounding. I note that it is well balanced between Democratic and Republican leaders, which confirms what I have sensed to be true about Q's intentions; it is not Democrat vs. Republican. It is lies vs. truth, and corruption vs. justice. Q's "intel" is the source supporting a potent movement for good to prevail over evil. My NVC training taught me to be radically compassionate and to think of "evil" as unconscious desperate attempts to meet universal needs, and perhaps much of it is. However, this topic of child sex trafficking is so utterly wrong in every way. It is pure evil.

My enthusiasm for Q and Trump remains strong, as he is seeking to put an end to human trafficking,[353] and I am puzzled as to why I have not heard of efforts made by any former president.[354]

2023 Reflection – What I Learned

Every former president, beginning with Clinton, took actions to fight human trafficking.[355]

The Storm (That Didn't Happen)

Long morning hikes become a cornerstone of my daily routine on the sandy red trails of Sedona. I put in my earbuds and listen to videos elaborating on QAnon theories or Q adjacent news for more than an hour most mornings while soaking in the sun and enjoying the natural beauty of Thunder Mountain. Listening to the various updates from QAnon influencers such as Stephen Ward, Young Pharaoh, MonkeyWerx, the X22 Report, and others is now an enlivening part of my morning routine, my morning dopamine fix. These updates are exciting and boost my trust in the Plan.

On one of those mornings in late September, my heart skips a beat as I hear a QAnon "intel insider" share the good news: The Storm is happening! The indictments have been opened, and Hillary Clinton, Barack Obama, and

Chapter 28: QAnon Themes

other members of the Deep State have been arrested. The video I'm watching shows pictures of various political figures wearing house-arrest ankle bracelets.

Oh my God! It's happening! The indictments are real! The truth is coming out! They are on house arrest! No one will be able to deny it now. No one will be telling me how wrong I've been.

My inner world is popping a bottle of champagne and tossing confetti as I celebrate this news. In my elation, my hike turns into a jog with an occasional skip. Everything is going to be okay now. My community will wake up. They'll understand why I didn't back down on my social media posts. I will be redeemed. Our world will not go through a genocide. The people I love will not die. Everything is going to turn around now. It's all going to be okay.

I can hardly contain myself, but I do upon returning home. I pretend to be nonchalant while inwardly I am in joyful anticipation for this news to hit the mainstream. I figure it will start with the right-wing channels, and the left will seek to hide it as long as possible but will ultimately have to talk about it. News this huge cannot remain hidden.

But to my extreme disappointment, this big news does not show up that day or in the days to follow. I do online searches to see if I can find any up-to-date news on Obama, Hillary, Bush, and the others named in this report.

There are updates. Obama does not seem any different than he has been at any other time in his political career. There is no sign whatsoever that he has endured any arrest or is at all concerned about an indictment. My heart sinks as this is *not* the redeeming moment I thought it would be. I have to face the fact that the news I have listened to is false. The Storm has not happened. I will have to continue enduring insults while I work to wake people up.

Shortly thereafter I hear in an X22 Report that "false reports are sometimes necessary to throw off those who would seek to undermine our country." With this update, and after consulting with another QAnon friend, I choose to take a deep breath and trust in God, trust in the Plan. This mantra is my anchor, along with the "Where we go one, we go all!" refrain. So long as I strive to be the change I want to see in the world, I maintain certitude that I am creating a ripple effect that benefits the collective.

Keep your head up! Keep your heart strong! I remind myself after accepting this crushing blow. I have got to believe that one day all my work will be seen. My friends and family will thank me because I never gave up on them. I loved them through all the hate and ridicule they threw my way. I never gave up.

While my self-talk helps me overcome my disappointment at this fake report, it doesn't feel good to be lied to, even if it was done to throw off the Cabal.

New Fears: Elections, CCP, Censorship, Vaccine Rollout

As the seasons change, so do the primary themes that come across my screen. At this time, little to nothing in my news feeds pertains to matters discussed in *Fall of the Cabal,* and as usual, I almost never independently check the website where the Q drops are posted.[356] To be honest, I have little to no interest in Q; I'm interested in how the world around me and those I love are affected by the matters that Q seeks to expose—and even then, only as expressed by online influencers I've come to follow.

The latest subject matter is the upcoming elections. Tucker Carlson and other conservative commentators are focusing on points that support Trump's victory, and the Young Pharaoh, Stephen Ward, and other QAnon intel insiders follow suit. Repetitive themes include the many ways in which the Deep State and the "radical left"[357] are seeking to take control of the election results. There are repeated warnings in increasing detail of the rise of the Chinese Communist Party (CCP). Pundits predict that a Biden presidency would result in China's yuan becoming the new world currency as the United States falls into an economic collapse worse than the Great Depression.

I am learning so much from the *Epoch Times* about the history of China through the Falun Gong perspective, and it's a disconcerting view. Falun Gong practitioners seem to be a deeply virtue-centered community.[358] It's hard to imagine why China sees them as such a threat. But according to *the*

🪷 Chapter 28: QAnon Themes 🪷

Epoch Times, Xi has captured many Falun Gong adherents, sending them to "reeducation camps" where they are tortured, used for slave labor, and murdered for the profitable industry of organ harvesting.[359] I learn this has also happened to the Uyghur people in China and that these camps hold over one million people who have no legal representation.[360] It seems the CCP is perhaps the most brutal of human traffickers. I am deeply grateful Trump is being tough on China, as the thought of the CCP taking over the US is now near the top of my current list of cataclysmic concerns.

Then Hunter Biden's laptop[361] comes to light, containing hundreds of images of Hunter drugged out and erotically engaged with underaged Asian girls[362] and evidence that the Biden family was well paid by foreign interests through Hunter's leverage of his father's role as vice president when making business deals.[363] These photos were reportedly taken during Hunter Biden's trip to China with his father, Vice-President Joe Biden, on government business. The conservative news channels present this as evidence to prove that Joe Biden is a pawn to China.[364] They assert the CCP has Biden by the balls and if he becomes President, they will control him via blackmail.

Meanwhile, the MSM is claiming the laptop is part of a massive fake news campaign,[365] and any mention of it is immediately erased from Facebook, YouTube, Twitter, and Instagram as part of the ever-growing efforts by the leftists to "end fake news."[366] It's completely obvious to me and everyone on the right that the Democrats' agenda is censorship, not only of highly charged, questionable information, but also of verifiably truthful information or even debate on certain topics. Shouldn't it at least raise an eyebrow that Hunter Biden is engaging in drugs and fornication with young Chinese women while his dad is meeting with President Xi? Is no one on the left concerned that China could be seeking to bribe and blackmail the Bidens? Are the MSM and their dark overlords (corporate sponsors) ending fake news?[367] Or are they covering up factual stories?

2023 – What I Learned and Personal Reflection

In March 2023, the BBC confirmed the laptop did belong to Hunter

> Biden.[368] By then, none of the Democrats I brought this up to were willing to pay attention or consider the possible ramifications. Meanwhile, viewers of conservative media had become outraged by the mass censorship of truthful information, especially given the enormous stakes of a presidential election. Many conservatives believe Trump would have won if this story hadn't been actively censored by the FBI.[369]

It is stunningly clear that all the left-wing-owned and -run social media platforms are involved in a coordinated effort in support of liberal political agendas. The way the MSM addresses the Hunter Biden laptop story clearly illustrates the complicity among the left, and also the relatively new tactic of "cancel culture,"[370] in which the "radical left" is ready to delete anything it does not agree with. It seems that right-leaning stories, even when merely reporting verifiable events, are increasingly flagged as disinformation, marked as false or misleading, or simply erased from all the major social media platforms.

I feel distressed by the ways in which this cancel-culture phenomenon is shutting down conversations, threatening freedom of speech, and burying stories that challenge the mainstream narrative. The Democrats and the American Civil Liberties Union (ACLU) used to be fierce protectors of the First Amendment, going so far (at one time) as to preserve the right of Ku Klux Klan[371,372] members to parade through a Jewish neighborhood, despite their violent and anti-Semitic stance and the distress it created in this neighborhood.[373] In March 2002, the ACLU published a clear warning: "History teaches that the first target of government repression is never the last. If we do not come to the defense of the free speech rights of the most unpopular among us, even if their views are antithetical to the very freedom the First Amendment stands for, then no one's liberty will be secure."[374]

I fear the potential loss of our democracy through censorship. I am concerned that this could play out like it has in China, where people are not free to speak their minds due to the mass surveillance blended with the CCP's social credit system. While my belief in the promised Storm has been

Chapter 28: QAnon Themes

seriously shaken, I have come to love and appreciate Trump. It is clearly evident to me that he is now filling stadiums with massive crowds as Bernie had done, while Biden and his fans are hardly showing up.

My engagement in exposing the vaccine agenda with #ExposeBillGates and the horrors of child sex trafficking with #SaveOurChildren has faded. I am now researching what's shaking down in regard to the upcoming election and keeping my eye on the "vaccine" rollout, as it seems this genocide project is imminent. I've learned that the mRNA technology does not qualify under the CDC's longstanding definition of vaccination; however, they have changed their definition over time, allowing for this new gene therapy to slide right in relatively unchallenged.

Prior to 2015 it was "Injection of a killed or weakened infectious organism in order to prevent disease." Then from 2015 to the present time the new (circular) definition reads, "The act of introducing a vaccine into the body to produce immunity to a specific disease." Pfizer and Moderna's new mRNA "vaccines" are neither killed nor weakened infectious organisms, and we are yet to see whether they will "produce immunity to a specific disease," or if they fail to generate sufficient immunity.

2023 Reflection – What I learned

In September 2021, the definition of vaccination changed yet again, to read "The act of introducing a vaccine into the body to produce protection from a specific disease."[375] The definition no longer must "produce immunity"; if it can be shown to provide some undefined quantity of "protection," it is now considered to be a vaccine.

In other news, Q has stated repeatedly that this battle for the future of humanity that Q and the White Hats are fighting is not about Democrats versus Republicans; however, it appears completely partisan now. The Q drops are filled with images and quotes from Donald Trump, deeming his election the only viable outcome on November 3, 2020.

> ### 2023 Reflection–What I Learned
>
> As most of my "intel" came from social media influencers, I was completely unaware that Q had posted nothing whatsoever about Bill Gates or vaccines in the drops. The pandemic was mentioned only in the context of accusing the left of actively undermining Trump's presidency by destroying the economy in the final year of his first term. Q also pointedly mentions the potential for election manipulation, especially with the use of mail-in ballots.

My primary concern has to do with the vaccine rollout, and I fear Biden might be owned by China and would make matters worse… perhaps even daring to roll out a social credit system in the United States. Given that Trump champions choice when it comes to vaccines, and that he is tough on China, I need him to win this election.

Chapter 29:
It Gets Personal

Blood Libel and Anti-Semitism

I've got so many thoughts and emotions stirring up as I learn more. I generally like to process out loud, to talk things through with people I trust. I don't do well holding it all inside of me. I am grateful my dad is willing to continue to engage with me. Years ago, he read a book about modern slavery and donated money to the cause of ending this dark industry. Given his interest in this topic, perhaps this is another angle I could try to see if he'll open to more. I begin another text exchange, sharing the latest articles and videos I've seen on this topic.

In response, Dad sends me an article entitled "The Dark Virality of a Hollywood Blood-Harvesting Conspiracy: A centuries-old anti-Semitic myth is spreading freely on far-right corners of social media,"[376] suggesting a new digital dark age has arrived.

He writes:

> *Katrina, the whole adrenochrome thing is way over the top for me, so I'll take a pass. I've been trying to tell you, this dark blood libel stuff has been circulating around Europe for centuries. It has stirred up virulent anti-Semitism with horrible consequences. I read up on it some time ago, and just sent you an article from Wired*

magazine that is well worth reading. It's good to gain historical perspective on some of these vicious rumors that potentially can lead to violent oppression of societal scapegoats.

Shortly after, he adds:

Please NEVER, NEVER promote this theory in the name of stamping out the evildoers. You'll be exposing yourself to ridicule that could seriously damage your credibility.

It does not in any way cross my mind that my dad would think I am implicating Jewish people by expressing my dismay over child sex trafficking. I'm half Jewish—this text boggles my brain! The thought of condemning myself and half my family for these atrocities is absurd.

Before reading the article, I write back:

I know that child trafficking is the second largest illegal industry in our world. I have seen documentaries of children being rescued by Operation Underground Railroad. So what if the adrenochrome rumors are true? Just like we didn't want to believe that Catholic clergy were molesting children, but now we can't deny it. What if it is true? I can't ignore it. I've seen too much evidence. Remember that disturbing video I sent you of the brother and sister talking about where their father kept the cleaver and skulls at church, and that he had told them to eat some of the baby?

Dad responds:

Katrina, there are real weirdos out there, but that doesn't mean that Satan-worshiping and cannibalism are widespread! The error is generalizing this psychotic behavior and linking it to a perverse power elite. Did you have a chance to read the Wired article? Generalizing perverted, disgusting, psychotic cult behavior and attributing it to a race or creed or position in society like Jews or priests or Gypsies, etc. is at the very heart of prejudicial beliefs that

Chapter 29: It Gets Personal

lead to outrages in the name of wiping out evil. In Hitler's Germany, the theory of blood libel greatly contributed to much of the citizenry of Germany coming to view a Jewish people as 'ugly cockroaches' that 'needed to be exterminated to cleanse the country.' You have distant relatives who were murdered in cold blood because they happened to be born into a Jewish family.

I read the article and respond:

Dad, I don't know what to say. I hear your concern about how this could be used to villainize groups of people, which creates a moral rationale that makes it easier for some people to justify slaughtering other people. I understand that concern. In NVC, it's called 'enemy images' and it is a way in which we are taught to dehumanize other people or groups of people, then use pejorative terms to demean them and validate violence. I understand that potential and it's very concerning to me too.

I did read the article and I believe it is possible that there is a very small handful of wealthy powerful corrupt psychopathic leaders, and a larger handful of sociopathic leaders, participating in blood libel and it's even possible that some of them might be Jewish. On the other hand, maybe none of them are Jewish. Who knows! At any rate, I am well-aware that that behavior is not at all representative of Judaism or any other religion for that matter.

My response seems to calm my father's concerns. He writes:

Well spoken. Generally speaking, we're on the same page. I am as horrified as anybody by the brutality, sadism and pathological beliefs that sometimes come to infect entire populations. And as for individual actors and small cults, whether they be comprised of billionaires or whomever, they should certainly be brought to justice. Your horror and abhorrence are absolutely understandable. The key at times like these, which are like a societal crucible, is to avoid painting with a broad brush lest we end up scapegoating and falling prey to mob psychology.

QAnon Week 18: Not Invited to Thanksgiving

A week later, I discover that my siblings, cousins, aunts and uncles are all invited to the family Thanksgiving on my father's side. I have not received an invitation. I receive no communication whatsoever. It's like I don't exist. I feel heaviness set into my chest, as I've never been excluded from family gatherings before. I understand they are all way more concerned about Covid than I am, but I'd be willing to get tested like everyone else, so why am I being left out?

Sadness and anger rise in me, as from my point of view the MSM has created division in my family by disseminating false information about the threat of this virus. My family members have fallen for the same indoctrination most everyone left of center has, hiding behind memes like "trust the science," as if media-sanctioned science is all that matters and any peer-reviewed research that comes to different conclusions is somehow unscientific. I am infuriated that open discourse and debate is being summarily blocked by the MSM, including social media channels, and any dissident voices, irrespective of credentials, are being mocked and censored.

My longing for understanding and comfort motivates me to call my dad once more.

"Hey Dad, I'm wondering if Aunt Sarah invited you to Thanksgiving this year?" I start.

"Hi, Katrina," his voice sounds cheerful. "Sarah knows we can't travel, so we weren't invited either."

"I don't know why Stephen and I weren't invited," I lament. "She's always included me, and I'd love to see the family. It hurts to be excluded. I'm guessing it's because I've been openly questioning the whole Covid narrative. I know the doctors on that side of our family all seem to be aligned with the MSM. I hate that all the propaganda could cause me to miss this family gathering."

Chapter 29: It Gets Personal

"For what it's worth Katrina, I'm sure it's not about Covid. They don't agree with your assessment of the vaccines, but I talked to Aunt Sarah recently and I believe she hasn't invited you because of other things you have posted."

"What do you mean?" I feel indignant.

"Our whole family is concerned about you. The things you believe, some of which you post on Facebook… We don't know what to do."

Inwardly I am rolling my eyes, but I remain silent as he continues, "I wish you could understand… These blood libel stories you continue to share are beyond disturbing. With the election right around the corner, our whole family feels we are facing an existential threat."

I implore him, "Dad, Trump does not pose an existential threat. If anything, he is seeking to end any existential threats, like the one we are facing with China and the threat of a technocratic authoritarian government controlling us by means of a social credit system."

"Katrina, I know you believe that, but please try to understand; you could be very wrong about this," he implores.

"Okay. Go on then. I'm listening," I say earnestly as my head drops and my emotions plummet. I do want to understand his perspective, and it pains me that it is so far from my own.

"Thank you. I know this is very hard for you to see, but from everything we can see, Trump is playing straight from Hitler's playbook. While I understand you are not connecting blood libel to the Jewish people, many other people who read and share the articles and videos that you watch do believe these crimes are being committed by Jews. The anti-Semitism we are seeing in our country is beyond anything it's been since World War II.[377] They are using the same tropes." My dad's voice is unusually shaky. I've never heard him express fear like this before.

"Dad, I hear that," I begin, "but what I am trying to tell you is that the media is lying to you and everyone in our family. Trump is not anything close to Hitler. I wish you could see that."

"Katrina, I know that is what you believe right now, and I wish I could get through to you to help you see something that seems to be beyond your visibility currently. Are you willing to hear me out?" he asks.

"Okay. Go ahead," I offer.

He chooses to take time to put his thoughts to paper:

Katrina, you know that your Grandma Anna was proud of having come from 'a long line of rabbis' dating back multiple generations. In the late 1800s and early 1900s some of your ancestors were scapegoated and brutally attacked during pogroms countenanced by the czarist regime of Russia. Some of their children, including your great grandmother Celia, fled to America to escape persecution. My father, your Grandpa Pete, was also Jewish. His grandfather and grandmother came to America from Germany to start a new life and raise a family around the turn of the century. Although genocide against European Jews under Hitler and the Nazis didn't take place until decades later, anti-Semitism was a cultural and political undercurrent in Germany dating back centuries. It generally rose to the surface during periods of economic stress and political instability.

During my college years I made a study of Hitler's rise to power in the 1930s. I was intent on understanding how one of the most well-educated and civilized countries in Europe could have fallen into the hands of a shrewd and ruthless psychopath and followed him in lockstep to a state-sponsored, mechanized slaughter of millions of innocent men, women, and children. I felt that if this horrific catastrophe could take place in Germany, then it could happen anywhere in the world in the decades to come. It could even happen here in the United States, as improbable as that may seem.

I had long ago come to understand that Donald Trump is a toxic narcissist, a pathological liar, a sociopath, and a first-class con man, so I was shocked by his unlikely rise to the presidency in 2016: the most powerful political position in the world. In the months and years that followed his inauguration, it became increasingly clear

Chapter 29: It Gets Personal

to me that his ambition was to take a wrecking ball to our democracy, smash through all institutional guardrails, punish his enemies, and fill his administration with abject loyalists whose sole purpose was to do his bidding.

To me, the reality of a Hitler wannabe doing whatever it takes to seize power, consolidate his grip, and initiate a dystopian dictatorship on the grave of our liberal democracy is a nightmare with echoes of Hitler's Third Reich. And Trump's penchant for energizing right wing extremists is giving license to all forms of scapegoating. I sense that anti-Semitism is about to raise its ugly head.

Trump has given voice to a strain in America's political and cultural life that has always existed in the shadows. Now this extremism is front and center and in danger of being adopted and "normalized" by a significant percentage of the voting population. An alarmingly large and growing number of Trump-loving extremists, many of them aligned with QAnon, are using the horrifying anti-Semitic myth of blood libel to rally people to their cause. People shrink in horror at stories of children being kidnapped, tortured and murdered for the purpose of harvesting adrenochrome, the supposed elixir of youth said to be consumed by Hollywood stars and Jewish-controlled global elites. These horrific stories are in keeping with the notorious Protocols of the Elders of Zion, a book that first appeared in Russia in the early 1900s and has done more to spread venomous lies and hatred against Jews than any other publication in modern times.

Please look it up. I will always love you, but some of our other family members feel so threatened by what you are saying, they might choose to end all contact with you. Please understand that you could be supporting a movement that could put your own life in danger and could slaughter so many people you love.

I am shocked into silence and don't know what to do. My dad is generally so easy going and tends to see the world through rose-colored glasses. I've never heard him share this much detail about our family history before. I am grateful he is helping me make sense of my relatives' choice to exclude me. And, it is painfully ironic to me that I feel like I've been trying to save them from a sinister fascist agenda, and yet from their perspective, they have every reason to think that I am the one who is holding an existentially dangerous allegiance—actively supporting a Hitler-like regime. I have not been invited because they are protecting themselves from me. I understand now with less bewilderment and more compassion, but it still hurts.

I agree to check out the *Protocols of the Elders of Zion*. It's reasonable for me to reach across the aisle and care for my relationship with my family in this way.

Protocols of the Elders of Zion

The United States Holocaust Memorial Museum website (USHMM)[378] states: "'*The Protocols of the Elders of Zion*' is the most notorious and widely distributed anti-Semitic publication of modern times. Its lies about Jews, which have been repeatedly discredited, continue to circulate today, especially on the internet. The individuals and groups who have used the Protocols are all linked by a common purpose: to spread hatred of Jews."

As for its origins, the website states, "It was first published in Russia in 1905 as an appendix to *The Great in the Small: The Coming of the Antichrist and the Rule of Satan on Earth,* by Russian writer and mystic Sergei Nilus." And "Although the exact origin of the Protocols is unknown, its intent was to portray Jews as conspirators against the state. In twenty-four chapters, or protocols, allegedly minutes from meetings of Jewish leaders, the Protocols 'describes' the 'secret plans' of Jews to rule the world by manipulating the economy, controlling the media, and fostering religious conflict."

I'm struck by how the mirroring between the religious predictions in those times and the current predictions are identical. Q is warning us of the rise of satanic forces, as did Sergei Nilus. While I once viewed satanic symbols not as any kind of real-world threat, but as an element of art, my time in QAnon has changed that. It seems there's something in our psyche that is inclined to believe in good versus evil, as if life were simply black

Chapter 29: It Gets Personal

and white and Q and this notorious piece of anti-Semitic propaganda effectively engage that human tendency.

My psyche is now wrestling with the fact that I too have fallen into beliefs about good and evil, inspired mostly by what seems to be layman's propaganda, despite my kinship with Rumi's quote, "Beyond the ideas of wrongdoing and rightdoing there is a field. I will meet you there." I recall my underlying value for and belief in spiritual oneness. Everyone is a part of me. Where there is evil, there is opportunity for love, compassion, and forgiveness. This does not mean we should allow people to enact harm. We can and we must actively work to prevent harm through the least violent means of force necessary, and still honor the humanity in everyone.

Or as Russian writer and prominent Soviet dissident Aleksandr Solzhenitsyn said, "The line separating good and evil passes not through states, nor between classes, nor between political parties either—but right through every human heart—and through all human hearts. This line shifts. Inside us, it oscillates with the years. And even within hearts overwhelmed by evil, one small bridgehead of good is retained."

Have I been projecting my shadow outward? Have I been denying my shortcomings? If so, how do I come back into full responsibility for my actions and their natural, karmic consequences?

I keep reading.

Another page on this site addresses the rumors. "The term blood libel refers to the false allegation that Jews used the blood of non-Jewish, usually Christian children, for ritual purposes. The Nazis made effective use of blood libel stories to demonize Jews, with Julius Steicher's newspaper Der Stürmer making frequent use of ritual murder imagery in its anti-Semitic propaganda."

The USHMM elaborates on this teaching saying, "Blood libel accusations often led to pogroms [raping and murdering Jewish victims and looting their property],[379] violent riots launched against Jews and frequently encouraged by government authorities."[380]

Tears soak my cheeks, as something in my genetic memory feels the horrors of my ancestral past. I am disturbed by how deeply that part of the QAnon narrative maps onto the *Protocols of the Elders of Zion*. I now understand that this propaganda was spread by Hitler's supporters in the rising tides that led to the Holocaust. I am somewhat horrified by the fact that I have been sharing these stories with others, given the history associated with them. I hate to think that the Cabal could be getting away with these horrible crimes, however, I know that blood libel is in no way part of the Jewish religion. The danger of this anti-Semitic literature is becoming clear to me now.

I feel brutally stuck between a rock and a hard place. I've already posted #SaveOurChildren, to my social media, and rather than people seeking to understand that there is a horrible and massive industry of stealing and selling kids for sex, they are labeling me as a racist, fascist, homophobic anti-Semite. And to make matters worse, the MSM is silent on this topic, choosing rather to focus on QAnon and dangerous conspiracy theories while practically ignoring the atrocious crimes against children.[381] Now if I post anything related to this topic, my character is immediately slammed. How do I express my care and support for the trafficked children without appearing to support anti-Semitism? While I know that rape and blood libel are distinct, they are both horrific and it must stop. And the distrust and hatred of Jews must stop too.

Reading these articles is humbling and nauseating to me. I am heartbroken by my new knowledge of Holocaust history. At the same time, I am grateful to have been willing to look at it, because I love my family. I value our connection. And now I understand why I cannot continue to entertain any adrenochrome stories. I need to be cautious about sharing anything that could be related.

That's a hard task, as it seems that any mention of child sex trafficking that I come across is quickly being scooped into the blood libel and conspiracy theory buckets, as if it were innately an anti-Semitic and therefore an immoral subject to discuss. I feel caught in a dilemma as I wish to honor my family lineage, and I am also deeply mourning the huge industry of child sex trafficking. Conflating it with anti-Semitism makes this horrific violation against our children exceedingly difficult to address. I stop talking about adrenochrome and become quiet in my enthusiasm and support for the work of Operation Underground Railroad.

Chapter 30:
Bridging the Political Divide

I rarely visit qanon.pub, a webpage dedicated to authenticated Q drops. But today I do, and in my scrolling, I find these:

> *The battle to prevent truth from reaching the people.*
> *The battle to maintain and push division.*
> *Divided you are weak.*
> *Divided you fight each other.*
> *Divided you pose no threat.*
> *System of control.*
> *Information warfare.*
> *Q*

> *This is not about R v D.*
> *This is about preserving our way of life.*
> *If America falls, the World falls.*
> *Patriots on guard.*
> *Q*

While most Q drops don't make much sense to me, these land as self-evident wisdom requiring no interpretation. They simply reflect the obvious antidote to the age-old "divide and conquer" war strategy, which stands in opposition to the idea of unity in "United we stand, divided we fall."

It seems to me that Q is seeking to create unitive strategies that align with my values. And yet I feel caught in the battles between Republicans and Democrats; I am striving to maintain a loving connection with my former liberal community while experiencing more connection with my new conservative friends. Having one foot in each world, I see that they are practically living in different realities. Most cannot fathom how on earth someone on the other side could see the world as they do. The accusations and ridicule that are part and parcel to political debates are anathema to me.

2023 Personal Reflection

While in QAnon, I was mostly unaware of how QAnon had quickly become a most divisive phenomenon in sharp contrast to the views of Democrats and Progressives. Later I would hear people compare these ideological differences to the ones that gave rise to the Civil War. From where I stood, instead of pitting the southern Confederacy and the northern Union against each other, this "war" of ideas pitted Republicans against Democrats.

I did notice that some QAnon influencers generated enemy images against Democrats, calling them "demonrats" and "satanists." According to these same influencers, however, Republicans are "God-loving people" and "true patriots." While I understood the general sentiment among QAnon is that Biden posed an existential threat to the world, these name-calling tactics did not sit well with me.

"Across the Aisle": A Rare Experiment in Peacemaking

Thankfully, a friend turns me onto a project designed by certified NVC trainer and mediator John Kinyon, called *Across the Aisle*. This weekly online community conversation welcomes people of all political affiliations to engage in a dialogue in which we hear each other's points of view and

Chapter 30: Bridging the Political Divide

practice empathic reflection, rather than the kind of reactive debate that has become the norm.

Kinyon describes the project in this way:

> *As tensions ratchet up around the US presidential election, and the phrase 'civil war' is heard more and more frequently, we need some way to bring the temperature down. We seem to be inhabiting different worlds of alternate realities, parallel universes of perspective, experience, and belief, with the very real potential for erupting into violence.*
>
> *I believe the way we reduce these tensions is through shifting from trying to convince each other out of what seem to be misinformed or even delusional beliefs, to seeing if we can hear and understand each other. What is key is to let go of seeking agreement on this level, while remaining grounded in our own sense of reality. From this understanding we can focus on what we each want, and ultimately what we all want—all of us around the country and around the world: safety, security, freedom, respect, inclusion, belonging, mattering, love, connection, peace, and honoring and protecting what we feel to be sacred.*
>
> *From this place of what we all want and need, we have the possibility of cooperation, even with all the disagreements and different realities still being there.*
>
> *For the past few months, a team of colleagues and I have been offering a weekly online public space that we call Across the Aisle: Open Conversation for Healing Our Political Divide. People show up to these events with a wide range of viewpoints. We take turns speaking, hearing, and reflecting back, until each speaker feels heard. There's no attempt to convince or persuade. Just speaking and listening.*

Perhaps this might be the medicine that could resolve the painful divide that is tearing apart the social fabric for many—including myself. I am eager to feel into the *Across the Aisle* experience. Wednesday evening is my introduction to this two-hour online experience.

Framework. The framework is simple. If you want to share a view that feels important to you, you raise your hand. From the raised hands, a participant is granted a turn to express. The chosen participant is asked to do the following:
1. Identify a single political issue that they feel is concerning.
2. Let the group know the personal meaning she or he (or they) gives to this issue.
3. Identify the feelings she or he (or they) has as it relates to this issue.
4. Identify the values that are "alive" in him or her (or them) when contemplating his or her (or their) stated topic.

Participation. In these sessions we agree to actively and compassionately listen to views that are very different from our own. The challenge is to do this with such skill that we can accurately reflect to the speaker what we've heard. We know we've been on target when the speaker says something to the effect of "Yes, that matches what I intended to express."

My commitment to listening through an empathic lens opens a door that had been shut in recent months, or at best only cracked open. I acknowledge inwardly that since my fall into QAnon, I have not been engaging in the reflective listening and speaking skills (verbal mirroring of other people's thoughts, emotions, and values) that I have honed with such care, for years. Instead, I have been reactive and eager to engage in fruitless debates.

This practice group helps me bridge the divide that lives within me. In most of my other interactions, friends and family members have been sharing left-of-center views with me, peppered with an occasional anti-Trump statement from Republicans Liz Cheney or Mitt Romney, as a way of trying to convince me that I am wrong, pointing out that even these hardcore Republicans agree with the criticisms against Trump. Their efforts

Chapter 30: Bridging the Political Divide

were futile, as I often responded passionately and decisively with my immediate comebacks rather than responding with empathy as I would do if I were implementing NVC. Nobody I know likes to be told they are wrong, even when some part of them knows their stance may not stand up to scrutiny.

I remind myself of the NVC wisdom to "connect before we correct." Or as my NVC colleague Scott would say, "Give empathy first, then count to a million before offering feedback." He also recommends asking permission and gaining authentic consent before giving any coaching or advice, or offering a reframe. While I have heard and taught these teaching points many times, it is easy to forget them in the heat of the moment. I am grateful for the *Across the Aisle* container, which helps me remember how powerful and healing these basic communication practices can be.

Most of the *Across the Aisle* sessions I attend are composed primarily of Democrats, with only an occasional Independent, Libertarian, or Republican. While this is not as well balanced as I had hoped, participants do express divergent positions. I observe how differences can be worked through amicably, and yet I feel hesitant to introduce my own ideas, which might stimulate negative reactions in the group. I am cautious as I toss in an unpopular angle to see how John holds the space for the group to navigate these challenges to their ideologies. It doesn't seem like anyone changes their minds; however, this conversational protocol does create an opportunity for people to talk about different perspectives with respect for everyone present. This is the first time in months I feel truly open to hearing an MSM-informed standpoint without being so prone to reactive debate. I come to trust that if I choose to share something from my right-leaning stance with the group, I will be treated with respect. Others in this practice group will seek to understand what I have to say rather than immediately dismissing my view of reality or attacking my character.

Facilitation. While I had professed to be keeping up with the mainstream news, it's interesting for me to hear what I've been missing. There are a couple of times in which someone who seems to be a QAnon also joins the Zoom calls.

Here is a summary of one such call:

After John's opening welcome, Kyle raises his hand to speak first, then says, "I see that Trump is a demagogue, and because of that I do not support him for president and want to see that he is no longer in office."

John reflects what he's heard and asks if we can "flesh it out" a bit more by looking at what feelings are "alive" in Kyle.

Kyle says, "I am worried about his desire to stay in power, especially when I hear that he would not concede the election in a peaceful transition of power. For me, that is a disqualification for someone to be president of the United States."

John then asks what values Kyle holds that lead him to feel worried, to which he responds, "I value healthy functioning of our government systems."

Heather asks to go next, and John coaches her to reflect back what Kyle has said so that he feels sufficiently heard and understood before expressing her view.

"Kyle, it sounds like you believe Trump is a demagogue and that you feel worried about his desire to stay in power. You want to have a healthy, functioning government. Is that right?"

"Yes. Thank you." Kyle affirms.

"Thank you both," John steps in. "That was a great demonstration of empathic mirroring. Heather, it's your turn now. What would you like to express?"

> *Kyle, I want to let you know that I share your feelings and values. I am concerned about the health of our government and how the system is functioning. I am a researcher who prefers to seek truth rather than popularity... the opposite of a demagogue, you could say. What I am noticing is that there is a lot of gossip going*

Chapter 30: Bridging the Political Divide

on, and name-calling. Calling someone a demagogue is a little bit beneath us, which is easy to do. I heard general terms, nothing specific in what you said. What I discovered about this president is that he supports choice when it comes to vaccinations. Given my background in health, this surprised me. So, I further looked into him and discovered that my assumptions about Trump were incorrect. As a lifelong Democrat I had invested a lot into mainstream media, but when I looked behind the curtain, I was surprised to see how much corruption is going on.

It seems that if left uninterrupted, she might keep going, so John steps in before she can say another word, giving her empathy for what she has shared and encouraging her to streamline her sharing.

Heather, it sounds like you have a very different view of Trump. I'd like to understand what the one key focus is that you want to share with the group. Is it about the news? Or name-calling? Or vaccines? Please clarify the part you would like to focus on for this share.

"I am tired of all the gossip," Heather states with an air of passion.

I want the truth. I go straight to the source. I read Trump's tweets and listen to his entire speeches, not just sound bites. I have listened to hundreds of hours of what he has to say, and he is impressive. He's guaranteed money to the Black colleges; he has ended our oil dependence; he has done hundreds of things that are good for our country.

I notice my physical energy increase and a sense of joy rise in my being as Heather shares her approach to making sense of reality with an enthusiasm that mirrors my own.

John again inserts himself with a jovial tone in his voice before Heather can start another sentence. He says, "Thank you for sharing all of this with us! Would someone like to go next and reflect back what they've heard?"

Larry raises his hand to go next.

> *Heather, it sounds like you are feeling frustrated and exasperated when you hear what you perceive to be gossip and misinformation about Trump. You value truth and going straight to the source rather than listening only to sound bites.*

John asks Heather, "How was that?"

She responds, "I would say he did very well considering he likely has a different position.

Everyone laughs.

"I think you did an awesome job, Larry." She says in completion.

"Larry, it's your turn now," says John.

Larry begins to share his view.

> *I obviously have some natural or internal pushback to some of the things Heather was saying and her characterizations of Trump. My bigger concern though is that our system of government and society is on the verge of collapse. I am neither a Democrat nor Republican. I am Independent. Although as an African-American, my interests have been served more by Democrats than Republicans over the years. I see what's happening as bigger than politics. Trump is not the problem; he's just a symptom. The problem though is in our willingness to identify with these polarities. To some degree, I agree with the evaluation that Trump is a demagogue, as I see him push the edges of the polarities rather than bridging solutions. This is a classic textbook description of what it means to be a demagogue.*

John reflects what Larry had expressed. Larry affirms he has been clearly heard and understood by John, then adds:

🪷 Chapter 30: Bridging the Political Divide 🪷

The part that is troubling to me is what Trump's original campaign lead, Steve Bannon, has said is the strategy, which is 'flooding the zone.'[382] Trump's strategic supporters are flooding people's minds with so much information they can't hold it all; it becomes overwhelming. And because the content is so emotional, it creates dysregulation, triggering the fight-or-flight system in the body, resulting in more conflict and widening polarization.

John asks Larry what he wants. Larry responds

I am afraid Trump will not agree with a peaceful transition of power. I've seen in my research that he will foment chaos and possibly civil war. I would love to see more cohesion and harmony where we can get back to constructive conversations for solutions that benefit everyone.

Larry happens to be a dear friend I've known for years. His expression makes an impact on me. What if he's right? I ask myself. While I am mostly immersed in conservative news, I maintain some of my left-of-center frames of reference. As much as I'm appreciating Trump, it does seem possible that if he does not immediately win the upcoming election, he could foment outrage and chaos.

My thoughts spin on this possibility. Conservative news has been warning its voters for months that the left is trying to rig the vote by using mail-in ballots, conveniently made more popular due to the pandemic. What's to keep the left from printing extra ballots and stuffing the boxes? What checks are in place to make sure all these ballots are connected to real and qualified voters? I don't know how elections work, but I haven't trusted them for quite a while. A few years ago, I watched the documentary *Hacking Democracy*,[383] which exposed the notoriously problematic Diebold (now Premier Election Solutions) voting machines. I am also aware that our voting process includes no original paper trail to leave hard-copy evidence of the actual votes. Instead, each ballot goes into a "black box," and three corporations ultimately count the votes.[384] That's a lot of power to put in the hands of a few private interests.

It's easy to imagine that if Biden wins this election, the results will be highly suspect by most Republicans. Trump's rallies have been enormous in size, and Biden seems to be hiding out in his basement. Those on the right side of the aisle have been seeing the left's election-rigging plans all over their predominant news channels for months. But what if Biden wins fair and square, and Trump along with other Republicans do not trust the results? I can only imagine outrage and chaos. I hope it does not lead to violence.

Alex is next. He expresses his concern as to how closely aligned our political discourse meltdowns reflect what Russian far-right political philosopher Aleksandr Dugin[385] taught in *Foundations of Geopolitics*,[386] also known as Putin's playbook, adding, "It's pretty disturbing to see what is discussed in that book, especially when you see what is playing out in our world."

His concern is apparent as he shares a quote from the book, reading:

"Russia should use its special services within the US borders to fuel instability and separatism. For instance, provoke Afro-American racists. Russia should introduce geopolitical disorder into internal American activity, encouraging all kinds of separatism in ethnic, social, and racial conflicts, actively supporting all dissident movement; extremist, racist, and sectarian groups, while destabilizing internal political processes in the US. It would also make sense to simultaneously support isolationist tendencies in American politics."

Alex expresses what meaning he gives this:

When I see that Russian intelligence is used as a primary source for information that is shared with the American public by people in our government, I feel alarmed. Lindsay Graham, for example, declassified a document, saying to Congress, 'This comes from Russia, and we don't know if it has validity or not.'

Chapter 30: Bridging the Political Divide

"When I hear that, I feel concerned," Alex admits, continuing with,

I have a need for stability and for truth. I can see that Russia has a particular interest in spreading disinformation and creating destabilization. It's almost as if certain people in our government are being used as willing participants and instruments in this spreading of disinformation. The last thing I'll say is that the shrugging off of this in our country by saying 'Russia, Russia, Russia' as a way to dismiss what's happening, versus taking it seriously, is concerning. I care about our country and the integrity of our political and social systems. The feeling I get around this is anger. I am angry this is being shrugged off.

I find myself naturally reflecting on this new information.

I am aware that Russia is influencing our media, but I don't know what does and does not come from that source. It does seem that all the white supremacists and most of the people who are intolerant of cultural or religious diversity are on the conservative side. I wonder how much the Russian KGB is working on each side of the aisle. Its influence seems more obvious in news channels like Fox, but in all likelihood, they are working the liberal side too.

This is uncomfortable for me to acknowledge, as I've been aligned with Trump and Republicans for the last eighteen weeks, and I still lean in that direction.

Questioning Everything

And while I've seen plenty of evidence that most Republicans are not anything close to being as racist or intolerant as I previously believed, I still see that any such groups *are* on the right. So, am I conservative? Or centrist? Or independent? I don't know anymore. All I know is that I am less certain of where I stand politically than I've ever been. I knew when I was a Democrat. I knew when I was a Berniecrat. And being a Trump-supporting QAnon has been clear to me too. But it is eye-opening to listen to Kyle as he shares that excerpt from Dugin's writings. I am more open than ever to considering that in all my research as a QAnon, I could be believing disinformation and misinformation propagated by Russia. And who knows what other countries have found their way into our independent media streams? I realize I need to be more suspicious of everything I have learned to date.

> ***I realize I need to be more suspicious***
> ***of everything I have learned to date.***

Alex's contributions are the last for this session before we engage in a debrief together, in which we acknowledge how deeply we are all longing for truth, and how difficult it is when each of us believes we have found a truth that others do not agree with. We sit together in mourning and frustration with the challenge of finding compelling, inarguable evidence that would support better sense-making, and the ability to establish a shared reality. And we celebrate that what we all want is greater cooperation, efficiency, and effectiveness in our efforts to contribute to the betterment of our government and our world.

I am drawn to participate regularly in this practice group. I notice how each session softens my grip on what I have held as "the truth." My mind is opening to different points of view from people who clearly take their research seriously.

Chapter 31:
QAnon Cracking and Crumbling

Where Is JFK Jr.?

With the election less than a week away, I am hopeful that JFK Jr. is about to make his presence known. It is clear to me that the future of our country and our world are at stake in this election. If he is alive and working closely with Trump to eliminate the threat of the Cabal, he will come out of hiding, as there's never been a more critical time in history for him to make himself known.

But he doesn't appear.

Not only that, but at this point I've heard news on several occasions that the Storm is happening and none of them have panned out. Where I was once excited to be in on the news, I am now aware that there are people who claim they have "insider intel" who are just plain wrong.

I wonder if that whole bit about JFK Jr. was manufactured by someone with deceptive intent. With that thought, my heart sinks. "If that was not real, who's behind Q?" I wonder.

These are thoughts I have been unable to entertain up until now. But at this point, given the disinformation I have seen among the QAnon influencers, it would be out of integrity for me not to ask these obvious questions.

The Election, Oil and Water

Several days before the election, I join a Zoom call with a small group of people with whom I practice NVC. My colleagues are naturally moved to share "what's alive in them" as it relates to the upcoming election. I let others go first. I am not surprised by where everyone else stands. They are generally feeling nervousness—hoping Biden can pull off a win—highly concerned about what might happen if he does not. I feel hesitant when asked to share my thoughts and feelings, however I have come to trust that I am safe in this group and can speak my subjective truth even when it is in discord with the beliefs of others.

I am slow and cautious as I begin. "To be honest, I am nervous about the possibility of a Biden presidency," I admit. "I'm concerned about his ties with China. I don't trust him to serve our best interest when it comes to the rising threat of the Chinese Communist Party." I pause to see how others are digesting my share.

"Wow. I feel surprised to hear this, Katrina," Joe offers. "I thought for sure you'd want Biden over Trump. Am I hearing you are hoping Trump wins?"

"Yes," I admit.

As the conversation continues, I am relieved that no one is becoming reactive or argumentative as is normal in most circles where Biden supporters and Trump fans mix as well as oil and water. Instead, they express curiosity and are able to reflect back what they understand my perspective to be, similarly to the way we have practiced in *Across the Aisle.*

Later that day, Laura and I share a bit of back and forth as we brace ourselves for the coming election.

She writes, "Are you as concerned as I am about Trump's stance on fracking and support of Big Oil in general? If he even nominally agreed we need to phase it out, I could feel a bit better… as if we have time to f#@k around with the environment… I'm relieved that so far there's no mass violence."

☸ Chapter 31: QAnon Cracking and Crumbling ☸

Laura adds a screenshot of a Trump tweet with a short video underneath headlined "Biden and Harris want to ban fracking and kill American jobs."

"I don't like fracking at all." I respond without hesitation. I had seen the documentaries *What the Frack*[387] and *Gasland: Can You Light Your Water on Fire?*[388] A few years ago and have no interest in using this strategy to harvest natural gas at the risk of our aquifers. The scenes of people's tap water lighting on fire have in my mind created plenty of evidence that this technology is *far* from harmless. It contaminates the water supply, making it unsafe to humans or any other form of life. In 2016, Yale researchers analyzed more than 1,000 chemicals used in hydraulic fracking and found that 157 of them, including arsenic, benzene, cadmium, lead, formaldehyde, chlorine, and mercury, were associated with either developmental or reproductive toxicity.[389] It seems that these, as well as flammable ingredients, leak into the aquifers as an inconvenient consequence of this natural gas harvesting technology.

As I contemplate the vital importance of our water supply, I am reminded of another documentary I had seen called *Blue Gold: World Water Wars*.[390,391] This video highlighted the growing problems of water scarcity[392] and corporate capture of the world's remaining water supply, suggesting that if we don't stop what these crony capitalists are doing, they will one day own and control every drop of water, essentially controlling the global population.

I realize I've lost sight of where Biden and Trump stand on a variety of issues. This one deeply matters to me, as did the attempt to stop the Dakota Access Pipeline project[393] The memory crosses my mind that Trump condemned the Water Protectors.[394] He was also personally invested in Energy Transfer Partners, the corporation behind this pipeline project.[395] And when he became president, one of the actions he took was to support the completion of the pipeline by unleashing the National Guard and law enforcement officers. The remaining protesters were forcefully evicted.[396,397] Trump did this without hesitation and despite righteous legal arguments from eighty-seven unified tribal governments and a clear demonstration that previous treaties were being violated by this act of building a pipeline on native land.[398]

I remember I hated Trump's actions at that time. Yet in the last almost five months, I had forgiven him because I understood his argument that for the sake of national security we had to get ourselves out of a situation of being reliant on other countries for oil. He would repeatedly say, "We have plenty at home and we should tap into it and use it." By becoming oil independent we have less need to continue fighting endless wars in the Middle East. It was easy to note that Trump was the only president in my memory who completed a term in office without adding to the war machine. To my understanding, against all odds, he had negotiated peace in North Korea and in the Middle East, fulfilling another core value of mine—peace.

At this point I don't know how to think of oil exploitation in our country, or in our world for that matter. It appears to be a necessary evil—until we have a truly environmentally friendly and sustainable solution for energy, which Q has promised will come once we free the patents that have been seized and locked up by the Cabal. But for now, we do not have good alternatives available.

But I can't support fracking. Water is life. We cannot risk our precious and dwindling water supplies with this highly environmentally damaging technology. I wish Trump understood that. I find myself hoping that maybe someone will get through to him and he'll realize the left has some things right. Fracking should be banned. I notice my enthusiasm for a Trump presidency is waning, but I am still so very concerned about China, and the rise of communism, that I lean toward him when Biden is the only other option we are given.

The Election

Then the election happens. Votes are cast, but the vote count, including all the mail-in ballots, create a five-day delay in the final tally. Trump is confident he has won, and initially he is in the lead. It appears he's got this election in the bag. Republican enthusiasm is high as people are preemptively celebrating Trump's victory. However, in the end and after all the

Chapter 31: QAnon Cracking and Crumbling

mail-in ballots are counted, Biden is declared the winner. Democrats are crying in relief as many Republicans are calling out foul play.

With all the rumors about dead people voting, duplicated mail-in ballots printed in China, and votes for Trump being found in dumpsters, I do not trust the way this election has been handled. I see gobs of evidence on my news feeds that there was foul play all over the place. The MSM is of course celebrating that this is the final vote count, asserting it will not be contested. Fox News affirms Biden's win, although Tucker Carlson is clearly not at all aligned with Fox's official announcement and continues to present information arguing that this election is far from over.

I know I have no personal power in what will unfold. Either Trump's team will expose corruption and Trump will be declared the true winner, or those efforts will fail, and Biden's win will prevail. With the passage of the next couple weeks, I begin to accept the possibility that Biden is the 46th president.

Maybe he won't be a disaster, I tell myself, in an attempt to relieve my anxiety. Maybe he'll ban fracking as promised. And it seems Bernie and Our Revolution have made an impact on Biden's campaign promises. Perhaps he'll lean in a positive direction as president. He's already acknowledged that Trump has made some appropriate decisions with China, so maybe he will stick with some measures that keep the United States protected, rather than undoing Trump's work. I can only hope Biden will do some good if he makes it through to the inauguration. I feed these thoughts by listening to friends who are deeply relieved Biden has won this election.

2024 Reflections

While I no longer carry anything close to the fear I had about Trump prior to being in QAnon, I am also aware of ways in which some of his actions are not in alignment with my values. I would imagine that even his most ardent supporters would (privately) agree that these aspects of Trump's record give reason to question his ability to make ethical choices, considerate of the common good.

- Trump hired the political consulting firm Cambridge Analytica to manage many aspects of his 2016 campaign, including micro-targeted advertising.[399] In 2018, the company was forced to shut down after the discovery that it had engaged in illegal data harvesting from an estimated 87 million Facebook users. It had also engaged in blackmail (also known as "honey-trap stings") of high-level leaders[400,401] and psychological operations to manipulate Americans to vote for Trump. Cambridge Analytica filed for bankruptcy, rapidly liquidating and closing up shop to avert criminal charges.[402]

- In February 2020, Trump hired former Cambridge Analytica head of product Matt Oczkowski[403,404] to oversee the data program for his second presidential campaign.

- During Trump's 2016 run for president he said, "I could stand in the middle of 5th Avenue and shoot somebody and I wouldn't lose voters."[405] While I do not believe Trump has homicidal ideations, he comes off as insensitive in this crass characterization of his die-hard fan base.

- While the cages at the border were built during Obama's time in office, they were used under the Trump Zero Tolerance Policy[406,407] to separate men, women, and children. I understand this is a very complex topic, as it was unknown which kids were arriving with family and which were coming in with traffickers. What is obvious is that this was devastatingly traumatic to thousands of children. There had to be a better way, and Trump failed to find it.

- On June 1, 2020, in response to Trump's request, law enforcement used tear gas and rubber bullets against people peacefully protesting police brutality, clearing the way so that the president could walk to St. John's Church and hold up a bible for a photo shoot.[408]

- Trump initiated the Covid lockdowns, which had an enormous number of "unintended" negative impacts, including trillions of dollars of increased national debt, small business closures, unprecedented unemployment, delayed or missed medical screenings and pre-

Chapter 31: QAnon Cracking and Crumbling

ventative care, worsened chronic health conditions, increased mental health issues (depression, anxiety, suicide), social isolation and loneliness, delayed development in children (social skills, emotional development), increased domestic violence, school closures and learning disruptions, widening educational equity gaps, and more.

- Trump had many disagreements with Fauci and could have replaced him. However, he allowed Fauci to continue to serve as the head of the White House Coronavirus Task Force. When Trump's supporters expressed their dissatisfaction with his Covid policies, he failed to take personal responsibility and instead used Fauci as a scapegoat.[409]

- Trump actively uses ambiguous and potentially incendiary phrases, such as "when the looting starts, the shooting starts,"[410,411] and "fight like hell!"[412,413] (The linked endnotes show how differently each side spins his words.) He has also said "I am your revenge president," and as I type this (spring 2024), he is portending "a bloodbath" if he doesn't win this November's election. While I know Trump is a showman, and the "bloodbath" remark is a warning about the impending downfall of the US automotive industry under Biden's policies, I feel concerned that that some of his supporters might be taking these comments as encouragement to take violent militant actions on US soil.[414]

Words carry power, and Trump's choice of words are inducing tremendous fear in so many people whom I love and who I know share many of the same basic values all Americans do: We want peace, a government that serves people over profits, safety, affordable housing, good education, fertile soil, clean water, clean air, health and well-being for everyone, support for strong families, and the ability to enjoy a good retirement. Trump's rhetoric is not bringing our country together; it is amplifying our tendencies toward further enemy images, division, and in some cases violence. It is a major contributor to the destruction of our nation from the inside. I wish he would stop using fear, threats, and insults to further polarize our population.

Trump's Loss Is Not Part of the Plan

I don't know what to do with the fact that Trump's election loss was definitely not part of Q's Plan. And it disturbs me that JFK Jr. never made himself visible. Was that whole story concocted to capture attention of people who love the legacy of the Kennedys? Certainly, I've not seen a scrap of evidence from any Kennedy family members indicating that they are hiding their knowledge of JFK Jr.'s living presence here on earth. If the future of the world is hanging on this election and JFK Jr. is alive, it's unthinkable that he would not reveal himself here and now. Perhaps that too was a lie, just like the three reports that the Storm was happening, but never did.

I'm now 21 weeks in as a QAnon, and I've got much less faith in the Plan than I did since discovering it in June. It's extremely uncomfortable to consider that either the Plan is falling apart, or Q is not what I thought it was. I've been waiting for the Great Awakening, and for my convictions to be publicly redeemed. I was sure it was real. I had put all my hope and faith into Q. The challenges happening in our world are so complex and severe. I needed a hero to feel any sense of hope and agency rather than falling into despair. I don't like considering the real possibility Q was fake, but I'm losing the ability to discount it.

And while Q may not be the superhero I imagined he/she/they/it was, I am still mentally and emotionally hooked by all that I've been exposed to in these last five months. I cannot see the MSM the way I once did. I see evidence that mainstream news is a propaganda machine, and there's no changing that now. I see that pedophilia and child sex trafficking are huge problems in our world, but I have no indisputable evidence that they are spearheaded by an organized crime syndicate with satanic cult ringleaders at the helm. I cannot prove that children are being bred in hidden underground tunnels and harvested for adrenochrome. I don't know to what degree that could be true or just a fabrication.

I recognize now that Obama's Kenyan birth certificate must have been a digitally altered fake. There's no way he could have been born outside of the US without anyone catching it. I can't believe I had entertained that idea, but I recognized that I considered all kinds of ideas while I was loading

Chapter 31: QAnon Cracking and Crumbling

myself daily with up to a dozen hours of emotionally charged content. I wonder, Was I actively flooding my own psyche, as Larry had mentioned in "Across the Aisle?" Is this the confusion and disorientation Steve Bannon intended to unleash on the population when he spoke about "flooding the zone with shit"? Could this same form of disinformation overload be part of the Q phenomenon? Could I have been duped along with so many others?

Larry said something to the effect of "This strategy, 'flooding the zone,' means that Bannon's team is actively seeking to flood people with so much information they can't hold it all. It becomes overwhelming. And because the content is so emotional, it dysregulates the mental processes of those individuals. That triggers the fight or flight system in the body, creating more conflict and widening the polarization."

Is that what has been going on with me? The thought of that possibility is so much more than unsettling. If that is what Q really is, I've got nothing to put my hope in—nothing to hold onto. I cannot go back to that reality. I can't live with that level of fear and despair. I just can't.

Chapter 32:
The Fear Roller Coaster Persists

The thought that Q is not JFK Jr. and may not be a truly heroic deep government insider is too unsettling for me to consider for long. Less than a day later, that idea falls into the background of my thinking as I continue to go online, seeking more information that might establish clarity and certainty about what is really going on.

- I want to know the truth about our elections. If Biden won fair and square, then he should be the president. But it seems there was foul play, so I keep a finger on the pulse as all the inquiries into election fraud unfold, taking special interest in the expertise I see from award-winning inventor Jovan Hutton Pulitzer, who is seeking to use one of his ballot-scanning inventions to detect the differences between valid ballots and stuffed ones.[415,416]

- Rumors are flying stating that China has been working diligently to fulfill its 100-Year Plan to overtake the US as the dominating world power. China is on track to fulfill its mission by 2049.[417,418] I have nightmares about Chinese invasions.

- I am concerned about accelerating climate events, which could impact our food and transport systems.

- I don't know how to prepare for the possibility of an electromagnetic pulse (EMP) attack that could take down our grid and do irreversible damage to all electronics (and our ability to transact in any way) in a heartbeat.
- I fear the possibility of a civil war, especially as I intend never to own or operate a gun, and neither will most people among my friends and family. I surmise that if war were to break out on our home turf, our chances of survival would be small when up against an armed populace.
- I don't know what to do with the news that our economy is on the verge of implosion and the banking system is continuing to engage in activities that created the 2008 financial collapse. Rumors abound that the Federal Reserve might intentionally generate this form of crisis as a step in its end goal of creating a New World Order, complete with an AI-run surveillance state, and enforced through control of global finance via a central bank digital currency, akin to "one ring to rule them all," in *Lord of the Rings*.
- I hate that I still feel completely helpless when it comes to our political system. I feel our democracy is close to a complete sham, with few threads of hope remaining. But maybe I am fooling myself. Maybe there is no hope. Maybe we've already driven off the cliff. Maybe we are already in free fall.
- The vaccines are now rolling out. No one in my family is eligible yet, but they will be soon, and they are eager to receive them. Are they somewhat safe? Do I want to live if they all die? Would I be able to at least be with them in their final hours? Or would I be somehow barred from being by their sides due to some other form of crisis or my vaccine status?

My mind is filled with these horrible scenarios.

We are back in the San Francisco Bay Area, where the lockdowns continue to be severe. It seems most people recoil instinctively with a frightened

🪷 Chapter 32: The Fear Rollercoaster Persists 🪷

look on their faces if I step into their six-foot radius. It's such a jarring reality after the wonderful sense of freedom I had in Arizona. Now that we are back home, I'm isolated again. It's hard to simply take a walk through the neighborhood without someone getting upset about it. And even if I could see my friends and family, I feel emotionally safe with only a rare few. While I know my family members love me, we cannot talk about anything meaningful without getting mired in emotionally charged and painful debates about politics and vaccines. I am once again alone, with a load of stress that is beyond what I can bear, hardly anything worthwhile to do, and plenty of time to investigate all of these potential hazards (and more) on the internet as I try to figure out how to prepare for the worst.

> *I am once again alone, with a load of stress that is beyond what I can bear.*

A Level-Headed Perspective

I'm learning so much about catastrophic possibilities in this twenty-third week of being a QAnon. I can't keep all this information to myself. I need to share it with Stephen. We need to figure out how we are going to plan and prepare together. However, Stephen is easily frustrated when I am spinning in fear and listing off possible scenarios that may never happen. It does not feel safe to express all that I need to say to Stephen currently. And yet I need to talk to someone. This time I reach out to another dear friend and mentor, Reverend Patrick McCollum. We make plans to meet in person.

I have not been open with Patrick about my radical shift in political beliefs, as I have feared he might say something critical of me, as so many others have done. I am feeling completely under-resourced and cannot handle another ounce of criticism for my beliefs. Rather than using a direct approach to address the topics that are frightening to me, I skirt around the edges, revealing that I am confused about all the right-wing and QAnon-connected rumors.

> *Patrick, you know I've been participating in Across the Aisle and seeking to check out and better understand the full political spectrum for a number of months. I don't know what to make of the*

accusations coming from conspiracy theories. It kind of makes sense that those who have the most power in the world—the banking families and most powerful oligarchs—are making decisions for the whole of humanity and have the financial wherewithal to do so.

I see those decisions having horrible impacts: those who are impoverished are struggling more than ever. And the middle class is shrinking rapidly, while the billionaire class is growing faster than ever. I understand that a loss of the middle class is a direct threat to our democracy. It's hard to believe that greed and the pursuit of more 'stuff' could be driving this insanity. It seems narcissistic and sociopathic. I'm curious what you think about the idea that it could be more sociopathic than we want to imagine. I'm sure you've been following the Jeffrey Epstein case and all the names on his flight logs. Do you think it's possible that the power elite are using underage kids and sex scandals to bribe, blackmail, and control our political leaders?

Patrick begins with his usual look of thoughtfulness,

You know, the whole idea that QAnon is presenting, accusing the elite and Democrats of being Satan-worshiping pedophiles is, an idea many people want to believe. It's a whole lot easier to think the world is full of good and evil, and that if we just vanquish the evil we will have a peaceful world, than it is to realize and accept the vast complexity of the challenges we are facing.

I feel caught, as he immediately names QAnon, but I keep my cool as if I am simply engaging in an exploration… not seeking to question or challenge what I had put all my faith into since the fateful night of June 12th. I remain silent and interested in what Patrick will say next.

There are three things I would encourage you to consider," he continues. "*Here's the first. You just can't keep people quiet, especially when a large group is involved. Child sex trafficking and the abuse and supposed use of child sacrifice is so dark, and QAnon*

Chapter 32: The Fear Rollercoaster Persists

claims there are hundreds, if not thousands of people involved. If something like that were happening, we'd be seeing dozens of whistleblowers. People would not be willing to remain silent about something like that, even if their jobs or lives were on the line. No one can control that many people to that degree. It's simply not possible. People would be coming out right and left to expose and end crimes happening on that level.

No doubt there is some level of horrible shit happening to kids, and we can see evidence of that as people are working to expose it and protect children. We can see how Jeffrey Epstein was caught too. But just because he was having sex with underage girls does not mean that everyone who visited his island participated or even knew what he was doing. And when he was found out, he was held to account. You'd better believe that if it were happening on a much bigger level as QAnon suggests, it simply could not remain hidden, especially in these times when video cameras are everywhere, and people are actively seeking to expose anything they can find.

This makes sense. After all, Edward Snowden, Daniel Ellsberg, and Bradley (now Chelsea) Manning were all whistleblowers who exposed government abuses of power that did not even involve children. I do believe most humans are good-hearted and well meaning, and that only a very small percentage are sociopathic—incapable of real love and compassion. If these people would put their lives on the line to expose government documents, I have to imagine that many more people would be willing to jeopardize their well-being to save children from the kinds of abuses that QAnon and its ardent followers have accused the elite cabal of participating in.

Patrick continues,

Here's the second piece I invite you to consider. I know you've never run a company, but you've worked with teams, which would give you a sense of how complicated it can be to get different personalities with different ideas to align for a common goal. I ran a company with several hundred employees. It's a very difficult job to keep employees organized and coordinated with respect to a goal they agree to work toward. Having had that experience, I can guarantee you, it is impossible for any small group, much less a large group, to coordinate, organize, and manipulate leaders in high positions of power in order to rule the world. It's simply impossible. People have their own ideas and will not fall into the fold in the way QAnon or so many of these other conspiracy theories propose.

And even if there were some kind of ruling elite that was attempting to control the world, there would be infighting among the leadership team, and fallout among the minions, which again would lead to information leaks all over the place. Practically speaking, even if the elites wanted to do this, they would not be able to pull it off.

Seriously? I think to myself. How could anyone have lived through the past couple years and not recognize how astonishingly easily people have 'fallen into the fold'? I return my attention to my friend, committed to hearing his opinion here.

He goes on:

And here's the third. Notice how QAnon is always shifting focus? If you want a movement that will really make a difference and change the world, you don't do it by adjusting your priorities every couple of months. However, QAnon always has a changing theme along with a new hashtag. Just this year it was #FollowTheWhiteRabbit, then #ExposeBillGates, then #SaveThChildren, then #DeepState, then #DrainTheSwamps, then #ElectionFraud ... it just keeps going. Nothing's getting solved; It just keeps people hooked in sensationalism.

My mind flashes back on the changing themes I've experienced in these last few months as I continue to listen to Patrick.

In his final words on this topic, he says:

❀ Chapter 32: The Fear Rollercoaster Persists ❀

They keep their followers grasping onto the new thing in order to maintain emotional hooks and engagement in the whole QAnon story. A whole industry has been built around online influencers, and they depend on perpetual drama to keep paying the bills. But no continued focus actually empowers followers to make a difference. All of it ultimately leads to 'Vote for Trump and he'll fix everything.' This makes it into a political ploy, manipulating people to fall into a dangerous cult-like mentality, blinded by their fears and driven to follow Trump, whom they believe will save them. Followers get engaged into thinking that by posting memes and hashtags they are 'digital warriors,' making a difference to 'fight evil.' However, the evil they are fighting is mostly made up, with a few points of truth to make it seem real.

Meanwhile, the real problems are not being solved in any way by their actions. In fact, we are losing the political ability to solve the problems we are facing because QAnon leads people to believe in a fantasy connected to alt-right ideology, which is gutting environmental protections, denying the existence of racism and sexism, cutting taxes for the elites, and cutting social services to the people who really need some support in an increasingly economically challenging world.

Oy. This conversation with Patrick reminds me of the perspective and values I held prior to having watched *Fall of the Cabal*. Despite my respect for Patrick and his sense of the world, the nature of humanity, and his dedication to peace, I don't believe I could have been open-minded to this conversation a month ago. Still, my beliefs are less stubbornly fixed than they were, and my journey with *Across the Aisle* has continued to establish a new pattern in which I am increasingly willing to listen to a broad spectrum of views.

What Shape Is the Earth?

My trust in Netflix has been shaken, as it seems to be supporting satanic themes. For a while I choose not to watch any of its streaming content. Recently, I've seen only the trailer for *American Horror Story*,[419] in which Lady Gaga plays the main character, a seductress and murderer who feasts on the blood of her victims, feeding it to her kids. The trailer with its many parallels to what QAnons say is really happening in our world is disturbing enough. And it swiftly triggers my recollection of her and Marina Abramovic sipping red liquid off of their spoons next to what appears to be a dead woman in a bathtub of blood. Now Netflix has a show called *Lucifer*,[420] too. Are they intending to normalize satanic themes? Or is there some kind of redeeming value in this form of "entertainment?"

Netflix intended to host a series called *Cuties*[421] last August, which seemed to sexualize prepubescent girls while claiming to empower them. That one was taken down before it had a chance to air due to an upset around the possibility that it was grooming young girls for pedophilia.

Despite my recent lack of ease with Netflix, I need a distraction from all the catastrophic scenarios that keep running through my mind. I've been searching online in my quest to discern fact from fiction for months now, yet I feel just as ill prepared for future disasters as I was at the start. So, again I turn to Netflix to see what's available.

As I flip through trailers, I am intrigued by one of the more popular documentaries: *Behind the Curve*.[422] According to the filmmaker, millions of people now believe the earth is flat. One person says "I just want to be comfortable with the things that I believe," and another person who seems to be an influencer says "We are coming to a point where it is starting to be accepted." The first one speaks again, saying "All of us want to connect to people around things that make us unique." Yet another voice chimes in: "Now we are holding an international conference. We want to prove that the earth has no curvature, and if we can do that, it's game over."

Other believers say, "We've all been called names," "I've lost friends," and "they say I'm an idiot. People give me strange looks, and that's fine. Let them think what they want. They are just asleep, going through life completely unaware of the truth." At the end of the trailer, the primary Flat

🪷 Chapter 32: The Fear Rollercoaster Persists 🪷

Earth influencer in this documentary says he likes to think of the world through a lens of "the glass is half full," but in this case "the glass is being controlled by some sinister group."

The parallels between what I see in this trailer and the experiences I've had with QAnon are exceedingly uncomfortable for me to admit to myself. However, at this point in my journey, I am willing to take a deeper look. Besides, this video is not about Q or QAnon; it's about Flat Earthers. I am stunned to learn that millions of people could go so far as to believe that the earth is flat, given all the scientific evidence including pictures, videos, and testimony from astronauts demonstrating the obvious fact that the earth is round. How in the world could Flat Earthers deny all that evidence?

The primary Flat Earth influencer in this documentary shares, "When you get bored with normal conspiracies, you look for something new." They believe that dinosaurs were made up, and that the moon landing and all NASA projects are a complete fake, designed to fool the public into believing the earth is round. I discover that they also believe in just about every conspiracy theory I have seen in QAnon, from questioning the Warren Report and the involvement of the CIA in President Kennedy's assassination, to beliefs that the Illuminati and Freemasons are secret societies connected to the global banking families in a shared quest to dominate all human beings on earth.

The bookcase belonging to this influencer flashes on the screen, and it is filled to the brim with every kind of conspiracy theory book I could imagine. The documentary reveals how these people are working hard to prove that the earth is flat. They believe that when they pull off this feat, the whole set of lies about the nature of reality and the dark group who is controlling all of humanity will be revealed. I notice the similarities with the way I've been banking on the return of JFK Jr, believing his presence will redeem my words and actions and mark the beginning of a definitive end to the rule of the Cabal.

(Spoiler alert!) In this documentary however, these Flat Earthers are unable to prove the earth is flat. In fact, their two best experiments demonstrate that the earth is round. However, they conclude that their tests did not take everything into consideration. With that assessment established, they continue to work to prove the earth is flat, as if the future of humanity depends on it. The camaraderie and sense of being part of a world-changing and growing community is palpable in this movie, just as it is in my QAnon world.

Not only that, but as we follow a couple of the biggest Flat Earth influencers, it is readily apparent that they have no professional qualifications for anything they say, outside of their wholehearted belief and passion for the Flat Earth movement. There is nothing scientific or grounded in their podcasts. It is opinion, belief, and entertainment, spoken with an air of authority that does not factually exist. And millions of people buy into it. *Oy vey...*

Seeing this reality of the Flat Earth movement has now got me seriously questioning the "Q Intel Insiders" in a whole new way. Who are Stephen Ward, the Young Pharaoh, MonkeyWerx, Simon Parkes, Dave at the *X22 Report,* and others? And why is it that I've been assuming they are trustworthy sources of news? Is it only because they are echoing what I want to believe? Affirming my cognitive bias? Could it be that some of the fact-checks and Wikipedia pages are more accurate than the so-called news I have been simmering in for months? I search for mainstream sources to discover who these characters are and cannot find anything that would make them credible with respect to world news and politics.

Oh my God. Have I had the wool pulled over my eyes this whole time? What is real and what is not? How can I discern truth from falsehood, propaganda, and just plain bullshit? I wonder in mild panic. I don't know what to think about all of this, but I have lost interest in most QAnon content and am only willing to listen to people who have real and confirmable qualifications now. I continue to tune in to Robert David Steele,[423] David Martin,[424] Michael Flynn,[425] Sidney Powell,[426] Tim Pool,[427] and Tucker Carlson,[428] who have at least some verifiable credentials as I track election rumors. I also seek to stay attuned to the so-called "Disinformation Dozen" and other experts, to keep tabs on Covid. My interest in remaining alert to catastrophic potentials, the election, and China does not wane. I want truth and I want safety.

Chapter 33:
Self-Induced Emotional Torture

On December 1, 2020, I send my dad three articles: the first is from HumansBeFree.com, titled "Stanford Professor of Medicine: Covid-19 Has a 99.95% Survival Rate for People Under 70";[429] the second one is from VaccineImpact.com, titled "Covid Vaccines: Biological Weapons of Mass Destruction";[430] and third, from Forbes, titled "Covid-19 Vaccine Protocols Reveal That Trials Are Designed to Succeed."[431] I continue to have deep distrust for the way this pandemic is being handled as I build evidence for my perspectives, hoping to protect the people I love.

    The next day my dad sends me an article from *Science* titled "Absolutely remarkable: No one who got Moderna's vaccine in the trial developed severe Covid-19."[432] He adds, "I don't know what to make of the second article you sent me. It's a deep dive into conspiracy theories that present themselves as facts. Some bits of it could be fact based, but a massive plot to depopulate and enslave the world is so draconian that I just can't let my mind go there unless I want to cultivate a paranoid mindset. I know that doing so would destabilize my emotional equilibrium, making my spiritual practices impossible to maintain. Why would I do that to myself? And just so you know, the third article from *Forbes* that you sent me is two months old. I just sent you an update."

I respond immediately, "The ruling-elite plan to vaccinate most Americans by late summer or early spring. The *New York Times* is great at predicting the future because it is owned by the global oligarchs who are creating what lies ahead. I do not trust this at all. What if it *is* draconian? Then we all die in the Armageddon together?" My body is shaking with fear.

Dad's response comes quickly, "Katrina, you're torturing yourself with these nightmare scenarios that you are driving into your consciousness. You are creating a neural network of fear. For the sake of your emotional well-being, it might be worth considering going off these themes entirely and cultivating uplifting topics to focus on in your life."

I send him a sad face then write, "I don't know how. To me it's like trying to put on rose-colored glasses as the Chinese Communist Party is setting up to take over everything and everyone. I'm resigned, depressed, disheartened, scared, and frustrated. I watch some of my friends from my health freedom[433] community take actions I want to take, but I can't. I just know that the criticism and hate I'll receive from most of my liberal friends is too great. I only have a dozen people from my old life who are seeking to sound the Covid alarm with me."

His encouragement continues, "You must develop a strong intention to go cold-turkey. Exert iron self-discipline until the wonderful thoughts, ideas, sentiments, and spiritual nutrients that you're feeding into your brain day in and day out create a deep neural network of joy, love for life, and a sense of the sacred enveloping you."

My dad's practical and spiritual guidance has been resonant for me more often than not. And I can hear the wisdom in his words. But I do not know how to move from where I am—spinning in stress and fear, to where he's suggesting I should be—attending first and foremost to my mental and emotional well-being.

"Dad," I retort, "they are seeking to create herd immunity, via mass vaccination of the population, by late spring. The agenda I've been warning you about for months is happening."

"Katrina, you are right. I didn't think the vaccine passport idea would ever fly, but it is. But that's not sufficient reason to put your emotional well-

Chapter 33: Self-Induced Emotional Torture

being in the gutter. You're up against an existential choice," he responds. "What you do will determine whether you rise up to new heights of spiritual awareness and self-actualization or succumb to the pervasive fear and paranoia that perpetuates the self-torment you're currently experiencing."

Despite his sage reflections and guidance, my fear is blocking my ability to connect with his reasoning.

"I feel like I am spinning my wheels here," I write back. "I'm alone. There's only virtual connection. I have no community and at this point very little family connection. Isn't it appropriate to act when one perceives existential threat? Right now, all the spiritual stuff seems like a bypass, a form of rose-colored glasses. What would you do if you could see Hitler rising to power? Meditate?" I ask as if the idea were absurd. For the moment I forget that this is exactly what he sees and fears with the possibility of another term with Trump as president.

Dad affirms, "Yes, spiritual action first and foremost. Fill your own cup first, then, take action to promote peace, joy, and love in your connections with others."

I still can't wrap my head around his words. Promote peace, love and joy while watching draconian agendas being fulfilled? Tell those who are walking into the Covid vaccine version of the gas chambers that this jab will save their lives so they can feel safe and happy before they are exterminated?

Dad continues: "Sweetie, do you think Jesus, the Buddha, Baha'u'llah, and so many other saints were wearing rose-colored glasses?" He asks, listing a few of the many spiritual masters whose wisdom has guided me in the past.

I answer, "No. They accepted the fact that there is suffering."

Dad adds, "And then transcended."

I seek to stick with his logic, although my responses continue to be colored by my current state of emotion. "Jesus accepted the crucifixion. I don't know how to transcend reality, except to die."

"What about Ammachi?" He asks, referring to the hugging saint from India.

"I haven't seen what she does through a genocide," I start. "But I don't think she is afraid of death. She probably tells people to seek God and comfort each other. But ultimately, she can't stop earthquakes or famines."

"Honey, we're not in a genocide right now." He writes, "Spinning horror stories about a possible future is the most efficient way to torture oneself."

Despite his efforts, my mind is still spinning in a multitude of fears.

"I see the vaccination agenda as the first major step," I assert. "It is rolling out as was predicted, with no alternative to the mRNA option. I'd much rather get the virus."

My dad stays with me. "Can you forget the vaccination theme long enough to take a moment, breathe deeply, and feel the sacred dimension of life? That's the path to freedom from fear, anger, and despair. Just take each moment and milk it for the beauty that's there if we attune ourselves to it."

"I have lost my feeling of connection to the sacred dimension. I used to find it with people in my community," I write, as I become present once again to all the social losses I've recently endured.

My dad tries a different tactic. "You're living in a horror movie. You have a choice to turn your mind's internal TV to a different station. At the moment, you're drinking spiritual arsenic."

> **You're living in a horror movie. You have a choice to turn your mind's internal TV to a different station. At the moment, you're drinking spiritual arsenic.**

I reply with a sad face.

He adds, "It's not easy, but vitally important."

"Okay" I write, feeling somewhat defeated.

He ends with, "I'm going back into meditation now. I love you and will always be there for you unconditionally."

"Thank you. I love you too." I write, feeling how much I really do.

•••

Chapter 33: Self-Induced Emotional Torture

Two days later I send him an article from CNBC.com, titled "Would you be willing to get a Covid vaccine in exchange for a $1,500 stimulus check? How one bold proposal would work."[434]

"Interesting!" Dad writes, adding, "How are your spirits today, Katrina?"

It's not the response I imagined I would get. And given yesterday's back and forth, I decide to try to avoid repeating our previous conversation.

"I'm taking it day by day and seeking to stay more emotionally balanced. I'm trying to ask myself 'what would someone who loves herself do right now?'"

Dad affirms, "That's a great way to bootstrap yourself back to a place of grace and ease. Find gratitude each day and in every moment consider what nurtures you."

Later in the day I send him an article from the *Wall Street Journal* titled "China Is National Security Threat No. 1."[435]

Dad does not respond.

The next day my tirade continues. "There is evidence that the global Covid response is in violation of the Nuremburg Code."[436]

Again, Dad does not respond, but it might be that his internet is down.

I try again a couple hours later, as I am feeling anxious once again and hope he might provide some co-regulation. "Hey Dad, I'm in another round of conflict with Stephen. This time his work is stretching him to the max, and he is continuing to lose patience with me, sometimes slipping into name-calling."

Dad still does not respond.

The next morning, now twenty-six weeks into my adventure down the QAnon rabbit hole, Dad writes, "How are things today?" Adding a heart to the end of his message.

I respond saying, "It's better than yesterday. He's not angry anymore, but has expressed concerned at the possibility that this level of stress could continue for years. How are you?"

"I'm well," he responds, adding several emojis.

Our chatter that day is short as I do not want to darken his happy state. Meanwhile, Stephen is on edge.

"Katrina, your anxiety is wearing on me. As much as I love you, I don't know how much longer I'll be able to endure being around you. If you don't get a handle on this, it's going to break me. It will break us." It's been almost six months. His patience is running thin.

Stephen's words land hard. I have no doubt he's speaking his truth. If the tables were turned, I wouldn't want to endure being around me either. This state of seemingly endless fear, anxiety, and paranoia is not only eating away at me, it's taking a toll on my ability to be present, loving, and attentive—not only to Stephen, but also to my now very small social circle of politically left-of-center Bay Area friends. I know I need to find a way to shift my state, but I don't know how to do that while adequately addressing all the things I am frightened might happen.

Chapter 34:
Free Yourself from Anxiety

A couple of days later my dad sends me a dharma talk from meditation and mindfulness teacher Jack Kornfield, entitled "Beauty and Human Goodness Amidst It All."[437] Kornfield starts off by acknowledging how easy it is to get lost in the problems and crises that we face, suggesting there is a bigger picture that is essential to grasp, especially in these divisive and uncertain times. He asserts that learning how to navigate this kind of predicament is at the heart of the teachings he received from his spiritual teacher, Mahasai Sayadaw.

Kornfield tells a story about his time in a monastery in Burma (around 1970), where he studied Theravada Buddhist meditation practices. Bombers often flew overhead, and explosions were regularly heard only a couple miles away. The students would ask the teacher what they should do and how they should prepare. The most common answer they received was a smile as he would say, "It's uncertain, isn't it?" before continuing with the lesson as if it were a non-issue. Kornfield's teacher embodied the ability to be calm and joyful, focused on the present moment and the immediate task of teaching, regardless of the obvious uncertainty of the situation. Kornfield goes on to express the wisdom of living peacefully in the midst of precariousness.

If Kornfield and his colleagues were able to cultivate inner peace and live relatively normal lives in a monastery while bombers were flying overhead and dropping explosives only a couple miles away, perhaps I can live in uncertainty too as my concerns are not imminent threats; they are mostly fearful projections into the future. I take a moment to recognize that no immediate threat is to be seen from the comfort of my home; the sun is shining, birds are singing, and the only airplanes flying overhead are passenger planes.

With this insight a door opens. I am one step closer to being able to live in uncertainty. However, even with this source of inspiration, my fears continue to spin, and I feel the constant effects of cortisol overload in my body. Despite my efforts to meditate and think positive thoughts, the fears keep creeping in, as are my compulsions to go online. At best, I curb my web time, attempting to keep it to social connection in order to feel less alone. But it seems that every time I go on the internet, I cannot help but to read or see something that restimulates all the dread that lies just under the surface, the fear I am trying to override.

Later that day, my dad sends me a conversation between Oprah and Eckhart Tolle called "Free Yourself from Anxiety."[438]

While many QAnon influencers do not like Oprah, I still do. I have seen nothing convincing that connects her to anything dark or corrupt. The only post of any substance I've seen from QAnon influencers is the one snippet where she talks about having been molested as a child. I've never seen anything else of substance, and this video does not paint her in a dark light in my eyes. It just means she's willing to talk openly about an adult touching her inappropriately when she was a child. She is not shaming or judging herself for what was done to her. She's bringing awareness to the fact that this does happen to children. She's making it safe to talk about this uncomfortable topic.

It takes a stretch of the imagination to begin to understand the view of her that many QAnons, including Janet Ossebaard, have—that she is near the top of the power structure with the Cabal and among the most protected—that she'll be one of the last to fall.

Chapter 34: Free Yourself from Anxiety

2023 Reflection – What I learned and personal reflection

While writing this book, I checked the website dedicated to Q drops and did a search to see what Q has posted about Oprah. Her name is mentioned only once in all the drops, and the message is simply "Oprah show." It includes no context and no link to which of her thousands of shows Q might be pointing to. Like most of the Q drops, it has no clear meaning and relies on the human phenomenon of "apophenia," the tendency to perceive meaningful connections between unrelated things. It's now obvious to me that whatever references I had seen connecting Oprah to the Cabal are fabricated.

In "Free Yourself from Anxiety," Oprah and Eckhart begin by discussing the way beliefs quickly become one's sense of identity. This is because of the ego. As Eckhart says, "Who you are—the deep 'I'—is consciouness. It is this mistaken sense of identity—people confusing their beliefs with their personal identity—that is generating the fierce divisiveness in our current political climate."

I now recognize how thoroughly I have been identifying with QAnon and the right. For months I have defended their pronouncements as if I were defending my sense of self. And my friends and family have been reacting to me, some distancing themselves from me, and others resorting to verbal abuse. They too have been clinging to their beliefs as if those beliefs define who they are. But at this point in time, my attachment to these QAnon political viewpoints is rapidly fading. They do not have the same grip on my mind as before.

Oprah and Eckhart continue their conversation, exploring how our minds can make other people appear to be monsters, overshadowing our ability to see another person's humanity. This is how mental constructs can dehumanize others, creating fertile grounds for violence against other human beings to occur.

I notice this is the same concept as NVC's "enemy images," which points out how mentally constructed judgmental stories can separate us from others. When we see someone else as an enemy, we are likely to automatically evaluate them as bad and deserving of punishment. This phenomenon is becoming increasingly obvious in the way QAnons relate to the rumors of a coming Storm.

Enemy images make cruel behavior easier.

As I look directly at Q drops, I note that Q has not clearly described what the Storm is. It's not even clear that the Storm is a slew of arrests, as QAnons assert it is. But the internet influencers have described what they think Q means in great detail. They have built piles of evidence by combining actual facts and fabricated rumors in support of their claims that the leaders they have identified are guilty criminals, pedophiles and satanists. These grand allegations include many well-known figures, but mostly Democratic politicians and Hollywood celebrities. Many QAnons hold the belief that the evidence against the people they list is overwhelming and it's only a matter of time before indictments are pursued and arrests are made.

It is becoming apparent to me that the promise of the Storm, and the way it is described among QAnons is feeding the all-too-human tendency to generate enemy images, driving followers toward violence as the necessary solution. At least one QAnon believed he had strong enough evidence to take justice into his own hands. Edgar M. Welch, the Comet Pizza shooter, believed he was rescuing children from Hillary Clinton's child sex trafficking ring. His reason for blasting into Comet Ping Pong would have been noble if only it were based on fact.[439] Any human with a heart would want to protect children from abuse. But as Welch, a man whose friends would describe as a loving father and good neighbor, would discover, "the intel was not 100%." He admitted his guilt and was sentenced to prison. The enemy images generated by the disinformation on Comet Ping Pong had caused real-world consequences, including traumatizing employees and patrons and sending a man with no prior convictions to prison.

Chapter 34: Free Yourself from Anxiety

It is coming to the forefront of my attention that factions of QAnon are not peaceful people as I previously imagined. I can also see how this tendency to dehumanize one another based on differences in political beliefs is a way our US society is being polarized and ripped apart. The "I'm right and you're wrong" sparring is being taken to the extreme. Republicans are accused of being racists and fascists. Democrats are accused of being pedophiles, satanists and communists. Everybody points their fingers at each other as if the other is to blame for a potentially cataclysmic future. People are gripped by dehumanizing beliefs about those who disagree with them. I too have been gripped by fears about the future and have noticed the rise of dehumanizing thoughts passing through my mind when feeling frustrated about those who disagree with me.

At the end of the conversation between Oprah Winfrey and Eckhart Tolle, Eckhart shares this: "The only thing you can take responsibility for is yourself—your own state of consciousness. In any situation, whether it has to do with a collective, political, personal, or any situation, what is primary is your state of consciousness with which you face that situation."

This message resonates with my inner sense of things. I understand what he is saying, what my dad has been saying, and what I need to do: I need to take complete personal responsibility for my state of consciousness.

Chapter 35:
False Evidence Appearing Real

The next day I still spin in fear. I seem to have become habituated to it. It is self-perpetuating. I don't know how to get my fearful thoughts to quiet down. I don't know how to redirect my attention and be at choice for my state of consciousness. Stephen notices I am unusually quiet and asks me what's going on.

"I don't know," I respond with nothing further to say.

The truth is I don't know how to address my fears. And I don't want to make him endure any more, especially given how he seems to be hanging only by a string to the love we have shared.

"I am sorry I lost my patience yesterday," he offers.

"It's okay," I respond, seeking to reassure him before giving him a window into what I am going through. "I understand I've been spinning in fear. I've hardly been present with you since we returned from Arizona. When we were there, I was able to distract myself from all the bad things happening, but now that we are stuck in our home again and hardly anyone in my community here sees the world as I do, I feel isolated and agitated. I want a human connection and a shared sense of reality—grounded in something that makes sense. I keep going online. Every time I do, I restimulate my fears. I know I need to get a handle on this. I know I need to learn how to be okay with the uncertainty of horrible things that could happen, but I don't know how to shift from where I am to where I need to be."

Stephen's strategic mind leads him to suggest, "Let's look at your fears, one by one, and see if we can address them so they have less of a grip on your mind."

> **Let's look at your fears, one by one, and see if we can address them so they have less of a grip on your mind.**

I feel a wave of relief. "Okay," I reply.

"So, what is the first one you want to work with?" he asks.

"Chinese invasions," I say. "I keep seeing reports that Chinese troops are establishing themselves in Canada and hiding out in New York. I know the People's Liberation Army (PLA) is huge, and we could be overrun if they successfully send troops here."

My fear has been heightened by recent Twitter posts from a QAnon backer with nearly 50,000 followers, which claim that tens of thousands of Chinese troops have assembled along Maine's border with Canada and that an F-16 fighter that crashed last week in Michigan was actually shot down—presumably by the Chinese.

Stephen responds, "Well, first off, I doubt China is an immediate threat, and I can't imagine they would send troops into the US. I bet if you look at the news sources, they are unverifiable. I have seen absolutely no evidence that Chinese soldiers are anywhere near our border. If they were, that would make the news and our military would be all over it. I suggest you check your sources, as this information is likely coming from highly unreliable reporters."

At this point, I am willing to use MediaBiasFactCheck.com (MBFC) as a part of my criteria for separating more trustworthy news sources from those that are simply opinion, misinformation, lies, or propaganda.

We take time together to do a bit of research. The first article I find is in the *Toronto Sun,* which verifies my claim to some degree. According to MBFC, the *Toronto Sun* is mostly factual. However, it is right- biased, uses

Chapter 35: False Evidence Appearing Real

loaded words, publishes misleading reports, and omits information that may damage conservative causes. This article reports that Trudeau allowed the PLA to train in winter warfare in Canada and received harsh criticism for having done this.[440] The title is ominous: "China's troops trained in Canada against which country?" However, there is no evidence they are targeting any country, only a suggestion that they are.

Next, we find an article from the *Military Times*.[441] MBFC assesses this news outlet as highly factual, saying "This source has minimal bias and uses very few loaded words. The reporting is factual and usually sourced."

This article begins: "It may seem like an updated version of the 1966 comedy 'The Russians Are Coming! The Russians Are Coming!'[442] but there is nothing funny about conspiratorial ravings from the Twitterverse that Chinese troops massed along the border with Maine were schwacked in an airstrike. While chatter about Chinese troops in Canada is steeped in fantasy, it is this kind of disinformation that presents a real threat, according to a couple of experts in the information battlespace."

"Okay," I voice with a sigh of relief and frankly a bit of embarrassment. "I'll admit this was another piece of disinformation I've been riled up about for a couple of months. I can let it go now."

I am grateful for Stephen's willingness to walk through my fears with me.

"So, what's the next one you want to tackle?" he asks.

"How about the possibility of an economic crash?" I offer.

"Katrina, here's the thing to know about that. The threat of an economic crash is almost always to be found somewhere in the news. People make money from these fear-laden prognostications. They try to make people feel financially vulnerable, then they offer enticing 'buy now' products or services. Usually, they'll try to convince you to buy silver or gold, but now it's cryptocurrency too. Sometimes people try to sell you 'insider information,' promising that if you follow their investment strategies, you will get rich when the stock market crumbles. There are all kinds of unethical ways in which some people try to make a buck at the cost of their customers. Sometimes people lose their fortunes to these schemes."

My mind is reeling as I see evidence for everything he is saying.

He continues; "I've been studying the financial world since my early twenties. You know that. There's so much to understand, it's really hard for most people to dedicate the time and focus required to understand how local and global markets work, so most people find experts they can trust—people who have long-standing records in the markets. I trust our financial advisor. He's fiscally conservative, which I appreciate, as he's taken great care of our portfolio. If you'd like, we can call him together and you can ask him any of your questions. In the meanwhile, I can assure you, I've done the research and while there will unfortunately be some kind of stock market correction in the coming years, it will not be nearly as severe as the news you are reading says it will be. It won't be happening any time soon. And even if it did, the right action to take is to stay in the market. It always has its ups and downs, and it consistently moves in an upward direction, which on average is generally close to 10% a year."

I know Stephen understands the markets far better than I do. While his response to me is reassuring, I take him up on his offer to chat with our financial advisor, Mark. Mark listens to my worries and suggests additional risk-management strategies we could entertain. However, he says we are generally well positioned for what the experts agree is happening in the market.

With this fear sufficiently addressed, Stephen asks me what's next.

"The vaccines." I state, knowing I need not say more.

"I understand you are highly concerned about these vaccines," he begins. "And I understand your reasoning. The testing was pushed through much quicker than is usual for vaccines. In addition to that, mRNA has been used to treat cancer but has not been used for this purpose. In that way, it is relatively new. While I am not nearly as concerned as you are, I am also hesitant to take this vaccine. I share your interest in tracking alternatives. However, neither one of us will even have the option to take it until some time in the spring or early summer. By then, tens of thousands of people will have taken it, so we will know if it has unwanted side effects."

I quickly add, "But we won't know about long-term ramifications."

Chapter 35: False Evidence Appearing Real

"It's true," he admits. "We won't know about possible long-term impacts for years. However, the worst side effects most commonly show up in the first few weeks after injection."

My fear is easing, but not sufficiently addressed. I express to Stephen what continues to drive my fears. "I can't get people to wait until we have more information. I am concerned about my parents and grandparents taking this vaccine as soon as it's available. It could kill them."

Stephen responds, "Katrina, I know this is hard to accept, but you can't get others to wait. Everyone has their own perspective of what is in their best interest. Based on what you've seen, which likely has some amount of misinformation," Stephen starts cautiously, as he chooses to be generous in assessing my information choices, "I understand that at this time you cannot even imagine taking the vaccine and you may never change your mind in this regard. That is fine, Katrina. As I have said previously, I will never force you to endure a medical treatment you do not wish to have."

He asserts, "Similarly, other people have come to their own conclusions and no matter what you say, you are highly unlikely to change their minds. What is much more likely is that your attempts to get them to avoid the vaccine will create stress and conflict in these relationships.

"We don't have complete information. There are many unknowns. And there is accumulating evidence that strongly suggests these vaccines will be as safe and effective as any previous one. Everyone needs to choose for themselves and live with the consequences of their choices," he says in resonance with my value for freedom of choice and personal autonomy.

He's right, I think to myself before I am willing to say this out loud. Just as I am deeply seated in my right to decline this vaccine, others have every right to choose for themselves.

"Okay," I say to Stephen. "I see your point. There is nothing I can do to prevent the people I love from taking this vaccine when their research has led them to want to take it. I pray it is not nearly as harmful as I fear it might be, and I can see that my fear is not helping the situation at all. I must let this go and let people do what they want to do. If they do have reactions, all I can do is show up to help them through whatever health challenges might arise."

"Yes, that is all you can do," he agrees. "What else is causing you fear?" he asks knowing there is more.

"I'm afraid of a civil war," I share. "I am afraid of how many people are buying guns and ammo. It seems we are being set up to fight each other, divided along party lines as we were in the first Civil War. I don't want to own a gun, and so I feel helpless when it comes to this possibility. I'm afraid of violent conflict, robberies, and shootings. I don't know what to do with that."

"It's true there is a lot of tension and divisiveness in our country right now," he begins, "but a civil war is not imminent."

We look into this together and acknowledge that according to Wikipedia many of the warning signs of a second civil war are present, including:

- Democratic decline, signs of anocracy, and authoritarian movements.
- The polarizing effect of a winner-takes-all[443] two-party system.[444]
- Radicalized citizenry with a record-high gun ownership rate.
- Irreconcilable beliefs about critical issues (such as media censorship and who won an election).
- Political tension within the U.S. military.
- Negative economic conditions (such as growing federal debt, income inequality, and inflation).
- A steady rise in political violence (particularly among far-right domestic terrorists).
- A loss of faith in the legitimacy of the government.
- And the normalization of open discussion of civil war.

However, as this Wikipedia page also points out:

"Skeptics claim that the occurrence of a civil war in the modern US is essentially impossible due to certain present-day conditions, including:

Chapter 35: False Evidence Appearing Real

- A lack of two organized standing armies.
- An absence of clear geopolitical lines (such as North versus South).
- A vastly nonviolent majority on both sides of the political spectrum.
- An absence of state-sponsored violence by political leaders.
- The nation's position as the wealthiest democracy in the world (which acts as a deterrent to the cost of war).
- Significant disincentives to interstate war (e.g., deeply shared economies across state lines)."[445]

These arguments demonstrating that a civil war could not happen any time soon are sufficient for my nerves to settle on this one… At least for now.

"What else have you got?" Stephen asks, seeming hopeful, but also practicing patience and perseverance in this exercise.

"An EMP strike," I say. He understands what I am talking about, as I've expressed my fear of an electromagnetic pulse attack to him previously. Such an offensive could wipe out all electronics and our energy grid, resulting in a loss of electrical power to most of the country. This would last for some unknown number of years before the transformers could be repaired or replaced. Given we are dependent on Chinese manufacturing for our transformers, we would be reliant on their goodwill to get our country up and running again.

"Katrina," he starts, "There are so many horrible things that could happen, and so many frightening potential events that have been predicted in the past. But as you've seen, none of them have happened. Remember how our parents went through nuclear bomb drills as kids? An alarm would go off and they were told to hide under their desks. But our country was able to successfully navigate the possibility of a nuclear attack. And remember when there was a hole in the ozone layer, and we were told that our atmosphere would be destroyed, and life may not survive? We figured that one out too."

I nod in agreement.

"Remember Y2K?" He asks. "There was so much fear that all our computer systems would fail as we moved from the 1900s to the 2000s. Hordes of people purchased extra food and emergency supplies preparing for the worst. And yet nothing bad ever happened. It was a non-event.

"There's always someone sounding the alarm that something horrible is about to happen," Stephen continues. "But most of the time these are false threats. Remember, fear stands for 'false evidence appearing real.' I assure you if a real threat is on the way, we will have time to respond."

With this last comment, my fears significantly subside. It seems what remains is the result of having been fearful for so long that my baseline cortisol levels have gone off kilter. But my fears are no longer backed by sufficient information to keep myself in this tailspin.

My fears are no longer backed by sufficient information to keep myself in this tailspin.

"Please don't spend your precious life worrying about things that will likely never happen," Stephen pleads with me. "You've got a beautiful life. You've got people who love you. You have a garden to tend, art projects to create, and clients to serve. Please spend your time caring for what is real— what is in your life now. It's beautiful out today. Get offline. Get some exercise, do yoga, meditate more, and get back into your affirmation practice. It seems that's been helpful before. Enjoy yourself, Katrina. The future is not guaranteed, but it never has been, and yet we are still here. Be grateful for the life you have right now!"

This is the final pep talk I need. I know I need to shift my focus, as well as the biochemical patterns of fear and stress I've been unintentionally cultivating in my body. I make a commitment to take myself off social media and stop reading world news. All I keep is my Instagram feed, which has no news whatsoever. On that channel I receive spiritual quotes, wisdom from a holistic psychologist, and athletic and nutritional tips. I also enjoy amazing performances in dance and acrobatic arts. I enjoy scrolling for maybe a half hour at a time, but don't get sucked in like I do with Facebook, YouTube, Twitter, or uncensored media platforms like Rumble, Bitchute,

Chapter 35: False Evidence Appearing Real

and Telegram. I remove all addictive social media apps from my phone and make a commitment not to open them on my computer. It's time to protect myself from any possibility of reentering into the fear-porn trance I've been marinating in for these past six months. It's time to reclaim my life.

"I love you, ya know." Stephen says with a smile.

"Yes. I know. Thank you, Stephen. I love you too."

PART 5:

ReQovery

Chapter 36:
Back to Life

Emotional and Biochemical System Reset

The next morning, I begin my day differently. Rather than picking up my cell phone and compulsively checking my text, email, and social media channels, I start with a twenty-minute meditation. Sitting in stillness proves exceedingly difficult, as my mind is still rapid-firing, and I can feel stress hormones circulating in my body. While I seek to focus all my attention on my breath, it proves nearly impossible. So instead, I focus on tracking my body sensations, which are uncomfortable but so distinct that they are easy to witness. They noticeably shift as I keep my awareness keenly upon them.

Having completed my meditation, I create a seat for myself in front of a mirror. I have a collection of affirmations with me that I had previously accumulated, from both from Louise Hay and Reverend Michael Bernard Beckwith at Agape International. I begin my practice using a basic technique Louise developed when she worked with terminal AIDS patients in the mid-1980s. The practice is one to cultivate self-love and positive energy. I follow the practice in the way she suggests; I look at myself in the mirror, making eye contact as I say to myself, "Katrina, I love you. I really, really love you!" I repeat this affirmation at least 10 times, generating the energetic frequency of committed love as a mother would speak to her beloved child.

While I have found this practice to be challenging, when I have managed to do it for several months in the past, it helped me out of a dark depression. That prior experience makes it easier to do now. I am no longer distracted by the immediate self-criticism of the voice inside my head pointing out the increasing number of gray hairs and wrinkles or how my skin tone isn't perfect. Instead, I stay present, maintaining eye-contact with myself and holding my heart as wide open as possible.

At first, I can tell that I do not believe the statement that I love myself. As much as I seek to generate love, the look in my eyes reveals distrust. But this is a familiar experience, and I know I'll eventually work through my own mental barriers. So, I stick with it, knowing this practice will help me generate the neurotransmitters responsible for the experience of love and relaxation. I keep faith that oxytocin, serotonin, and dopamine will eventually override my stress hormones.

Spiritual Wisdom

"There is a big difference between loving yourself and being selfish. When you truly understand what it is to know and love yourself, you cannot help but to love and serve others. When you understand this at the core level of your being, you will be on the path Home."
~ author unknown (Hidden Hand material)

After completing this practice, I continue with my affirmations:
- I am willing to release the need for this condition.
- I am worth loving.
- I relax and enjoy life.
- I know whatever I need to know is revealed to me in the perfect time.
- I recognize the presence of Universal Love as my own precious life.

Chapter 36: Back to Life

- Cosmic energy restores my body-temple and my mind.
- The sacred space of Divine Love is my dwelling place.

I repeat each of these affirmations, generating positive emotional energy while maintaining eye contact with myself.

I feel a shift in my body after only 20 minutes of doing this mirror work. I am noticeably more calm and joyful. I revisit these quotes later in the day, further anchoring new thoughts and feelings into my mind and body as I replace stress with peace and joy.

Next, I work out while watching a TV series on Netflix that is entertaining and heartwarming, with messages about friendship, loyalty, and virtue. It is a welcome escape from the stress I have been experiencing. And the cardiovascular exercise supports my sense of well-being.

I finish it off with a smoothie before carrying on with my day.

I notice how I've ignored my garden for too long. Some of the plants are clearly suffering, and weeds have taken over. I remove my shoes and enjoy being barefoot as I begin the cleanup work, delighting in the warm rays of the sun on my body. The gentle breeze feels delightful on my skin as I catch the fragrance of jasmine growing nearby. I don't know how long it's been since I've noticed the birds singing, but it's such a sweet sound. Ahhh… how have I lost track of all of this? This is what it's like to live in peace and joy. It's hard to believe I've been missing out on these simple pleasures for so long.

Dealing with My Post-Q Mind

I am now highly skeptical of anything coming from QAnon influencers. And while I question whether any aspects of Q may be legitimate, I cannot prove or disprove who or what Q is, nor can I prove or disprove the facts surrounding most conspiracy theories that have (rightly or wrongly) become connected in some way to QAnon. Stephen reminds me that we cannot and do not know what is real, other than what we can see, touch, and feel directly in front of us; everything else is subject to manipulation, exaggeration and outright lies. He asserts, "So many people claim they know the truth, but very few, if any, really do."

> *So many people claim they know the truth,*
> *but very few, if any, really do.*

I wonder if there could be governments and political figures around the world involved in supporting and benefiting from the industry of child sex-trafficking. I wonder about the reality of human beings engaging in satanic practices, and whether or not they do so as individuals or in some organized way. I wish I knew whether Fauci and Gates are actually seeking to end the pandemic and develop medicines for the benefit of humanity or if they have been lying to the public and profiting from their investments in vaccines. I want to know if the Covid vaccines are safe or not.

Intelligent, well-educated people and authority figures hold diametrically opposed views on so many topics. All I know is that it is a waste of my precious mental and emotional well-being to keep trying to separate the wheat from the chaff. All that effort has led me to is an overwhelming burden, characterized by conflict, anxiety, and depression.

But I don't know how to simply eliminate all the influences impressed upon my mind. I've succumbed to tens of thousands of impressions over the course of these last six months. Any topic connected to politics or Hollywood stirs up associations, thoughts, and beliefs that still have some grip on me. I can't help but see news stories come across the screen of Stephen's phone or computer. When I go out, seeing people wearing masks is a constant reminder of what feels like a dystopian technocratic future I hope to avoid. My recent addiction to learning more online compels me to check the news on my cell phone even though I know I won't like what I see. It seems I am unable to block the MSM from my phone. I recognize that I need to discipline myself to choose another focus rather than falling prey to the habitual and unhealthy impulses that have hijacked my mind.

As a way of calming myself down, embracing uncertainty, and building new habits, I adopt a new mantra: "I don't know what the fuck is going on, and that's okay." This statement acknowledges my confusion and frustration

Chapter 36: Back to Life

while bringing a bit of humor and acceptance into the mix. Repeating it regularly does wonders for me.

January 6th

Three weeks have passed since I made a firm commitment to going cold turkey on the news and engaging in my morning practices. I feel worlds better. Today is January 6th, 2021, the day of the official final vote tally. Congress is meeting to certify the electoral college vote. While I have mostly taken a sabbatical from the news, I choose to watch the live coverage with Stephen. I am aware President Trump and his supporters are continuing to assert election fraud and Republican members of congress will likely begin to build their cases for recounts in at least several key states. Stephen just wants to see Biden's count confirmed so as to end the danger he believes another Trump term would mean for our country and perhaps for the world.

The electoral count is done alphabetically, and there are no arguments about the count in Alaska or Alabama, but Arizona is contested by Paul Gosar and Ted Cruz. Because of this objection, the joint session adjourns to allow each chamber to debate and vote on the objection in accordance with the electoral vote count process. However, one hour later, news breaks that Trump supporters have stormed the Capitol, and the electoral count is put on hold as members of the Senate and the House are evacuated.

"Can you believe they just stormed the Capitol?!" Stephen's voice expresses disbelief and outrage.

"Of course I can." I respond in a matter-of-fact way. "Trump's supporters believe he won the election. They think the mail-in ballots were printed in China and ballot boxes were stuffed. They are convinced that many were illegitimate, and Fox News has been validating this belief since the election. There are swaths of people who believe this was a fraudulent election. Conservative news outlets have been saying for months that the Democrats were going to use the pandemic to manipulate the vote through mail-in ballots, so—"

"I don't want to hear it, Katrina," Stephen's intense statement cuts me off. "There is no excuse for this behavior. It is outrageous. It's an attack on our democracy." He marches out, swinging the door with more force than is needed as it slams shut.

The me of six weeks earlier would have gone into a tailspin in reaction to Stephen's comments. I would have felt upset, frustrated, and irritated. My longing for truth and fairness would have catapulted me into another online fact-hunting frenzy with general distrust of the MSM, and resonance with Tucker Carlson and similar voices. However, I am in a different place now, and my well-being is my top priority. With this in mind, I tune out January 6th, figuring anything I need to know I will learn in time.

News About the Insurrection

Over the next few days, I hear differing reports. Stephen tells me that Congress reconvened, completed its process, and Biden has secured the electoral votes he needs to be president. I also learn from friends on the right that Republicans in Congress lost their commitment to challenge election results in several states after having narrowly escaped the riot. They did not want to see more violence, so they were eager to simply get the count done. Only the Arizona and Pennsylvania objections were debated, and in the end, both were denied. Many Trump supporters maintain the belief that the election results were fraudulent and feel cheated of their basic right to fair elections, although plenty of Republicans, including more than eighty conservative judges, do not share those views.

I feel mixed and perplexed by what's going on. What's the truth and what's corruption and deception? Before my mind wastes time on these questions, I remind myself: I don't know what the fuck is going on, and that's okay.

I do know two new bits of information that helps me distance myself further from QAnon and Trump, as I witness undeniably factual evidence about this movement and this president that are contrary to my personal values.

The first is this: while no doubt there were many regular people at the Capitol that day, there were also neo-Nazis, white supremacists, and militia, who were armed and ready to fight. I had been trying to convince people

Chapter 36: Back to Life

that Trump is not a racist. While I have plenty of videos to prove my point, these neo-Nazis and white supremacists must believe Trump is on their side. Why else would they be present that day waving Trump flags?

I have wanted to believe that Trump has sufficiently denounced white supremacy and the KKK, and I have seen and heard him denouncing them,[446] However, it seems this might have happened only in the context of little-seen interviews, not during speeches that would be seen by his white supremacist supporters. Is he more committed to keeping their votes than doing what is right? Given the reality that these fringe groups showed up in support of Trump on January 6th, carrying military weapons with readiness to fight, it appears that Trump's denouncing of white supremacy is disingenuous. Had he really meant it, he would have done so in a way that would have driven these groups away from proudly advertising their outrageously racist presence in support of him on this day.

The second is this: there were Trump supporters among the crowds threatening to hang Mike Pence. Others claimed it was their right to arrest and bring to justice or kill Democrat politicians who they believed to be connected to the Cabal. As the Storm hadn't happened, some believers were ready to make it happen by their own hands.

I have assumed QAnons to be "true patriots" who love our country and our Constitution. But how many of them have ever read it? Have they forgotten the essential precept of "innocent until proven guilty?" Are they ready to forget that due process is a core tenet of our justice system and that everyone in a criminal case has a right to trial by jury? The thought that these constitutionally mandated protections are simply being ignored and overrun by an outraged mass of QAnon-influenced Trump supporters, a number of whom are carrying weapons, is more than disconcerting.

I feel the way my attention to the events and drama of January 6th has knocked me off center and quickly reengaged my fear and anxiety. I resume my self-care practices and let Stephen know I don't want to hear him talk about politics within an earshot of me. He understands my sensitivity and is happy to keep it to himself, taking sufficient space so that I cannot hear him when he wants to discuss politics with others.

Conversations with John Kinyon

In mid-January, I take a small but meaningful risk and send a text request for a chat to John Kinyon.

"Hey Katrina, thanks for reaching out! I've really enjoyed your participation in *Across the Aisle*. Your ability to give empathy to some of the more conservative views has been impressive to me. I'll admit, as much as I seek to do that, I notice I get triggered by some of the content they bring to our sessions. It's sometimes hard for me to reflect them back clearly, but you seem to have a knack at it. I've learned a lot from your example over these last few months."

I had taken a couple workshops with John prior to *Across the Aisle*. I feel comfortable with him. I trust he is able to receive what I have to share with compassion and as little judgment as anyone on the left of the political spectrum. He knows I have been generally aligned with the progressive politics that are common in the Bay Area. And he knows I have a passion for NVC and mediation work.

"Thank you, John," I begin, feeling warmth and appreciation. "I've been challenging myself to understand the viewpoints of Republicans this last year after I recognized I was relating to them through a highly judgmental bias. My prejudices against them fell short of my values for understanding or compassion, so I challenged myself to understand politics through their eyes, rather than through my biased lens."

This is a truthful statement; however, it is hiding how deeply I entered and came to understand Republican political perspectives. When I think of the six months I spent as a QAnon, I feel ashamed. I am not eager to expose that aspect of my journey, but at the same time I know I can't hide such a huge part of my life experience and still be as open, authentic, and connected with my community as I'd like to be.

John responds, "That's fantastic, Katrina! I'm intrigued to know what you've been doing that helped you work through the resistance and reactive tendencies that most people on the left have when hearing right-wing talking points?"

Chapter 36: Back to Life

"Well, it's a long story," I begin, "but I'll tell you the short version and if you want to hear more of the details, I'd be happy to share them with you. How does that sound to you?"

John responds, "That sounds great. I'm very interested to hear your story, as this work of building bridges across our political divides has become my passion. I intend to deepen this work to see how I can expand it in this time of need."

"Alright." I take a breath before I continue. "It started last May for me. I noticed I was deleting a bunch of Facebook friends from my list, and I felt internally confronted and torn, as I could tell this was reactive and out of alignment with my dedication to live and embody the NVC principles of compassionate consciousness."

"That sounds familiar, and I understand that challenge. I know it's a growth edge for many of us, including many NVC certified trainers," he acknowledges.

"That totally makes sense," I affirm. "I'll just cut to the chase. Last June, after successfully giving empathic feedback to a couple of my right-leaning friends, then watching a disturbing and curious video series called *Fall of the Cabal*, I had an overnight flip and became a QAnon. It's only been about a month since I left the rabbit hole.

"Wow! That must have been quite the experience," he states.

I feel relieved by his initial nonjudgmental statement. However, given my experience of John's work, I expect nothing less. My confidence in his capacity to hold space for people to share whatever their authentic expression may be provides me with a sufficient sense of emotional safety, despite the shame I carry as it relates to my participation in QAnon.

John continues, "I'm very interested in hearing as much as you'd like to share about this topic."

Over the course of several phone calls, I recount the events of the last six months. In the end, he expresses gratitude for my willingness to share so openly and vulnerably and lets me know our conversations have added richness and clearer context to his desire to understand polarizing dynamics and the challenges of our current political climate. I'm feeling grateful as well. This is my first tiny step out of the QAnon closet. It is my first experience of openly talking about what happened with someone outside of Stephen, my dad, or the therapist Stephen encouraged me to work with over these last few months.

Chapter 37:
QAnon Casualties

A week later a good friend of mine sends me an article from *Cosmopolitan* entitled "The Unlikely Connection Between Wellness Influencers and QAnon."[447]

> **2024 Note:**
>
> This article was at some point renamed, replacing "QAnon" with "Pro-Trump Rioters."

    This article strikes several chords in me as I feel a kinship to "Jennifer's" story of falling down the rabbit hole via the path of New Age spirituality. She was in a vulnerable mindset and stuck at home during the pandemic, scrolling endlessly online as I was. She enjoyed uplifting memes such as "Trust the Plan" and "Light Is Coming to Dark." She read phrases that appeared to support personal empowerment, such as "Put on your critical thinking hats; this just doesn't make sense," alongside questions about government schemes, Covid-19, and vaccines.

    As I read Jennifer's story, I see many elements that directly mirror my own experience. It's eerie as I begin to realize that many people in the wellness world got swept up into QAnon as I was. I am intrigued, as this *Cosmopolitan* story reveals the existence of a forum on Reddit called QAnonCasualties, created by Jitarth Jadeja, who exited QAnon in the fall of 2019. Jitarth's story[448] has been shared publicly on many news channels. QAnonCasualties is a place where people who have been impacted by QAnon can post their experiences, seek support, and give support. The site has 75,000 members, up from the 44,000 it had only a couple months earlier.

2024 Reflection – What I Learned

This *Cosmopolitan* article has been edited since its first publication. QAnonCasualties is no longer mentioned in the article, but it is still very much an active forum (or "sub" as they are called) on Reddit. The group doubled its membership in the spring of 2021 and, as of spring 2024 it counts 275,000 members. Unfortunately, as moderators were unable to keep up with the barrage of content, it has become increasingly toxic as pain and anger fuel reactive and deeply polarized comments.

The existence of this Reddit sub piques my curiosity, and I log in to check it out. The top post is titled "My QMom Died Today and Everything is Worse."[449] This post by someone I'll call Elizabeth (Reddit handle u/elizabethanelevator) is a poetic memorial—an ode to the mother who adopted her when she was only one week old. Elizabeth describes how, after Biden won the election, her mother elected to commit suicide in the bathtub. This gut-wrenching post begins with:

"I lost my mom today."

Her bio-mom was Korean, and her bio-dad was a Black American soldier. When this girl endured racist statements at school, her adopted mother would comfort her with the words, "The blacker the berry, the sweeter the juice, my love. You're the nicest lady I've ever met!"

The mother who raised Elizabeth sounds like me in many ways, except that I was not sexually abused as a child. She was passionate about holistic health, buying organic, and avoiding modern medicine as much as possible.

Chapter 37: QAnon Casualties

She had a "coexist" bumper sticker on her car, which uses various religious symbols in place of each letter as a way of symbolizing an embrace of all faiths. She followed Bernie Sanders before getting hooked by the pedophilia narrative connected to QAnon, as she too fell down the rabbit hole.

Elizabeth highlights how potently QAnon changed her mom's personality. Whereas this woman once loved and doted on her daughter, her loving spirit shifted radically as a result of entering the Q trance.

Elizabeth writes:

> *I showed her the photos of Trump and Epstein, I sat her down to try to explain that these things that had taken over her mind were false. I begged her to see reason and she immediately turned on me. I didn't see her hand flying at my face. I barely felt the slap and the rake of nails down my neck that took my breath away and knocked me off my chair. My mother wasn't standing before me. Instead, there was a red-haired demon wearing the kaftan I'd once hidden in. 'The blacker the skin, the faster it rots!' It spat out at me as it wrung its hands. Then she did it, she was the only person who had ever done it, she called me a nigger and I think that's what killed me inside more than anything else had.*

I feel my heart in anguish with this young woman, Elizabeth, who is between semesters in her undergraduate studies. Tears stream down my face, and I can barely continue reading. I have to face the facts: This and many more "QAnon Casualties" are the real-life consequences of the larger QAnon narrative. This gruesome ending, and many like them (though usually not quite this horrific) are connected to the movement I have given six months of my life to and have been desperately trying to get others to join. Holy crap! How could this mom turn on her daughter? How could I have not seen this before?

Based on what I've learned about social media, my mind weaves together an answer. QAnon is like a buffet, but you don't have access to seeing all the offerings. You take what you want and leave the rest. And when you take something, the algorithms feed you more content resonant with what it discovers you are naturally motivated to pay attention to.

I have ignored the blatantly racist messages I have seen in QAnon, faulting those messages on the remnants of racism in our country, not on Q. As I have not engaged with those posts, I have received very few of them. Most of my feed has consisted of what is considered to be the softer, kinder "Pastel Q" version of the overall narrative. But it has been ignorant of me to pretend that my experience of QAnon and other variations of it are entirely separate.

My head is spinning, and my heart feels as though it is breaking. But I must keep reading. I need to see this. I need to understand that QAnon is not just another wacky theory trying to explain and solve all that is wrong in our world. It has devastating real-world consequences. I read on.

Elizabeth never had the opportunity to reconnect with her mother before her death. She laments:

> *I think [her calling me nigger] broke a little part of me that can never be repaired because we never had the time to reconcile over that and I swear, if I could have spoken to her, I would have forgiven her immediately. I loved her that much. I thought she'd come to the light.*
>
> *I wish there was a warning on the sites she'd go to desperately find more information on Q. There should be. A simple 'Abandon all hope, ye who enter here' would be a sufficient warning to those who decide to delve into the deep and immerse themselves in a world of deception. My mother was so focused on finding the sexual predators that she didn't realize that she had been completely taken over by a different sort of predator that ended up taking her life.*

Toward the end of her post, she wrote:

> *Today I will sit down and write her obituary for her, I'll wash the blood off the marble, and I'll pick up what pieces I can before I call to order her headstone.*

❦ Chapter 37: QAnon Casualties ❦

I am devastated to imagine this young woman's twofold loss of her mother's love, and then her mother's life. I am a ball of tears, feeling the emotional agony of Elizabeth's lived experience. I begin to understand why many experts call QAnon a cult.[450] People fall under its spell, then they do things that are damaging to themselves and others. They engage in activities that they never would have considered if it hadn't been for the influence and social phenomenon that arose with Q.

I read the next few stories. A woman with three kids is on the verge of divorcing her husband who went down the QAnon rabbit hole three years ago and now is paranoid and carrying guns. Another woman who was once very close to her sister can no longer talk to her, as the sister is constantly talking about pedophiles and trying to convince her that Pizzagate is real.

Each story moves me to tears as I discover the harsh truth. Families are being torn apart because of the conflict driven by these QAnon stories. This is *far* from the nonviolent movement Janet Ossebaard had described in *Fall of the Cabal*. This is the most destructive set of beliefs I've encountered in my lifetime, and it plays upon people's anxieties and fears. I discover estimates that there could be tens of millions who believe in at least some part of the many narratives broadly associated with QAnon. QAnon has a way of hooking people across the spectrum with respect to race, class, and education. It has now woven itself into the fabric of our American society, luring people into its web via an array of narratives that hook them first then lead them to greater and greater radicalized content. Instead of bringing us together, it's tearing us apart.

How can I have missed this? How is it I haven't seen the damage QAnon is causing so many families and threatening my own? How is it I could have believed this was a nonviolent movement and some kind of spiritual awakening? How could I have been so blind? My heart hurts as the harsh reality—the shadow side of QAnon—becomes clearly visible.

Sweet Stephen

"Sweetheart, what's going on?" Stephen's voice surprises me, as I had no idea he had entered the room.

"I just found this website," I start, but Stephen cuts in before I catch my breath.

"I thought you were taking a break from all the news, Katrina. You know it's not good for your emotional well-being," he begins.

"I know. But this is different," I say. "I found this group on Reddit called 'QAnon Casualties,' and the stories about how QAnon has impacted families are horrendous." Consoling me in my obvious distress, Stephen understands that what I've read is supportive of my determination to pull myself out of any remaining mental grip the QAnon experience has on my mind.

"Do you want to talk about it?" He offers.

As I reread the first story to him, I feel a surge of tears along with a deepening recognition—the fact Stephen stuck with me is nothing to be taken lightly. I have been unconsciously undermining my relationships, straining my familial bonds. Through my very active participation in polarizing debates in which I was the clear minority, I have unwittingly generated my own experience of alienation. And if Stephen had not stuck closely by my side, with as much acceptance, communication, patience, and persistence as he brought, I could have gone much further. I could have left California, distancing myself from the nourishing roots I had enjoyed for decades of my life. I could have become at least as much of a zealous supporter of Trump and a poster child for the pastel version of QAnon as I had been a diehard Bernie supporter for the previous five years. I have been emotionally hooked. I have been blind. I have been practically impermeable to my friends' and family's many attempts to pop me out of my trance and help me discern reality from the fantasy world cast about my mind.

> **I have been blind. I have been practically impermeable to my friends' and family's many attempts to pop me out**

Chapter 37: QAnon Casualties

***of my trance and help me discern reality from
the fantasy world cast about my mind.***

Between my sobs, these words escape my mouth: "Stephen, thank God you stuck with me." I am deeply humbled. Having woken up to the socially destructive impact the rise of Q is having on families, friendships, and the social fabric of our world, I am incredibly grateful for Stephen and the handful of others who committed to staying loving and close to me despite my time as a passionate QAnon. Never before have I felt such deep mourning and gratitude simultaneously. I almost lost what matters most to me—I almost lost many of the relationships I hold most dear. I don't take it for granted that Stephen didn't give up on me as so many others could easily have done. Thank God he chose to stay connected—to find ways to help me see the unintentional damage I was doing.

These words of thanksgiving would be repeated many times in the days, months, and years to come.

Chapter 38:
Lemons and Lemonade

I am overwhelmed by emotion as I come to terms with the painful dichotomy between the beautiful movement I thought I was in and the reality of the other people's experiences I am reading on Reddit. I am compelled to engage with someone about it all. But as I am emotionally fragile, and I still feel ashamed enough to want to hide in a closet, I make an ungrounded judgment call: I believe it will be safer to anonymously seek the connection I long for via this Reddit sub than to reach out to the remaining people in my life who know and love me.

I realize I am taking a risk. I might be verbally slammed, but I like to think I'll receive support similar to what I see others receiving on this sub. The vast majority of the people here have suffered their own horror stories. People they love who were sucked into the QAnon rabbit hole have at times been cruel, as I glean from stories I have read. The emotional pain and outrage on this page is overwhelming. But I can think of no other place where I can express myself anonymously, receive some amount of empathy and support, and perhaps share some insight that might help others who are struggling.

As I choose to move past my feeling of vulnerability, I post a stream of thoughts to the sub. I acknowledge that I was a QAnon adherent and share a bit of my story. Responses start piling in quickly. Some of the messages are kind, supportive and congratulatory. Others are coaching or advisory in nature. However, the ones that quickly rise to the top are the most cutting, reactive, and cruel. I am unprepared to read the most popular, scathing comments. Those posts linger for days before the sub's moderators catch and delete them.

One comment not caught by the moderators is this one, which echoes the most widely held sentiments among this group:

I don't understand why you're being coddled and congratulated for doing the absolute bare minimum. You were racist and harmful and bigoted. Now you don't want to be attacked because you snapped out of it?! You helped to be a part of a terrible problem. You don't deserve forgiveness; you do deserve all the mean names you've been called. You shouldn't be afraid of people attacking you on here. You're an idiot, and an asshole for seeking comfort from people who are being traumatized by people like YOU every day.

You don't deserve a pat on the back for not being violently stupid. All the people who are coddling you and preaching forgiveness are part of the reason we got here–by handling racists with kid-gloves. It's your own fault you were sucked in by stupidity. You deserve every ounce of hate you receive.

I feel panic rise in my chest as my mind goes into a tailspin. Is this the backlash I'm going to face as I begin taking risks to reconnect with my community? Will anyone be left? Will I be an outcast for years to come? Will I have to hide the fact that I was a QAnon in order to have any friends? How will anyone with a left-leaning political view feel genuine love, acceptance, or trust in me after my time in QAnon? Will my continued distrust of corporate-sponsored media and mRNA vaccines remain as a reason to shun me?

No doubt I can fall back on my new friendships with people who have conservative political views, but that would also make me more prone to

Chapter 38: Lemons and Lemonade

staying hooked on right-wing propaganda. I fear that if I were to do that, it would compound the mess I am already in, keeping me in a state of perpetual disconnect from those who are closest to my heart.

> ## 2021 Personal Reflection
>
> It's easy for me to understand why most QAnons never escape this matrix. As I began reaching out in spring of 2021, I discovered that I was far from alone in this harsh phase of exiting QAnon. As Jitarth Jadega put it:
> "The pain and shame that came with the disillusionment were overwhelming. I couldn't look people in the eye. I felt like I had committed a violent crime and was running for my life. I was terrified that someone would find out my secret and my life would be ruined forever."

It's crushingly humbling to step out of the QAnon trance and realize I've been associating with something that has such a deep and dark shadow, is doing incredible harm, and has so many data points that could be easily debunked if I had only had access to my critical thinking faculties.

> *It's crushingly humbling to step out of the QAnon trance and realize I've been associating with something that has such a deep and dark shadow.*

But I haven't had access. I have been driven by emotions—most prominently fear, but also love, hope, and exhilaration. I have been driven by a need to make sense of the world and to feel some sense of agency and safety. While QAnon is filled with nonsense and has a clear political agenda, I have completely lost trust in the intellectuals and authorities who could debunk it. The simplified story of good and evil, with a hero I could place my hope and faith in, who would save humanity from the depths of darkness and bring about a world of peace and beauty, has had potent emotional appeal to me. My fears have eclipsed my rational mind.[451] And now I have to pay the price for having fallen victim to this cult-like trap.

Steeped in Self-Loathing

My inner critic is spewing an avalanche of self-negation and self-hatred on a daily basis. When I think of reconnecting with members of my extended community, I notice I have lost any sense of personal dignity and am in a state of emotional collapse. I continue to wrestle with this every day, lifting myself up with affirmations, meditation, and life-affirming activities in order to cultivate and keep my precious mental and emotional health.

However, when I read these kinds of scathing comments on the Reddit sub, I feel at risk of falling into depression, despair, and a complete loss of self-confidence. I work to quiet the suicidal fantasies that pop up in my mind almost daily. I know I will never act on them, but somehow these thoughts seem to be an appropriate form of self-punishment for having been weak, gullible, and stupid.

Part of me knows these evaluations are only stories held by my mind, generating unnecessary suffering. Part of me knows I can look at times in my life when I've been remarkably strong and perceptive. However, that part feels so distant to me while the aspect of me that perpetuates pain, suffering, and disconnection has a vice-like grip on my mind. I do not have what it takes yet to overcome the incessant self-judgment. I am struggling to reestablish my self-respect and well-being.

Will I recover from this? Have I lost my community forever? Will I ever feel safe around people again? How does a person recover from an experience like this?

Answers to these questions are not forthcoming. All that is obvious to me is that hundreds of thousands of people have been hurt by the spiraling impact of Q. Many of those same people are quick to assume that anyone who has ever fallen down this rabbit hole must be a racist, sexist, anti-Semitic, violent, deranged, stupid idiot who should be punished for having participated in such a vile belief system. How does one regain a positive self-regard and renew a sense of belonging within a community when these dehumanizing evaluations are the entrenched views of those who have experienced harm at the hands of QAnon?

❀ Chapter 38: Lemons and Lemonade ❀

I do receive one especially supportive message on Reddit, from someone who is also an ex-QAnon:

> *Hey, I want to let you know that the people here responding to your story negatively don't know the pain of being sucked into a cult. If they're giving you shit about 'sounding like a victim,' they are out of line. I know they've been hurt by Q people, but they need to understand that Q gets good people right in their hearts. It is HARD to wake up from that, and you are doing a great job. Your family is doing a great job. I am speaking as a recovering Q person, too.*

I read this one a dozen times over. This is what I need to remember. I am not alone. Others have gone through something like this. Recovery *is* possible.

I also receive another encouraging message:

> *Your story matters and perspective matters. It takes a lot of strength and introspection to pull oneself out of that rabbit hole. As long as you stay committed to becoming the best person you can be, affecting positive change in the world, and being a champion of truth, you have my support. Your unique experience makes you uniquely qualified to speak in this forum and help solve these issues. Don't be concerned that this community may not accept you. This community needs you.*

And privately, I receive a message on the Reddit chat from a user I will soon discover is Jitarth. He apologizes for the hatred spewed at me on the QAnon Casualties sub and congratulates me on exiting QAnon, encouraging me to reach out to him whenever I want.

Making Lemonade

When life serves you mega-lemons, make mega-lemonade, *right?* The shame I am feeling about having been involved with QAnon is a serious mega-lemon, yet I know it's given me and my fiancé insights that are rare and needed as people attempt to heal their relationships with loved ones. But making lemonade from these bitter lemons is not straightforward.

As the weeks progress, I receive many requests from researchers and reporters via Reddit, as well as questions on QAnonCasualties from people who are seeking to understand the strange beliefs of their QAnon friends and family members, in hopes that insights might help them deal with the pain and perhaps support their loved ones to exit QAnon.

Among the requests comes one from Channel 4 News in the UK. The reporter, Milena Dambelli, expresses the quality of empathic care I was hoping to receive when I posted on Reddit. Connecting with her alleviates some pain in my heart. She lets me know she's interested in my story, but uncertain as to whether or not it's a fit for their news channel and asks me if I am open to talking with her further to see where this goes. Her warmth and genuine interest are touching, as she expresses appreciation for my willingness to talk openly about my experience. She interviews me for a couple hours, then talks to Stephen and my dad before telling me that their news channel is excited about my account and ready to fly their team out to my home to create a short piece for a broadcast.

I am both delighted and hesitant. She believes my story could make a difference for many people who are struggling with QAnon, and my desire to contribute to others compels me to want to say yes. However, I told her that based upon the backlash I have already received on Reddit, I can only do it if they are willing to blur out my face, alter my voice, and change my name. She lets me know that it is against their policy to do anonymous pieces, as they want their viewers to know that this is a real person—not something made up. As much as I'm wanting to share in a way that might support the healing of others, the idea of rapidly coming out of the closet scares me.

It seems like a perfect time to reach out to Jitarth, as he has chosen to say yes to many news reporters, making his face public as an ex-QAnon. When I share my dilemma with him, he suggests it could be very liberating to be out in the open about my experience but also gives me insight on what to expect. Here's what he writes:

꧁ Chapter 38: Lemons and Lemonade ꧁

You will be called a moron, attacked, thanked, disrespected, respected, asked for advice, and shamed as someone no one should ever listen to. People on the left will hate you for being a Qultist even in the past, people on the right will hate you for not being a Qultist. But others will thank you; they will go out of their way to tell you how brave you are, how they cried when they heard your story, how you touched them deeply, how important it is, and how grateful they are for what you're doing. You'll be a hero and a villain. Neither is true. Don't do it for them; do it for you. Admitting you were wrong is a powerful thing, really, and the more I talk about it, the less shame I feel. Most of all, people will pity you and your situation, when in truth they should be so lucky to have the opportunity to be so human. Coming out as an ex-QAnon is the best decision I ever made.

I can feel how much I want to be out of the closet, to speak openly and to make a difference for those who are ready to hear. But I am certainly not ready for the kind of hate Jitarth says will be coming my way. I decline all video-based news outlets and say yes to only a few people writing articles and books in which my identity will be kept anonymous.

Over the next year, I talk to a few reporters who are willing to guarantee my anonymity. I engage with a half-dozen researchers, including psychologists, sociologists, and a professor in terrorist studies. And I participate anonymously in several podcasts. I follow my desire to contribute to society in a meaningful way; however, I cannot imagine going public with my story. I need time to heal and reestablish my life.

Chapter 39:
Healing and Reconciliation

Healing My Mind

"Healing is making whole… Whole means a sense of being sound, being able to function as the person someone is— whole in an individual sense."

~ Eric J. Cassell, *The Nature of Healing*

Fast forwarding to 2024, it took time and commitment for the symptoms of my post-Q mind to subside and fall away enough that I could feel whole once again. More than a year passed before I began to feel safe again with old friends or was able to hear news without mapping it onto all that I had learned in those six months down the rabbit hole. I had to remind myself regularly that many people choose to wear masks for their personal sense of safety or to protect others, rather than allowing my thoughts to immediately associate masks with the dark influence of the Cabal, forced vaccinations, violations of our US Constitution, and general compliance with a rising totalitarian takeover.

My time in recovery was a period of inward reflection, still driven by a desire to make sense of reality, but to do it in a way that could keep me out of the QAnon rabbit hole rather than have me falling back in. For a couple years I became an introvert as I recovered from the social trauma, not ready to risk being in the company of old friends I hadn't seen since before the lockdowns. I had only a very small handful of people with whom I trusted I could speak openly about the unique challenges I was facing as an ex-QAnon. It was a time of going back to the basics: meditation, affirmations, healthy eating, exercise, gardening, focusing on my work, and engaging in activities that were nourishing to my spirit, like singing, playing guitar, dancing, and other forms of art, as I slowly began rebuilding my social life.

But I could not make all the impressions on my mind simply go away. Questions pertaining to fears about the future faded with my commitment to reminding myself that I don't know what (the F) is going on, and that's okay. I had to actively work through other mental imprints relating to QAnon theories, including basic questions like who or what is Q, really? And how did a series of cryptic posts on an obscure messaging board give rise to what had become widely known as QAnon? I discovered many videos on the Vice media channel[452] that answered these questions to my satisfaction, even though there was never a conclusion on who created and propagated the Q drops.

Evil As Teacher

But the one lingering form of generalized dread that plagued me the most was the possibility of any number of catastrophic future realities that could arise at any given moment, at the hands of intentionally evil people. I could easily understand that unhealed trauma can cause people to act in unconscionable ways, and that under some circumstances good people can choose to engage in harmful actions as was made evident in Hitler's Germany. But I had reasoned that even these types of atrocities arise from fear, pain, and ignorance–not consciously intentional evil.

2024 Personal Reflection

I highly recommend listening to a ten-minute video from Daniel Schmachtenberger: "Why Good People Comply with Evil."[453] His explanation, along with looking at this issue through a modern-day lens of complex and interconnected global systems, is to-the-point, eye-opening, and timely. Daniel's insights have been instrumental to my desire for make sense out of reality in a grounded and objective way.

Chapter 39: Healing and Reconciliation

Prior to QAnon, the existence of evil as a living presence on earth was an idea I would brush off as religious folklore. But having watched *Fall of the Cabal* and having been immersed in an ocean of alternative media that confirmed most of its darkest claims, I could no longer do so. No longer thinking that Q is legitimate, or Trump is chosen by God to vanquish evil and drain our nation and the world of "swamp creatures" in politics and government, I had to find an alternative way of thinking about all of this in order to calm the fear and anxiety that would otherwise consume me.

To that end, I turned my attention to three precepts that help rest my soul:

1. I believe evil is real only in this "earth school," but that on the other side of this temporal experience of life, only love is real.
2. I have long taught that our character strengths (including things like patience, integrity, and the ability to love) are shaped, solidified, and refined when they are tested.
3. My cosmology has always included the knowing that there is no light without darkness, no night without day, no life without death, and the like. An extension of this is the truth that I would have no ability to see, feel, or experience the fullness of love and goodness without knowing the contrast of fear.

From this perspective, I can strive to view darkness and evil, in all their manifestations, as my master teachers necessary for my realization of love and cultivation of what are often considered divine qualities of human virtue.[454]

Choosing Love

This way of thinking about evil led me right back to my passion for actively participating in the creation of peace and empowering my friends, community, and clients to find and remove the barriers to love they have built within themselves. My work here is to keep my focus on love in every way possible, not allowing the circumstances of life to separate me from the divine love that is my true essence. The art of cultivating loving and harmonious relationships has been my north star for almost two decades of studying, practicing, and teaching NVC. NVC has been essential to my recovery, and it affords me a rich tool kit from which to offer healing to a shattered world.

You may have noticed that Stephen and I have some unusual relating tools and practices. They are largely informed and shaped by NVC and we are both grateful for the ways that NVC has allowed us to weather very serious storms together. It is clear to me that I would have unconsciously generated a whole lot more social harm, and I would not have had the tools and support to reconcile my relationships, had I not been deeply trained in its philosophy. If our story has inspired you, the principles and practice of core NVC concepts are widely and readily available, both in print and online. A great place to start is the NVC Academy.[455]

> *You may have noticed that Stephen and I have some unusual relating tools and practices…*
> *We are both grateful for the ways that NVC has allowed us to weather very serious storms together.*

Changing Channels

Even with close to two decades of working with the NVC skill set, reconciliation has been a long and vulnerable process, which began with letting go of my impulse to attempt to shift the perceptions of others.

It didn't take me long to realize that in order for me to enjoy harmonious connection with my Democrat and Progressive friends, I had to be willing to stop talking about controversial topics at a moment's notice, should I sense any sign that they did not want to engage in that conversation. I had overstepped their boundaries too many times under my Q trance, and I knew that rebuilding trust would require me to stop that behavior immediately and prioritize connection over anything else.

> *In order to enjoy harmonious connections,*
> *I had to be willing to stop talking about*
> *controversial topics at a moment's notice.*

Where conspiracy theories, politics, and Covid once dominated my thoughts, time, and interactions, it was time to commit to changing those channels. It became clear to me that digging into online sources in my

Chapter 39: Healing and Reconciliation

attempts to prove what was true and what was not was detrimental to my mental and emotional health, and ultimately a futile and time-wasting activity.

If I wanted to recover my mind and my relationships, which I was highly motivated to do, these topics had to be set aside consistently. I actively reminded myself that as much as my mind and biology continued to want to discern objective truth from propaganda, misinformation, and disinformation, there is more wisdom in learning to live in uncertainty—to know that no matter how much I learn, there is so much I don't know, including broader contexts, which have more than once changed conclusions I had thought were final.

I reminded myself that the only way I can live happily in the face of so much uncertainty is to repeatedly acknowledge that I can't ultimately know what is going on, and arguing with others over discordant beliefs is not worth the effort, or the predictable fallout.

With this clear internal guidance, I was able to shift my focus and habits toward optimizing my health, going to the gym, working in the garden, continuing with my professional training goals, and engaging in other life-serving activities. I became intentional about bringing these to the forefront of my conversations with others as I worked to diminish the grip of old thoughts and fears on my mind. Slowly, the new thoughts and goals gained more real estate in my mental landscape than the previous anxiety-generating impressions.

Reconnecting

My closest family members and friends were relatively quick to embrace me with open arms, celebrating my departure from the QAnon trance. Our relationships have deepened as a result of our reconciliation work, which isn't to say it's all been smooth or easy. It was essential for me to hear and understand how each of them was impacted by my time in QAnon, and we needed to navigate having different political perspectives, as well as differences in the ways we still view and address our respective Covid concerns.

It was essential for me to hear and understand how each of them was impacted by my time in QAnon.

Early on after my exit from QAnon, I began engaging regularly with colleagues in my NVC community, starting with the certified trainers whom I had been closest to. As noted earlier, I had been in contact with John Kinyon through his *Across the Aisle* workshops and with Jim Manske, who is both a mentor and friend. I felt seen, heard, and appreciated by both of them. These conversations helped my nervous system relax into the possibility that I could one day feel safe to talk more openly about this whole chapter of my life. I then began contacting individuals in my NVC trainer candidate group. As vulnerable as this topic was for me, I trusted I would be received with compassion and care among most of these people who take the NVC teachings to heart, and I was right.

Over the first two years after my exit from QAnon, I was cautious about admitting to friends that I had been involved. It was obvious to a number of people in my close community, but not to everyone. However, in the first couple of months I did open up to about a dozen friends.

Reconciliation

In early 2023, as I began the work of writing this book, I challenged myself to reach out and open up to people whom I had been avoiding due to my fears and untested predictions of what they might say.

I contacted a number of people, including several Facebook friends, with the same basic apology:

I want to say thank you for trying to get through to me when I fell into QAnon in June of 2020. I am writing a book about my experience now, so I am looking back on communications and appreciating how intelligently you were seeking to assist me to snap out of it. Unfortunately, I was entirely unreceptive to anything that challenged the QAnon narrative. It seems my psyche wouldn't allow it. Looking back, I feel tears welling up as I reread attempts people made to reach me. My tears combine the shame I still feel (which I am working my way through), regret over the

Chapter 39: Healing and Reconciliation

impact I had on others, and gratitude for the many people who tried to use kindness and reason to help me find my way out. In short, I am sorry, please forgive me. And thank you.

While my "conscious community" included plenty of people who were far from empathetic to my experience of QAnon, their values for compassion, kindness and forgiveness shone clearly in their responses to my outreach.

In response, Stuart wrote:

Hi Katrina, it's so good to hear from you. I breathed a sigh of relief when Stephen gave me the update. I'm so sorry for what you went through. When I was deep in conspiracy theories it took me losing friendships to shift my perspectives. So, I get it. And I had limited capacity when I was trying to get through to you. I had eight Covid cases in my family, and one person died. My younger sister, who also got Covid, is in a hospital every day working to save people's lives, so it felt more personal and urgent for me. I found myself instantly shutting off anybody, even though I know empathetic conversation is the only true solution. I just didn't have the space for that, and I apologize. I hope you know it wasn't personal. I have nothing but love and respect for you.

This first response was especially relieving to me as months earlier Stuart had tried to persuade Stephen to leave me, asserting I was a lost cause and needed to hit rock bottom in order to see the error of my ways. While I had previously known Stuart to practice empathic connection, I wasn't sure if that quality had disappeared in his relationship to me. This note from him reassured me that he had been caught up in his own pain and fear, but the underlying care he had for me had not been lost. Stuart's message gave me more optimism that it was likely safe to reach out to others.

Tony responded with:

Thank you for your kind words. Welcome out of the rabbit hole! I'm happy to forgive you, though I don't really think you did anything to me that would require forgiveness. There's one thing you can do for me though. Please be gentle with yourself. Be tender. I can't be there to give you a hug, so please give yourself one. And when you are ready, please forgive yourself.

Amanda wrote:

Thanks for reaching out. I'm sure it wasn't easy. I'm glad you are feeling better. There are definitely no hard feelings and I wish you nothing but the best. Xoxo.

And Rick responded:

I'm so happy that you reached out now. And it feels sweet and warm to be remembered by you as someone who used both kindness and reason with you, whether it was effective at the time or not. I remember you as a warm-hearted, loving, quite intelligent being, and I'm really glad to be able to welcome you home. You are not only forgiven by me, you are so warmly welcomed back. Thank you for reaching out with your message.

Each of these messages brought soothing relief to my emotionally sunburned heart. While part of me was pleasantly surprised to receive such kind responses, another part of me remembered that this had been the normal tone of our friendships pre-pandemic.

As of the writing of this book, I believe I have been thorough in my reconciliation process (similar to the "amends" steps in 12-Step programs), and I am grateful to be experiencing abundant love and harmony with my closest friends and family. I continue to see the world and politics through a less polarized lens than most of the people in my social circles. While we are able to openly acknowledge our differences in perspective, we do not allow these variances and dissimilarities (or even outright disagreements) to escalate into the kind of conflict that could undermine our basic values for mutual care and respect, or for our friendships.

Chapter 39: Healing and Reconciliation

"Connection Over Correction"

"War mentality saturates our polarized society, which envisions progress as a consequence of victory—victory over a virus, over the ignorant, over the left, over the right, over the psychopathic elites, over Donald Trump, over white supremacy, over the liberal elites. Each side uses the same formula, and that formula requires an enemy. So, obligingly, we divide ourselves up into us and them, exhausting 99% of our energies in a fruitless tug of war, never once suspecting the true evil power might be the formula itself."

~ Charles Eisenstein, "Find the Common Thread"

Through this tumultuous ordeal, I now realize that I have received another great gift: the lived experience of seeing the world through the eyes of people I thought I opposed. And to my surprise, I found that the opposition was all in my head, spoon-fed to me by the media and echoed by my social circles.

The opposition was all in my head, spoon-fed to me by the media and echoed by my social circles.

With this new clarity, I have been able to release the prejudices I once held about people with political views that are different than my own. My mind and heart are now more open than ever to discovering (and seeking out) points of common connection. I can learn from diverse points of view, which broaden my perspective and assist me in seeing a bigger picture of our world and the complex problems we face together. This is a striking consciousness shift—from my prior mental state (in which I unknowingly perpetuated separation and division based on politically progressive ideologies) to one in which I feel and experience myself as part of a much larger human family. Conservatives are no longer the "frustrating other"; they are my friends and allies, as we all desire a world that works for humanity. Frankly, I can't believe now that I ever thought otherwise.

Even when opposition is starkly real—such as the two-sided debates surrounding white-hot topics such as Ukraine and Russia, Israel and

Palestine, the right to bear arms and the argument for gun control, pro-life and pro-choice—we always have the option of turning to connection over correction (or as NVC puts it, "empathy before education").

This is a radically different approach to interacting with people who see the world differently. Rather than rushing into scolding and trying to convince them they are wrong, genuine empathetic listening requires slowing down enough to truly hear them—not only what they are saying, but *what they care about*, underneath the words (which may be very hard to hear). NVC describes this as "leaning in, softly, with a willingness to be changed by what we hear." This empathetic form of communication assists us to build bridges rather than walls. Whether I agree is not the most important factor; in bridge-building, we have the opportunity to respond with "I see that X really matters to you."

> *Whether I agree is not the most important factor;*
> *in bridge-building, we have the opportunity to respond*
> *with "I see that X really matters to you."*

I view this as a spiritual practice that is not easy or natural in a fast-paced, hair-trigger world. I can take a moment to metaphorically walk in the shoes of the other, imagining the emotions I might feel or the values that I might seek to express through this alternative viewpoint. We can agree to disagree and still value and respect each other.

Undoing Social Conditioning That Fosters Conflict

"Dominator culture has tried to keep us all afraid, to make us choose safety instead of risk, sameness instead of diversity. Moving through that fear, finding out what connects us, reveling in our differences; this is the process that brings us closer, that gives us a world of shared values, of meaningful community."

~ Bell Hooks, *Teaching Community: A Pedagogy of Hope*

The difficult truth is that we have been socially conditioned to dehumanize and disparage each other, and this social programming serves structures of control, colonialism, or "empire," as some people call it. We have been actively influenced for generations to use strategies of dominance and

Chapter 39: Healing and Reconciliation

submission, imposing power over and power under relationships, rather than engaging in the far more respectful dynamic of power with. Respect cannot flourish in unbalanced power dynamics; "power with" is a prerequisite to harmonious relationships.

> **Respect cannot flourish in unbalanced power dynamics.**
> **"Power with" is a prerequisite to**
> **harmonious relationships.**

This topic of social conditioning contains far more than can be adequately addressed here. However, Dr. Marshall Rosenberg, the founder of the Center for Nonviolent Communication, wrote a comprehensive introductory book *Nonviolent Communication: A Language of Life,*[456] which delves deeply into this meaty and important issue.

In chapter 2, Marshall introduces a topic which he calls "communication that blocks compassion."

In Marshall's own words:

> *Most of us grew up speaking a language that encourages us to label, compare, demand, and pronounce judgments rather than to be aware of what we are feeling and needing. I believe life-alienating communication is rooted in views of human nature that have exerted their influence for several centuries.*
>
> *Life-alienating communication both stems from and supports hierarchical or domination societies, where large populations are controlled by a small number of individuals to those individuals' own benefit. It would be in the interest of kings, czars, nobles, and so forth that the masses be educated in a way that renders them slave-like in mentality.*
>
> *The language of "wrongness," "should," and "have to," is perfectly suited for this purpose: the more people are trained to think in terms of moralistic judgments that imply wrongness and badness, the more they are being trained to look outside themselves—to outside authorities—for the definition of what constitutes right, wrong, good, and bad.*

> *When we are in contact with our feelings and needs, we humans no longer make good slaves and underlings.*

> **[We are] educated in ways that render [us] slave-like in mentality… When we are in contact with our feelings and needs, we humans no longer make good slaves and underlings.**

Marshall goes on to expose how we've been trained to accept that those who are bad or wrong are deserving of punishment. Social acceptance of these constructs supports hierarchical power structures, leading us to believe (and to stop questioning) that what we are told is right and just. People who disobey authority can then be punished, censored, or canceled for their actions, ensuring peer-pressure-supported compliance among the masses.

Consider how these tactics are used to create conformity in various power hierarchies, such as religious institutions, governments, and large corporations.

- In *life-supporting cultures,* people in official capacities act *in service to* the populations they represent—they are authoritative, not authoritarian.
- In *life-negating cultures,* questioning authority figures is generally unwelcome and often punished. In this way, those on top maintain their unquestioned (illegitimate) power over others, who must submit and comply or "face the consequences."

Marshall also asserts that the way out of these domination paradigms is through "contacting our feelings and needs." This orientation away from moralistic judgments and toward discerning universal needs offers us a bridge to connect in our humanity. It is our access to establishing the foundation necessary to seek collaborative win/win solutions to every conflict or problem we face.

Chapter 39: Healing and Reconciliation

Dehumanization

The dehumanizing of those who disagree with us, through use of name-calling, judging, or otherwise labeling, is the precursor to entering into this slave-like trance of life-alienating communication. Sadly, this form of communication has become especially prevalent in social media commentary, leading to a toxicity online that most everyone has experienced at one point or another. The object of disdain is too White or too Black, too rich or too poor, too Christian or too non-Christian, etc.

It is painfully common for conservatives to attack liberals as libertards and the other all-to-familiar pejoratives. This does nothing to create connection. It only keeps us down, while the abusive power structures which we all are made to endure continue to accumulate power and control. Similarly, the common name-calling attacks of liberals against conservatives, which start with racist and runs the gamut of stereotyped enemy images, does nothing to support seeing our shared underlying humanity. They breed only contempt among people who would otherwise be naturally motivated to work toward the same basic values.

The common name-calling attacks... breed only contempt among people who would otherwise be naturally motivated to work toward the same basic values.

We all want safety, security, a sense of belonging, a healthy planet, health for ourselves and those we love, clean water, the freedom to be ourselves, truth, justice, fairness, and so much more. And yet with all this name calling, judging, labeling, criticizing, blaming, and shaming, we are infighting as opposed to devoting our precious time and energy to collaborating on solutions that could work for everyone.

Rehumanization

The only way to mend our social fabric, including the painful discord between QAnons and their "casualties," is to return to what connects us all—what makes us all human. This can be accomplished through empathic dialogue. NVC teaches that we all have the same range of feelings, and we all share the same universal needs (which could also be called heart-centered values). Where we differ is in the strategies we use to meet those needs. Our highest work is to begin considering the needs of others, even our adversaries, and to ensure that we don't harm others in our attempts to get what matters to us.

> *We all have the same range of feelings, and we all share the same universal needs. Where we differ is in the strategies we use to meet those needs.*

As basic as this is, empathic dialogue is the cornerstone, and the building blocks, for reconnection, healing, and harmony.

In reading this book, you now know the story of one ex-QAnon, a story I trust represents many. *If you have hated QAnons previously, do you still? Or has your heart and mind opened just a bit more, to consider that those who have fallen into it are not what you've been made to believe they are?*

> *"The only way you can hate people is not to know them and not to see them as human. Empathy is everything."*
> *(~ my friend Laura)*

The Art of Peace

Peacemaking has been my life's mission. As a result of this bizarre set of circumstances, I now find myself uniquely positioned to facilitate mutual compassionate understanding across stark divides, addressing one of the most contentious cans of worms in our modern world. Like Mosab Hassan Yousef, the disowned son of a Hamas cofounder who spent ten years as a spy for Israel,[457] I have the broad perspective and unusual experience of living on both sides of the divide. This, combined with my NVC training, has added depth and meaning to my mission that I could never have planned or anticipated, and would never have chosen. But as they say, hindsight is 20/20, and in retrospect I see the perfection.

I am one of many professionals offering workshops, coaching, and facilitation in the art and practice of NVC. There are hundreds of NVC trainers worldwide, and dozens of them are also skilled mediators. However, I am one of the relative few who has actively worked to build connection across

Chapter 39: Healing and Reconciliation

the political divide, taken courses to understand my role as a White person as it relates to the humanitarian work of undoing racism (and other isms that perpetuate unjust power dynamics), and to have trained in other modalities that support trauma healing.

There are *many* easy-to-find resources available for those who are called to assist in the establishment of peace—a world that works for everyone—where the diverse human family is honored and revered, never forced into compliance under the thumb of a dictating authority. And while NVC is not the only tool in support of true social harmony, it is a powerful one that has gained traction globally, and one I cannot recommend highly enough.

Peace in relationships is not something that ever comes from "out there." Trying to make someone be other than the way they are is *not* the path to peace. Peace starts inside. It starts with acceptance and compassion. It starts with our hearts and minds. It starts at home with the way we treat ourselves and our loved ones. From there, it can extend to our friends, neighbors, communities, cities, states, countries, and ultimately to the world.

"Hate cannot drive out hate. Only love can do that."

~ Dr. Martin Luther King Jr.

If we cannot embrace personal responsibility for co-creating harmony with the people we love or have once loved, we are fooling ourselves to think there is any other route to peace. Truly peaceful families—where everyone is heard, seen, and understood, and where everyone's needs matter—are the cornerstones of a peaceful world.

*"The end is reconciliation; the end is redemption;
the end is the creation of the beloved community.
It is this type of spirit and this type of love that can
transform opposers into friends. The type of love that I
stress here is not eros, a sort of esthetic or romantic love;
not philia, a sort of reciprocal love between personal friends;
but it is agape which is understanding goodwill for all men.
It is an overflowing love which seeks nothing in return.
It is the love of God working in the lives of men.
This is the love that may well be the salvation
of our civilization."*

~ Dr. Martin Luther King Jr.

Please join me in co-creating a world of peace.

Peace begins with me.

Appendix A:
Questions and Answers

I received many questions from Reddit users, most of which I have answered in this book. However, there were a number of questions that came in months after my exit, which I will share here.

Question: What makes Q get its hooks into people? Does it have a psychological basis? Is it driven by social media AI algorithms?

The best answer I've seen to this is from an article called *A Game Designer's Analysis on QAnon*,[458] which I view as a must-read for anyone who wishes to understand the QAnon phenomenon. According to this article, it seems that QAnon originated as a "live action role play" (LARP), an online fantasy game blended into the real world in creative ways. However, based on the research done by Vice reporters in their video series *QAnon 101: Search for Q*,[459] this particular LARP appears to have been created by a small group of diehard Trump supporters. The core group behind Q appears to have over time included high-level military insiders, most notably Michael Flynn. This LARP quickly spun out into the phenomenon that would later become known in the media as QAnon.

Q's first "drop" on 4Chan, a cryptic messaging board known for hosting pornography and hate group memes (which I knew nothing about until after exiting QAnon), was posted on October 28th, 2017, only a couple weeks after Trump stood for a photo op with military generals, cryptically saying, "You guys know what this represents? Maybe it's the calm before the storm."[460]

Most QAnons describe Q similarly, as a small team of Trump supporters within the military and government. They believe that one or more of these people has top ("Q-level") government clearance, which gives them access to seeing the roots of corruption clearly. This mysterious collective called Q is said to be working to help humanity see the darkness that has infiltrated our government as well, so that we might have the collective will to reclaim our republic and liberate humanity.

This intention hooked into people's sense of urgency, as we all have a biological drive for survival. And the clues generated a sense of intrigue, adventure, and even camaraderie as Q's following grew. What more potent driver could there be than one in which you believe you are working on behalf of good, and against evil? Is it any stretch of the mind to see how enticing it is for so many people in our primarily Christian nation to believe their team has God on its side (which of course implies that the other team has Satan on its side)? Imagine you are in on the great secrets hidden from the masses for all the previous generations, and now is the time for The Great Awakening. If you really get into it, not as an abstract idea, but as a lived experience, the idea is exhilarating. That's QAnon.

All that aside, LARPs in general have an addictive quality because they support a human behavior I first mentioned in chapter 8, called apophenia. This is the tendency to draw parallels among various items that have no intrinsic connection. All LARPs blend online gaming with real-world experiences, dropping clues or puzzle pieces both virtually and in the material world for their players to put together as they are led on a mystery-solving adventure to a final destination. Only this Q-generated LARP does not have the safety features most LARPs must have (as spelled out clearly in the article mentioned previously), nor does it have a clearly defined end goal. What it *does* have is humongous political influence.

☸ Questions and Answers ☸

When people see clues and assemble pieces in a way that makes sense to them, regardless of whether or not those pieces are put together the way Q intended, the players are rewarded with a dopamine rush similar to what they might experience if they hit a slot-machine jackpot. But the QAnon players do not at all see this as a game of fantasy. They see it as an online window into hidden truths in which they are special because they see "behind the curtain."

Many view themselves as "digital warriors," heroes chosen by God who are collectively fighting a sinister force in our world. Participating in this LARP, which they believe has critically important real-world stakes, might be a way they restore a sense of personal agency in an otherwise increasingly despairing world, with alarming and accruing catastrophic risks.

The AI-based social media algorithms multiply the effects of this game, as those who participate in Q's LARP actively search online for information related to the Q drops.

The way the various AI algorithms work is consistent for everyone. You will be rewarded with more and more of whatever you seek online. With great efficiency, the AI algorithms study your patterns and compare them to those of others, predicting what will catch your interest before you even think of what to search for. In combination with the social media algorithms, the dopamine rush of having one's cognitive bias affirmed, plus the social dynamics that commonly occur among QAnons and other people, create a quicksand that grabs a potential believer by any number of potential hooks. These sticky traps include Pastel Q themes such as protecting children from sex abuse, standing up for natural health and body autonomy, and protecting freedom of speech, as well as a range of other snares (UFO cover-ups, 9/11, JFK's assassination, White Christian nationalism, survivalist strategies, potential for financial collapse, etc.) and sink them quickly into the world of QAnon.

Question: Why are QAnons so insistent on sharing their "research" with everyone?

I believe most QAnons are completely convinced that they are seeing information that is essential for you to know in order to stand a chance against the evil in our world and survive what is to come. They love you and want the best for you. The more deeply they love you and are attached to your survival, the more committed they can be to getting you to see what they see as soon as possible, because the thought of losing you to any of the numerous methods of genocide led by the Cabal is a crushing one.

It is easy for me to imagine some QAnons have gone into a state of despair and numbness, believing their loved ones to be doomed to the coming Cabal-created threats and disasters. Sharing their "research" could be viewed as ways in which they continue to try to hold onto hope that you might wake up and do what they believe is needed not only to survive, but to turn the challenges around, to stand up to the evil Cabal and restore a world that serves humanity. If they succeed in convincing you, it would also meet their values for shared reality, connection and partnership.

They also believe in collective momentum: If strangers wake up, the ones they love are more likely to wake up, too. And the sooner we reach critical mass, the sooner evil will be defeated, and truth and virtue will be restored.

They also could be compelled to share their research so as to prove to you than they are not crazy. QAnons are generally triggered by being called crazy over and over and over again, as these accusations, when repeated over time, generate self-protective trauma responses. Calling them "crazy" is a dialogue stopper. They do not view themselves as crazy at all, and they long to be seen clearly and for the things they have uncovered to be heard and understood.

The impasse arises because it is challenging to meet them halfway. It is hard for people on the outside to see people caught up in QAnon clearly and to validate their "research." That is why the approach Stephen took proved most effective for me. He acknowledged my sincere desire to help others

☸ Questions and Answers ☸

and did research *with* me to address my most potent concerns. He also dialogued with me to place my concerns in their proper perspectives.

Question: Was there a sort of turning point, or eye-opening experience that you had, that really changed your mind on Q and Trump? Was it a Netflix documentary? Just wondering if there's a useful bit of information, or a conversation, that can help pull people out of this.

There were multiple turning points along the way.

- Stephen said he was willing to acknowledge that he may be wrong about some of what he believes to be true. He then took a long pause before asking me if I was willing to do the same. I said, "Yes." And, I meant it.
- Stephen expressed willingness to check out my "research" with me for only two hours a week. He encouraged me to be selective and share with him only what I believed was most relevant to our lives, and factually true. This motivated me to check my sources and seek opposing viewpoints (in anticipation of his doing so) before sending content his way. As a result, I realized that much of what I was seeing had flimsy evidence, if any at all.
- JFK Jr. never appeared. I had consumed enough false content to become convinced he was still alive. I was banking on his reappearance.
- I heard several reports that the Storm was happening, and quickly discovered they were all false. That shattered my trust in the QAnon influencer channels that were reporting about the ever-imminent Storm.
- I had to face the fact that my engagement in QAnon was taking a toll on all my closest relationships. I realized that was not a price worth paying.
- I participated in conversations called *Across the Aisle*, facilitated by professional NVC mediator John Kinyon. These conversations helped me remember that people whose views conflict with the

ones I had been holding as absolute truth could be grounded and intelligent.
- I watched two Netflix documentaries, *The Social Dilemma*[461] and *Behind the Curve*[462], both of which influenced my eventual exit, especially the latter.
- I began to realize that some QAnons were "taking justice into their own hands" in unlawful and dangerous ways. That was against everything I stand for.
- I came to understand that the adrenochrome conspiracy theory is very similar to the *Protocols of the Elders of Zion* propaganda used by Hitler in the Holocaust to turn his followers into a nightmare for Jewish people. This had a huge impact on my willingness to be associated further with QAnon.
- I realized my engagement in online content was very unhealthy and was generating severe anxiety and depression. I recognized that if I didn't change my habits, these problems could get worse, not only impacting my well-being, but also taking a further toll on my relationships.
- After exiting QAnon, it became clear to me that white supremacists and Nazi sympathizers are among Trump's major supporters. While I have heard him repeatedly denounce racism and white supremacy, it is clear that they still view him as sending them dog whistles— ultimately supporting their cause. I condemn white supremacy and fascism, so I do not want to have any personal associations with these ideologies.
- I discovered the Reddit sub r/QAnonCasualties and came to the realization that QAnon is not a nonviolent movement. Instead of promoting world peace, it is a highly divisive mobilization, intensifying political polarization and generating severe social breakdown. My desire to distance myself from QAnon grew as I came to realize how families are being destroyed over the increasing

🪷 Questions and Answers 🪷

political divides. I finally understood that QAnon is playing an enormous role in this dysfunction.
- As a part of my deprogramming efforts, I watched everything Vice Media has produced on the topic of QAnon. Those videos were eye-opening. I also took time to read several dozen articles from the mainstream news on the topic of QAnon, which provided me with a much different context than the one I had seen while I was caught up in it.

All that said, I had to come to the personal realization that my belief in QAnon was causing more harm than good. I had to recognize that it was problematic. I had to *want* to change.

Question: Was there anything your fiancé did or said that helped? I'm in a similar bind with my ex-fiancé. It's hard to talk to him without getting into arguments.

I've asked Stephen to answer that question for you. Here's what he wrote:

The first critical question to answer for yourself is: 'How important is this relationship to me?' If this is a relationship that you feel strongly you want to save, then you can do that. It will require putting some of your own beliefs aside—at least for the time being—so you don't spend precious energy arguing about things you clearly disagree about.

Patience is key. *This may be a phase, and this may be long term—even a forever shift. You just can't know. I was advised to contemplate this two ways:*

One: *Think of this akin to something far less contentious, like a nonreligious person finding Jesus and becoming a Born Again Christian or embracing some other evangelical belief system. Once converted, the world is different for them. They see reality through a different lens, and no matter how hard you try you will NOT shift their view. So don't even try. You have to accept that this is their* view, and no amount of logic, science, pleading, or anything else will change their mind.

Two: The second way of thinking about this is as an illness or an injury. Some would say falling down this rabbit hole is similar to a psychotic break. Taking that view, how would you show up for your fiancé if he broke his leg or had a head injury? Show up the same. Be loving. Be caring. Stay close so he doesn't hurt himself or others, and be his protector to the extent he will allow it. Encourage him to be reflective enough not to make decisions or take actions that can have significant negative consequences while he is in an alternative reality or ungrounded state.

Next, if you want to work this through, here are some keywords that may become your gospel: patience, curiosity, balance, love, and support.

Curiosity: This was a hard one for me, but I signed on to it and did my best. Essentially, put your mind in a place of childlike curiosity. I had to constantly remind myself that no one really knows the objective truth. No one has enough information to be absolutely sure of their position. Therefore, can you leave room in your mind for the potential that what you have come to believe may not be so? If you can hold that and then listen to your beloved with curiosity, that will go a long way. I would also make an agreement with him—that he should not be seeking to change your views just as you commit not to try and change his. You will simply agree to share information with each other, but not debate.

Balance: I suspect your fiancé is deep in the rabbit hole and for him there is little else to focus on. It is almost a compulsive disorder. It is designed to be addictive. I suggest working hard to get him to focus on being present in life with you, focusing on

☸ Questions and Answers ☸

aspects of being alive that are happening here and now. What do you enjoy doing together? What projects are important? What activities that have nothing to do with being online are essential to your well-being and enjoyment of life?

The discussion of beliefs and time spent 'doing research' needs to be limited to maybe one to two hours a day. Encourage him to stay aware of how his time spent scrolling online is taking away from his life, including connection with you, family, career productivity, etc. See if you can motivate and inspire him to strike a balance. That needs to be his commitment; to maintain balance and well-being in his own life, and to give energy and attention to nurturing your relationship together. Again, your work is to meet him with curiosity—to accept where he is at, rather than reacting to and judging him.

Love: *Focus on your love and your dreams for your future. Remind him why the two of you have chosen each other. All of that still exists. It has been overshadowed by Q, but it is still there, and the balance will hopefully bring him back to remembering.*

In the end, I needed to accept that my beloved might never come back to her old self. I needed to see if I could find a way for life to be good even if that was the case. I gave myself six months to see if we could find our way through, but I did not tell her. In that time, I needed to prove to myself that life with her could still be good. During that time, I fervently hoped she would return to the Katrina I remembered. I feel fortunate beyond words that she 'came around' almost exactly six months after she went down the rabbit hole. However, if she hadn't, we had still worked out a way to be together. But life is much better with her back out of the rabbit hole.

Support: *Find a network of people to support you. This will be very hard on you. And you want to show up as best you can—and so you need to have people you can turn to for strength,* *compassion, empathy, and the occasional shoulder to cry on. Find people who care about both of you, who will not judge him for his new beliefs but can have some understanding for the fact that this trap has pulled hundreds of thousands of people into it. Many good-hearted, intelligent people with the best of intentions have unwittingly slid down the rabbit hole, and once you are in, no one on the outside can save you. You have to get yourself out. Best to find support people who can have compassion for both of you, as judgment will likely drive him further away.*

Friends, family, and my therapist were all important to our success, and I am indebted to their patience with me.

Question: If you don't trust the science, how can I believe you are not still a QAnon?

I *do* trust the scientific process, but I do not trust what I see as a "trust the science" propaganda campaign which denies the integrity of scientific standards. According to what I've seen from the liberal media, there should be no debate because their media pundits argue that there was sufficient scientific consensus that the virus should be addressed as guided by Dr. Fauci and the emergency authorized vaccines were safe and effective. As Dr. Fauci famously said, "Attacks on me quite frankly are attacks on science."[463]

> ***"Blind belief in authority is the greatest enemy of truth."***
>
> ~ Albert Einstein

However, *real* science remains inherently a self-correcting and dynamic process, where conclusions are always open to reevaluation as new evidence becomes available. This openness is what allows for the advancement of our understanding of the natural world.

According to Rupert Sheldrake, PhD, "The 'science delusion' is that science already understands the nature of reality in principle… it's the kind of belief system of people who say, 'I don't believe in God, I believe in science'… science has come to inhibit and restrict the free inquiry, which is the very life blood of the scientific endeavor."[464] The fallacy of "trusting the science" is the assumption that the science on Covid and the vaccines was established with clear and inarguable truth. In effect, 'science delusion' is a scientific dogma that undermines the fundamental scientific process.

Debate is not just a part of the scientific process; it is *essential* for ensuring robust and comprehensive scientific inquiry. It helps to clarify uncertainties, test the validity of findings, and ensure that scientific advancements are both sound and ethical.

> **Debate is not just a part of the scientific process; it is <u>essential</u> for ensuring robust and comprehensive scientific inquiry.**

While I have empathy and understanding for those who "trust the science" they've been given by their trusted news sources, I have not seen sufficient proof to believe that the critiques of these assertions should be ignored. Tens of thousands of top experts in virology, immunology, epidemiology and other related fields of study, many of whom hail from top-rated universities, strongly disagree with the MSM's statements on "the science."[465] Many doctors are so resolute in their convictions that they have been willing to lose their careers and endure shaming, smearing, and loss of income so as to maintain integrity with their oath to do no harm to their patients. Much of what they have to say has been highlighted and backed by countless studies in Robert F. Kennedy Jr.'s book, *The Real Anthony Fauci.*[466,467]

I am appalled to see how rigorously the voices of these highly credentialed experts have been silenced, censored, and written off as "fringe," "anti-vaxxers," or "conspiracy theorists." And I have seen far too many studies which completely challenge the "safe and effective" claim. The website "Real Not Rare" is one of many online portals where people upload their written accounts and videos, evidencing the injuries, deaths, and chronic conditions they now face after taking what they believed to be safe and effective Covid vaccines.[468]

> *"I would rather have questions that can't be answered than answers that can't be questioned."*
>
> ~ Richard Feynman, PhD, prominent theoretical physicist known for his work in quantum mechanics.

I know each person must do their own form of study and come to their own conclusions, and I respect plenty of people who have come to different conclusions than my own. And I would hope that we can all come together in our desire to see the scientific process at its best. This debate could be settled if the MSM were to host a long series of conversations between the best experts in the field who at this time hold diametrically opposing views. Let's get them in a room together and allow the public to see science in action with transparent debate and the studies to back any claims made.

As for the QAnon question, it seems most people who trust mainstream sources think QAnon and Covid-questioning activities are for all intents and purposes one and the same, but they are not. In short, QAnon believes that a secret Cabal of Satan-worshipping pedophiles rule the world. Most people who mistrust the Covid narrative do not believe in (or haven't even heard of) this very basic QAnon premise. They are two separate topics that happened concurrently, and some fell into both, as I did. I have exited QAnon, and I continue to be distrustful of the mainstream narrative, the NIH, CDC, Fauci, Gates, and the WHO when it comes to the topic of handling global pandemics in a *truly* safe and effective way.

QAnon believes that a secret Cabal of Satan-worshipping pedophiles rule the world. Most people who mistrust the Covid narrative do not believe in (or haven't even heard of) this very basic QAnon premise.

In a June 2024 interview with Chris Cuomo, former CDC chief Dr. Robert Redfield, arguably one of the top experts on the topic of Covid vaccines, stated a number of points that run counter to the way the pandemic was handled. He did not support the lockdowns or mandatory vaccinations, especially for young healthy people. He explained that these vaccines did *not* prevent infection; however, for those over age 65 and with pre-existing comorbidities, they did prevent serious injury and death.[469] I appreciate his balanced perspective and highly recommend watching his full interview.

Question: Do you have a sense as to why so few ex-QAnons are willing to come out?

It seems we are a very small number, but perhaps many have exited quietly, preferring to pretend they were never in it rather than risk the vulnerability of admitting to having ever been engaged in QAnon information streams.

What I suspect is that most QAnons were Republicans first. I've spoken with several Republicans who have no idea what QAnon is. When I describe it to them, I usually hear something like "Well, that's weird," but otherwise they don't really seem to care. I would imagine integrating back into those communities is relatively easy.

The experience of a Democrat or progressive falling into and climbing out of QAnon is far different. More people on the left rely on mainstream news for information. This leads them to believe (rightly or wrongly) in at least two existential threats that are amplified by QAnon.

The first is that Trump poses an indisputable danger to democracy. And it seems many on the left view him as a fascist threat emulating Adolf Hitler or modern dictatorships like Viktor Orban or Vladimir Putin. People who are terrified of Trump returning to the presidency may tend to harshly judge anyone who supports Trump, believing that person to be an enabler.

The second major threat many see is the tendency for politically conservative people (not necessarily Trump supporters) to be more likely to question the Covid narrative,[470] along with its challenge to the idea that the vaccines were the best strategy for stopping the spread and saving lives. According to the view of many on the left that I've come across, anyone who questions that narrative, refuses to wear a mask, or chooses not to get the Covid vaccine and subsequent boosters is a threat to public health. More personally, they might view people like myself as a threat to someone they love who they believe (perhaps rightly so) is vulnerable to debilitating sickness or death from this virus.

When a person perceives an existential threat, the part of their brain responsible for compassion tends to be overridden by the "reptilian" or limbic brain, which is responsible for survival reactions: fight, flight, or freeze. In conversation, especially online, this can manifest as verbal combat or violence.

If a QAnon believer shares his or her political views openly with people who are anti-Trump, the chances of receiving negative reactions, including accusations of being a racist, sexist, fascist, homophobe, nut job, etc. are high. Many people are far from eager to put themselves in a position where they will predictably receive cutting remarks. And many who receive verbal attacks react by snapping back, creating an escalation that leads to more pain, stress, and frustration across the board. This only deepens the feelings of alienation, loneliness, and even despair for an ex-QAnon who is seeking reintegration with people they love and have lost among their former community. So why take the risk to share?

I have taken the risk because I trust that when I have time to pause and reflect, I have sufficient ability to listen to others and respond in a way that demonstrates care and validation of their concerns. I know there are people who are genuinely seeking to understand the QAnon phenomenon in a way that might give them a better chance at healing their relationships. I am sharing my story for those people.

Question: How did your QAnon experience change you?

- I have appreciation for all political perspectives now, whereas before I was clearly on team blue and resistant to other points of reference.
- I now have friends across the political aisle.
- I am far less interested or engaged in politics than I was before.
- I am keenly aware of how quickly political conversations can devolve in ways that are harmful to social bonds and so am much more hesitant to engage in these conversations or post anything political on my social media feeds.

Questions and Answers

- I am much more aware of how rampant disinformation has become, on *all* sides of contentious issues.
- I actively choose media that uplifts, inspires, and educates me in topics that support my life.
- I have a much more consistent spiritual practice and enjoy listening to wisdom talks regularly.
- I am active in my garden and learning more about how to grow and nurture plants.
- I have picked up the guitar and love how practicing soothes my emotions and brings me joy.
- When politics arises in conversation with others, I am attentive to acknowledging the other person's beliefs, regardless of whether they align with mine. I do this using empathetic reflection, a basic Nonviolent Communication (NVC) tool, to deepen the way in which I am able to give the other the sense of being deeply heard, seen, understood and that their core values matter.
- I have also learned that it's best to gently excuse myself from a political conversation or ask to change the topic as soon as I, or the person I am talking to, feels discomfort. Connection, love, and respect are my priorities.

Question: What do you think would have happened if Stephen hadn't worked so hard to turn you around?

Stephen's consistent efforts in my six months as a QAnon clearly altered my trajectory. In retrospect, it's easy for me to imagine the permanent damage I might have done to my relationships if Stephen had not steadfastly committed to working this through with me.

Not only was I losing the community I had actively cultivated for the previous two decades, but I was also losing connection with my closest friends and family, due to our different political perspectives. I kept falling prey to the unhealthy impulse to argue that I was right, rather than prioritizing understanding, love, and connection. I was rapidly moving in the direction of destroying my entire social network. Part of me was aware I was losing my social bonds. Another part of me thought that I needed to build a new community because the one I had might be killed off by the Cabal, despite my best attempts to prevent that outcome.

Stephen engaged in damage control efforts, reducing my tendency toward making potentially irreversible social errors while reminding me how deeply I value other aspects of my life. He encouraged me to pay attention to my health and fitness, our garden, my coaching work, and an uplifting and mutually enjoyable quality of connection with my family, friends, and community.

I have read so many heartbreaking accounts of people losing their closest friends, family, and loved ones to QAnon, and I can see that I was also on that train. Thank goodness Stephen stuck with me. Having gone through this together, I know I have been blessed by his love and support.

Question: Have you considered starting a support group for other ex-QAnons?

I have, and yet it is so very complex and certainly not a project I could take on alone. I would need to pull together a team of people whom I trust have the skill set necessary to be successful in this form of service. To date I have been unable to locate anything close to an effective support group for ex-QAnons. However, I do offer professional NVC coaching and mediation sessions, which assist people in building mutual compassionate understanding when their relationships have broken down due to the challenges of navigating differences in belief.

Question: Are you willing to consider that some of the content you seem to believe is factual may not be true?

Yes. I would like to continue to align my beliefs with what can be clearly discerned as factually true.

Question: How can I reach you?

Through the website for this book: www.ReQoveryBook.com

Appendix B:
Glossary of Terms from the QAnon Lore

4Chan, 8Chan and 8Kun

4Chan, 8Chan and 8Kun are all online anonymous and encrypted message boards upon which Q first appeared and all the Q drops were posted.

adrenochrome

Adrenochrome is a real chemical compound created through the oxidation of adrenaline. It is also a fictionalized drug which has made appearances in several Hollywood films and in a couple books. QAnon adherents believe that adrenochrome is harvested from the blood of tortured children and used by elites as a nontoxic fountain of youth.

Anons

Anon is a broad term applied to anyone who follows Q or Q-adjacent topics. Anons began as anonymous people (similar to those who post on Reddit, but with deeper, untrackable anonymity) who found the early Q posts (beginning in late 2017) on the 4Chan and 8Chan message boards and began to interact with those messages. A subset of Anons, sometimes referred to as "Bakers," devote significant time and energy to analyzing the Q posts (aka "Q drops," or "crumbs"), seeking to discover patterns and concoct connections between them and random real-world topics and events, to create a better understanding of the clues and information they reveal. Some Anons have amassed thousands of online followers, becoming influencers who continue to shape and lead the QAnon movement today.

Cabal

QAnons assert that an amorphous "Cabal," composed of top-tier power elites around the globe, use fear and manipulation to gain total control over the human population. For these (almost exclusively) men, greed and material gain are not enough; they wield their power and control in pursuit of a "prison planet"—a total surveillance state where every thought and action of the common person is tracked and sanctioned or punished (modeled after the existing Chinese social credit system). While some QAnons point fingers at famous people, accusing them of being members of this Cabal, other QAnons believe the members of this Cabal include nonhuman beings as well. Some believe they are extraterrestrials from the Draco star system who have been controlling humanity since before the dawn of civilization.

calm before the Storm

This phrase was used by Donald Trump only weeks before Q posted its first drop. Other anonymous posters on the 4Chan board also used this phrase prior to Q's arrival. It is a statement QAnons hear as an indication that the Storm is near.

crumbs

Crumbs are synonymous with Q drops. They are the clues Q posted on anonymous and encrypted message boards.

Glossary of Terms: QAnon Lore

Deep State

The Deep State is a term used by some people to describe the parts of the US government in which people hold unelected positions of power with no term limits. This includes leaders among the FBI, CIA, NSA, NIH, CDC, and regulatory agencies. However, in QAnon lingo, the Deep State (also referred to as Globalists or Black Hats) is a secret organization created by the Cabal for the purpose of fulfilling the Cabal's dark agenda.

"drain the swamp"

According to Wikipedia, "drain the swamp is a phrase which has frequently been used by politicians since the 1980s and in the US often refers to reducing the influence of special interests and lobbyists." In QAnon stories, this meme is similar to the Storm, but focuses on eliminating those who are believed to be corrupted politicians and administrators from the federal government.

GESARA

The global version of NESARA is "a plan to reset planet earth and humanity on a sustainable governance foundation."

Great Awakening

The Great Awakening is a meme that has been used in many circles, including spiritual groups. However, among QAnons, this idea describes what adherents believe is an awakening to the lies spread by the MSM and to the dark reality of the Deep State or the swamp.

jab

A British-inspired term used by people to talk about Covid vaccines in a way that expresses distrust in their safety and efficacy.

med beds

This technology is not proven to exist, although those who believe in it believe it will magically heal any condition or disease by use of plasmatic energies and healing frequencies.

NESARA

The National Economic Security and Recovery Act is a set of US economic reforms that was proposed in the 1990s. Although never introduced before Congress, QAnons (and many before them) believe that this act was secretly passed by Congress in 2000 and that it is only a matter of time before its legal status implements massive fiscal changes, including:

1. The end of the IRS and income taxes (to be replaced by a 14% flat-rate sales tax on new/nonessential items only—e.g., not groceries, rents/leases, insurance, and medical services).
2. Forgiveness of credit card, mortgage, and other debt, as remedy for bank frauds.
3. A US treasury banking system and precious-metals-backed "rainbow currency."
4. Cessation of all aggressive US military actions and establishment of peace, worldwide.
5. Release of more than 6,000 patents on suppressed technologies that are being withheld from the public under the guise of national security, including free energy devices, antigravity, and sonic healing machine.
6. Restoration of constitutional law... and much more.

Q

Q is a reference to Q-level security clearance, which is required to access top-secret restricted data within the Department of Energy. Q is also the alias under which someone, or some group of people, posted content to the 4Chan (and later 8Chan) online message boards. These posts would later be called

"Q drops" and would become the basis for the growing phenomenon of QAnon.

QAnons

QAnons (plural) is a general term for people who follow Q and/or the online influencers who share any of the many Q-related or Q-adjacent topics covered in this book (and more). This term does not actually exist in the QAnon lexicon as Q made it clear that "QAnon" was created by the MSM and is not representative of the intended movement.

Q drops

Q drops are the posts from the alias "Q" that gave rise to the QAnon phenomenon.

the Storm

This is an event that is highly anticipated by QAnons and is a central theme to the way they believe the Plan of the White Hats will play out. The QAnon lore says that the Justice Department is holding hundreds, if not thousands, of sealed indictments against members who are active pawns for the plans of the Cabal, promising many will be tried for treason and for sex crimes, especially crimes of child sex trafficking. The Storm is the time in which these indictments will be unsealed, and all the criminals connected to the Cabal will be arrested and imprisoned, freeing humanity from the source of all evil.

"trust the Plan"

QAnons believe that Trump and the White Hats have created a brilliant and foolproof plan, which is destined to end the rule of the Cabal, ending suffering for all of humanity. While QAnons do not know what the Plan is and have never seen it articulated, adherents believe that it exists and place their faith in the idea that all is unfolding according to said Plan.

Where we go one, we go all (WWG1WGA)

"Where we go one, we go all!" is the most popular QAnon slogan, expressing solidarity and the power of the individual to make a difference in our world. In the QAnon mythos, this slogan is believed to have been etched into a bell on a sailboat owned by JFK Jr. While fact checks disagree with this assertion, we do know that these words appeared on a bell in a 1996 Hollywood movie called *White Squall*.

White Hats

In the QAnon lexicon, White Hats are the good guys and gals working within our government systems to end corruption and restore integrity to our constitutional republic and to end the impacts of evil on earth.

Appendix C:
Final Reflections and Learnings

In the first years after exiting QAnon, I sought to understand more deeply what happened to my mind, what QAnon really is, and what's going on with our information streams, including news outlets and social media. Since not everyone reads from cover to cover, I'm hoping that chapter hoppers and bottom-liners will at least lay eyes on this final section where I've collected some of the most eye-opening aspects of what I learned in my recovery process.

Here's what's on tap:

- A Stressed and Polarized Mind Is Unstable
- Theories on QAnon's Ability to Change People's Minds
- Q Drops Versus QAnon
- What Is QAnon, Really?
- War on Humanity
- Disinformation, Cyberwarfare, and Propaganda
- Popping Our Filter Bubbles (No One Is Immune)
- Building Immunity to the QAnon Rabbit Hole
- Living With Uncertainty
- The Serenity Prayer

A Stressed and Polarized Mind Is Unstable

It is stunning to me how completely my cognitive bias flipped overnight, although after further research into the workings of the mind under intense stress, it's beginning to make more sense. While writing the first draft of this book, I went through periods of feeling vulnerable, as I had thought my mind was more stable than that. I imagine many others are under that same illusion. However, I have come to understand that a polarized mind is by nature unstable. This knowledge leads me to believe that one of the best ways I can care for my mind is to seek to exit the trap of political polarization, which for me also means unplugging from the news. For those like me who seek not to choose sides, but instead want to find a common path toward peace, this presents a formidable challenge.

Theories on QAnon's Ability to Change People's Minds

I have seen people posit ideas as to how the flip into QAnon has happened for so many people. Among the most common theories from those on the left is that QAnon is a far-right psychological operation, carefully designed to promote alt-right ideology, perhaps with Russian support. Along this line of thinking is the idea that calculating minds have been refining the art of propaganda, researching, and determining the most effective ways to hijack the limbic brain to sway it in some intended direction. Many theorize that President Trump was actively working with whomever posted the Q drops; however, QAnon influencers (many of whom may well have merely jumped on the bandwagon to capitalize on the trendy topics, having nothing whatsoever to do with the allegedly organized person or group that created the Q drops) promoted material from many murky sources.

Limbic Hijack and the Basic Need for Safety: The science supporting the idea that QAnon utilized a "limbic hijack" (when intense emotions override rational thought processes, leading to impulsive reactions and making an individual more susceptible to believing misinformation due to diminished critical thinking) is strongly validated in a webinar led by neuroscience educator Sarah Peyton. In March 2021, she hosted a 90-minute webinar entitled "Conspiracy Theories and Political Extremism: Understanding Brain Behavior in an Uncertain World."[471] In this presentation, Sarah cites the many ways in which the combination of intensely polarized politics, a pandemic, and climate changes, can stimulate states of fear, making many brains ripe and receptive to conspiracy theories.

Conspiracy theories can serve an intrinsic need to make sense of life when authoritative information sources are propagating narratives that are diametrically opposite. Our minds have a hard time dealing with this disconnect, as we are compelled to make sense of our surroundings in order to support our biological drive for survival. For this reason, Sarah advises that when talking to a person who is spinning in fear and swept up by conspiracy theories, it is vitally important to establish for them a sense of safety, security, and agency, to calm these potent emotions associated with the perception that life is out of control. When these basic human needs for safety and security are not met, people are likely to remain in the fear state, which reduces their access to rational thinking and keeps them in a stressed emotional state, prone to reactivity.

> *When talking to a person who is spinning in fear and swept up by conspiracy theories, it is vitally important to establish for them a sense of safety, security, and agency.*

Q Drops Versus QAnon

In my recovery, I wanted to know: How do the claims of the MSM accurately or inaccurately portray the reality of QAnon? I wanted to know what originated with Q, in contrast to what was added in by the "Anons," social media influencers and other preexisting and newly generated media. It wasn't until 2023 while writing this book that I reviewed the Q drops from top to bottom, doing word searches to scan for specific topics, to see which of the beliefs I picked up during my foray into QAnon were clearly derived from Q, and which ones came from elsewhere. I estimated that 95% of all the information I gathered in my six months as a QAnon came from various influencers, not the Q drops.

✤ ReQovery ✤

I estimate that 95% of all the information I gathered in my six months as a QAnon came from various influencers, not the Q drops.

Here's what I discovered:
- The only mention I saw of JFK Jr. among the drops was one posted December 12, 2018, in which a QAnon asked Q if JFK Jr. is still alive and Q simply responded "No."
- I saw many mentions of pedophilia, but only one mention of child sex trafficking.
- I did not find any mentions of adrenochrome.
- I saw only one photo of Lady Gaga, none of Marina Abramovic, and no mentions of spirit cooking.
- I saw 45 local news reports of various arsonists who had been arrested for starting fires in California in 2020.
- I did see criticism of George Soros, the Rothschild family, and a Democratic politician, all of whom are Jewish; however, I also saw criticism of many other politicians who are not Jewish. The majority of those who are heavily criticized in the Q drops are Christian; however, Q is clearly supportive of Christian beliefs, as many drops quote directly from the Bible. Given that, I did not see anything that clearly demonstrated racism or anti-Semitism.
- Q repeatedly stated that to be patriotic is to rise in unity despite the forces that would seek to divide us by race, sex, religion, political affiliation, or class.
- Q posted a number of drops with photos, articles, and video links asserting that Trump is not a racist.
- Q never said that Covid-19 or the mRNA vaccines were a genocide project, nor was there any mention of a bioweapon in the drops.
- Q did suggest that the Covid virus may have been released intentionally in order to generate a pandemic, crash the economy, and reduce the possibility of a Trump reelection.

☸ Final Reflections and Learnings ☸

- Q also said the pandemic created excuses for Democrats to champion the use of mail-in ballots, which could easily be manipulated to make sure Trump would not win reelection.
- Reptilian shapeshifters, time travel, and villains among English royalty were mentioned by Janet Ossebaard, but not by Q.
- Q said nothing about underground tunnels where babies are bred for the Cabal to use in satanic practices without leaving a record of these births or deaths.
- Nor was anything in the drops about the World Health Organization, Bill Gates, the World Economic Forum, Klaus Schwab, Agenda 2030, or Event 201.

But the algorithms fed me all of these topics and more as a QAnon.

Initially much of what I came to believe was stimulated by watching *Fall of the Cabal*. Then over time it became compounded by social media algorithms. It appears that the most outrageous QAnon claims were generated by influencers who were profiting from internet traffic and selling products via their social platforms. They had loads of fodder to choose from, as the web was already filled with conspiracy theories.

I'd like to think that separating fact from fiction might soften the fear of and anger against others who have fallen into QAnon, but I also remember that as a Democrat, I once believed that all Republicans shared the ideology of white supremacy to one degree or another. So, I do understand that the indoctrination of one group against another runs deep. However, for those who are interested in looking beyond propaganda and clarifying fact from fiction, the Q drops can be read and keyword searched by anyone (while avoiding the toxic 4Chan and 8Chan boards), at qanon.pub. While you might find the drops mostly nonsensical and boring (as I did), feel free to check your assumptions against what you find there, and you'll know the difference for yourself.

While Q's communications are a collection of "drops" posted to online messaging boards, what I call QAnon is something else. It's not just a collection of almost every conspiracy theory I'd ever come across woven into one massive mega-theory; it carries many non-conspiracy-theory topics under its umbrella as well. QAnon is a runaway train. It is a magnet for some of the most outrageous, terrifying, and divisive claims that appear in our online space. This content is a melting pot of information that includes fact and falsehoods, news and propaganda (misleading partisan rhetoric, designed to generate enthusiastic support for Donald J. Trump). Its vast reach includes:

- Right-wing news.
- Everything supporting Trump.
- Everything questioning the coronavirus narrative and vaccine push.
- Everything addressing sexual deviation, pedophilia, and child sex trafficking.
- Information on Planned Parenthood and the unlawful under-the-table sales of fetal organ tissues.[472]
- Information on Planned Parenthood's roots in the eugenics movement[473] and its promotion of abortion in non-White and impoverished communities.[474]
- The allegedly gargantuan organ trafficking industry, which in China alone is estimated to be over $1 billion annually, fueled by harvesting the organs from China's population of over 1.5 million humans currently held in its "re-education camps."[475] These inmates are primarily minorities and dissenters, including Muslims, Uyghurs, Falun Gong practitioners, and those who dare to observe religious or spiritual traditions that are not approved by the CCP.[476,477]
- China and Ukraine's alleged bribery of the Biden family.[478]
- China's takeover of the Hollywood film industry.[479]
- Biblical references to the End Times.
- References to lesser-known ancient religious texts from the Dead Sea Scrolls,[480] including *The Book of Enoch*, also known as *The Book of Giants*.[481]

❀ Final Reflections and Learnings ❀

- Information on UAPs, and ET races.
- Information on new technologies like AI, human cloning, the fast-emerging central bank digital currencies (CBDCs), Bitcoin, and other blockchain-based alternatives to the CBDC.
- Warnings against the predictable trajectory of transhumanism.[482,483,484]
- Opposition to issues surrounding gender identity, especially biological males (assigned at birth) participating in women's sports or using women's bathrooms.
- Opposition to the liberal strategy of including Critical Race Theory in the public school curriculum.[485]
- Information on the World Economic Forum (WEF), the UN's 2030 Agenda for Sustainable Development and the WEF's Great Reset initiative[486] ("Agenda 2030").
- Information on survival strategies and "prepping" for any number of catastrophic eventualities.
- And so much more.

And while these might seem like disparate topics, they all somehow fit together. I was flooded with so much new information I felt like I had entered an alternate universe, one that had always existed, underlying the reality of everything I previously thought I knew.

I needed to separate fact from fiction in this regard because most people don't care to take the time to do the research of discerning the difference between the cryptic posts from Q, and other concurrent issues (many of them very much valid and pressing) that got lumped into QAnon in the public mind. Most everyone I know on the left believes what the MSM reports about the nature of, and beliefs surrounding QAnon, which pulls it all together as if there is no distinction. However, this is another example of a mistaken conflation, which only harms the potential for healing.

Other (valid and pressing) concurrent issues got lumped into QAnon in the public mind. This mistaken conflation only harms the potential for healing.

Harmful QAnon Distortions

I continue to be amused at how few Republicans have ever heard of QAnon, and yet this is simply another example of how disparate the left-leaning and right-leaning news channels have become. Every Democrat I know has some sense of what QAnon is and is distraught by what he or she has learned about this cultish phenomenon.

As part of their current censorship strategy, Facebook and Instagram have eliminated almost everything connected to QAnon. If a user wishes to understand why this decision was made, they are referred to an article published by the Global Network on Extremism & Technology (GNET) as an authority on the topic of QAnon, and some of what I read on that page bears no resemblance to my personal experience.

According to GNET's website, "QAnon is a militant and anti-establishment ideology rooted in a quasi-apocalyptic desire to destroy the existing 'corrupt' world order and usher in a promised golden age. This is reminiscent of numerous violent anti-government, white nationalist, and neo-Nazi extremist organizations across the globe."[487]

While I saw videos of current and former military officers express their agreement with some QAnon-related topics, I experienced nothing militant. QAnon generally opposes the political establishment, but most voters (on both sides of the aisle) have completely lost trust that this establishment cares at all about the needs of the people, so I don't blame QAnon's desire to expose and combat existing corruption connected to what it sees as a dystopian version of a new world order (a notion espoused by several American presidents and other heads of state since the time of Woodrow Wilson).[488] And there's certainly nothing wrong with holding a vision akin to the mythical idea of the Golden Age—a time when goodness prevails and humanity lives peacefully on a vibrant planet where nature is thriving and technology supports life. My experience of QAnon was not in the least bit

❁ Final Reflections and Learnings ❁

violent, white nationalist, or neo-Nazi. I find the allegations on this website are infuriatingly false. They might point to a reality about a fringe element of QAnon, but they are far from representative of what I saw while steeped in the QAnon experience.

> *My experience of QAnon was not in the least bit violent, white nationalist, or neo-Nazi.*

If GNET is at all representative of what people believe to be true about QAnons, there's very little chance of healing relationship bonds, as this description is every bit as preposterous as the absurd assertion that Democrats are satanists and pedophiles. The enemy images are too thick. Even with my wholehearted commitment to compassion, I could never associate with anyone who fits the above description. And yet, others who did not really know me, (and even Stephen to some degree), believed that this is what I had become and what I represented.

Inclusion Redefined

While I am no longer a QAnon, I have no problem being friends with people who are, so long as they share my values for peace and a world that works for everyone. From my limited experience as a "Pastel Q," I believe there are plenty of QAnons who share these core values, and only a small fringe who fit the description used by Facebook to censor speech.

Similarly, the prejudices I had against Republicans and Trump supporters, fed to me by liberal media channels, represent only the darkest and most incoherent fringe of the Republican party; they are nothing close to being accurate representations. To those who have been on the receiving end of this form of ignorant verbal attack, I am sorry. Please forgive me.

> *To the Republicans who have been on the receiving end of this form of ignorance, I am sorry. Please forgive me.*

Now I have a much more highly diverse community, which spans not only the cultural, race, class, creed, gender and socioeconomic spectrums, but also easily and naturally includes friends across the various ideological divides. Walking the talk of the inclusion I claimed to value has opened my life in unexpected directions, freeing me to see the humanity in people I once dismissed. While I don't agree with everyone's politics, and while it seems we are all grappling with our unmet desires to come together in shared reality based clearly on objective and undeniable truths, I have yet to meet anyone on the right whose values so diverge from mine that I need to remove myself from their presence.

There is a way in which my spirit has expanded, knowing that our differences in perspective no longer generate enmity in me. It's truly okay to agree to disagree and move forward with mutual respect and care. I wish the masses around me could have this breakthrough in social harmony too.

If this still seems unlikely to you, I invite you to enjoy this 3-minute video clip.[489] In it, a young Democrat with "empathy" on his t-shirt did something I'm sure his friends considered courageous (or crazy). He walked into a Trump rally to see how he would be received as a liberal and test his assumptions. To his surprise, he was met almost exclusively with warmth and kindness, and the energy was decidedly one of living peacefully among diversity.

Watch this video from Dr. Phil's YouTube channel: "This Liberal Went to a Trump Rally"

To be clear, I am *not* encouraging you to watch this with any hope that it would turn you into a Trump supporter. Rather I fervently wish we could all stop judging people we don't know. Or as Rodney King said on the third day of the 1992 Los Angeles riots in his emotional plea for peace, "Can we all get along?"

Although I just watched videos and never went near a Trump rally, this dynamic was very much my experience as well. Learning how off base I had been about people across the aisle is one of the great gifts that this QAnon experience gave me—one that will inform my entire life, going forward. Although I had already devoted conscious study to the practice of regarding people without prejudgment and seeing their light, I was blind to the ways I had been building walls until this six-month digression showed

Final Reflections and Learnings

me how much farther I could stretch into the values I claimed to hold. While some people's experiences may surely not have been as positive, this short video genuinely reflects mine.

War on Humanity

As I shared in the introduction to this book, "divide and conquer" is a strategy as old as politics and war. It is clear as day that we are being divided. While we are distracted in conflict with one another, it is harder to see all the things that are going on to strip us of our basic human rights to life, liberty and the pursuit of happiness. The metaphor of "boiling the frog" applies to the situation in which we as a human family find ourselves now.

Our water sources are accumulating increasing amounts of toxic chemicals from industrial corporate dumping, agrochemicals, pharmaceutical residue, fracking, and more. Our soil is being depleted by monocropping and decades of chemical spraying. An average of 200 highly toxic "persistent organic pollutants" exist in the umbilical cord blood of babies as they develop in the womb;[490] chemically compromising us before birth. Our health is degenerating, as can be seen most notably by the meteoric rise of autism, obesity, diabetes, ADHD, cancer, depression, and suicide in our kids.

Meanwhile, our economy is being drained through endless wars and the complete failure of Anthony Fauci's strategies to protect the public health during the Covid pandemic. Our national debt, which was already at $17 trillion, doubled between 2016 and 2024, with Trump and Biden adding similar amounts to this already incalculably enormous burden. Now Medicare and Social Security insolvency are "right around the corner,"[491] and our grown kids are burdened by outrageous college debts with which they obtain degrees that hardly help them to stay financially afloat, and that give them little to no hope of ever owning a home. This is in sharp contrast to only fifty years ago, when one person working a full-time job could afford a home and a car, provide for a family of four, and pay for their kids to go to college.

We are steeped in a deep pot, and it's coming to a boil. Our health is in decline as degenerative diseases are on the rise and no pharmaceuticals can cure the problem of a toxic environment leading to spillover "toxic body burden." Our finances are increasingly strained, censorship is on the rise, and our freedom to simply leave our homes can be taken away in an instant—just as soon as the WHO sounds the alarm for the next Public Health Emergency of International Concern.

What do we have left of the sacred promise of life, liberty, and the pursuit of happiness? And yet we cannot move forward because we are fighting each other based on cognitive distortions we hold about each other—enemy images spread by way of our media and various online influencers. I had thought the Republicans and the people who support Trump were the culprits destroying our country. Now I see that I was woefully wrong.

> *"Our country is being ransacked right now, and the people who are ransacking it, their best interest is to have us all fighting each other— with Blacks fighting Whites and Republicans vs. Democrats— because then we're not keeping an eye on what's happening in Washington D.C."*
>
> ~ Robert F. Kennedy Jr.

Disinformation, Cyberwarfare, and Propaganda

We are living in times when AI disinformation is becoming exponentially more challenging. Fabricated news is part of the modern world. People and organizations have learned how to weaponize this technology,[492] destroying countries from within by sowing seeds of misinformation, division, and hatred, and calling for violence. Some even say we are already in WWIII; however, it is not a kinetic war. It is a war on the mind—a psychological cyberwar.[493]

Lieutenant General H. R. McMaster, who served as the United States National Security Advisor from 2017 to 2018, has gone so far as to say "It's the war that Russia, China, and other hostile foreign actors are fighting

🪷 Final Reflections and Learnings 🪷

against us—weaponizing social media to undermine our faith in each other, our government, and democracy itself."[494] From what I can see, it goes far beyond our own country. Propaganda campaigns are sowing seeds of division and hatred around the globe as power brokers do backroom deals to accumulate and consolidate more power.

Many sources of disinformation, misinformation, and factual information, paired with clear bias, are being generated and disseminated by a wide range of sources including commercial, religious, political, ideological, and international interests. And while those who did not fall for QAnon might believe themselves to be impermeable to mental and emotional manipulation, anyone can fall prey to malicious mind-control campaigns.

By amplifying extreme positions that do not represent the majority of a group, propaganda campaigns have been designed to divide us into "us against them." For example, Democrats are led to believe that Republicans support policies that would be disastrous for climate change, send women's rights back to the 1950's, and turn a blind eye to issues of systemic racism. And Republicans are led to believe that Democrats support policies that would destroy families, crash our economy, and give rise to a genderless society. Notice how prevalent these beliefs have become—practically unquestioned—and highly divisive.

> *By amplifying extreme positions that do not represent the majority of a group, propaganda campaigns have been designed to divide us into "us against them."*

Devious tactics have been designed by a number of sources with the objective to hack our minds and hijack our beliefs. This makes us all prone to the increasing risks of escalating global violence, as people around the world lose faith in each other and their elected officials and lose sight of the vision for a peaceful and prosperous future for all.

Ideological subversion originating from Russia has been called a "firehose of falsehoods." It has been running full blast since the end of the Cold War.[495] And the Chinese Communist Party is another big player in the arena of spreading fake news and accounts that serve its own interests.[496]

Iran, North Korea and Venezuela have been known to target the United States as well.[497]

But nations aren't the only entities creating and disseminating propaganda that tears apart our social fabric. Far-right white supremacist groups also create and spread this toxic form of communication.[498] Similarly, The Heritage Foundation has been accused of spreading propaganda that could install a far-right fascist-style of political leadership in the US through Project 2025, which is designed to "rescue the country from the grip from the radical Left."[499,500] These examples, and many more, make it obvious to liberals that conservative media spin is real.

On the flipside, conservatives feel equally troubled by indoctrination they see on the left. For example, the right calls into question both Black Lives Matter and Antifa, as many conservatives consider them to be domestic terrorists due to their (openly acknowledged) Marxist[501,502] and pro-Communist,[503] roots, and their inclination to promote violent protest strategies.[504,505] Thus, both sides, for different reasons, regard the other with great urgency to be "a threat to our democracy."

Artificial Intelligence in Media: Creation and distribution of news narratives with the wide reach to influence entire populations was once the domain of a limited few in what is now known as "legacy media" (print, film, music, advertising, radio, and television). Now, however, with the rise of user-friendly AI tools like Dall-E 2 and Midjourney in this decade, anyone with a computer can hop on the disinformation-creation train, further flooding the internet with hordes of falsehoods and half-truths, including highly realistic AI-generated photos and videos of bombings that never happened, gatherings that never occurred, and people who never existed.[506,507] Just look up "AI generated deepfake" and you'll see numerous compelling examples of this modern technology, all of which can be produced in a matter of minutes.[508,509]

In 2024, with the development of advanced multimedia creation tools like Sora,[510] the ability to create realistic deepfakes where people can appear to be saying anything in their own voice, speaking style, and mannerisms, is on the horizon. Even with current tools, it's easy to depict anyone anywhere, though not yet with speech. Once that capability is perfected, it will be nearly impossible to distinguish an actual video from one created with AI.[511,512,513,514]

A Note on Censorship: Censorship has been on a sharp and notable rise since 2020, validated by the necessity to protect the public from the massive rise of disinformation. Some experts say it is the only way to effectively deal with the vast amount of toxic garbage influencing our population. Others say the best way to combat the harmful effects of untruths is not with censorship but with better information.

While I would agree that we need far better strategies to safeguard our population from informational spins designed to cause harm, and while censorship on the surface appears to be a commonsense solution, it doesn't take much to look deeper and recognize that this tactic would predictably set us up for enormous troubles ahead. Freedom of speech does not exist in authoritarian governments. There is a crucial reason it is clearly protected in our first amendment. The American Civil Liberties Union published a document on March 2, 2002 called "Freedom of Expression," stating:

> *History teaches that the first target of government repression is never the last. If we do not come to the defense of the free speech rights of the most unpopular among us, even if their views are antithetical to the very freedom the First Amendment stands for, then no one's liberty will be secure.*[515]

The freedom to criticize government is a cornerstone of democracy; without it those who rise to power would have the ability to determine what we are and are not permitted to say. And anyone who criticized their abuses would be forcefully silenced as democracy died. Without freedom of speech, we are lost.

We must therefore tackle the complexity head-on. We are swimming in a chaotic sea of information, and some of it is intentionally designed to generate emotions and convictions that encourage conflict and violence.

Separating truth from falsehood is becoming increasingly difficult, even for the most grounded and well informed among us. It is impossible to stay up to date on the rapid evolution and implications of AI technological advances, even for the experts and teams at the Center for Humane Technology, who actively seek to do just that.[516]

But we can take steps to build our immunity to content designed to cause harm. We can reduce our engagement with social media directly and indirectly by not only enjoying more time offline, but also choosing not to engage in live conversations that echo divisive online content. We can build media literacy, gaining clearer discernment when it comes to finding trustworthy sources of information. We can burst our filter bubbles and gain a much wider perspective on a variety of issues. And we can choose to focus on building harmony in our relationships, agreeing to disagree with mutual care and respect, rather than giving in to impulses toward conflict and violence.

Popping Our Filter Bubbles (No One Is Immune)

On top of the massive persuasion campaigns crossing our screens regularly, AI-based "Inconspicuous Filter Bubbles" as described in chapter 11 are still very much operational.[517] This ubiquitous design feature of social media increases the effectiveness of propaganda from all sources.

Awareness of this phenomenon helps us to exercise greater discernment with respect to the information streams that pop up on our social media channels. All of us who spend time in these spaces are living in digital echo chambers that affirm our cognitive biases. If we've fallen into propaganda traps, our minds will continue to be influenced by those jaws until we actively work to exit them.

> *All of us who spend time on social media are living in digital echo chambers that affirm our cognitive biases.*

I found a website called AVID Open Access, which has an entire section on *digital citizenship* (which involves safely and responsibly navigating digital environments while actively and respectfully participating in these spaces) and *media literacy* (the skill of critically evaluating the content in mass media, assessing its credibility and accuracy). It lists these ten ways to pop a filter bubble:[518]

- Understand that information is being filtered.
- Intentionally seek out opposing viewpoints.
- Seek news from a variety of sources.
- Evaluate the credibility of information sources.
- Watch for bias.[519,520]
- Seek out less-biased news outlets.
- Don't avoid the hard conversations; engage in them.
- Don't unfriend those who disagree with you.
- Listen with the intent to learn.
- Question your own perspectives.

> *Don't unfriend those who disagree with you.*
> *Listen with the intent to learn.*

Whew, I can only imagine what kind of world we would live in if the curiosity to learn from those with disparate viewpoints replaced our knee-jerk habit of rejecting and disparaging them.[521] And let's not forget that we can (gasp!) simply unplug from technology and plug back into nature and connection with each other at any time.

Building Immunity to the QAnon Rabbit Hole

Many people have asked me what I am doing to reduce the risk of ever stumbling into something like QAnon again. And, they ask "how could you have ever fallen for something like that?" Honestly, if I hadn't gone through it myself, I'd be just as bewildered as they are. But having lived it, I no longer believe any of us is immune to this kind of AI-enhanced mind control.

> *I no longer believe any of us is immune to*
> *this kind of AI-enhanced mind control.*

I would encourage you to check out this short video clip from mind control educator Jason Christoff, as he shares another astonishing example of thought hacking, which was accomplished in just five minutes by world-renowned mentalist Max Major on "America's Got Talent."[522] (And if you didn't catch the first Christoff clip I shared in chapter 17, I'd like to bring it to your attention again: Search YouTube for "Justin Wilman: Influencing the Influencers" to watch the tables get turned on three savvy and successful young social media influencers, who find themselves influenced—into a lockstep behavior that leaves them dazed and bewildered in a "How could this have happened to me!?" stupor… one that I know so well.) According to Christoff, "80% of mind control is repetition." Consider for a moment the repetitive messages we've all received in recent years, via text, sound, and imagery. If a human can control mass behavior to this level in five minutes, it's scary to imagine what AI-driven media is doing to all of us, especially over much longer periods of time.

I plummeted into QAnon at a time that I was unusually mentally and emotionally vulnerable. My trust in our political system was at an all-time low, and I, along with most of the world, was socially isolated and stressed to the max, three months into the Covid lockdowns. The way the pandemic was handled in California created mental health challenges that made many people prone to online propaganda. It is perfectly human to want to find some hope—solutions that will make things right. Given my knowledge of this vulnerability, my mental and emotional health are top priority for me now.

One immediate step I took to stay alert to the possibility of reentering a harmful mental trap was to agree to listen when my close friends and family think I might be descending into something unhealthy again. If someone who loves me expresses concern, we address it together. And I take a whole lot more time to check my sources, knowing that even the best references are prone to error. I hardly take anything online or in conversation with others at face value anymore.

Early on in my recovery, I went cold turkey on all forms of news and almost all social media, as so many associations risked quickly throwing my mind back into a QAnon-style frenzy. To be honest, I feared that writing this book might stir it all back up again. As I wrote the first draft, I got mentally and emotionally stimulated at times and felt the addictive tendency to go online and learn more. But as I am well aware of the toll that took on me during my time in QAnon, I have strong motivation to replace those unhealthy impulses with a version of my mantra which helps me find inner peace amidst uncertainty: "I don't understand what's going on and that's okay." Staying attentive to my tendency to go into an addictive trance is essential to my ability to build immunity to QAnon or anything like it.

Screen Time Addiction: However, this addictive trance is not solely a QAnon phenomenon. Screen time addiction, particularly related to social media and online gaming, is a growing concern (and becoming an emergency[523] among the current generation of young people) due to the integral role digital devices play in our daily lives. This type of addiction is characterized by excessive and compulsive use of social media platforms and online games that negatively impacts an individual's mental, emotional, and even physical health.

This behavior is driven by several interrelated factors. The design of social media platforms leverages intermittent reinforcement; sporadic and unpredictable rewards such as likes and comments stimulate the brain's reward centers, encouraging continual engagement. Games each have their own sets of virtual rewards. Fear of missing out (also known as FOMO), compels users to constantly check their devices to stay connected and avoid missing important updates or social interactions. Additionally, social media often prompts users to engage in social comparison, which can lead to feelings of inadequacy and a compulsive need to seek validation online. Finally, many turn to social media and online gaming as an escape from boredom or anesthetize negative emotions, reinforcing habitual and excessive use as a coping mechanism. These elements collectively foster a cycle of dependency that can be challenging to break.

The consequences of social media and online gaming addiction are multifaceted and profound. Prolonged engagement can lead to issues such as anxiety, depression, and a pervasive sense of loneliness, as the virtual connections often do not provide the same quality and fulfillment as face-to-face interactions. It can disrupt sleep patterns, distract people from attending to basic self-care practices and daily activities, strain the eyes, and create chronic pain due to poor posture.

Addressing this prevalent addiction involves a combination of personal discipline, lifestyle adjustments, and possibly professional help, particularly when the behavior significantly interferes with daily functioning or well-being.

While I can take all of these preventative measures as an individual, other immunity-building strategies require collective action. I learned from the 2020 documentary "*A Social Dilemma*" that AI had already learned plenty about human weaknesses on its way to eclipsing human intelligence.[524] It has come a long way since then. Highly sophisticated AI is being massively deployed this year (2024) to manipulate our minds and our emotions, and with that our words and actions. It is imperative that we demand ethical regulations on AI development, to whatever extent that is possible, as it has both the power to create miraculous solutions to the many problems of our modern age and also the potential to enslave us.[525] I encourage people to support the work of the Center for Humane Technology and Nicole Shanahan,[526] both of whom are working to establish ethical development of this powerful and rapidly self-evolving technology and to contact your congressional representatives, demanding they address the growing threat of poorly regulated AI tech development.

Staying immune to QAnon or anything like it is similar to staying healthy. It takes daily awareness and consistent action in alignment with my desired results. If I revert to harmful habits, I can notice and pick myself up again. Having a supportive and healthy community of friends and family makes all the difference, and much can be done to create healthy relationships.

❀ Final Reflections and Learnings ❀

The Liberating Gift of Embracing Uncertainty

Accepting that life is full of unknowns was the final piece I needed to break free from QAnon's grip. Yet the battle wasn't (isn't) over, as QAnon is just one source of anxiety-inducing fixations. Calamitous potentialities (both imminent and imagined) come at us daily, dominating media headlines, activist rhetoric, and a good chunk of what passes as "entertainment." The reality of uncertainty is deeply woven into the human experience, perhaps now more than ever due to the accelerating pace of change in our modern times.

We can shore up our capacity for living on shaky ground by various means, such as strengthening our personal relationships, engaging in spiritual or religious practices, or advocating for policies that aim to mitigate risks. We can take actions to become increasingly self-sufficient—less dependent on external systems for our basic needs such as water, food, and electricity. We can develop skills which are valuable and tradeable, remembering that money is not the only form of transactional currency, building an abundance that can be shared in community should the necessity arise. And we can do all of this while living in peace, gratitude, and joyful connection with each other and Mother Earth.

Our future will always be fraught with looming catastrophes, but true inner peace cannot exist in the relentless frantic dread of scenarios that might never come to pass. I am not advocating for pretending everything in life is normal; it's not. We are living in tumultuous times, and engaging in individual and collective emergency preparedness is wise. However, living in unceasing fear robs us of the blessings and joys that are here with us today. In our anxiety, we miss countless opportunities to love ourselves and uplift others, to revere our natural world, and to be in service to life and the people around us.

My journey of recovery has gifted me with a lightness of spirit and a calmness of mind, where I embrace the present moment amidst life's uncertainties. This path is open to everyone.

The Serenity Prayer

In closing, I'd like to say that I still don't know what (the fuck) is going on—and that's okay! As I accept the uncertain nature of our modern-day reality, this abbreviated version of the Serenity Prayer by the late Reinhold Neibuhr is my (more life-serving) go-to mantra:

"God grant me the Serenity to accept the things I cannot change, the Courage to change the things I can, and the Wisdom to know the difference."

About the Author

Katrina Vaillancourt is a certified Nonviolent Communication (NVC) trainer, mediator and life coach. Her work includes a variety of personal and relationship growth tools including NVC, Authentic Relating, compassionate inquiry, role-play dialogues, inner child work, use of positive affirmations, and more. She is the creator of Love Smart Cards, an educational tool that aids in the rapid learning and practical application of the basic principles in NVC and Positive Psychology, most notably the cultivation of empathy. In her free time, she enjoys yoga, meditation, outdoor sports, time with her family, and many forms of creative arts, including dancing, devotional singing, and tending her garden.

Endnotes and References

The full endnotes are also available on our website:
www.ReQoveryBook.com/Endnotes

All these links were active as of May 2024.

[1] Center for Nonviolent Communication
http://ww.cnvc.org

[2] "Satan is real, Pope Francis says"
https://www.catholicnewsagency.com/news/41160/satan-is-real-pope-francis-s

[3] The Social Dilemma (documentary about social media AI-algorithms to drive user attention)
https://www.thesocialdilemma.com/

[4] Bill Moyers article comparing Trump to fascism
https://www.commondreams.org/views/2020/06/06/we-hold-truth-be-self-evident-its-happening-our-very-eyes

[5] DNC apologizes to Bernie Sanders amid convention chaos in wake of email leak
https://www.theguardian.com/us-news/2016/jul/25/debbie-wasserman-schultz-booed-dnc-fbi-email-hack

[6] Wikipedia: The Great Hack (documentary about Cambridge Analytica and the 2016 election)
https://en.wikipedia.org/wiki/The_Great_Hack

[7] "Cloak and Data: The Real Story Behind Cambridge Analytica's Rise and Fall"
https://www.motherjones.com/politics/2018/03/cloak-and-data-cambridge-analytica-robert-mercer/

[8] "Trump isn't the only Republican who gave Cambridge Analytica big bucks"
https://www.cnn.com/2018/03/20/politics/cambridge-analytica-republican-ties/index.html

[9] "Cambridge Analytica parent firm SCL Elections fined over data refusal"
https://www.bbc.com/news/technology-46822439

[10] "Mercer sisters liquidate beleaguered Cambridge Analytica"
https://apnews.com/article/64280ae1f30c44eb8b82049f6875dddd

[11] Oxford Reference: Manufacture of Consent
https://www.oxfordreference.com/display/10.1093/oi/authority.20110803100132197

[12] Wikipedia: The Corporation (2003 film)
https://en.wikipedia.org/wiki/The_Corporation_(2003_film)

[13] Wikipedia: Citizens United v. FEC
https://en.wikipedia.org/wiki/Citizens_United_v._FEC

[14] *** "Dark Money: Citizens United unleashed unlimited spending in our elections, and groups can now spend hundreds of millions without disclosing their sources of funding. We advocate for greater transparency in election spending."

https://www.brennancenter.org/issues/reform-money-politics/influence-big-money/dark-money

[15] "Will Covid-19 End the Age of Mass Protests?"
https://www.csis.org/analysis/will-covid-19-end-age-mass-protests

[16] "The Coronation" by Charles Eisenstein
https://charleseisenstein.org/essays/the-coronation/

[17] "In Their Own Words: The 'Water Protectors' Of Standing Rock"
https://www.npr.org/2016/12/11/505147166/in-their-own-words-the-water-protectors-of-standing-rock

[18] Wikipedia: TigerSwan
https://en.wikipedia.org/wiki/TigerSwan

[19] "LEAKED DOCUMENTS REVEAL COUNTERTERRORISM TACTICS USED AT STANDING ROCK TO "DEFEAT PIPELINE INSURGENCIES": Internal TigerSwan documents provide a detailed picture of how the mercenary firm surveilled Dakota Access Pipeline opponents and infiltrated protest camps."
https://x/theintercept.com/2017/05/27/leaked-documents-reveal-security-firms-counterterrorism-tactics-at-standing-rock-to-defeat-pipeline-insurgencies/

[20] "Standing Rock: A Case Study in Civil Disobedience"
https://www.americanbar.org/groups/gpsolo/publications/gp_solo/2018/may-june/standing-rock-case-study-civil-disobedience/

[21] Plandemic 1 (documentary with Dr. July Mikovits)
https://plandemicseries.com/plandemic-1/

[22] Tony Robbins: "COVID-19 Facts from the Frontline: Unmasking the Science You Aren't Hearing On TV"
https://www.youtube.com/watch?v=YgP_Au5RZVw&feature=youtu.be

[23] "Why is the Gates foundation investing in GM giant Monsanto?"
https://www.theguardian.com/global-development/poverty-matters/2010/sep/29/gates-foundation-gm-monsanto

[24] *** **New England Journal of Medicine, Feb. 28, 2020, Dr. Anthony Fauci: Covid CFR** *"may be considerably less than 1%"*
https://www.nejm.org/doi/full/10.1056/NEJMe2002387

[25] Antibody Tests Point To Lower Death Rate For The Coronavirus Than First Thought"
https://www.npr.org/sections/health-shots/2020/05/28/863944333/antibody-tests-point-to-lower-death-rate-for-the-coronavirus-than-first-thought

[26] "Infection fatality rate of COVID-19 inferred from seroprevalence data"
https://pubmed.ncbi.nlm.nih.gov/33716331/

[27] American Race: White Privilege in America [CLIP] | TNT
https://youtu.be/pgUCGo5kUXk

[28] Wikipedia: 13th (documentary about the 13th amendment and systemic racism)
https://en.wikipedia.org/wiki/13th_(film)

[29] Deeyah Khan: "White Right: Meeting the Enemy" (documentary about White supremacy in the US)
https://deeyah.com/blog/white-right-meeting-enemy/

Endnotes and References

[30] ABC News: "Hacker Group, Anonymous, Hits Federal Reserve"
https://www.youtube.com/watch?v=iknsdj34LIM

[31] Wikipedia: Anonymous (hacker group)
https://en.wikipedia.org/wiki/Anonymous_(hacker_group)

[32] How a tree can burn from the inside
https://www.sciencealert.com/watch-this-devil-tree-in-ohio-is-burning-from-the-inside-out

[33] NIH Pichichero: Mercury concentrations and metabolism in infants receiving vaccines containing thiomersal: a descriptive study
"Interpretation: Administration of vaccines containing thiomersal does not seem to raise blood concentrations of mercury above safe values in infants. Ethylmercury seems to be eliminated from blood rapidly via the stools after parenteral administration of thiomersal in vaccines.")
https://pubmed.ncbi.nlm.nih.gov/12480426/

[34] **NIH Burbacher: Comparison of Blood and Brain Mercury Levels in Infant Monkeys Exposed to Methylmercury or Vaccines Containing Thimerosal**
"Knowledge of the biotransformation of thimerosal, the chemical identity of the Hg-containing species in the blood and brain, and the neurotoxic potential of intact thimerosal and its various biotransformation products, including ethylmercury, is urgently needed to afford a meaningful interpretation of the potential developmental effects of immunization with thimerosal-containing vaccines in newborns and infants. This information is critical if we are to respond to public concerns regarding the safety of childhood immunizations."
https://www.ncbi.nlm.nih.gov/pmc/articles/PMC1280342/

[35] **NIH Kern: Examining the evidence that ethylmercury crosses the blood-brain barrier**
"In total, these studies indicate that **Thimerosal and** ethylmercury-containing compounds **readily cross the BBB**, converting, for the most part, to **highly toxic inorganic mercury-containing compounds**, which significantly and persistently **bind to tissues in the brain**, even in the absence of concurrent detectable blood mercury levels."
https://pubmed.ncbi.nlm.nih.gov/31841767/

[36] Geoengineering Whistleblower ~ Ex-Military ~ Kristen Meghan, Hauppauge, NY, January 18th, 2014
https://environmentaljusticetv.wordpress.com/2022/08/22/geoengineering-whistleblower-ex-military-kristen-meghan-hauppauge-ny-january-18th-2014-4/

[37] CDC: Toxicological Profile for Sulfur Trioxide and Sulfuric Acid
https://wwwn.cdc.gov/TSP/ToxProfiles/ToxProfiles.aspx

[38] EYE ON THE SKY: Digging deep on the facts versus fiction of chemtrails & contrail cirrus and how to pragmatically deal with sky pollution and geoengineering.
https://climateviewer.substack.com/p/eye-on-the-sky-del-bigtree-and-jim

[39] Photos of the Vatican
https://www.vatican.va/content/francesco/en/events/event.dir.html/content/vaticanevents/en/2022/1/5/udienzagenerale.html

[40] Pope Francis: "The serpent that kills and the one that saves"
https://www.vatican.va/content/francesco/en/cotidie/2016/documents/papa-francesco-cotidie_20160315_the-serpent-that-kills-and-the-one-that-saves.html

[41] Photo of the large bronze "Resurrection" sculpture in the Vatican
https://www.aljazeera.com/mritems/images/2013/3/17/2013317144445897894_8.jpg

[42] "The story behind the Vatican's colossal sculpture of Jesus rising from nuclear destruction"
https://www.americamagazine.org/arts-culture/2022/08/29/fazzini-resurrection-sculture-vatican-243642

[43] Popular Science: "Lucifer Instrument Helps Astronomers See Through Darkness to Most Distant Observable Objects"
https://www.popsci.com/science/article/2010-04/devil-named-telescope-helps-astronomers-see-through-darkness/

[44] Politifact: "No, the Vatican doesn't own a telescope called Lucifer"
https://www.politifact.com/factchecks/2021/nov/22/facebook-posts/no-vatican-doesnt-own-telescope-called-lucifer/

[45] Constantine: The Man Who Invented Christmas
https://www.bbc.co.uk/mediacentre/proginfo/2011/52/constantine-the-man-who-invented-christmas

[46] Wikipedia: Catharism
https://en.wikipedia.org/wiki/Catharism

[47] Wikipedia: Loose Change (documentary about 9/11)
https://en.wikipedia.org/wiki/Loose_Change

[48] Architects & Engineers for 9/11 Truth
https://www.ae911truth.org/

[49] "21 Completely Filthy Hidden Sex References in Disney Movies"
https://www.cosmopolitan.com/entertainment/celebs/g19587585/disney-movies-sex-references/

[50] Snopes: "Was a Phallus Purposely Added to the Artwork for 'The Little Mermaid' VHS Cover?"
https://www.snopes.com/fact-check/phallus-purposely-added-artwork-little-mermaid-vhs-cover/

[51] Business Casual: "How Soros Made a Billion Dollars and Almost Broke Britain"
https://www.youtube.com/watch?v=WBZnau8Px5E

[52] "Migrant border crossings in fiscal year 2022 topped 2.76 million, breaking previous record"
https://www.nbcnews.com/politics/immigration/migrant-border-crossings-fiscal-year-2022-topped-276-million-breaking-rcna53517

[53] "Title 42: What is the immigration rule and why has it ended?"
https://www.bbc.com/news/world-us-canada-65477653

[54] "Under Biden More Illegal Immigrants Have Entered Through the Southern Border Than the Population Of 36 States"
https://www.gop.gov/news/documentsingle.aspx?DocumentID=728

[55] "The 'Baby Foreskin Facial' Is a Real Thing"
https://www.bostonmagazine.com/health/2015/04/14/baby-foreskin-facial-boston-hydrafacial/

[56] "Fact check: List of US patents is not evidence that viruses are manmade"
https://www.reuters.com/article/idUSKBN27C1OT/

[57] **"Parents can't sue drug firms when vaccines cause harm, Supreme Court says"**
"A federal law grants drug companies immunity from certain lawsuits from injuries or deaths tied to vaccines, the US Supreme Court affirmed Tuesday."
https://www.csmonitor.com/USA/Justice/2011/0222/Parents-can-t-sue-drug-firms-when-vaccines-cause-harm-Supreme-Court-says

🪷 Endnotes and References 🪷

[58] John Hopkins: **Event 201 (October 18, 2019)**
https://centerforhealthsecurity.org/our-work/tabletop-exercises/event-201-pandemic-tabletop-exercise

[59] Center for Health Security: Event 201 video series
https://youtu.be/AoLw-Q8X174

[60] "Pandemic simulation exercise spotlights massive preparedness gap"
"That center's latest **pandemic simulation**, **Event 201**, dropped participants right in the midst of an **uncontrolled coronavirus outbreak** that was spreading like wildfire ... As fictional newscasters from "GNN" narrated, the immune-resistant virus ... was crippling trade and travel, sending the global economy into freefall. **Social media was rampant with rumors and misinformation**, governments were collapsing, and citizens were revolting."
https://hub.jhu.edu/2019/11/06/event-201-health-security/

[61] Science Daily: "When did the first COVID-19 case arise?"
"Using methods from conservation science, a new analysis suggests that the **first case of COVID-19 arose between early October** and mid-November"
https://www.sciencedaily.com/releases/2021/06/210624141537.htm

[62] **Gates** Notes, April 30, 2020: "What you need to know about the COVID-19 vaccine"
"**My answer is always the same:** when we have an almost perfect drug to treat COVID-19, or when **almost every person on the planet** has been **vaccinated** against coronavirus."
https://www.gatesnotes.com/What-you-need-to-know-about-the-COVID-19-vaccine

[63] Gates Notes: April 6, 2021: "Meet an epidemiologist fighting to make vaccines work for communities of color"
"If there's one thing the world has learned about COVID-19 over the last year, it's this: the pandemic will only end when almost everyone on the planet has been vaccinated against the virus."
https://www.gatesnotes.com/Heroes-in-the-field-Dr-Stephaun-Wallace

[64] Wikipedia: Citizenfour (documentary about whistleblower Edward Snowden)
https://en.wikipedia.org/wiki/Citizenfour

[65] "Here's Why the Patriot Act Is So Controversial" (end of privacy)
https://www.history.com/topics/21st-century/heres-why-the-patriot-act-is-so-controversial-video

[66] "Agent Orange: Background on Monsanto's Involvement"
https://www.business-humanrights.org/en/latest-news/agent-orange-background-on-monsantos-involvement/

[67] Wikipedia: Glyphosate
https://en.wikipedia.org/wiki/Glyphosate

[68] "Millions Against Monsanto" (AKA "Billions Against Bayer)
https://organicconsumers.org/campaigns/millions-against-monsanto/

[69] "Bayer agrees to $10.9bn settlement over Monsanto's weedkiller Roundup: Numerous lawsuits have been brought against the pharmaceutical subsidiary over claims the chemical causes cancer"
https://www.theguardian.com/business/2020/jun/24/bayer-109bn-settlement-monsanto-weedkiller-roundup

[70] "Robert F. Kennedy Jr. wins historic $290 million case against giant Monsanto and Roundup weed-killer"
https://www.irishcentral.com/news/robert-f-kennedy-case-monsanto-roundup-weed-killer

71 Bayer's Billions in Roundup Verdicts Increase Pressure for New Legal Strategy
https://www.bloomberg.com/news/articles/2024-01-30/bayer-roundup-verdicts-increase-pressure-for-new-legal-strategy

72 *** "The 'Revolving Door' between Regulatory Agencies and Industry: A Problem That Requires Reconceptualizing Objectivity"
https://research.ncsu.edu/ges/files/2017/11/2011-Kuzma-Revolving-Door-between-Regulatory-Agencies-Agricultural-and-Environmental-Ethics.pdf

73 "Revolving doors: Monsanto and the regulators"
link.gale.com/apps/doc/A21269224/AONE

74 "Glyphosate Lawsuit"
"those injured as a result of exposure to glyphosate may be able to file a Roundup lawsuit for compensation"
https://www.sokolovelaw.com/product-liability/monsanto-roundup/glyphosate/

75 "FOODS MOST LIKELY TO CONTAIN GLYPHOSATE"
https://www.organiclifestylemagazine.com/foods-most-likely-to-contain-glyphosate

76 "Why Glyphosate Is Used on Non-GMO Crops"
https://www.onlyorganic.org/why-glyphosate-is-used-on-non-gmo-crops/

77 "Why is the Gates foundation investing in GM giant Monsanto?"
https://www.theguardian.com/global-development/poverty-matters/2010/sep/29/gates-foundation-gm-monsanto

78 "Indian Farmer Suicides: A Lesson for Africa's Farmers"
https://archive.foodfirst.org/publication/indian-farmer-suicides-a-lesson-for-africas-farmers/

79 "Seeds of suicide and slavery versus seeds of life and freedom: Contrary to its claims, Monsanto's monopoly on seeds in India are the root cause behind the sharp increase in suicides." By Vandana Shiva
https://www.aljazeera.com/opinions/2013/3/30/seeds-of-suicide-and-slavery-versus-seeds-of-life-and-freedom/

80 "Common weed killer glyphosate increases cancer risk by 41%, study says"
https://www.cnn.com/2019/02/14/health/us-glyphosate-cancer-study-scli-intl/index.html

81 "America dropped 26,171 bombs in 2016. What a bloody end to Obama's reign" by Benjamin Media, founder of Code Pink
https://www.theguardian.com/commentisfree/2017/jan/09/america-dropped-26171-bombs-2016-obama-legacy

82 "After 8 Years Of Unbroken War, Obama Hands Over Conflicts To Trump"
https://www.npr.org/sections/parallels/2017/01/18/510447582/after-8-years-of-unbroken-war-obama-hands-over-conflicts-to-trump

83 "Barack Obama Is a War Criminal" by Prince Williams
https://harvardpolitics.com/obama-war-criminal/

84 *** US National Archives: Eisenhower's "Military-Industrial Complex" Speech Origins and Significance (Warning to all Americans)
https://www.youtube.com/watch?v=Gg-jvHynP9Y

꧁ Endnotes and References ꧂

[85] "Obama's Weak Defense of His Record on Drone Killings"
https://www.theatlantic.com/politics/archive/2016/12/president-obamas-weak-defense-of-his-record-on-drone-strikes/511454/

[86] *** "Daniel Sheehan Presents: Trajectory of Justice: Rulers of the Realm. A History of America's One Percent... and Their Influence on American Policy (Both Overt & Covert): 1776--2016"
https://www.danielpsheehan.com/ucsc-2016-rulers-of-the-realm/

[87] *** Johnny Harris: "The 'Deep State' Explained"
https://youtu.be/tWxh2oS7Ays

[88] *** "Citizens United Explained: The 2010 Supreme Court decision further tilted political influence toward wealthy donors and corporations."
https://www.brennancenter.org/our-work/research-reports/citizens-united-explained

[89] "More money, less transparency: A decade under Citizens United"
https://www.opensecrets.org/news/reports/a-decade-under-citizens-united

[90] "Scalia, Thomas and Citizens United"
https://www.politico.com/story/2011/01/scalia-thomas-and-citizens-united-047855

[91] Nonviolent Communication: "Transforming Enemy Images in the Workplace"
https://www.nonviolentcommunication.com/resources/articles-about-nvc/enemy-images-workplace-ilasater

[92] Wikipedia: List of Pedophile Advocacy Organizations
https://en.wikipedia.org/wiki/List_of_pedophile_advocacy_organizations

[93] "Satan is Getting Hot as Hell in American Pop Culture"
https://www.newsweek.com/satan-getting-hot-hell-american-pop-culture-1790669

[94] "A Taste for Cannibalism: A spate of recent stomach-churning books, TV shows and films suggests we've never looked so delicious — to one another."
https://www.nytimes.com/2022/07/23/style/cannibalism-tv-shows-movies-books.html

[95] "How did Jeffrey Epstein make his money and get so rich?: The multi-millionaire sexual predator owned luxury houses around the world."
https://www.cosmopolitan.com/uk/reports/a32824007/jeffrey-epstein-wealth/

[96] Wikipedia: Adrenochrome
https://en.wikipedia.org/wiki/Adrenochrome

[97] "Untangling the Conspiracy Theories Around Adrenochrome"
https://science.howstuffworks.com/adrenochrome.htm

[98] "Lady Gaga's Panda Costume: Gagapanda Embraces Japan (VIDEO)"
https://www.huffpost.com/entry/lady-gagas-panda-costume_n_886766

[99] Wikipedia: N,N-Dimethyltryptamine
https://en.wikipedia.org/wiki/N,N-Dimethyltryptamine

[100] "DMT: The Spirit Molecule: A Doctor's Revolutionary Research Into the Biology of Near-Death and Mystical Experiences"
https://ajp.psychiatryonline.org/doi/10.1176/appi.ajp.159.8.1448

[101] "Satan is real, Pope Francis says"
https://www.catholicnewsagency.com/news/41160/satan-is-real-pope-francis-s

[102] "Pope says Satan is More Intelligent than Humans & the Muslim Times' Response"
https://themuslimtimes.info/2017/12/15/pope-says-satan-is-more-intelligent-than-humans/

[103] "Never underestimate the devil, he's smarter than we are, pope warns: Satan is real and more intelligent than human beings, says Francis. 'He will turn your head.'"
https://www.timesofisrael.com/never-underestimate-the-devil-hes-smarter-than-we-are-pope-warns/

[104] Wikipedia: Satanic Panic
https://en.wikipedia.org/wiki/Satanic_panic

[105] Wikipedia: Catholic Church sexual abuse cases
https://en.wikipedia.org/wiki/Catholic_Church_sexual_abuse_cases

[106] Wikipedia: Jeffrey Epstein
https://en.wikipedia.org/wiki/Jeffrey_Epstein

[107] Epstein's full flight logs - UNREDACTED
https://archive.org/details/epstein-flight-logs-unredacted_202304

[108] Wikipedia: Yellow vests protests
https://en.wikipedia.org/wiki/Yellow_vests_protests

[109] Wikipedia: Q Clearance
https://en.wikipedia.org/wiki/Q_clearance

[110] "NXIVM Leader Keith Raniere Has Been Convicted for Keeping Women as 'Sex Slaves.' Here Are the Major Players in the Case"
https://time.com/5568135/nxivm-allison-mack-raniere/

[111] Wikipedia: Apophenia
https://en.wikipedia.org/wiki/Apophenia

[112] Wikipedia: Confirmation bias
https://en.wikipedia.org/wiki/Confirmation_bias

[113] "KENNEDY'S PLANE LOST: THE POLITICS; Kennedy Rebuffed Overture In Senate Race, Torricelli Says"
https://www.nytimes.com/1999/07/20/us/kennedy-s-plane-lost-politics-kennedy-rebuffed-overture-senate-race-torricelli.html

[114] "The last day: The final 24 hours of J.F.K. Jr.'s life were a typical whirl for someone used to the limelight. But in that very ordinariness lay the seeds of disaster"
https://www.cnn.com/ALLPOLITICS/time/1999/07/26/jfk.last.day.html

[115] Wikipedia: George (magazine)
https://en.wikipedia.org/wiki/George_(magazine)

[116] "Bodies of Kennedy, Bessettes Brought to Shore"
https://www.washingtonpost.com/wp-srv/national/longterm/jfkjr/stories/kennedy072299.htm

[117] Wikipedia: John Perkins (author)
https://en.wikipedia.org/wiki/John_Perkins_(author)

[118] Wikipedia: Confessions of an Economic Hit Man (book by John Perkins)
https://en.wikipedia.org/wiki/Confessions_of_an_Economic_Hit_Man

❧ Endnotes and References ❧

[119] George Magazine: Survival Guide to the Future, pg. 8-9
https://archive.org/details/george-magazine-february-1997-survival-guide-to-the-future-bill-gates-interview/page/n7/mode/2up

[120] George Magazine: Survival Guide to the Future, cover
https://archive.org/details/george-magazine-february-1997-survival-guide-to-the-future-bill-gates-interview/mode/2up

[121] "Vince Fusca, who some suspect of being a Kennedy, is running for Senate as his own man"
https://www.wesa.fm/politics-government/2022-03-07/vince-fusca-who-some-suspect-of-being-a-kennedy-is-running-for-senate-as-his-own-man

[122] "Lizard people, deadly orgies and JFK: How QAnon hijacked Hollywood to spread conspiracies"
https://www.latimes.com/california/story/2021-12-07/how-QAnon-has-hijacked-hollywood-movies-for-conspiracy-theories

[123] Wikipedia: Media conglomerate
https://en.wikipedia.org/wiki/Media_conglomerate

[124] "These 6 Corporations Control 90% of the Media in America"
https://www.businessinsider.com/these-6-corporations-control-90-of-the-media-in-america-2012-6

[125] "The Media Monopoly Crisis: Our new special issue takes on the out-of-control consolidation that is squeezing out independent voices and controlling what we read"
https://www.thenation.com/article/society/media-consolidation-monopoly-big-5/

[126] "How a Company Called BlackRock Shapes Your News, Your Life, Our Future"
https://commonreader.wustl.edu/how-a-company-called-blackrock-shapes-your-news-your-life-our-future/

[127] "Tesla: Life and Legacy: The Missing Papers"
https://www.pbs.org/tesla/ll/ll_mispapers.html

[128] "Elvis Presley Died 40 Years Ago. Here's Why Some People Think He's Still Alive"
https://time.com/4897819/elvis-presley-alive-conspiracy-theories/

[129] "Michael Jackson death anniversary: Conspiracy theories around his death"
https://www.wionews.com/photos/michael-jackson-death-anniversary-conspiracy-theories-around-his-death-308523

[130] "Prince still alive?"
https://en.mediamass.net/people/prince/alive.html

[131] "John F. Kennedy Jr.'s Close Friends Speak Out About the Emotional Impact of QAnon Lies: Extremists claim the late Kennedy is alive, a falsehood devastating those who knew and loved him."
https://www.townandcountrymag.com/society/politics/a39787446/john-f-kennedy-jr-q-anon-friends-speak-out/

[132] "Marina Abramović Satanism Controversy, Explained: Why Right-Wing Outlets Think She Is in a Cult"
https://www.artnews.com/art-news/news/marina-abramovic-satanism-controversy-explained-1202684150/

¹³³ Lady Gaga and Marina Abramovic at an art gala benefit highlighting culinary treat that appears as a red liquid in a tub of blood with a naked female body playing dead
https://dress.yournextshoes.com/lady-gaga-leather-dress/

¹³⁴ "How Tony Podesta, a Washington Power Broker, Lost It All"
"The Democratic lobbyist had money, connections and a rarefied art collection. Then came a divorce, Paul Manafort and Donald Trump, and his world came crashing down"
https://www.wsj.com/articles/how-tony-podesta-a-washington-power-broker-lost-it-all-1524065781

¹³⁵ "The paintings depicted are the work of Serbian artist Biljana Đurđević, and some are owned by Podesta's brother, Tony Podesta."
https://www.newsweek.com/john-podesta-art-balenciaga-scandal-1763960

¹³⁶ "Pedo symbols at Disney World!"
https://imgur.com/a/ZAmAc

¹³⁷ Pedophilia (boy lover) symbols on Disney's Chief Zephyr
https://disney.fandom.com/wiki/Chief_Zephyr?file=Chief_Zephyr.png

¹³⁸ "HUGGIES Little Movers Diapers pedo symbols"
https://vigilantlinks.com/2023/04/huggies-little-movers-diapers-pedo-symbols/

¹³⁹ "Pedophile symbols on children's toys?"
https://midmichigannow.com/news/videos/pedophile-symbols-on-childrens-toys

¹⁴⁰ Pedophile (girl lover) symbol used by Good Humor
https://logos.fandom.com/wiki/Good_Humor#2003–2009

¹⁴¹ "Pedophiles use codes and symbols to communicate"
https://www.ispybutterfly.com/2011/11/pedophiles-use-codes-and-symbols-to.html

¹⁴² Justin Trudeau's previous logo
https://christianobserver.net/wp-content/uploads/2018/01/trudeau2.jpg

¹⁴³ "Boy Lover" Symbolism? Francis' World Youth Day Vestments seem to feature Pedophile Logo
https://novusordowatch.org/2019/08/francis-wyd-vestments-pedophile-logo/

¹⁴⁴ Wikileaks: FBI pedophile symbols
https://wikileaks.org/wiki/FBI_pedophile_symbols

¹⁴⁵ Tony Podesta party with red shoes
https://www.huffpost.com/entry/tony-podesta-has-a-party_n_333819

¹⁴⁶ Wikipedia: Papal shoes
https://en.wikipedia.org/wiki/Papal_shoes

¹⁴⁷ the Consilience Project (How to Mislead with Facts)
https://consilienceproject.org

¹⁴⁸ Johnny Harris: "I Deep Faked Myself, Here's Why It Matters"
https://youtu.be/S951cdansBI

¹⁴⁹ Marina Abramovic, "Spirit Cooking," disturbing "art", Tony Podesta, Bill Gates, Lord Rothschild…
https://247sports.com/college/west-virginia/board/103782/Contents/have-you-ever-read-the-podesta-emails-on-spirit-cooking-147514241/

⚜ Endnotes and References ⚜

[150] Controversial art mimicking cannibalism
https://www.artforum.com/diary/linda-yablonsky-at-the-la-moca-gala-29517

[151] "MARINA ABRAMOVIC SPIRIT COOKING"
https://youtu.be/3EsJLNGVJ7E

[152] Lady Gaga and Marina Abramovic at an art gala benefit highlighting culinary treat that appears as a red liquid in a tub of blood with a naked female body playing dead (repeat link)
https://dress.yournextshoes.com/lady-gaga-leather-dress/

[153] Lady Gaga Artpops in at Watermill Benefit
https://wwd.com/eye/parties/gallery/lady-gaga-artpops-in-at-watermill-benefit/watermill-2013-lady-gaga-marina-abramovi263-robert-wilson-7069558-landscape/

[154] "DEVIL'S HEAVEN : The 20th Annual Watermill Center Summer Benefit"
https://museemagazine.com/culture/culture/art-out/20th-annual-watermill-center-summer-benefit-2

[155] "The Artist Who Painted Jeffrey Epstein's Portrait of Bill Clinton in a Dress Tells Us Why She Made It, and What It Means"
https://news.artnet.com/art-world/artist-epstein-clinton-painting-1628953

[156] "Addressing the resurrected conspiracy claims, Tony Podesta confirmed that he does own some of the Serbian artist's the work but told Newsweek that claims tying his brother to it are false. 'I own the work and John has nothing to do with this,' Tony Podesta said."
https://www.newsweek.com/john-podesta-art-balenciaga-scandal-1763960

[157] Wikileaks: Clinton emails
https://wikileaks.org/clinton-emails/emailid/30489

[158] "The WikiLeaks-Russia connection started way before the 2016 election"
https://www.vox.com/world/2017/1/6/14179240/wikileaks-russia-ties

[159] Wikipedia: Moloch
https://en.wikipedia.org/wiki/Moloch

[160] "The True History of Moloch, The Ancient God of Child Sacrifice"
https://allthatsinteresting.com/moloch

[161] Wikileaks: FBI pedophile symbols (repeat link)
https://wikileaks.org/wiki/FBI_pedophile_symbols

[162] "Pope vestiges with alleged pedophile symbol for boy lover"
https://www.rcdea.org.uk/east-anglia-group-join-pope-and-600000-at-wyd-vigil/

[163] "Hampstead Christ Church Satanic Ritual Child Abuse Cover-Up Police Testimonial of Child 1" (reuploaded)
https://www.bitchute.com/video/xvOTmZcxBKUp/

[164] "Police Testimony of Child 2 – Hampstead Christ Church Satanic Ritual Child Abuse Cover-Up"
https://www.bitchute.com/video/Ahy1nys1xYXQ/

[165] *** "Digital Media Literacy: How Filter Bubbles Isolate You"
https://edu.gcfglobal.org/en/digital-media-literacy/how-filter-bubbles-isolate-you/1/

[166] Wikipedia: Filter bubble
https://en.wikipedia.org/wiki/Filter_bubble

[167] Wikipedia: The Social Dilemma (documentary)
https://en.wikipedia.org/wiki/The_Social_Dilemma

[168] Wikipedia: Red pill and blue pill
https://en.wikipedia.org/wiki/Red_pill_and_blue_pill

[169] George Magazine February 1997: "Survival Guide To The Future" Bill Gates Interview JFK JR
https://archive.org/details/george-magazine-february-1997-survival-guide-to-the-future-bill-gates-interview/page/n1/mode/2up

[170] Unify: Harmonic Convergence 2020 (playlist)
https://www.youtube.com/playlist?list=PL5Jez5v4qMCefHZVqWFtq6_SdJZnRWsy4

[171] Wikipedia: Satya Yuga
https://en.wikipedia.org/wiki/Satya_Yuga

[172] Lakota "Rainbow Warriors" prophecy
https://www.lakotatimes.com/articles/rainbow-warriors/

[173] Eagle and the Condor prophecy
https://threadsofperu.com/blogs/blog/an-ancient-legend-meets-modern-times-the-eagle-and-the-condor

[174] Baha'i Teachings: "The Lesser Peace and the Most Great Peace"
https://bahaiteachings.org/lesser-peace-great-peace/

[175] Baha'i Teachings: Peace
https://www.bahai.org/library/authoritative-texts/compilations/peace/2#139834699

[176] "Our Universe may have a fifth dimension that would change everything we know about physics"
https://www.sciencefocus.com/space/fifth-dimension

[177] "Awakening to the Fifth Dimension" (book excerpt)
https://static.macmillan.com/static/smp/awakening-to-the-fifth-dimension/AWAKENING_TO_THE_FIFTH_DIMENSION_excerpt.pdf

[178] *** **"A Man of Great Influence" infographic**
https://robscholtemuseum.nl/wp-content/uploads/2020/05/Bill-Gates-A-Man-of-Great-Influence-foto-Twitter.png

[179] Corbett Report: "Who is Bill Gates?" (video series)
https://www.corbettreport.com/gates/

[180] Wikipedia: United States v. Microsoft Corp.
https://en.wikipedia.org/wiki/United_States_v._Microsoft_Corp.

[181] *** NIH: "The grand impact of the Gates Foundation. Sixty billion dollars and one famous person can affect the spending and research focus of public agencies"
https://www.ncbi.nlm.nih.gov/pmc/articles/PMC2373372/

[182] *** "How is the World Health Organization funded, and why does it rely so much on Bill Gates?"
https://www.euronews.com/next/2023/02/03/how-is-the-world-health-organization-funded-and-why-does-it-rely-so-much-on-bill-gates

❀ Endnotes and References ❀

[183] *** "**How Bill Gates and partners used their clout to control the global Covid response — with little oversight**"
"Four health organizations, working closely together, spent almost $10 billion on responding to Covid across the world. But they lacked the scrutiny of governments, and fell short of their own goals"
https://www.politico.com/news/2022/09/14/global-covid-pandemic-response-bill-gates-partners-00053969

[184] "CDC Foundation Receives $13.5 Million in Grants for Global Health"
"I am pleased to announce the award of three grants to the CDC Foundation, totaling $13.5 million, from the Bill & Melinda Gates Foundation."
https://www.cdcfoundation.org/blog-entry/cdc-foundation-receives-13.5-million-grant-from-gates-foundation

[185] DAVOS, Switzerland -- "The Bill & Melinda Gates Foundation today announced a $200 million grant to establish the Grand Challenges in Global Health initiative, a major new effort and partnership with the National Institutes of Health (NIH)."
https://www.gatesfoundation.org/ideas/media-center/press-releases/2003/01/grand-challenges-in-global-health

[186] "Ninth Global Health Workshop Held with Gates Foundation"
(with photos of Bill Gates sitting next to Dr. Anthony Fauci at the workshop)
https://nihrecord.nih.gov/2023/01/06/ninth-global-health-workshop-held-gates-foundation

[187] GAVI: "The Bill & Melinda Gates Foundation"
"Gates Foundation pledged US$ 750 million to set up Gavi in 1999. The Foundation is a key Gavi partner in vaccine market shaping."
https://www.gavi.org/operating-model/gavis-partnership-model/bill-melinda-gates-foundation

[188] FUNDING TO UNIVERSITIES BY THE BILL & MELINDA GATES FOUNDATION
https://www.universityphilanthropy.com/bill-and-melinda-gates-foundation-funding

[189] "How Bill Gates pulled off the swift Common Core revolution"
https://www.washingtonpost.com/politics/how-bill-gates-pulled-off-the-swift-common-core-revolution/2014/06/07/a830e32e-ec34-11e3-9f5c-9075d5508f0a_story.html

[190] "Gates Institute awarded grants totaling $71.3M to support sexual, reproductive health interventions"
"The Bill & Melinda Gates Institute for Population and Reproductive Health at the Johns Hopkins Bloomberg School of Public Health has been awarded two grants totaling $71.3 million—$36.3 million from Bayer AG and $35 million from the Bill & Melinda Gates Foundation—cover a four-year period ending in December 2025."
https://hub.jhu.edu/2021/11/18/gates-institute-funding-for-sexual-reproductive-health/

[191] "Prime Minister and Bill Gates launch £400m partnership to boost green investment"
https://www.gov.uk/government/news/prime-minister-and-bill-gates-launch-400m-partnership-to-boost-green-investment

[192] "Bill & Melinda Gates Foundation: $93k grant to Oxford"
https://www.gatesfoundation.org/about/committed-grants/2020/04/inv016778

[193] "Prime Minister and Bill Gates launch £400m partnership to boost green investment"
https://businessinsider.com/bill-gates-connections-jeffrey-epstein-mit-donations-ronan-farrow-2019-9

[194] *** **"Documents show Bill Gates has given $319 million to media outlets to promote his global agenda"**
https://thegrayzone.com/2021/11/21/bill-gates-million-media-outlets-global-agenda/

[195] Eugenics in America: "The Legacy of Sanger and Gates"
https://catholicstand.com/eugenics-in-america/

[196] MIT project: "Storing medical information below the skin's surface"
"Specialized invisible dye, delivered along with a vaccine, could enable "on-patient" storage of vaccination history"
https://news.mit.edu/2019/storing-vaccine-history-skin-1218

[197] "Invisible Ink Could Reveal whether Kids Have Been Vaccinated"
https://www.scientificamerican.com/article/invisible-ink-could-reveal-whether-kids-have-been-vaccinated/

[198] "Want doors to open with a wave of your hand? Chip in."
https://www.chicagotribune.com/2017/08/18/want-doors-to-open-with-a-wave-of-your-hand-chip-in

[199] "You will get chipped — eventually" (published August 2017)
https://www.usatoday.com/story/tech/2017/08/09/you-get-chipped-eventually/547336001/

[200] "China is tracking schoolchildren with chips embedded in uniforms"
https://siliconangle.com/2018/12/26/china-tracking-school-children-chip-embedded-uniforms/

[201] "Chinese schools scanning children's brains to see if they are concentrating"
"US-made devices could be used to collect data on 1.2m pupils"
https://www.independent.co.uk/tech/china-schools-scan-brains-concentration-headbands-children-brainco-focus-a8728951.html

[202] *** **Google Patents: Cryptocurrency system using body activity data (filed by Microsoft Technology, June 2019)**
https://patents.google.com/patent/WO2020060606A1/en

[203] *** **Microsoft: "Partnering for a path to digital identity"**
"As discussions begin this week at the **World Economic Forum**, creating universal access to identity is an **issue at the top of Microsoft's agenda**, and we think technology can be a powerful tool to tackle this challenge. It was last summer that Microsoft took a first step, collaborating with Accenture and Avanade on a **blockchain-based identity prototype** on Microsoft Azure. Together, we pursued this work in support of the **ID2020 Alliance** – a global public-private partnership dedicated to aiding the 1.1 billion people around the world who lack any legal form of identity. To say that we were encouraged by its mission would be an understatement. We were inspired by it."
https://blogs.microsoft.com/blog/2018/01/22/partnering-for-a-path-to-digital-identity/

[204] "ID2020 partners with Digital Impact Alliance to promote people-centric digital ID"
https://www.biometricupdate.com/202308/id2020-partners-with-digital-impact-alliance-to-promote-people-centric-digital-id

[205] *** **"Scientists caution against new digital identity"**
"Big tech companies and governments are promoting the advent of a new digital identity for everyone. The corona crisis is fast-tracking this agenda. Experts warn against the consequences. 'This is the end of freedom.'"
"if major parties have their way, 'a surveillance state could emerge in which everything will be stored in order to steer people in various ways, both politically and commercially'."
https://www.ftm.eu/articles/scientists-caution-against-new-digital-identity

☸ Endnotes and References ☸

[206] "China's 'social credit' system ranks citizens and punishes them with throttled internet speeds and flight bans if the Communist Party deems them untrustworthy"
https://www.businessinsider.com/china-social-credit-system-punishments-and-rewards-explained-2018-4

[207] *** "China ranks 'good' and 'bad' citizens with 'social credit' system"
https://youtu.be/NXyzpMDtpSE

[208] Wikipedia: Nineteen Eighty-Four (famous George Orwell dystopian novel about "Big Brother" technocratic authoritarian future – similar to China's current "social credit system")
https://en.wikipedia.org/wiki/Nineteen_Eighty-Four

[209] "China's Chilling 'Social Credit' Blacklist: A lawyer is barred from buying a plane ticket because a court found his apology 'insincere.'"
https://www.hrw.org/news/2017/12/12/chinas-chilling-social-credit-blacklist

[210] *** "China's 'social credit' system ranks citizens and punishes them with throttled internet speeds and flight bans if the Communist Party deems them untrustworthy"
https://www.businessinsider.com/china-social-credit-system-punishments-and-rewards-explained-2018-4

[211] "China's digital currency will help CCP punish or coerce citizens with social credit system"
https://sociable.co/government-and-policy/chinas-digital-currency-help-ccp-punish-coerce-citizens-social-credit-system-cnas/

[212] Federal Reserve: Central Bank Digital Currency (CBDC) FAQs
https://www.federalreserve.gov/cbdc-faqs.htm

[213] WHO: "Pandemic prevention, preparedness and response accord"
https://www.who.int/news-room/questions-and-answers/item/pandemic-prevention--preparedness-and-response-accord

[214] Kim Iverson: "How the Fed Plans to Control and Surveil You Using Digital Currency"
https://youtu.be/7u0F63KyrTk

[215] NIH: "Vaccines in the United States: a systematic review on history of evolution, regulations, licensing, and future challenges"
"The approval procedure for vaccines in the United States is regulated by the Center for Biologics Evaluation and Research."
https://www.ncbi.nlm.nih.gov/pmc/articles/PMC7445324/

[216] Yale Medicine: "**Emergency Use Authorization Vs. Full FDA Approval: What's the Difference?**"
"Put simply, an emergency use authorization (EUA) is a tool the Food and Drug Administration (FDA) can use to expedite the availability of medical products, including drugs and vaccines, during a public health emergency. **An EUA can only be granted when no adequate, approved, available alternatives exist, and when the known and potential benefits outweigh the potential risks.** An EUA also only lasts as long as the public health emergency for which it was declared."
https://www.yalemedicine.org/news/what-does-eua-mean

[217] British Medical Journal: "Covid-19: FDA authorizes Moderna vaccine as US starts vaccinating health workers"
"COVID Vaccination Studies: From Double-Blind to Hardly-Blind?"
https://www.bmj.com/content/371/bmj.m4924/rr-6

[218] red pill and blue pill: symbolism
https://www.britannica.com/topic/red-pill-and-blue-pill

[219] Wikipedia: Walter Cronkite
https://en.wikipedia.org/wiki/Walter_Cronkite

[220] Agricultural Hero: Vandana Shiva
https://www.oneearth.org/agricultural-hero-vandana-shiva/

[221] "Bill Gates is continuing the work of Monsanto," Vandana Shiva tells FRANCE 24
https://www.france24.com/en/20191023-bill-gates-is-continuing-the-work-of-monsanto-vandana-shiva-tells-france-24-1

[222] "Speaking The Righteous Truth!!!!!This Doctor Exposed Bill Gates Wicked Agenda" | Viable Tv
https://youtu.be/w9_hRczpcaA

[223] Corbett Report: Episode 380 – "Meet Bill Gates"
https://corbettreport.com/meetgates/

[224] Rose/Bigtree: Digital Freedom Platform: "The Coronavirus Agenda"
https://freedomplatform.tv/the-coronavirus-vaccine-agenda-exposing-the-dangerous-truth-of-big-pharmas-master-plan-del-bigtree/

[225] "Perspectives on the Pandemic" | The (Undercover) Epicenter Nurse
https://youtu.be/UIDsKdeFOmQ

[226] *** After Skool: "Why Good People Comply with Evil" - Daniel Schmachtenberger (including insights on Nazi Germany) https://youtu.be/9g6w2f3ttMM

[227] Dr Marshall Rosenberg: "Amtssprache: The Most Dangerous Language in the World
https://youtu.be/QYR9qGVtBXQ

[228] "ROSE/ICKE 1: THE TRUTH BEHIND THE CORONAVIRUS PANDEMIC, COVID-19 LOCKDOWN & THE ECONOMIC CRASH"
https://freedomplatform.tv/the-truth-behind-the-coronavirus-pandemic-Covid-19-lockdown-the-economic-crash-david-icke/

[229] Wikipedia: The Hunger Games (film series)
https://en.wikipedia.org/wiki/The_Hunger_Games_(film)

[230] "How does The Hunger Games Criticize American Society?"
"The Hunger Games offers a broad anti-capitalist critique of western society. Specifically, Collins replicates America's vastly expanding rich-poor divide through the juxtaposition of the obscenely wealthy Capitol and the impoverished Districts."
https://medium.com/@meganxburbage/how-does-the-hunger-games-criticise-american-society-729cd9d73bb6

[231] IMDB: "The Hunger Games" (movie)
https://www.imdb.com/title/tt1392170/

[232] Robert Reich: "The Rise of the 1%"
https://youtu.be/ppLaVpdKQd4

[233] "ROSE/ICKE 2: THE CORONAVIRUS CONSPIRACY: HOW COVID-19 WILL SEIZE YOUR RIGHTS & DESTROY OUR ECONOMY"
https://freedomplatform.tv/the-coronavirus-conspiracy-how-Covid-19-will-seize-your-rights-destroy-our-economy-david-icke/

[234] Wikipedia: Kary Mullis
https://en.wikipedia.org/wiki/Kary_Mullis

Endnotes and References

[235] *** "**DR KARY MULLIS, THE WINNER OF A NOBEL PRIZE AND THE INVENTOR OF THE PCR TEST**"
https://www.bitchute.com/video/Jh4dFU54u3bq/

[236] *** "**KARY MULLIS PCR TEST INVENTOR EXPLAINS THE TEST**"
https://www.bitchute.com/video/DXFe2zYyivlI/

[237] "US CDC Real-Time Reverse Transcription PCR Panel for Detection of Severe Acute Respiratory Syndrome Coronavirus 2" (published August 2020)
"Test Algorithm: …we considered a specimen to be positive for SARS-CoV-2 if all assay amplification curves crossed the threshold line within 40 cycles (Ct <40)."
https://wwwnc.cdc.gov/eid/article/26/8/20-1246_article

[238] "**Your Coronavirus Test Is Positive. Maybe It Shouldn't Be.**"
"Any test with a cycle threshold above 35 is too sensitive … I'm shocked that people would think that 40 could represent a positive … A more reasonable cutoff would be 30 to 35, or even less. Those changes would mean the amount of genetic material in a patient's sample would have to be 100-fold to 1,000-fold that of the current standard for the test to return a positive result — at least, one worth acting on."
https://www.nytimes.com/2020/08/29/health/coronavirus-testing.html

[239] "Fauci On PCR Test Cycle Threshold - False Positives"
https://youtu.be/esNQZXu17U8?t=41

[240] "How are COVID-19 deaths counted? It's complicated" (Feb. 2021)
"Last April, Deborah Birx, MD, coordinator of the **White House Coronavirus Task Force, said this when asked about people who have COVID-19 but die from preexisting conditions: 'If someone dies with COVID-19, we are counting that as a COVID-19 death.'**"
https://www.aamc.org/news/how-are-Covid-19-deaths-counted-it-s-complicated

[241] "ROSE/ICKE 3: 1,000,000 PEOPLE FIGHTING FOR FREEDOM"
https://freedomplatform.tv/1000000-fighting-for-freedom/

[242] "Marx and the Middle Classes"
"'The internal enemy' of the proletarian … is constituted first and foremost by the lower middle classes."
https://www.marxists.org/archive/kun-bela/1918/05/04.htm (Part II)

[243] Wikipedia: Joseph Stalin
https://en.wikipedia.org/wiki/Joseph_Stalin

[244] Wikipedia: Mao Zedong
https://en.wikipedia.org/wiki/Mao_Zedong

[245] "Marxism In America"
https://www.nas.org/academic-questions/35/1/marxism-in-america/pdf

[246] Wikipedia: Communist state
https://en.wikipedia.org/wiki/Communist_state

[247] Wikipedia: Excess mortality in the Soviet Union under Joseph Stalin
https://en.wikipedia.org/wiki/Excess_mortality_in_the_Soviet_Union_under_Joseph_Stalin

[248] "ROSE/ICKE 4: WE WILL NOT BE SILENCED"
https://freedomplatform.tv/rose-icke-iv-we-will-not-be-silenced/

249 "All I See Is Part of Me" (Children's book read out loud)
https://youtu.be/97WRYcFgdIA

250 "The Century of the Self - Part 1: 'Happiness Machines'"
"The story of the relationship between Sigmund Freud and his American nephew, Edward Bernays. Bernays invented the public relations profession in the 1920s and was the first person to take Freud's ideas to manipulate the masses. He showed American corporations how they could make people want things they didn't need by systematically linking mass-produced goods to their unconscious desires."
https://youtu.be/DnPmg0R1M04

251 *** **Justin Wilman: Influencing the Influencers–A demonstration in mind control**
https://www.youtube.com/watch?v=4RksLFJ7A2M

252 Wikipedia: Alan Watts
https://en.wikipedia.org/wiki/Alan_Watts

253 "Predictive Programming"
"Predictive Programming is theory that the government or other higher-ups are using fictional movies or books as a mass mind control tool to make the population more accepting of planned future events."
https://u.osu.edu/vanzandt/2018/04/18/predictive-programming/

254 "2012 LONDON OLYMPICS OPENING SATANIC RITUAL - COVID 19 PREDICTIVE PROGRAMMING"
https://www.bitchute.com/video/X5cCG4Eh9Xal/

255 "The Inner Language of the Subconscious: A picture is worth a thousand words."
"When we access and spend time within the subconscious, we are released from the confines of our logical, practical minds."
https://www.psychologytoday.com/us/blog/in-flux/201301/the-inner-language-of-the-subconscious

256 Google Adreno Chrome 666
https://docs.google.com/document/d/1EH2EOi-GT-76EtSOS5OV5SyfyB-mPhM2GwfjdRZ8OYE/

257 Satanic/Lucifarian Hand Sign
http://whale.to/b/hand.html

258 "Face Recognition Software Shows Improvement in Recognizing Masked Faces"
https://www.nist.gov/news-events/news/2020/12/face-recognition-software-shows-improvement-recognizing-masked-faces

259 "Mask Up and Shut Up"
https://www.theatlantic.com/ideas/archive/2020/08/wear-your-mask-and-stop-talking/615796/

260 **"Fauci to Congress: 6-Foot Social Distancing Guidance Likely Not Based on Data"**
"In closed-door congressional testimony, former chief White House medical adviser Anthony Fauci said that federal social distancing guidance during the pandemic was likely not based on any data, and conceded that the lab leak hypothesis of COVID-19's origins isn't a conspiracy theory… The repeated federal recommendation that people keep six feet of distance between themselves and others 'sort of just appeared,' said Fauci"
https://news.yahoo.com/fauci-congress-6-foot-social-174529265.html

261 *** **Congressional Subcommittee on the Coronavirus Pandemic: on Dr. Fauci's transcribed interview**

Endnotes and References

- "**Dr. Fauci** claimed that the "6 feet apart" social distancing recommendation promoted by federal health officials was likely not based on any data. **He characterized the development of the guidance by stating "it sort of just appeared."**
- "**Dr. Fauci acknowledged that the lab leak hypothesis is not a conspiracy theory**. This comes nearly four years after prompting the publication of the now infamous 'Proximal Origin' paper that attempted to vilify and disprove the lab leak hypothesis.
- Dr. Fauci admitted that America's vaccine mandates during the COVID-19 pandemic could increase vaccine hesitancy in the future. Previously, **Dr. Fauci advocated that "when you make it difficult for people in their lives, they lose their ideological bullshit, and they get vaccinated."**
https://oversight.house.gov/release/wenstrup-releases-statement-following-dr-faucis-two-day-testimony/

[262] *** Great Barrington Declaration (published October 2020)
"**As infectious disease epidemiologists and public health scientists we have grave concerns about the damaging physical and mental health impacts of the prevailing COVID-19 policies** and recommend an approach we call Focused Protection.
"Coming from both the left and right, and around the world, we have devoted our careers to protecting people. Current lockdown policies are producing devastating effects on short and long-term public health. The results (to name a few) include lower childhood vaccination rates, worsening cardiovascular disease outcomes, fewer cancer screenings and deteriorating mental health – leading to greater excess mortality in years to come, with the working class and younger members of society carrying the heaviest burden. Keeping students out of school is a grave injustice. **Keeping these measures in place until a vaccine is available will cause irreparable damage, with the underprivileged disproportionately harmed."**
https://gbdeclaration.org/

[263] Children's Health Defense: Robert F. Kennedy Jr.
https://childrenshealthdefense.org/about-us/our-team/

[264] *** "THE TAKING OF AMERICA" (The Kennedy Assassination and more)
https://www.cia.gov/library/abbottabad-compound/11/1183CF937B8095F6A96DB7C9468BDE2A_The_Taking_of_America_-_Richard_Sprague.pdf

[265] Wikipedia: Allen Dulles (VERY shady former head of the CIA)
https://en.wikipedia.org/wiki/Allen_Dulles

[266] Attorney Daniel P. Sheehan: JFK Assassination lecture series
https://www.danielpsheehan.com/ucsc-2013-jfk-assassination/

[267] Warren Commission Report
https://archives.gov/research/jfk/warren-commission-report

[268] COUNTERING CRITICISM OF THE WARREN REPORT
https://ia601007.us.archive.org/3/items/CIADOC1035960/CIA%20DOC%201035-960.pdf

[269] "The Paranoid Style in American Politics" by Richard Hofstadter
"I call it the paranoid style simply because no other word adequately evokes the sense of heated exaggeration, suspiciousness, and **conspiratorial fantasy** that I have in mind."
https://harpers.org/archive/1964/11/the-paranoid-style-in-american-politics/

[270] Hoaxed (movie)
http://hoaxedmovie.com

[271] "Read Hillary Clinton's 'Basket of Deplorables' Remarks About Donald Trump Supporters"
https://time.com/4486502/hillary-clinton-basket-of-deplorables-transcript/

272 "Robert Kennedy Jr. Exposes Big Pharma, Fauci and the Danger of a COVID-19 Vaccine"
https://21stcenturywire.com/2020/05/16/robert-kennedy-jr-exposes-big-pharma-fauci-and-the-danger-of-a-covid-19-vaccine

273 "Disinformation Dozen" (censorship of all speech questioning the predominant Covid narrative) "Center for Countering Digital Hate is calling on Facebook and Instagram, Twitter and YouTube to completely deplatform the disinformation dozen they believe are dangerous and instrumental in creating vaccine hesitancy at a crucial moment in the pandemic."
https://www.theguardian.com/world/2021/jul/17/covid-misinformation-conspiracy-theories-ccdh-report

274 "Revealed: Dark Money Funders Behind 'Disinformation Dozen' Report"
https://childrenshealthdefense.org/defender/dark-money-center-countering-digital-hate-disinformation-dozen-report/

275 "9 'Dark Money' Sources Funding CCDH: A Foreign 'Digital Hate' Group Which Used the White House to Quash Free Speech"
https://greenmedinfo.com/blog/9-dark-money-sources-funding-ccdh-foreign-digital-hate-group-which-used-white-hou1

276 *** **"Biden administration coerced social media giants into possible free speech violations"**
https://www.usatoday.com/story/money/2023/09/08/biden-administration-coerced-facebook-court-rules/70800723007/

277 "Home Run King Hank Aaron Dies of 'Undisclosed Cause' 18 Days After Receiving Moderna Vaccine"
https://childrenshealthdefense.org/defender/hank-aaron-dies-days-after-receiving-moderna-vaccine/

278 "Tip of the Iceberg? Thousands of COVID Vaccine Injuries and 13 U.S. Deaths Reported in December Alone"
https://childrenshealthdefense.org/defender/thousands-covid-vaccine-injuries-13-deaths-reported-december/

279 "Health Officials Push Pregnant Women to Get COVID Shots, Despite Known Risks"
"With no data showing COVID vaccines are safe for pregnant women, and despite reports of miscarriages among women who have received the experimental Pfizer and Moderna vaccines, Fauci and other health officials advise pregnant women to get the vaccine"
https://childrenshealthdefense.org/defender/health-officials-push-pregnant-women-covid-vaccine/

280 "653 Deaths + 12,044 Other Injuries Reported Following COVID Vaccine, Latest CDC Data Show"
https://childrenshealthdefense.org/defender/vaers-injuries-covid-vaccine-cdc-data/

281 "Why a Judge Ordered FDA to Release Covid-19 Vaccine Data Pronto"
"That is not a typo. The FDA wanted court approval to have up to 75 years to publicly disclose this information."
https://news.bloomberglaw.com/health-law-and-business/why-a-judge-ordered-fda-to-release-covid-19-vaccine-data-pronto

282 Wikipedia: You'll own nothing and be happy
https://en.wikipedia.org/wiki/You%27ll_own_nothing_and_be_happy

283 Wikipedia: Richard Hofstadter
https://en.wikipedia.org/wiki/Richard_Hofstadter

Endnotes and References

[284] Wikipedia: Apocalypticism
https://en.wikipedia.org/wiki/Apocalypticism

[285] "The Paranoid Style in American Politics" by Richard Hofstadter
"It had been around a long time before the Radical Right discovered it—and its targets have ranged from "the international bankers" to Masons, Jesuits, and munitions makers."
https://harpers.org/archive/1964/11/the-paranoid-style-in-american-politics/

[286] *** **"Goebbels' Principles of Propaganda" (also known as Hitler's Playbook)**
https://www.physics.smu.edu/pseudo/Propaganda/goebbels.html

[287] *** **Wikipedia: IT-backed authoritarianism (also known as techno-authoritarianism, digital authoritarianism or digital dictatorship)**
https://en.wikipedia.org/wiki/IT-backed_authoritarianism

[288] *** **"TECHNO-AUTHORITARIANISM: PLATFORM FOR REPRESSION IN CHINA AND ABROAD"**
https://www.cecc.gov/events/hearings/techno-authoritarianism-platform-for-repression-in-china-and-abroad

[289] Nonviolent Communication Academy: Feelings and Needs word lists
https://nvcacademy.com/media/NVCA/learning-tools/NVCA-feelings-needs.pdf

[290] "DOCTOR DEMONSTRATES WHY FACE MASKS DO NOT & WILL NOT STOP COMMUNITY SPREAD OF COVID"
https://www.bitchute.com/video/JfUhTjoOF5vz/

[291] JP Sears: "How to Get Angrier at People You Disagree With" (comedy)
https://youtu.be/cVFiqY7T5Gl

[292] Wikipedia: Antifa (Germany)
https://en.wikipedia.org/wiki/Antifa_(Germany)

[293] Wikipedia: Stalinism
https://en.wikipedia.org/wiki/Stalinism

[294] "Police find 51 of 76 missing children in Michigan sweep"
https://www.wthr.com/article/news/nation-world/police-find-51-of-76-missing-children-in-michigan-sweep/531-e366da5e-4009-45c2-be89-47c6c9b1322e

[295] "Cuomo, facing criticism for COVID handling, blames Trump for virus coming to New York"
https://www.foxnews.com/politics/cuomo-covid-handling-blames-trump-ny

[296] "Trump: The Tonight Show with Jay Leno - 1999 - Running for POTUS"
https://youtu.be/Q2-5Wy_CMIE

[297] Larry King Live: "(2005) Donald and Melania Trump as newlyweds"
https://youtu.be/q4XfyYFa9yo

[298] "Anatomy of Delusion: How Otherwise Conscious People Descended into the Darkness" by Stephen Dinan
https://stephendinan.medium.com/anatomy-of-delusion-how-otherwise-conscious-people-descended-into-the-darkness-e3acd73cb08f

[299] The Shift Network - Transformational Education, Media, and Events
https://theshiftnetwork.com

³⁰⁰ Is "Trump Derangement Syndrome" a Real Mental Condition?
https://www.psychologytoday.com/us/blog/talking-about-men/201901/is-trump-derangement-syndrome-real-mental-condition

³⁰¹ JP Sears "Spiritual People Thinking Out Loud" (comedy)
https://youtu.be/M6f7KWpBrGE

³⁰² JP Sears "What to do When You Run Out of Toilet Paper" (comedy)
https://youtu.be/o0kydrA1-04

³⁰³ JP Sears "Blue Pill People" (comedy)
https://youtu.be/dC_IZLzCrOI

³⁰⁴ "US protests: More riots and lawlessness in cities across nation"
https://www.foxnews.com/us/us-protests-more-riots-and-lawlessness-in-cities-across-nation

³⁰⁵ "CNN slights Mount Rushmore as 'monument of two slaveowners' after extolling its 'majesty' in 2016"
https://www.foxnews.com/media/cnn-mount-rushmore-monument-two-slave-owners

³⁰⁶ "Trump, in fiery Mount Rushmore address, decries rise of 'far-left fascism,' calls on Americans to rise up"
"The president asserted that recent attacks on the nation's monuments, alongside "cancel culture" and the rise of the Marxist ideology of the Black Lives Matter (BLM) movement, were **symptoms of a 'left-wing cultural revolution'** that was threatening to "overthrow the American Revolution." **BLM explicitly advocates the destruction of the 'nuclear family structure,'** which Trump said was in fact the 'bedrock of American life.'"
(https://nypost.com/2020/09/24/blm-removes-website-language-blasting-nuclear-family-structure/)
https://www.foxnews.com/politics/trump-in-fiery-mount-rushmore-address-decries-rise-of-far-left-fascism-calls-on-americans-to-rise-up

³⁰⁷ "Who Wants to Tear Down Mt Rushmore?"
https://www.foxnews.com/politics/who-wants-tear-down-mt-rushmore

³⁰⁸ Wikipedia: KGB
https://en.wikipedia.org/wiki/KGB

³⁰⁹ *** **"Former KGB Agent, Yuri Bezmenov, Warns America About Socialist Subversion"**
https://youtu.be/Z1EA2ohrt5Q (13-min excerpt)
https://youtu.be/5It1zarINv0 (Full interview)

³¹⁰ Daniel Schmachtenberger "Existential Risk and Phase Shifting to a New World System"
https://www.ucl.ac.uk/global-governance/podcast/12-daniel-schmachtenberger-existential-risk-and-phase-shifting-new-world-system

³¹¹ "The Most Shocking Aspect of RFK Jr.'s Anti-Semitism" (hit piece)
https://www.theatlantic.com/ideas/archive/2023/07/rfk-kennedy-covid-anti-semitism/674727/

³¹² "Democrats try to censor, remove RFK Jr. at hearing on censorship"
https://www.foxnews.com/politics/democrats-censor-remove-rfk-jr-hearing-censorship-despicable-comments

³¹³ Debbie Wasserman Schultz – **false accusations** against RFK Jr at hearing on censorship
https://youtu.be/ir68tdhR3Uw

³¹⁴ "King George III" (King of England)
https://www.pbs.org/wgbh/americanexperience/features/adams-king-george-III/

☸ Endnotes and References ☸

[315] *** Yale University: "COVID-19 Vaccine Messaging, Part 1" (study on coercion techniques)
https://clinicaltrials.gov/study/NCT04460703

[316] "Persuasive messaging to increase COVID-19 vaccine uptake intentions"
https://pubmed.ncbi.nlm.nih.gov/34774363/

[317] "Plandemic 2: Indoctornation" (full movie)
https://plandemicseries.com/plandemic-2-indoctornation/

[318] ACLU: "How the 1994 Crime Bill Fed the Mass Incarceration Crisis"
https://www.aclu.org/news/smart-justice/how-1994-crime-bill-fed-mass-incarceration-crisis

[319] "Biden's description of Obama draws scrutiny"
https://www.cnn.com/2007/POLITICS/01/31/biden.obama/

[320] *** "Trump's Censored Video – Tribute to George Floyd" (why was this censored?)
https://www.bitchute.com/video/AyzaK5EEzznG/

[321] Wikipedia: First Step Act (Formerly Incarcerated Reenter Society Transformed Safely Transitioning Every Person Act – signed into law by Trump in December 2018)
https://en.wikipedia.org/wiki/First_Step_Act

[322] Wikipedia: Violent Crimes Control and Law Enforcement Act
https://en.wikipedia.org/wiki/Violent_Crime_Control_and_Law_Enforcement_Act

[323] "Trump signs bill restoring funding for black colleges"
"President Donald Trump on Thursday signed a bipartisan bill that will permanently provide more than $250 million a year to the nation's historically black colleges and universities, along with dozens of other institutions that serve large shares of minority students."
https://apnews.com/article/c4834e48841d97c5a93312b1bf75302a

[324] "Before Trump, There Was Jesse Jackson"
https://www.bloomberg.com/view/articles/2015-12-29/before-trump-there-was-jesse-jackson

[325] "Donald Trump, Jesse Jackson, Al Sharpton at launching of Rainbow Coalition's Wall Street Project at the WTC – 1996"
https://www.reddit.com/r/HistoryPorn/comments/4uisjn/donald_trump_jesse_jackson_al_sharpton_at/

[326] "Remember when Spike Lee loved his friend Donald Trump"
https://twitter.com/MarkSimoneNY/status/1099899320529313792

[327] "A Timeline of Snoop Dogg & Donald Trump's Relationship"
https://www.billboard.com/music/rb-hip-hop/timeline-snoop-dogg-donald-trump-feud-7727893/

[328] Getty Images: Donald Trump and Oprah Winfrey
https://pyxis.nymag.com/v1/imgs/7c9/402/be6e978eeaaa9756ce35e7f61ef7386b68-08-trump-oprah.rsquare.w700.jpg
https://content.fortune.com/wp-content/uploads/2018/02/gettyimages-804769714.jpg
https://www.telegraph.co.uk/content/dam/politics/2018/01/12/TELEMMGLPICT000150471125_trans_NvBQzQNjv4BqD6uUf9vQfNJ4dalFWbgSkIVse9JsN00kzbUr3IXHaGo.jpeg

[329] "Donald Trump Just Ruined 14 of Your Childhood Heroes" (Donald Trump with Famous People)
https://www.gq.com/story/trumps-famous-friends

ReQovery

[330] "This Is the Woman President Trump Wants to Be the First Female African-American Marine General"
https://time.com/5237828/first-african-american-woman-general/

[331] YouTube: Walk Away Campaign
https://www.youtube.com/@WalkAwayCampaign

[332] YouTube: BlexitAmerica
https://www.youtube.com/@BLEXITAmerica

[333] "Rose/Icke 5: The Answer"
https://freedomplatform.tv/rose-icke-v-the-answer/

[334] "Zeitgeist: The Movie" 2007, Part 1
https://youtu.be/XVYIxHteUMs

[335] Thrive (movie series)
https://closed.thrivemovement.com

[336] "The Great Lockdown: Worst Economic Downturn Since the Great Depression"
https://www.imf.org/en/Blogs/Articles/2020/04/14/blog-weo-the-great-lockdown-worst-economic-downturn-since-the-great-depression

[337] ABC News "'Maybe they're not that crazy': Preppers reflect on panic buying amid COVID-19 lockdowns"
https://youtu.be/5lt2Oo3LrHU

[338] "Billionaire Bunker Owners Are Preparing For The Ultimate Underground Escape"
https://www.forbes.com/sites/jimdobson/2020/03/27/billionaire-bunker-owners-are-preparing-for-the-ultimate-underground-escape

[339] NIH: "COVID-19 outpatients: early risk-stratified treatment with zinc plus low-dose hydroxychloroquine and azithromycin: a retrospective case series study"
https://www.ncbi.nlm.nih.gov/pmc/articles/PMC7587171/

[340] "Hoaxed Official Trailer"
https://youtu.be/0BEyAT8Npxk

[341] "Candace Owens: Democrat Laws Negatively Impact Minorities"
https://youtu.be/3Y_LI_u5WLA

[342] "George Carlin - It's a Big Club and You Ain't In It! The American Dream" (comedy)
https://youtu.be/kXhZyAOuyhE

[343] "China Has 'First-Strike' Capability To Melt U.S. Power Grid With Electromagnetic Pulse Weapon"
https://www.forbes.com/sites/jamesconca/2020/06/25/china-develops-first-strike-capability-with-electromagnetic-pulse

[344] "Fact Check: Kamala Harris eligible to be president despite misleading posts"
https://www.reuters.com/fact-check/kamala-harris-eligible-be-president-despite-misleading-posts-2023-10-18/

[345] Definition: Birtherism
https://www.merriam-webster.com/dictionary/birtherism

[346] Wikipedia: Motte-and-bailey fallacy
https://en.wikipedia.org/wiki/Motte-and-bailey_fallacy

❧ Endnotes and References ❧

[347] "Veep debate: Fact-check on Kamala Harris as California prosecutor"
https://calmatters.org/politics/2020/10/fact-check-debate-kamala-harris-california-prosecutor/

[348] TIME: "Rep. Gabbard Challenged Sen. Harris' Record While Serving as Attorney General Of California"
https://youtu.be/VxaRt-LIpEk

[349] Media Bias Fact Check
https://mediabiasfactcheck.com/

[350] Operation Underground Railroad
https://ourrescue.org/

[351] "When a Dream Bucket Leads to Change | Tony Robbins & Operation Underground Railroad"
https://youtu.be/gF8yaBlaPcg

[352] Q Drop (No.10504503 and 10504508): List of politicians and activists found guilty for pedophilia crimes
https://docs.google.com/document/d/1F7A-JsokI33naMVbCPU9niBvy5SCvRAOnQZayfjD2BQ/

[353] "The Trump Administration Is Committed to Combating Human Trafficking and Protecting the Innocent"
https://trumpwhitehouse.archives.gov/briefings-statements/trump-administration-committed-combating-human-trafficking-protecting-innocent/

[354] "Obama Administration Efforts to Combat Human Trafficking"
https://obamawhitehouse.archives.gov/blog/2017/01/13/obama-administration-efforts-combat-human-trafficking-0

[355] "Post Distorts History of Presidential Efforts to Fight Child Sex Trafficking"
https://www.factcheck.org/2023/03/post-distorts-history-of-presidential-efforts-to-fight-child-sex-trafficking/

[356] Website with compiled and searchable Q Drops
https://QAnon.pub

[357] Trump's definition of the "Radical Left"
https://youtu.be/l7q_-IcN0ng

[358] Wikipedia: Falun Gong
https://en.wikipedia.org/wiki/Falun_Gong

[359] "CCP Persecution of Falun Gong Adherents Extends From Doctoral Candidates to Elementary School Students"
https://www.theepochtimes.com/china/ccp-persecution-of-falun-gong-adherents-extend-from-doctoral-candidates-to-elementary-school-students-5597422

[360] Amnesty International "Up to one million detained in China's mass 're-education' drive"
https://www.amnesty.org/en/latest/news/2018/09/china-up-to-one-million-detained/

[361] Fox News: "Hunter Biden email story: Computer repair store owner describes handing over laptop to FBI" (Oct 14, 2020)
https://www.foxnews.com/politics/hunter-biden-emails-computer-repair-store-owner-john-paul-mac-isaac

[362] Biden Laptop Media
https://bidenlaptopmedia.com

363 CBS News Channels 3: "Timeline: Allegations and evidence surrounding Hunter Biden's business dealings" (Oct. 23, 2020)
https://www.wwmt.com/news/nation-world/timeline-allegations-and-evidence-surrounding-hunter-bidens-business-dealings

364 Epoch Times: "Senate Investigators Seek Hunter Biden Records"
https://www.theepochtimes.com/article/senate-investigators-seek-hunter-biden-records-3549783

365 "What We Know and Don't About Hunter Biden and a Laptop"
https://www.nytimes.com/2020/10/22/us/politics/hunter-biden-laptop.html

366 "Facebook and Twitter Dodge a 2016 Repeat, and Ignite a 2020 Firestorm: The companies have said they would do more to stop misinformation and hacked materials from spreading. This is what that effort looks like."
https://www.nytimes.com/2020/10/15/technology/facebook-twitter-nypost-hunter-biden.html

367 Wikipedia: Fake news
https://en.wikipedia.org/wiki/Fake_news

368 "Hunter Biden sues repairman over release of personal data from laptop"
https://www.bbc.com/news/world-us-canada-64991918

369 "Zuckerberg tells Rogan FBI warning prompted Biden laptop story censorship"
https://www.bbc.com/news/world-us-canada-62688532

370 Wikipedia: Cancel culture
https://en.wikipedia.org/wiki/Cancel_culture

371 ACLU: "The Skokie Case: How I Came To Represent The Free Speech Rights Of Nazis"
https://www.aclu.org/issues/free-speech/skokie-case-how-i-came-represent-free-speech-rights-nazis

372 Wikipedia: Ku Klux Klan
https://en.wikipedia.org/wiki/Ku_Klux_Klan

373 "Why American Civil Liberties Union Defends Free Speech for Racists and Totalitarians"
https://www.aclu.org/wp-content/uploads/legal-documents/4156_ri_1978.pdf

374 *** ACLU: "Freedom of Expression"
"History teaches that the first target of government repression is never the last. If we do not come to the defense of the free speech rights of the most unpopular among us, even if their views are antithetical to the very freedom the First Amendment stands for, then no one's liberty will be secure."
https://www.aclu.org/documents/freedom-expression

375 "Experts say changes to CDC's vaccination definition are normal"
"**three definitions for the word 'vaccination'** ... One was labeled 'pre-2015' and described vaccination as: 'Injection of a killed or weakened infectious organism in order to prevent disease.' Another was dated 2015-2021 and said: 'The act of introducing a vaccine into the body to produce immunity to a specific disease.' The third was from September 2021, calling vaccination: 'The act of introducing a vaccine into the body to produce protection from a specific disease.'"
https://apnews.com/article/fact-checking-976069264061

🪷 Endnotes and References 🪷

[376] "The Dark Virality of a Hollywood Blood-Harvesting Conspiracy"
https://www.wired.com/story/opinion-the-dark-virality-of-a-hollywood-blood-harvesting-conspiracy/

[377] "The State of Antisemitism in America 2020: AJC's Survey of American Jews"
https://www.ajc.org/AntisemitismReport2020/Survey-of-American-Jews

[378] United States Holocaust Memorial Museum (USHMM) "Protocols of the Elders of Zion"
"The Protocols of the Elders of Zion is the most notorious and widely distributed antisemitic publication of modern times. Its lies about Jews, which have been repeatedly discredited, continue to circulate today, especially on the Internet. The individuals and groups who have used the Protocols are all linked by a common purpose: to spread hatred of Jews."
https://encyclopedia.ushmm.org/content/en/article/protocols-of-the-elders-of-zion

[379] USHMM: "Pogroms"
"Pogrom is a Russian word meaning 'to wreak havoc, to demolish violently.' Historically, the term refers to violent attacks by local non-Jewish populations on Jews in the Russian Empire and in other countries."
https://encyclopedia.ushmm.org/content/en/article/pogroms

[380] *** **USHMM: "Blood libel"**
"The term blood libel refers to the false allegation that Jews used the blood of non-Jewish, usually Christian children, for ritual purposes. The Nazis made effective use of the blood libel to demonize Jews, with Julius Steicher's newspaper Der Stürmer making frequent use of ritual murder imagery in its antisemitic propaganda."
https://encyclopedia.ushmm.org/content/en/article/blood-libel

[381] "US election 2020: 'QAnon might affect how my friends vote'"
https://www.bbc.com/news/blogs-trending-54440973

[382] "'Flood the zone with shit': How misinformation overwhelmed our democracy"
https://www.vox.com/policy-and-politics/2020/1/16/20991816/impeachment-trial-trump-bannon-misinformation

[383] Hacking Democracy (movie)
https://www.hackingdemocracy.com/

[384] *** **Black box voting**
https://vimeo.com/181771227
https://trustthevote.org

[385] Wikipedia: Aleksandr Dugin
https://en.wikipedia.org/wiki/Aleksandr_Dugin

[386] Wikipedia: Foundations of Geopolitics
https://en.wikipedia.org/wiki/Foundations_of_Geopolitics

[387] Trailer: "What's The Frack?" (documentary)
https://youtu.be/5uWV7xoEZHE

[388] Trailer: "Gasland" (documentary)
https://youtu.be/YmB0iTfug_g

[389] "Chemicals in fracking fluid and wastewater are toxic, study shows"
"In a large analysis, YSPH researchers found that many substances used in fracking have been linked to reproductive and developmental health problems."
https://news.yale.edu/2016/01/06/toxins-found-fracking-fluids-and-wastewater-study-shows

❀ ReQovery ❀

---

390 Wikipedia: Blue Gold: World Water Wars (documentary film)
https://en.wikipedia.org/wiki/Blue_Gold:_World_Water_Wars

391 Trailer: "Blue Gold: World Water Wars" (documentary)
https://youtu.be/Ikb4WG8UJRw

392 Wikipedia: Water scarcity
https://en.wikipedia.org/wiki/Water_scarcity

393 Wikipedia: Dakota Access Pipeline protests
https://en.wikipedia.org/wiki/Dakota_Access_Pipeline_protests

394 "President Trump Says the Dakota Access Pipeline 'Serves the National Interest,' Yet It Threatens Indian Rights and the Drinking Water of 18 Million People"
https://www.aclu.org/news/racial-justice/president-trump-says-dakota-access-pipeline-serves

395 "Dakota Access pipeline company and Donald Trump have close financial ties"
https://www.theguardian.com/us-news/2016/oct/26/donald-trump-dakota-access-pipeline-investment-energy-transfer-partners

396 "Trump advances controversial oil pipelines with executive action"
https://www.cnn.com/2017/01/24/politics/trump-keystone-xl-dakota-access-pipelines-executive-actions/index.html

397 "Police remove last Standing Rock protesters in military-style takeover"
https://www.theguardian.com/us-news/2017/feb/23/dakota-access-pipeline-camp-cleared-standing-rock

398 "Stand with Standing Rock"
https://cases.open.ubc.ca/standing-with-standing-rock/

399 "Leaked: Cambridge Analytica's blueprint for Trump victory"
https://www.theguardian.com/uk-news/2018/mar/23/leaked-cambridge-analyticas-blueprint-for-trump-victory

400 *** Channel 4 News: "Cambridge Analytica Uncovered: Secret filming reveals election tricks"
https://youtu.be/mpbeOCKZFfQ

401 "Former Cambridge Analytica chief receives seven-year directorship ban"
https://www.theguardian.com/uk-news/2020/sep/24/cambridge-analytica-directorship-ban-alexander-nix

402 "Cambridge Analytica Is Dead, Long Live Our Data"
https://www.bostonreview.net/articles/law-justice-david-carroll-cambridge-analytica/

403 Matthew Oczkowski – former staff at Cambridge Analytica hired by Donald Trump" "oversaw data strategy, research, and predictive modelling programs for Donald Trump's Presidential Campaign"
https://www.leadingauthorities.com/speakers/matthew-oczkowski

404 "Trump campaign hires alum of controversial data company"
https://www.politico.com/news/2020/02/19/trump-cambridge-analytica-oczkowski-114075

405 "Trump: I could 'shoot somebody and I wouldn't lose voters'"
https://www.cnn.com/2016/01/23/politics/donald-trump-shoot-somebody-support/index.html

⚜ Endnotes and References ⚜

[406] Separated Immigrant Families, Zero Tolerance
https://www.texastribune.org/series/separated-immigrant-families-zero-tolerance/

[407] "The Trump Administration's "Zero Tolerance" Immigration Enforcement Policy"
https://sgp.fas.org/crs/homesec/R45266.pdf

[408] "Peaceful Protesters Tear-Gassed To Clear Way For Trump Church Photo-Op"
https://www.npr.org/2020/06/01/867532070/trumps-unannounced-church-visit-angers-church-officials

[409] "Trump knocks Fauci: 'I inherited him'"
https://thehill.com/homenews/administration/514523-trump-knocks-fauci-i-inherited-him/

[410] "The History Behind 'When The Looting Starts, The Shooting Starts'"
https://www.npr.org/2020/05/29/864818368/the-history-behind-when-the-looting-starts-the-shooting-starts

[411] Fox News: "Exclusive interview: Trump sits down with Harris Faulkner" (addressing "When the looting starts the shooting starts")
https://youtu.be/5g4cAskc-Jk

[412] "Trump Says His 'Fight Like Hell' Speech Before Capitol Riot Was Actually 'Extremely Calming'"
https://www.rollingstone.com/politics/politics-news/trump-fight-like-hell-speech-extremely-calming-1270504/

[413] The Independent: "Trump defense uses video to call Democrats 'hypocrites' over word 'fight'"
https://youtu.be/ScAJxneYBnY

[414] "Donald Trump warns of 'bloodbath' if he loses 2024 election while talking about the auto industry"
https://youtu.be/pwP2mlcJJSw

[415] "Forensic Audit Aftermath: Top 12 Lies and Truths" (Jovan Pulitzer's assessment of the election)
https://www.bitchute.com/video/u0IsVA3U4w6O/

[416] Jovan Pulitzer
https://jovanhuttonpulitzer.org

[417] "The Hundred-Year Marathon: China's Secret Strategy to Replace America as the Global Superpower" (book)
https://thehundredyearmarathon.com/

[418] "China's Grand Plan To Take Over The World"
https://www.forbes.com/sites/johnmauldin/2019/11/12/chinas-grand-plan-to-take-over-the-world

[419] Wikipedia: American Horror Story (TV series)
https://en.wikipedia.org/wiki/American_Horror_Story

[420] Wikipedia: Lucifer (TV series)
https://en.wikipedia.org/wiki/Lucifer_(TV_series)

[421] "How 'Cuties' Is Fueling the Far Right's Obsession With Pedophilia"
https://www.rollingstone.com/culture/culture-commentary/cuties-netflix-far-right-controversy-pedophilia-1057736/

⚜ **ReQovery** ⚜

---

[422] "Behind the Curve" (documentary)
https://www.behindthecurvefilm.com/

[423] Wikipedia: Robert David Steele
https://en.wikipedia.org/wiki/Robert_David_Steele

[424] David Martin
https://www.davidmartin.world

[425] Wikipedia: Michael Flynn
https://en.wikipedia.org/wiki/Michael_Flynn

[426] Wikipedia: Sidney Powell
https://en.wikipedia.org/wiki/Sidney_Powell

[427] LinkedIn: Tim Pool
https://www.linkedin.com/in/timothy-pool-7228ba25/

[428] Tucker Carlson
https://tuckercarlson.com/about/

[429] https://humansbefree.com/2020/11/stanford-professor-of-medicine-covid-19-has-a-99-95-survival-rate-for-people-under-70.html (this article has been removed. Check out a similar article on this professor and topic here - **https://www.ihmc.us/stemtalk/episode-151/**)
"Back in early days of the COVID-19 pandemic, Dr. John Ioannidis wrote an article in March of 2020 questioning government statistics about the fatality rate associated with COVID-19. The backlash was swift and brutal and John's reputation as one of the most influential scientists in the world took a beating.
"Today, John makes his second appearance on STEM-Talk to discuss his extensive research into the COVID-19 pandemic as well as the public shaming he received in 2020 for questioning the World Health Organization's prediction of a 3.4 percent fatality rate associated with COVID-19.
"**John also talks about his most recent peer-reviewed paper that looked at the age-stratified infection fatality rate of COVID-19 in the non-elderly population. The study found that the pre-vaccination fatality rate for those infected may have been as low as 0.03 percent for people under 60 years old, and 0.07 percent for people under 70, far below the World Health Organization's prediction of a 3.4 percent fatality rate."**

[430] "'COVID Vaccines 'Biological Weapons of Mass Destruction' says Wyoming Medical Doctor and Manager for Wyoming's State Public Health Department'"
https://vaccineimpact.com/2020/covid-vaccines-biological-weapons-of-mass-destruction-says-wyoming-medical-doctor-and-manager-for-wyomings-state-public-health-department/

[431] "Covid-19 Vaccine Protocols Reveal That Trials Are Designed To Succeed"
https://www.forbes.com/sites/williamhaseltine/2020/09/23/covid-19-vaccine-protocols-reveal-that-trials-are-designed-to-succeed

[432] "'Absolutely remarkable': No one who got Moderna's vaccine in trial developed severe COVID-19. Biotech will ask FDA for emergency approval as final results from efficacy trial back up initial claim of vaccine success"
https://www.science.org/content/article/absolutely-remarkable-no-one-who-got-modernas-vaccine-trial-developed-severe-covid-19

[433] Citizen's Council for Health Freedom
https://www.cchfreedom.org/

[434] "Would you be willing to get a Covid vaccine in exchange for a $1,500 stimulus check? How one bold proposal would work"

৬ Endnotes and References ৬

https://www.cnbc.com/2020/12/03/1500-stimulus-checks-for-covid-19-shots-how-one-plan-would-work.html

[435] "China Is National Security Threat No. 1"
https://www.wsj.com/articles/china-is-national-security-threat-no-1-11607019599

[436] "Why Is the Nuremberg Code being used to oppose Covid-19 vaccines?"
https://fullfact.org/health/nuremberg-code-covid/

[437] Jack Kornfield: "Beauty and Human Goodness Amidst It All Dharma Talk"
https://youtu.be/FUAEpT9bElY

[438] Oprah: Supersoul Podcast: "Oprah's and Eckhart Tolle Free Yourself From Anxiety"
https://www.oprah.com/own-podcasts/eckhart-tolle-free-yourself-from-anxiety-stress-and-unhappiness

[439] "The Comet Ping Pong Gunman Answers Our Reporter's Questions" (Pizzagate)
https://www.nytimes.com/2016/12/07/us/edgar-welch-comet-pizza-fake-news.html

[440] "Fatah: China's troops trained in Canada against which country?"
https://torontosun.com/opinion/columnists/fatah-chinas-troops-trained-in-canada-against-which-country

[441] "No, Chinese troops are not on the Canadian border — and the dangers of misinformation"
https://www.militarytimes.com/news/your-military/2020/12/15/no-the-chinese-are-not-on-the-border-of-maine-and-the-dangers-of-misinformation/

[442] IMDB: "The Russians are Coming The Russians are Coming!" (movie)
https://www.imdb.com/title/tt0060921/

[443] Wikipedia: Plurality voting
https://en.wikipedia.org/wiki/Plurality_voting

[444] Wikipedia: Two-party system
https://en.wikipedia.org/wiki/Two-party_system

[445] Wikipedia: Second American Civil War
https://en.wikipedia.org/w/index.php?title=Second_American_Civil_War&redirect=no
(This page has since been deleted.)

[446] Trump Disavows Racism
https://www.bitchute.com/video/MWDhu4eEXXkM/

[447] "A new book explains how QAnon took hold of the GOP — and why it's not going away"
https://www.cosmopolitan.com/health-fitness/a35056548/wellness-fitness-influencers-QAnon-conspiracy-theories/

[448] "I Left QAnon in 2019. But I'm Still Not Free."
https://www.politico.com/news/magazine/2021/12/11/q-anon-movement-former-believer-523972

[449] "My QMom died today and everything is worse"
https://www.reddit.com/r/QAnonCasualties/comments/l3dpek/my_qmom_died_today_and_everything_is_worse/

[450] Distinguishing Cults Versus Non-Cults
https://docs.google.com/document/d/1mKWnFLpmw0aEMDOihilz4DqVJ5eRPEjwraXhSkJ8Zys/edit

⚜ ReQovery ⚜

---

[451] "5 Things You Never Knew About Fear"
https://www.nm.org/healthbeat/healthy-tips/emotional-health/5-things-you-never-knew-about-fear

[452] Vice Media: videos about QAnon
https://video.vice.com/en_us/search?q=qanon

[453] *** **Before Skool: "Game Theory, False Narratives, Survival, Life Advice - Daniel Schmachtenberger"**
https://youtu.be/LSx8j8ISewA (full interview)

[454] "Faith Forum: What makes one morally virtuous?"
https://www.rgj.com/story/life/2016/06/09/faith-forum-what-makes-one-morally-virtuous/85670768/#

[455] Nonviolent Communication Academy
https://nvcacademy.com/

[456] "**Nonviolent Communication: A Language of Life**" by Dr. Marshall Rosenberg **(full book)**
https://ccpgc.usmf.md/sites/default/files/inline-files/Nonviolent%20Communication_%20A%20Language%20of%20Life_%20Life-Changing%20Tools%20for%20Healthy%20Relationships%20%28%20PDFDrive%20%29.pdf

[457] Sky News Australia: "'Enough of this': Hamas co-founder's son speaks out"
https://www.youtube.com/watch?v=k2BSDLFVT74

[458] *** **"A Game Designer's Analysis Of QAnon: Playing with Reality"**
https://medium.com/curiouserinstitute/a-game-designers-analysis-of-qanon-580972548be5

[459] Vice Media: "QAnon: The Search for Q"
https://www.vicetv.com/en_us/show/QAnon-the-search-for-q

[460] "What Did President Trump Mean by 'Calm Before the Storm'?"
https://www.nytimes.com/2017/10/06/us/politics/trump-calls-meeting-with-military-leaders-the-calm-before-the-storm.html

[461] *** **"The Social Dilemma" (documentary)**
https://www.thesocialdilemma.com

[462] "Behind the Curve" (documentary about "Flat Earthers")
https://www.behindthecurvefilm.com

[463] "Dr. Fauci On GOP Criticism: 'Attacks On Me, Quite Frankly, Are Attacks On Science'"
https://www.forbes.com/sites/carlieporterfield/2021/06/09/fauci-on-gop-criticism-attacks-on-me-quite-frankly-are-attacks-on-science/

[464] After Skool: Scientific Dogma (Banned Ted Talk)
https://youtu.be/sF03FN37i5w

[465] "The Great Barrington Declaration" (doctors and scientists speak out against the Covid lockdown policy)
https://gbdeclaration.org **(repeat link)**

[466] "The Real Anthony Fauci Intro to the book"
https://www.slideshare.net/planginc/the-real-anthony-fauci-intro-to-the-book

❀ Endnotes and References ❀

467 "RFK Jr.'s 'The Real Anthony Fauci' Is a Record-Smashing Bestseller — But Mainstream Media Pretends It Doesn't Exist"
https://childrenshealthdefense.org/defender/rfk-jr-the-real-anthony-fauci-record-smashing-bestseller/

468 *** "Search Hundreds of Covid Vaccine Injury Stories"
https://www.realnotrare.com

469 *** Chris Cuomo: "Ex-CDC Chief Dr. Robert Redfield Reveals COVID-19 Truths"
https://youtu.be/oMlhvnMpRU0?si=P4Vjw-NdUkbEIRU_&t=1744

470 Mainstream Covid narrative
https://www.psychologytoday.com/us/blog/talking-about-health/202107/defining-the-covid-19-narrative

471 *** "Conspiracy Theories and Political Extremism: Understanding Brain Behavior in an Uncertain World" (webinar)
https://sarahpeyton.com/product/conspiracy-theories-and-political-extremism-understanding-brain-behavior-in-an-uncertain-world/

472 Snopes: "Does This Video Prove Planned Parenthood Sells Fetal Tissue Illegally?"
https://www.snopes.com/fact-check/pp-baby-parts-sale/

473 "Reckoning With The Feminist, Eugenicist Founder Of Planned Parenthood"
https://www.huffpost.com/entry/margaret-sanger-eugenics-birth-control-planned-parenthood_n_5f1f2a40c5b638cfec4893a8

474 Planned Parenthood: "Our History"
https://www.plannedparenthood.org/about-us/who-we-are/our-history

475 "Cotton, Coons, Colleagues Introduce Bill to Hold China Accountable for Forced Organ Harvesting"
https://www.cotton.senate.gov/news/press-releases/cotton-coons-colleagues-introduce-bill-to-hold-china-accountable-for-forced-organ-harvesting

476 Amnesty International: "Up to one million detained in China's mass 're-education' drive"
https://www.amnesty.org/en/latest/news/2018/09/china-up-to-one-million-detained/

477 Wikipedia: Xinjiang internment camps
https://en.wikipedia.org/wiki/Xinjiang_internment_camps

478 "Analysis of Hunter Biden's hard drive shows he, his firm took in about $11 million from 2013 to 2018, spent it fast"
https://www.nbcnews.com/politics/national-security/analysis-hunter-bidens-hard-drive-shows-firm-took-11-million-2013-2018-rcna29462

479 "How China Captured Hollywood"
https://www.theatlantic.com/international/archive/2022/02/china-captured-hollywood/621618/

480 Dead Sea Scrolls
http://www.gnosis.org/library/scroll.htm

481 Book of Giants
http://www.gnosis.org/library/dss/dss_book_of_giants.htm

482 "Transhumanism: World's Most Dangerous Idea"
https://myrepublica.nagariknetwork.com/news/transhumanism-world-s-most-dangerous-idea/

❀ ReQovery ❀

---

483 "Transhumanism and the Metaverse, an audio essay by Charles Eisenstein"
https://youtu.be/7_qqmnP4XLQ

484 NIH: "Transhumanism, medical technology and slippery slopes"
https://www.ncbi.nlm.nih.gov/pmc/articles/PMC2563415/

485 Time: "'Critical Race Theory Is Simply the Latest Bogeyman.' Inside the Fight Over What Kids Learn About America's History"
https://time.com/6075193/critical-race-theory-debate/

486 Wikipedia: Great Reset (World Economic Forum)
https://en.wikipedia.org/wiki/Great_Reset

487 Global Network on Extremism & Technology (Facebook's reference for QAnon)
https://gnet-research.org/2020/10/15/what-is-qanon/

488 Wikipedia: New world order (politics)
https://en.wikipedia.org/wiki/New_world_order_(politics)

489 *** **Dr. Phil: "This Liberal Went to a Trump Rally"**
https://youtu.be/0ko7m8PVOGk

490 "Tests Find More Than 200 Chemicals in Newborn Umbilical Cord Blood"
"Study commissioned by environmental group finds high levels of chemicals in U.S. minority infants"
https://www.scientificamerican.com/article/newborn-babies-chemicals-exposure-bpa/

491 "Medicare and Social Security insolvency is right around the corner"
https://www.cnn.com/2023/02/09/politics/medicare-social-security-what-matters/index.html

492 *** **"Pentagon opens sweeping review of clandestine psychological operations"**
"The Pentagon has ordered a sweeping audit of how it conducts clandestine information warfare after major social media companies identified and took offline fake accounts suspected of being run by the U.S. military in violation of the platforms' rules."
https://www.washingtonpost.com/national-security/2022/09/19/pentagon-psychological-operations-facebook-twitter/

493 "Psychological Warfare"
"Psychological warfare involves the planned use of propaganda and other psychological operations to influence the opinions, emotions, attitudes, and behavior of opposition groups."
https://www.rand.org/topics/psychological-warfare.html

494 Center for Humane Technology: "Is World War III Already Here? Guest: Lieutenant General H.R. McMaster"
https://www.humanetech.com/podcast/45-is-world-war-iii-already-here

495 "The Russian 'Firehose of Falsehood' Propaganda Model"
https://www.rand.org/pubs/perspectives/PE198.html

496 "The Expansion of Chinese Communist Party Media Influence since 2017"
https://freedomhouse.org/report/special-report/2020/beijings-global-megaphone

497 "Two Iranian Nationals Charged for Cyber-Enabled Disinformation and Threat Campaign Designed to Influence the 2020 U.S. Presidential Election"
https://www.justice.gov/opa/pr/two-iranian-nationals-charged-cyber-enabled-disinformation-and-threat-campaign-designed

꧁ Endnotes and References ꧂

[498] "White Supremacist Propaganda Soars to All-Time High in 2022"
https://www.adl.org/resources/report/white-supremacist-propaganda-soars-all-time-high-2022

[499] The Heritage Foundation: Project 2025
https://www.heritage.org/conservatism/commentary/project-2025

[500] Wikipedia: Project 2025
https://en.wikipedia.org/wiki/Project_2025

[501] **BLM Cofounder Patrice Cullors: "We are trained Marxist"**
https://www.bitchute.com/video/EQ4IqURxuvlF/

[502] **"'Unashamedly Marxist' founder of BLM resigns"**
https://youtu.be/d6Eo1umdScg

[503] "The real history of Antifa"
https://centerforsecuritypolicy.org/the-real-history-of-antifa/

[504] Wikipedia: Post-World War II anti-fascism
https://en.wikipedia.org/wiki/Post–World_War_II_anti-fascism

[505] "'Mostly Peaceful': Countering Left-Wing Organized Violence"
https://www.congress.gov/event/118th-congress/house-event/115946/text?s=1&r=54

[506] "It Costs Just $400 to Build an AI Disinformation Machine"
https://www.wired.com/story/400-dollars-to-build-an-ai-disinformation-machine/

[507] "Fake AI-generated image of explosion near Pentagon spreads on social media"
https://www.theguardian.com/technology/2023/may/22/pentagon-ai-generated-image-explosion

[508] "AI-Generated Images: Trump and Biden Being Best Friends"
https://www.sadanduseless.com/trump-and-biden-as-best-friends/

[509] "Midjourney 5: The Most Realistic AI Generated Images
https://www.streamline.us/blog/midjourney-5-most-realistic-ai-generated-images/

[510] "Introducing Sora—OpenAI's text-to-video model"
https://youtu.be/HK6y8DAPN_0

[511] "AI-generated deepfakes are moving fast. Policymakers can't keep up"
https://www.npr.org/2023/04/27/1172387911/how-can-people-spot-fake-images-created-by-artificial-intelligence

[512] "AI Generated Videos Just Changed Forever"
https://youtu.be/NXpdyAWLDas

[513] "23 of the best deepfake examples that terrified and amused the internet"
https://www.creativebloq.com/features/deepfake-examples

[514] "I Deep Faked Myself, Here's Why It Matters"
https://youtu.be/S951cdansBI

[515] ** ACLU: "Freedom of Expression"
"History teaches that the first target of government repression is never the last. If we do not come to the defense of the free speech rights of the most unpopular among us, even if their views are antithetical to the very freedom the First Amendment stands for, then

no one's liberty will be secure."
https://www.aclu.org/documents/freedom-expression

[516] Center for Humane Technology
https://www.humanetech.com

[517] *** "How Filter Bubbles Isolate You"
https://youtu.be/pT-k1kDlRnw

[518] *** "Pop the Filter Bubble: To create well-informed citizens, we need to recognize filter bubbles and the impact they have on our information universe."
https://avidopenaccess.org/resource/pop-the-filter-bubble/

[519] "Acknowledge and Identify Bias: To be effective consumers of digital information, students need to be able to acknowledge and identify bias in all forms of media."
https://avidopenaccess.org/resource/acknowledge-and-identify-bias/

[520] Media Bias Fact Check
https://mediabiasfactcheck.com

[521] *** After Skool: Why Smart People Believe Stupid Things
(curiosity as an antidote for rationalizing false ideas)
https://youtu.be/5Peima-Uw7w

[522] *** "Max Major REVEALED How He Influenced Millions on Americas Got Talent
https://youtu.be/FdsPoe5m_8Q

[523] "Dark future of iPad kids"
https://www.youtube.com/watch?v=nTvKo1buDck

[524] "The Social Dilemma" (documentary)
https://www.humanetech.com/the-social-dilemma

[525] RFK Jr. "AI Should Be Controlled, But Also Harnessed"
https://youtube.com/shorts/yGbWZq3bU_8

[526] "Nicole Shanahan on Risks of AI"
https://youtu.be/2GgLzVnZVf0

May Peace Prevail on Earth